SEXAGON

Sexagon

Muslims, France, and the Sexualization
of National Culture

MEHAMMED AMADEUS MACK

Fordham University Press
NEW YORK   2017

the
modern language
initiative

THIS BOOK IS MADE POSSIBLE BY A COLLABORATIVE GRANT
FROM THE ANDREW W. MELLON FOUNDATION.

Visit us online at www.fordhampress.com.

Library of Congress Cataloging-in-Publication Data available online at
http://catalog.loc.gov.

Printed in the United States of America

19 18 17   5 4 3 2 1

First edition

MIX
Paper | Supporting
responsible forestry
FSC® C013604

To my immigrant parents, Mark and Faiza

CONTENTS

Sexagon

Introduction: Enter the Sexagon

Among the sensitive questions involving Muslims living in the West, and in Europe most singularly, there is the position of Islam on homosexuality. In certain contexts, this question would be the sole and unique key to the possible "integration" of Muslims in Western culture. As if European cultures and values could be reduced to the acceptance or rejection of homosexuality.

TARIQ RAMADAN[1]

Sexagon explores the broad politicization of sexuality in public debates about immigration and diversity in France and traces said politicization in French discourses and cultural productions in an attempt to challenge common perceptions that Muslims maintain unmodern attitudes about sexuality. Specifically, the book focuses on examples from literature, film, psychoanalysis, ethnopsychiatry, and pornography, as well as feminist, gay, and lesbian activist rhetoric to examine where sexualized representations of communities of immigrant origin take a political turn. The book also examines the rhetoric of French establishment figures who have expressed their frustrations with the changing demographics in their "familiar" France by questioning the "Frenchness" of Arab and Muslim minorities born in France—not because of linguistic or civic barriers, but because of perceived conservative attitudes about gender and sexuality. This frustration, I argue, gravitates around the concept of *virilism*—that is, a mixture of toughness, hardness, unruliness, assertiveness, and sometimes aggression which is projected onto male and female immigrants and their offspring. In the eyes of many French observers and commentators, virilism not only animates the "difficult" Arab, black, and Muslim boys featured in sensationalized newscasts, it also defines their neighborhoods in the suburbs or *banlieues*,[2] their religion of Islam, and the notion of immigration itself. This virilization of the Arab *other* naturally requires a feminization, and in some cases an androgenization, of the host country: France, which has been called the hexagon (because it has six distinct sides), increasingly has come to resemble what I term a *sexagon*, because of the way its borders increasingly have come to be defined through values such as gay-friendliness, secular feminism, and metrosexuality, on the one hand, and the condemnation of immigrant and working-class machismo on the other. This perceived virilism is seen as all the more dangerous as it appears to include citizens who are often targeted as ideal candidates for cultural assimilation because they are thought to be antagonistic to virilism: women and homosexuals. The official discourses under investigation here are crucially inflamed by a defining element of these virility cultures: their clandestinity. Mirroring the secret and underground qualities of "illegal" immigration, both gay and straight proponents of clandestine cultures choose to withdraw from official scrutiny into ethnic shelters that are anathema to the French Republic's desire for universalism and transparency. One of the most prominent and damning books on the subject of homosexuality, homophobia, and the multiethnic banlieues—journalist Franck Chaumont's *Homo-ghetto*—establishes in its very title that banlieue homosexuals are the unassimilated "clandestines of the Republic."[3]

Attitudes about women's liberation, sexual violence, homophobia, excision, polygamy, youth sexuality, the hijab (or headscarf), and family size have emerged as flashpoints in recent debates about immigration to France, leading many self-appointed guardians of French culture, as well as cultural chauvinists, to assert a stance of sexual enlightenment over France's Arab and Islamic communities. At a time when French citizens of Arab and Islamic descent—French for generations—can no longer be accused of nonassimilation on linguistic grounds, they appear to have been subjected to a new form of citizenship test that is predicated on the perceived fitness of their views on sexuality. Thus, a cultural divide, once bridged when these children of immigrants became French citizens, seems to have reemerged with political and sometimes legal consequences. This type of cultural xenophobia, however, ignores the many ways through which African and Arab minorities in France have *queered* or deviated from normative French understandings of sexuality, both heterosexual and homosexual.

Indeed, sexuality has emerged as a new battleground in the public debates about whether postwar immigration from the former colonies has eroded French identity. Since the 1990s, long-standing concerns about religious or ethnic diversity increasingly have been accompanied by a sexualized rhetoric that accuses Muslim immigrants of advocating rigid gender norms and being intolerant of homosexuality. *Sexagon* pushes the conversation into the cultural arena of representations and explains how sexuality constitutes a prism through which to establish the existence of non-European difference, which is often expressed in terms of being uncomfortable with gender fluidity (for men, not women), effeminacy, transparency, and "being out." The integration of immigrants and their descendants within the national fabric increasingly has been defined in terms of a set of "appropriate" attitudes toward gender and sexuality that have been proclaimed to be long-standing French values, but which in reality have been embraced only recently.

European Islam and Gay-Friendliness

In this context of the nationalization of sexual liberty, the Swiss theologian Tariq Ramadan has drawn negative media attention for his "inappropriate" attitudes about homosexuality. In May 2009, Ramadan weighed in on a polemic that was taking shape in the Western European media surrounding the alleged homophobia of Muslims in general, and European Muslims in particular. Journalists and politicians, he argued, were increasingly tying attitudes about sexuality to the question of Muslim integration in Europe. Himself a proponent of a French and more largely European Islam, Ramadan has chronicled in books and blogs the formation of European Muslim identity. He has stressed that Muslims have set roots in postimmigration European society and that French Islam exists independently of influences from the Islamic countries of origin: French Islam expresses itself in French rather than Arabic and responds to Muslim European concerns. A telegenic polyglot, Ramadan enjoys a demographically significant following among Muslim youths in France and beyond.[4] It is precisely due to his being at home in Europe that he has been met with aggressive skepticism by both secular European politicians and conservative elements in the Muslim diaspora who share the desire to unveil his "hidden" agenda.[5] His followers, many of whom hope for and believe in Euro-Islam, are all the more dispirited when, in their eyes, the theologian most willing to seek compromise between Islamic and European customs faces an opposition more stalwart than that faced by foreign fundamentalists preaching in France: Ramadan's assimilative potential thus makes him all the more dangerous for being already so similar. The progressive branch of Muslim communities in France faces particular demands for a tolerance that is rarely afforded to them in kind, as is evident in the "cascading series of terms—respect, accept, defend, embrace, promote—that interpellate them," all of which create a disproportionate "representational burden" around French Muslims who, for example, must disavow signs of homophobia and sexual intolerance, whether responsible for them or not.[6] This increased pressure exists not because progressive Muslims' beliefs are problematic, but rather because progressive Muslims choose exposure and existence in the secular mainstream, in the media, and in plain view of those who assess them. Therefore, progressive Muslims aiming to engage the French center face an opposition that is sometimes stronger than that faced by fundamentalists.

Journalists and politicians invoking the need to protect *laïcité*, France's form of secularism, have criticized Ramadan's advocacy of women's right to wear the hijab, as well as his encouragement of Islamic feminism, considered a paradox by the staunchest secularists. The critiques culminated in a televised debate with then presidential candidate Nicolas Sarkozy, in which the politician aggressively presented himself as a defender of women's freedoms against Ramadan, whom he alleged to be misogynistic.[7] When Sarkozy was elected president in 2007, he made the unprecedented move of appointing three female ministers of color (Rama Yade, Rachida Dati, and Fadela Amara) who all shared a Muslim background, albeit one they had either criticized or distanced themselves from. Some commentators declared that this groundbreaking move toward diversity and the inclusion of minority women's voices (however limited they turned out to be) were secured on the condition that these women use their voices to criticize Islam.[8] Caroline Fourest, a prominent journalist and former president of the Gay and Lesbian Center in Paris, devoted a book-length study to unpacking what critics have called Ramadan's "double-speak," or his supposed tendency to say one (palatable) thing to a French or English-language audience and another (unpalatable) one to a Muslim.[9] The fact that Ramadan has become a darling of Muslim reformists and proponents of Muslim reconciliation with Western values has not staved off critique; if anything it has increased it, as Ramadan has been portrayed as a wolf in sheep's clothing. Ramadan's pushback, as well as the fact that some of his most prominent opponents have invoked LGBT rights in their critiques, shows that the issue of homophobia has become a significant flashpoint in the debates about immigration and Islam and its leadership in France and other European countries. More radical critics and politicians have called for limits on immigration from Islamic countries so as to defend against sexual intolerance. For Ramadan, however, a key problem with the political rhetoric emphasizing Muslim "homophobia" is that it has penetrated private Muslim consciousness, calling for rejection of, rather than reconciliation with, religion.[10] Ramadan shows awareness of what can be called "sexual demonization" and its more political corollary "sexual nationalism": the deployment of an otherwise progressive feminist and LGBT-rights agenda for anti-immigration purposes.

Ramadan's characterization of the Islamic stance on homosexuality is a controversial element in this debate. Ramadan, citing the French author Isabelle Lévy, states that homosexuality is religiously "condemned and forbidden," and that this is "largely, the majority opinion of all spiritualities and of all religions, to which Islam is no exception."[11] Elsewhere he has adopted an attitude similar to the Christian promise to "hate the sin, love the sinner," while also commenting that Muslims in the Western imaginary have gone from being overly sexual (harems, bisexuality, sodomy) to overly prohibitive within a century.[12] However, when Ramadan condemns homosexual practices, does he also condemn homosexual identity (which is what he is accused of doing by his Western secular critics)?[13] Why doesn't a theologian who has previously called for interpretation instead of dogmatism when it comes to women's rights do the same for sexual orientation, an identity marker intelligible and relevant to his young followers? Whether in their own biographies or in their interactions with gay friends and coworkers, many young European Muslims seek a progressive Islamic verdict on the question from a trusted guide, one who would neither settle for hard-hearted rejection nor for a rewriting of Islamic scripture. Some critics of the rejection of homosexuality from Islamic culture have pointed out that it rehistoricizes Arab-Islamic culture so that all the myriad elements of same-sex desire are erased: this extraction would come in response to a history of Western representations that place disproportionate stress on the "perversion" of these desires.[14] This historical operation is an example of the "double phantasm" that occurs when a subject or group is falsely represented, and then defines itself in counterpoint to that false representation, creating a third representation that may have little to do with reality. In this way, Muslims rejecting homosexuality might be doing so not because of Islamic teachings and customs, but rather because of their own embarrassed reactions at having been portrayed as sexual deviants in previous cross-cultural accounts.

This anecdote about Ramadan sheds light on the difficulty of assessing and judging Muslims' alleged intolerance of homosexuality as well as the "intolerance of intolerance" exhibited by their critics. This assessment is complicated by the fact that in France, just as in many other Western countries with minority populations, tolerance is demanded of the marginalized, not very well tolerated minority.[15] By contrast, tolerance traditionally is not demanded of the more powerful majority, whose intolerances, if they are acknowledged at all, appear too intractable to combat and thus less of an issue.[16] Though some have portrayed Ramadan as intolerant of sexual diversity, he has consistently stressed (to the dismay of other conservative Muslim theologians) that one can be "homosexual and Muslim": "a person who pronounces the attestation of Islamic faith [*shahada*] becomes Muslim and if, besides this, they practice homosexuality, no one has the right to reject them from the faith. A behavior considered reprehensible according to moral rules does not suffice to excommunicate an individual."[17] While this stance remains distant from the inclusivity demanded by most gay rights activists, it is a far cry from the death sentence rhetoric commonly circulated in conversations about Islam and homosexuality.

European Muslims who embrace a homosexual identity occupy a most difficult position. They often find themselves alienated by an LGBT mainstream that seems hostile to conjugating religious and sexual identities, which calls for exiting religion and community as rites of passage toward a mature homosexual identity. Emergent groups such as the Homosexuels Musulmans de France (HM2F) have tried to articulate visions of inclusivity and a hybrid identity: the group condemns Islamophobia, homophobia, noninclusive secularism, and sexism.[18] Often neglected in characterizations of the Muslim community in France as a monolith, however, are the unique relationships and solidarities between homosexual Muslims and their heterosexual allies. Euro-Muslim cultural output features narratives about Muslim homosexual men who gravitate toward women, sisters, and mothers as confidantes. Other narratives describe how gay Muslims may pass unnoticed in sex-segregated spaces thought to be homophobic, or even secure valorized positions in these orders (see chapter 3). While many activist groups lump Muslim women and Muslim gay men together in a shared oppressed status, they are united in other ways beyond victimhood. Both have to deal with the perception that they kid themselves if they believe they can profess their gay or feminist identities while Muslim. Against such aspersions of false consciousness, gay Muslims have copied Islamic feminists' strategies and forms of resistance tested against a second-wave feminism skeptical of their sincerity.

Vocabularies of Race and Desire

The various disagreements about what Ramadan and his critics mean by homosexuality and tolerance reveal the potential for controversy in one's word choice. This book employs a purposefully shifting vocabulary to describe highly hybridized concepts and subject positions. In describing North African and Muslim populations in France, the choice of the term *virility* over *masculinity* is deliberate. In my perhaps nontraditional usage, virility variably includes elements of vigor, assertiveness, combativeness, and ambition that may be absent from *masculinity*. Though *virility* does contain the Latin root *vir-* referring to "man," the term can be understood in a sex-neutral way, as women too have independently produced the elements of virility outlined earlier. This does not necessarily entail a sacrifice of femininity, as I document portrayals of women with virile linguistic and sartorial qualities, who maintain a physical investment in traditional gendering practices and in heterosexual relationships (as is the case, for instance, with the female gang member or the veiled woman who is said to "erase" her femininity in chapter 1). While virile women have often been the subject of negative criticism, they have found increasing acceptance in banlieue spaces, according to various sociological and documentary sources. These gender performances have been subject to the most intense debate when they are seen as indicative of banlieue social disorders. *Sexagon* also examines how the pejorative connotation of virility is manipulated or displaced by banlieue subjects, as well as how a supposedly "heterosexist" virility is adopted for strategic or pragmatic reasons by sexual minorities purported to be victims of heterosexism. Furthermore, the book highlights how the various actors deploy said characteristics and epithets to contest or reinforce gender boundaries. Etymology provides an initial answer as to why North African immigration in France has been conceived mainly in terms of the male, as evidenced by the term *diaspora*.[19] My account seeks to divorce *diaspora* from this male investment—not by writing in its missing female elements, but by showing how women contribute to and define the virile institutions of diasporic creation in the banlieues and ethnic enclaves, such that it no longer makes sense to talk of virility as male.

As in any study dealing with successive waves or generations of immigrants, the terminology used to refer to these subjects is always in flux. Nomenclature shifts according to whether it is informed by self-nomination (what the subjects call themselves) or nomination from the outside (what they are called by politicians, journalists, sociologists). From the precolonial era to the postcolonial context of multiethnic France, peoples hailing from North Africa have variously been called indigenous, French, Arab, Berber, Kabyle, *pied-noir*,[20] European, Muslim or French Muslim, Jewish, Sephardic, Christian, Maghrebi, North African, Franco-Arab, *beur*,[21] *rebeu*,[22] visible minority, or racial minority, or they been named according to nationality (e.g., Algerian, Moroccan, or Tunisian). The choice of one term over another is politically and culturally informed, and in my discussion I supply the historical and political context for each shift in terminology as it comes up while remaining sensitive to the subjects' self-nominations.

One term, however, appears more often than others in my description of French citizens of North African descent: Arab, more specifically, Franco-Arab. As Nacira Guénif-Souilamas explains in *Des beurettes*, the term *Maghrebi* has been used over the last few decades as a way to bypass racial self-designations (*beur, rebeu, arabe*) or to eclipse older designations now considered problematic, such as the nonsecular colonial category of "French Muslims" or a pejorative and outmoded epithet such as *bougnoule*.[23] In her argument, the word *Maghrebi* marks erasure and also self-effacement; as it is less particular in regards to race, it avoids the more rallying term *Arab*.[24] Guénif-Souilamas concludes that *Maghrebi* is strongly connected to a hegemonic, centralized, French republican color-blindness that avoids statements of ethnic attachment and pride. Opting for Franco-Arab or Arab-French allows one to mirror the frequency of French North Africans referring to themselves as Arab (implicit in the terms *beur* and, more recently, *rebeu*).[25] The epistemic violence involved in not using the term *Arab* appeared to me greater than that involved in using it. However, where the subjects of North African descent choose to identify according to a non-Arab marker (usually Berber or Kabyle), that designation will be observed.

Beyond the question of the regional or national origin of immigrants and their descendants, I reflect on what can be termed *banlieusard* experience—that is, the lives of the residents in the multiethnic, usually working-class suburbs, an environment that has generated its own sartorial, verbal, and social codes. This multifaceted social category of shared experience has prompted some scholars to forgo traditional ethnographic approaches by which only one ethnic group becomes representative for a highly diverse space or neighborhood (as has often been the case with the banlieues where those of North African or Islamic origin have tended to eclipse the multiplicity of other ethnic groups that populate these areas). Fatima El-Tayeb uses the more polyvalent "Europeans of color" or "minorities of color in Europe" to describe social formations that unite racially diverse populations whose shared experience consists of a myriad possibility of strands that range from a colonial past, stories of migration, religious difference, and police surveillance or brutality to being perceived as in need of (sexual) education.[26] Other scholars have focused on the commonality of religion, which unites racially diverse subjects (North Africans, Sub-Saharan Africans, Turks, Levantines, and converts) within a common category, and attached it to citizenship in France, as in Mayanthi

Fernando's use of "Muslim French." The social group I examine is in close relationship with the urban and the peri-urban. The presence of multiethnic populations is most contested where the density of urban life leads to conflict in close quarters and narratives of contagion and invasion,[27] as in, for example, fearmongering accounts of Islamization and Sharia in the Goutte d'Or neighborhood of Paris. In many instances, I prefer the terms *banlieusards* or *Europeans of color* over *Arab* or *Muslim*; in other instances, I favor *Arab* and *Islamic* over designations that refer to geography.

The group *banlieusards* can also include individuals who, in a North American context, could be more easily designated as white or Caucasian, epithets that have not been employed to the same extent in contemporary French discourse. Using the term *white*, however, is not entirely satisfactory for designating European immigrants who preceded the wave of immigrants from North and West Africa: many Southern Europeans, for example, who in a strict sense might be considered white, have faced instances of racial discrimination in France, and furthermore may be partially and distantly connected to North Africa dating to the period of Islamic expansion.[28] However, a growing community of French activists, scholars, and minorities has now resorted to using these terms—as well as the field of "critical whiteness studies"—in opposition to officialized French republican color-blindness. My preference for using the hyphenated term *Franco-Arab* experience, however, does not imply that I accept the much more controversial category "Franco-French." The term *Franco-French* is not merely synonymous with white or Caucasian. The term has been increasingly employed by xenophobic authors—in parallel with the recent rise of the far-right National Front party—to mark an often tenuous difference between people descended from one of the "original" French peoples within the borders of the hexagon, and people who arrived in France via one of the more "recent" waves of immigration (which since the 1960s have been majority Muslim). Numerous factors trouble this attempted distinction. Without giving a lengthy history of settlement and population movements in the land mass now known as France, the "original" peoples invoked by French purity groups themselves descended from a the proverbial "melting pot."[29] This patchwork of origins—stretching through wars, annexations, colonialism, and mass immigration—makes up what is an essentially uncategorizable object called multiethnic France, mapped out to dizzying extent in historian Gérard Noiriel's *The French Melting Pot*.[30] One of Noiriel's most revelatory statistics discloses that one-fourth of the respondents in a nationwide study had a foreign grandparent.

The Sexualization of Ethnicity, Now and Then

Tracing the evolution of nomenclature naturally brings up the question of historical parameters. I focus on a contemporary period that stretches from the early 1980s to the 2010s. I demarcate this period for reasons having to do with the emergence of antidiscrimination, antiracist, and immigrant rights movements. Over the course of this period, the politicization of sexuality within immigration debates has reached a critical mass in France. The 1980s bore witness to the March for Equality and Against Racism, also dubbed the March of the *Beurs*, during which populations of North African descent began to make demands in their own name. That decade also saw the creation of the state-sponsored antidiscrimination group SOS Racisme, and important reforms regarding immigrant residency papers under a Socialist government. The 1990s gave rise to the *sans papiers* (undocumented) movement—in which West African immigrants played a more prominent role—triggering a national conversation, under a right-wing presidency, about the notion of hospitality and the evolving status of France as a land of asylum. After 2000, riots gripped the multiethnic suburbs, launching a debate about lack of security and what to do about it. Organizations advocating for increased minority visibility in the media and at the workplace—such as the Conseil Représentatif des Associations Noires (CRAN)—were formed and achieved significant gains. Bans on Islamic headscarves in public schools were legislatively approved in 2004 under President Jacques Chirac. Under the right-leaning President Nicolas Sarkozy, the government reexamined *laïcité* (secularism) within a collective and often controversial conversation about national identity and, in 2010, passed another ban on conspicuous religious symbols (the niqab, a cloth that covers the head and hair as well as the face). In the aftermath of the Arab Spring, Syria's civil war, and the turmoil in Iraq and Afghanistan, 2015 saw a refugee crisis and two terrorist attacks that prompted a continental conversation about tightening borders: these restrictions threatened the freedom of movement within Europe secured by the Schengen Agreement and its associated visa.[31]

The 2000s and 2010s are key for my analysis, because during this historical juncture the hexagon becomes the sexagon. This sexualization of national inclusion and exclusion occurs because, I argue, sexual vocabularies became the best platform in postmulticulturalist Europe to symbolically strip those who had already become French of their "Frenchness." The early 2000s witnessed events and media interventions that seemed to associate sexual intolerance with specific ethnicities and religions. Exposés about sexual violence and gang rapes in the suburbs proliferated in the French media. Gender and sexual "refugees" from Islamic societies such as Ayaan Hirsi Ali or Chahdortt Djavann found sudden prominence. Multicultural Holland witnessed in shock the assassination of provocateur filmmaker Theo Van Gogh and right-wing gay politician Pim Fortuyn.[32] Coupled with the French riots of 2005–2006, this was a pivotal moment when the multicultural sympathy of old for the Arab or Muslim male was exhausted (see chapter 1). The negative image of the Muslim male reached depths not seen since the 1970s, when, during France's economic crises, immigrants were cast as job thieves or unemployed burdens on the state. An important motivation for the "sexualization of ethnicity" is that it allowed anti-immigrant and antiminority forces to keep the threat of Arab, African, and Islamic difference persistent, even though today the differences between the descendants of immigrants and French citizens of "European" origin at the level of linguistic competence and civic integration are negligible. The 2010s saw a prolongation of this debate with the legalization of gay marriage in France (2012) and the *mariage pour tous* (Marriage for All) bill. Though it is officially forbidden in France to collect statistics about racial and religious origins,[33] French Arabs and Muslims are widely believed to be collectively opposed to gay marriage. Mayanthi Fernando asserts that in the eyes of the larger French public, Muslim opposition to gay marriage was considered more dangerous than the highly visible Catholic opposition during the Manif pour Tous (Protest for All) demonstrations, organized as a rejoinder to *mariage pour tous*. Muslim opposition was also deemed more problematic than the strident and biologically essentialist critiques of gay marriage articulated by the center-right Union for a Popular Movement (UMP) party.[34] Jasbir Puar and other scholars have pointed out that gay marriage has become an "insurance premium" in Europe which allows the distance between Muslim and Christian Europeans to persist for just a bit longer, however statistically unfounded this difference of opinion may be.[35]

The sexualization of immigration is apparent, moreover, in a number of immigration controversies: the polygamous marriage practices (real or alleged) of Muslim, and especially West African Muslim, immigrants; rape and sexual violence in multiethnic banlieues; the homophobia (real or imagined) of immigrants and banlieue youth; arranged marriages; custody battles over children hailing from mixed marriages; male and female prostitution; machismo; perceptions of repressed homosexuality and clandestine bisexuality; Islamic patriarchy; and suggestions that France is being transformed at an alarming pace due to intermarriage and softly coercive religious conversion. Yet, what is politically condemned can also be culturally in demand as manifest in the exotification and fetishization of often-denounced figures such as the Arab macho and the veiled Muslim woman in cinema, sports, music (especially hip-hop), or pornography (both heterosexual and homosexual).

The recent sexualization of ethnicity in France recalls other periods in the twentieth century during which recent arrivals to France were sexually demonized. Historian Todd Shepard, whose work examines France and Algeria from the colonial period to the 1970s, explains how North Africans caused various panics in a France reeling from the Algerian War.[36] Kristin Ross discusses in *Fast Cars, Clean Bodies* how—in a 1960s France severing itself from its former colonies—colonial "energy" originally intended for managing North and West Africa was redirected at the female consumer, new access to housing, domestic space, and the matter of national hygiene;[37] thus, a still "male" France could continue to protect women and the feminized interior of France from the implied "dirtiness" of the colonial experience, of which immigration from North Africa would be an inescapable and constant reminder. In the early 1980s, North Africans started to speak up and demand better living and work conditions. Around that time, France was cast as an allegorical female figure at risk of invasion. The mostly male immigrant threat is drummed up again in the late 1970s and early 1980s after the oil crises and the rise of mass unemployment, a situation in which immigrants appear to xenophobes as excessive male intruders and interlopers. This return to sexual vocabularies in one way echoes the Ross and Shepard periodization—that is, a return to the unfinished business of decolonization—but it also changes the narrative in that the failure of multicultural acceptance in the 1990s recasts the national bogeyman as an Arab or black teenager, rather than an immigrant father who wants to settle with his family in France.

Perspectives: A Note on Methodology

This study is anchored in the analysis of cultural forms and speech rather than in the anthropological examination of society. When I cite journalists, politicians, social scientists, and psychiatrists, I do not aim to explain or dictate the reality of French diversity; instead, I use discourse analysis to analyze regimes of knowledge that purport to document social reality and I trace the figures and patterns that these regimes create. The project's perspective differs from a cultural anthropology approach by focusing on cultural media and the ways in which they convey messages about sexuality, gender, race, nationality, and class. My approach is aligned with the methods of cultural studies to the extent that it looks at representations and debates unfolding across different media as manifestations of a single set of anxieties about immigrant sexuality.[38]

Much of my analysis targets debates, discourses, and rhetoric in keeping with the cultural studies approach of using a textual and linguistic bridge to unify commentary about a multifaceted phenomenon with disparate components stretching across disciplinary boundaries.[39] In many instances, I document the coalescing of voices, at a particular moment and for particular reasons, around the intersection of sexuality and immigration. I opt to look at debates because many of the flashpoints discussed in this book are controversies that take a dialectical form, with counter-representations and also counteressentialisms—not necessarily symmetrical—that struggle over the image of the immigrant or *banlieusard*. While this breakdown perhaps entails that there is no space outside of controversy or politics for exploring the cultural expression of sexuality and ethnicity, I do discuss several examples that withdraw from the explicitly political, which seek evasion from the repetitive tropes of social anomie, violence, and poverty by changing the subject. Other examples escape the patterns of misery literature and the culture of poverty through a "killing off of psychology," representing a revolt against the special kind of psychosis that can result from French Arabs, Muslims, and *banlieusards* overdosing on news reports that present them as a "problem," a revolt against the convenient recourse to psychological complexes to explain their "failures." One might say that such withdrawals from politics are themselves political, a vote of no confidence of sorts. However, counter-representations differ from alternative representations in that the first more explicitly reacts to and is therefore informed by an original representation; the second is a "killing off of psychology" through indifference. Moreover, factors besides politics play a role in politicizing culture; cultural artifacts such as films, books, and documentaries too can launch national debates about the sexual attitudes of immigrants and minorities.

This project stands on the shoulders of much important scholarship in the fields of *beur* and banlieue studies. Sociologists such as Abdelmalek Sayad taught readers to be sensitive to the plight of the solitary immigrant worker from North Africa, and warned us not to confuse different generations of immigration.[40] Loïc Wacquant accounted for the banlieue's unique codes and legitimated it as an object worthy of anthropological exploration, while being careful not to conflate the term with the transatlantic *faux ami* (false friend) of the ghetto.[41] Alec Hargreaves gave an exhaustive portrait of the massive, demographic postcolonial changes that have led to what he calls "multiethnic France."[42] Carrie Tarr explored the representation of the banlieue on screen, and Kathryn Kleppinger studied how *beur* cultural actors crafted their own image in the media.[43] Guénif-Souilamas pushed *beur* studies into the territory of documenting the inner and outer life of the Franco-Arab young woman in the banlieues and elsewhere, before exploring the "bad reputation" of an intertwined figure most often presented as her tormentor, the "Arab boy."[44]

This project also engages with that purposefully enigmatic, intellectual, and activist production: queer theory. I employ the Franco-Arab context and its set of particularities to test the line between queer theory's shifting status between nontheory and theory. This matter is especially germane to the corpus at hand, in which sexual liberation and diversity activists dictate what Arabs' appropriate attitudes toward sexuality should be only to pronounce themselves resolutely against all forms of gender dictatorship and sexual policing. Rooted in the work of Michael Warner, Eve Sedgwick, Judith Butler, and Gayle Rubin, queer theory has been subject to definitions, redefinitions, and refusals to give definitions. Rather than offer a one-size-fits-all meaning, I volunteer a multiplicity of epithets that have characterized this discourse over time: transgressive, context shifting, subversive, strangeness producing, willing to reimagine, in touch with frontiers of sexuality and gender, engaged with difference, resistant to sedimentation, noncanonical, liberatory, conscious of hierarchies of power (yet willing to play with them), nondogmatic, humorous. While queer theory is relatively young, it has been consistently challenged and pushed in new directions, something which its proponents salute as the mark of its success: the realization of its purpose.

Not Queer Enough

"*Queering* queer theory"—to borrow an expression from Jarrod Hayes —is a way of reminding us that the so-called queer is also in danger of sedimenting itself, that it must take into account the differing sexual practices and notions of the other in the continuous elaboration of what is queer. In his book *Queer Nations*, Hayes demonstrated how sexual formations located in a seemingly traditional non-Western culture (that of the Maghreb in his example) have much to teach the West about sexual diversity.[45] The act of queering has often been unidirectional, that is, radiating from Euro-America outward. I describe the way that Franco-Arab and *banlieusard* sexual subcultures may exist in opposition to mainstream understandings of homosexual emancipation as well as queer theory's first wave. This mostly has to do with the primacy of the "closet," in that both queer theory and mainstream gay and lesbian activists "argue with great rigor and sophistication that the binary between closeted and uncloseted sexual desire is a primary determinant of modernity and modernism."[46] Banlieue and Franco-Arab sexual subcultures remind this branch of queer theory of its regressive alignment with homonormative politics, in its unquestioning acceptance of the closet as the primary category of sexual intelligibility, such that the queer potential of the banlieue's willfully clandestine sexualities may never be known.

Clandestinity is problematized differently in each chapter of this book. The term has usually been employed in the context of clandestine or "illegal" immigration, seen as an underground phenomenon avoiding public space. *Sexual clandestinity*, however, branches from that meaning to include phenomena such as the refusal by men who have sex with men and women—including the married men among them—of an openly gay identity, Muslim and Arab subjects' rigorous adherence to the public-private distinction, and an eroticism based on the "secret" rather than the "exhibitionistic." When the gay mainstream has placed all bets for its betterment on a politics of recognition, what does *chosen invisibility* mean? In his analysis of an unpublished chapter of Ralph Ellison's *Invisible Man*, Roderick Ferguson writes, "[for Ellison] invisibility is not only antithetical to a logic of recognition and acceptance; it is antagonistic to that logic that helps to form the alliance between canonical formation, national identification, and ethical development under liberal capitalism."[47] In my analysis of the French gay community's internal divisions along color lines, I find that many nonhomonormative men of color choose clandestinity and retreat from otherwise liberatory forms of exposure as a form of national dissent. They dissent not only from dominant gay visual culture and the imperative of hyperexposure, but also from agreements between minorities and the mainstream that put minority sexual diversity on the path toward homogenization and stabilization. "Down low" men of color, for example, may find public spaces of gay sociality judgmental, uniform, or boring. The prospect of sexual homogenization is dependent on the assent of minorities and secured when the clandestine make themselves visible. Invisibility, in this context, means staying a while longer in an unregulated space of sexual diversity, liberatory or not.[48]

As sociologists and anthropologists (such as Sayad, Guénif-Souilamas, and Fernando) have shown, Franco-Arab cultures and subcultures may privilege group attachments over individualism: this puts pressure on the imperative of transgression, subversion, and antisocial isolationism that characterize a sometimes imperial version of queer theory that devalues community while glorifying atomization. While working on the American case, Ferguson helped identify forms of Anglo and white privilege within the first generation of queer theorists.[49] I intend to use the particularity of Franco-Arab sexual subcultures to unmoor queer theory from a too comfortable perch in the Anglo-American context. Ferguson's study of class, internal migration, and sexuality in *Aberrations in Black* proves especially helpful here: the process by which the nation, in its quest to affirm itself, consistently associates nonheteronormative pathological sexualities with a given racial minority, while simultaneously returning these sexualities to migrant origins, finds several parallels in postcolonial France—with the important difference that this process moves from a national to an international stage. Gayatri Gopinath maps the terrain where the queer meets the international in her theory of the "queer diasporic framework." She explains how, just as the queer is always seen as an incomplete imitation of the heterosexual, so too is the diaspora cast as the queer interior of the nation.[50] Applied to the context of France, both heterosexual and homosexual Muslims can be considered queer for their nonalignment with nationally approved sexual normativities, as in the large (heterosexual) African family or the "closeted" homosexual Arab man in a heterosexual marriage, for example.[51] This equation has a special resonance on the French terrain I am describing, as this dual operation of a simultaneously nationalist and heterosexist expulsion is one that particularly affects Arabs in France, as they may face rejection both for their immigration status and for unfit attitudes about sexuality. Even the gay mainstream, in its condemnation of Franco-Arab men who eschew an openly gay lifestyle, reproduces internally an expulsion from the norm that homosexuals were once victims of (see chapter 1). As Hayes puts it, the Arab and Maghrebi could have the potential to "queer" queer theory if not disqualified from the start by cultural arbiters. Gopinath, like Ferguson, belongs to a growing wave of queer of color theorists who question the normativity of gay scholarship and commentary that aims to cast the "queer, nonwhite, racialized, and/or immigrant subject" as insufficiently modern and politically unaware.[52]

Scholar Lisa Duggan deployed the term *homonormativity* to describe increasingly conservative tendencies among formerly oppressed sexual minorities in neoliberal societies. This occurred at the particular moment when (mainly white) homosexual men were courted by capitalist interests in the rush to exploit the lucrative new prize of the "gay market."[53] Strangely enough, homonormativity contributes to heteronormativity by policing sexual diversity in the homosexual camp. In my argument, homonormativity functions in France to stave off the threat of change that a serious consideration of Muslims' sexual subcultures would effect in the homosexual mainstream. Oftentimes, in France as in the United States, this reproach of political ignorance against queers of color concerns their nonenthusiasm about gay marriage; however, the ignorance of their critics in terms of racial justice, diversity, and empire never becomes as pressing a problem in these reciprocal expectations.

The incredible media firestorm around "dangerous" Arab and black *banlieusards* at times has made it seem like rape has an ethnicity, or that it was invented in the banlieues. Guénif-Souilamas analyzes the figure of the "Arab boy" as constructed by journalists, politicians, and activists: she retraces how *banlieusard* youth sexuality became a countermodel to officialized sexual education campaigns encouraging a healthy rapport between the sexes. Other interlocutors include Joseph Massad, whose work on misrepresentations of Arab sexuality in Western scholarship helps us locate the lingering influence of Orientalism in contemporary French depictions of despotic Islamic patriarchies in the banlieues. Houria Bouteldja, member of the activist group Les Indigènes de la République (The Republic's indigenous),[54] has recently brought Massad's analyses regarding the Arab world to bear on the French context, underlining a lack of enthusiasm among banlieue youth for France's marriage equality campaign. The factors behind this lack (which emanates from internal divisions similar to those opposing queers of color and the gay mainstream in the United States) have to do with the perception that the campaign appeals mostly to white, upwardly mobile homosexuals and allies and is far removed from the daily concerns of *banlieusards* and queers of color.[55]

This study does not aim to cast the practices of European populations of immigrant origin as always other, that is, in constant tension with Western ways of being, especially in a globalized age. However, we can observe that the same critics who call for Franco-Arabs to embrace race-blindness and republican integration actually return them to their origins when they cast them as nonqueer for reasons of Arab difference. Even thinkers assumed to be in the service of sexual liberation have suggested that queerness stands outside the reach of Arabs, Muslims, and other French minorities (see chapter 1 for examples of why the damning sentence of "never queer" is misleading, incomplete, or even antiqueer).

Rarely has republican integration been presented as a threat to the sexual diversity of Muslims and residents of color in the banlieues. Rarely have European youths of color been understood as victims or resisters of a sexual civilizing mission. The infrequent occasions on which they can be heard speaking on their own behalf are usually incriminating, edited, unsophisticated, or embarrassing. *Sexagon* attempts to address this defenselessness at several junctures by reading the filmic and literary portrayals of youths of color against the grain, while highlighting alternative representations outside the dominant culture. Defenses of European men of color against racist attacks usually aim to address discrimination based on skin color and religion rather than sexual demonization. Still other defenses engage in a depoliticized cultural relativism ("sexism is everywhere") so as to perform damage control whenever these subjects are caught making offensive statements. The supposedly entrenched sexual essentialism of banlieue men is questioned less often as an essentialist verdict of its own—obviously it is sexist to think that all banlieue men are sexist, but this statement mainly goes unchallenged in the media. French and American cultural productions have deployed a familiar sexual victimology to frame the experiences of Muslim women (see, for example, Coline Serreau's *Chaos* or the American television series *Homeland*); Muslim men cannot be thought of as victims (unless avowedly homosexual) because this framing depends on them as victimizers. Hence, it is often difficult—within the existing European vocabularies of sexual repression—to imagine what it might be like to be on the receiving end of sexual stereotyping, to face assumptions of machismo, or to occupy a disadvantaged position in the marriage market. This one-way perspective applies to queer persons of color and banlieue youths as well; they can be the recipients of sexual enlightenment and education from the gay mainstream but certainly not agents of queer innovation, let alone content sexual minorities happy to remain attached to their communities and religions.

Solid versus Fluid Identities

Black queer critique in the United States has already enumerated the ways in which bodies of color are used as the stable comparative foundation for "fluid" sexuality's experimentation and nonessentialism.[56] This notion of solid versus experimental sexualities helps explain the incredible dearth of queer readings of banlieue citizens of color, who are counted on to serve the roles of countermodels to a queer fluidity now carrying a geographical specificity in the metrosexual city center. Among the French "outlaw" figures that might demonstrate the queering potential of subjects deemed nonqueer are female gang members in the banlieues and homosexual *cailleras* (thugs); both incarnate a combative type of urban virility, but in different ways. Through a queer reading of these figures, we can reinterpret the recourse to virility in postimmigration generations as a form of nonnormative performance.

Queer theory has often sought to destabilize essentialist identity politics. The sexual and ethnic minority figures under study here, however, do make strident identity-based assertions about their ethnic, urban, and religious pride: as *banlieusards*, as Muslims, as Moroccans, as butch, and sometimes, irreverently, as *cailleras*. These assertions would seem to have little to do with the self-critique and self-shattering one usually thinks of when it comes to queer dispositions. I maintain, however, that the solidity of identity these subjects aim for actually sheds its normativity in light of the circumstances of immigration, postimmigration, and life as a minority in France. When compared to an increasingly homogenous gay mainstream, outwardly phallocentric "homo thugs" deviate from acceptable norms, though their respect for virility might seem normative in the heterosexual mainstream. In some instances, well-meaning gay activists call for queering banlieue or Islamic identities to achieve a liberatory or dissident outcome, a queering whose ultimate consequence is a community-breaking disarmament. The queering most often demanded of banlieue homosexuals is an interrogation of virility and an exploration of sensitivity. However, the normative quality of virility varies according to context. For instance, the practice of hypervirility by banlieue homosexuals of immigrant background signifies differently from the virility exhibited in traditional or patriarchal societies or in those same subjects' ancestral homelands. Queering the first as opposed to the second virility would entail consequences disproportionate in terms of power relations, because the first virility belongs to an embattled minority that may use it for expressive and resistant purposes, while the second virility only comforts what are presumed to be majority attitudes in those societies. The same can be said about decisions to wear the hijab in a postcolonial European context as opposed to within an Islamic society where the majority of women wear it. The traditional, when surfacing in contemporary contexts, is rarely just traditional, as seen in the highly heterogeneous mixtures of the traditional and modern in phenomena such as Islamic Internet dating or gay marriage. These reflections are part of a larger examination of how certain encouragements to *queer* can be incorporated within a national agenda that finds in (distorted) queering a useful weapon against minority or Muslim assertions of identity politics.

Transgressive is a buzzword that factors in much recent coverage of Islamic and Arab sexual cultures, and it is the implicit goal of the type of top-down queering just mentioned. Academic scholarship is not immune from this insistent focus on the transgression of Islamic cultures, as though these cultures were only recoverable or worthwhile if they contained transgressive elements. Oftentimes this scholarship does not reflect on how calling for transgression in a climate where transgression stands as an integration imperative is hardly transgressive.[57] The potential for queer scholarship to examine what happens when norms are inhabited, engaged, or played with—often with unexpected outcomes—has rarely been examined in the case of French subjects with Islamic roots, a gap that motivates my study.[58]

Sexual Nationalism and the Rape of Europa

The imperative of transgressing Islamic sexual values comes about in the aftermath of important shifts in the meaning of so-called European values. In the last decade, sexuality has been tied to modernity and, more largely, European identity. Xenophobic politicians and groups have portrayed the presence of Muslims in Europe as a sexualized invasion or rape, whose aim is to bring about the *grand remplacement* (great replacement), a dystopia in which the complexion of Europe changes for the darker. In France this portrayal has surfaced in the rhetoric of the far-right Front National party and more expansively in the recurrent images of a feminized Republic—that takes the form of a veiled Marianne or Joan of Arc—threatened by Muslim patriarchy. From the postdecolonization period to the 2000s, Western European countries saw the increased institutionalization of women's rights concurrent with the homogenization of the European Union, paving the way for European laws on gender equality and sexual rights equality. Sociologist Nilüfer Göle, often asked to speak on Turkey's possible accession to the European Union, alludes to the proliferation of contact zones between Europe and the Islamic world as she introduces the notion of their "interpenetrations." Interpenetrations exist, Göle argues, because there is a "corporeal, sexed, and also forced, violent aspect in this communicative encounter. Muslims are forcing their presence onto Europe." She concludes that "the candidacy of Turkey and its desire for Europe are perceived by Europeans not only as suspect, but also as an intrusion within the geographic, historic, and religious borders of Europe."[59] Within this imagery, the "desire for Europe"—whether felt by pro-accession Turks or by *harragas* (i.e., North African immigrants traversing the Mediterranean in makeshift boats in search of a better life)—is met by the protectors of "Fortress Europe" with the suspicion that normally greets men too eager for sexual relations.

The tying together of nationalist, xenophobic politics with a sexual liberation or LGBT agenda has been termed "sexual nationalism" and also "homonationalism." This fair-weather convergence between political entities that have previously clashed (US homosexuals and the military, for example) has been the object of several books as well as a high-profile 2011 conference in Amsterdam. Dubbed "Sexual Nationalisms," the conference called attention to an international trend by which upwardly mobile sexual minorities were increasingly expressing nationalist, militaristic, or anti-immigration politics and being recruited by right-wing parties ready to accept them into their fold.[60]

The situation in Europe is all the more special because of the "modern sexual illogic" that seems to break through political entrenchments that have long alienated enemy camps from one another.[61] Both the Left and the Right align in the sexualization of racial difference, spurred by fair-weather friendships between anti-immigrant patriotism and liberal secularism, as has been the case in the Netherlands, Denmark, and Germany.[62] Within these friendships, the issue of immigrant homophobia has arisen as a political convergence point. The Netherlands released an official study in 1996 that explicitly compared and contrasted gay friendliness with the presence of migrants in the country, and an official report that depicted "gays of color" as especially representative of the cultural tensions (and even schizophrenia) that divide neighborhoods in these globalized European centers.[63] Ultranationalists have warned about the "danger" of admitting male Muslim migrants (who they perceive as potential rapists lusting after the nation's daughters) into a spineless, submissive, and feminized France made vulnerable by its unwillingness to forsake tolerance and social welfare in the name of security (see chapter 2). Some left-wing thinkers, on the other hand, have warned of the influx of patriarchal values concurrent with African immigration that might imperil decades of feminist and, more recently, LGBT victories. With an exhausted and exasperated tone, they warn of the necessity of having to fight old battles over again, because of "antimodern" immigrants.[64]

Sexual nationalism has its share of critics, who take their cues from reflections on "imperial feminism." Jasbir Puar and others have called attention to how the plight of Afghan women under the Taliban was often cited as a justification for the 2001 invasion of their country. Eric Fassin, a co-organizer of the "Sexual Nationalisms" conference, alludes to how the believers in a so-called clash of civilizations have expanded the telos of irresistible neoliberal democracy to include women's rights.[65] Both Nick Rees-Roberts and Maxime Cervulle have written about how in France the tolerance of homosexuality has coincided with the rejection of figures such as the veiled woman or the male immigrant, "sexual-racial others" banished from sexual modernity.[66] Branching from sexual nationalism, Puar offers up the term "homonationalism": a national, patriotic homosexuality that emerges from American exceptionalism and imperialism, rejecting and demonizing Muslim "sexual-racial others" as a way of asserting its superiority.[67]

In many ways, the "sexual-racial others" Puar refers to have a corollary in the outlaw African and Arab sexualities mentioned earlier, which, by counterpoint, help solidify the ideal French "national homosexual subject." In France this happens not on military but on cultural terrain; indeed, a version of nationalist homosexuality runs through the corpus of various cultural guardians—including writers, philosophers, and journalists—whose outspoken defense of French literature, values, and identity often seeks to reinforce the endangered contributions of homosexuals to French culture. The writer Renaud Camus and the journalist Caroline Fourest, for example, highlight the menace of Muslim immigrants to both sexual diversity and French culture.

A term such as *homonationalism*, which is not specific to France, needs to be nuanced before it is applied to the French context. In some instances, the *banlieusard* phenomena I study exceed the parameters of what the term describes and necessitate new vocabularies. Puar's argument is specifically linked to American exceptionalism: with a cut-and-paste application to France, Puar's homonationalism might lose in specificity when it turns into a catch-all term applied to processes outside the Anglo-American context. The same could be said about Fassin's use of "sexual nationalism," which may signify differently outside of France where it is used to condemn *banlieusard* subjects already part of the French nation. The "sexual nationalism" awakened in the West at the sight of an Afghan woman wearing a burqa is quite different from that which surfaces at the sight of a French teenager wearing a bandanna or hoodie as a covert hijab in a secular banlieue high school. Similarly, one must remain guarded against reactions and condemnations that vary little when one switches from the Middle East and North Africa (MENA) to the banlieue: European commentators who condemn the homosocial exclusivity of male groups in sex-segregated Saudi Arabia, may try to draw a parallel when they make similar commentaries about "packs" of young black and Arab men donning hip-hop attire and strutting with confidence through central Paris. There are further differences between the contexts of the MENA region and postcolonial France, such that comparison, even if on a continuum, becomes difficult. Religion, for some French Muslim youth, has gone from being an intimate practice behind closed doors to a vector of a political identity and resistance. Sartorial expressions of Islamic modesty can become expressions of Islamic exuberance. Stereotypes about Muslims' attachment to the private sphere of domestic life signify differently in a French postimmigration situation: private life can become impossible in the surveillance state of the vertical banlieue housing projects and must therefore seep out into the public sphere, such that public spaces become domestic spaces for many banlieue youth (see chapter 3).

The Banlieue as Laboratory

My study identifies two cultural formations emergent in the banlieues that exceed the traditional parameters of both homonationalism and sexual nationalism: nongendered virility and chosen homosexual clandestinity. These formations are attached of course to figures who exemplify these notions in practice. The discreet "homo thug" (often referred to in French parlance as *caillera gay*) and sexually clandestine Arabs and Muslims reject an openly gay lifestyle (even when it is available to them) and public (but not private) effeminacy, as well as the draw of the city center; instead, they may prefer to explore their sex lives in ethnic enclaves and banlieues. The female gang member, the female "soldiers" of Islam, and the preponderance of banlieue women who adopt clothing styles and manners of speaking that the dominant society at large associates with masculine swagger, all exemplify how virility has been divorced from men and identified with immigration. These banlieue figures are interrelated in the sense that they ostensibly reject as culturally other what some might find to be progressive advances in the domain of women's and sexual minorities' freedoms, for reasons of identity-based demarcation and sometimes Islamic affirmation. These figures, immediately rejected as backward and patriarchal, are in my argument the main examples of a queer of color backlash against homo and sexual nationalisms that has less to do with the MENA region than with the cultural and social dynamics of contemporary France. For this reason, these formations might be better seen as *proregressions* in their forward-thinking embrace of sexual dispositions misunderstood as regressive by critics who believe them to incarnate old forms of patriarchy, rather than contemporary reactions to a feminist and gay rights movement that does not always include minorities. On the one hand, this is evident in how some banlieue and Muslim women trade in, master, and also contribute to a virility traditionally associated with men, making the association between the male and the virile irrelevant. On the other hand, banlieue and Muslim men indicate proregression when they purposefully choose to enter clandestine worlds removed from the scrutiny of openly gay life for reasons that have little to do with internalized homophobia and more to do with contemporary desires for the affirmation of cultural difference in a world of increasing gay homogenization. Internet possibilities of selective disclosure have informed this proregression, allowing participants in banlieue subcultures to craft their desired degree of outness, which is often influenced by a Franco-Islamic view of the public and the private (see chapters 1 and 2). These are not formations produced by nostalgia for Islamic or North African ways of understanding sexuality but arise in the specific conditions of dense urban living in Europe.

Choosing clandestinity as an object of analysis naturally presents certain epistemological problems: how does one study that which is meant to stay hidden? Is it disrespectful to expose sexual subcultures to a harsh outside atmosphere that might lead to their endangerment or extinction? What to do in the face of this subculture's indifference to how it may be perceived by those critics who find that secrecy is a thing of the past? Who can stand to represent these subcultures when most participants choose anonymity? This conundrum calls for a cautious and nuanced approach that requires the researcher, on occasion, to break with conventions of academic distance and access private spaces to gain "insider" knowledge. This approach respects the right to indifference and anonymity, but intervenes when this subculture's participants are criticized in media forums where, for privacy reasons, they refuse to appear and are therefore unable to mount a defense. Though part of this respect involves *not* telling a story about *banlieusard* sexual subcultures when disclosure is demanded (so as not to play secondhand native informant), at times, only alternative storytelling can quell the one-way stream of unanswered critique that colors so many representations of clandestine subcultures.

An Eventful Home Life

The valorization of clandestinity at a time of great change in urban planning, housing, and gentrification naturally leads to the revision of "home" as a concept. Queer of color theorists have spoken of how progress narratives about diaspora often define the western host country as one of sexual liberty and the eastern or southern home country as a space of sexual repression.[68] Most interesting for the case of cultural depictions of Franco-Arabs living in the banlieues, is that very often this equation is reversed: private homes and immigrant enclaves become the most hospitable space for sexual expression, while public spaces in the city center traditionally designated as meeting places are avoided (see chapter 1). The queer innovation that these subjects are so often accused of lacking, I argue, occurs inside, and not outside, the home. The narrative of gay emancipation that locates gay men's upward mobility in their departure from "home" is often neither desirable nor available to banlieue men for whom separation from family or community is not a priority.

The home spaces that Muslim and banlieue men have queered in this way, create a new "exotic" curiosity that has recently become the object of gay tourism and cruising (see chapters 1, 3, and 5). What Hiram Perez calls "gay cosmopolitan tourism" mostly flows in one direction, however, with mobility allowed for tourists to meet "poor communities of color" on their own terms, but not vice versa.[69] Hegemonic gay tourism conceives of these communities as resources of "labor, food, sex, and other commodities valued by the consumer citizen."[70] In the urban agglomeration of Paris, this reading also applies to ethnic enclaves within the city limits that are rapidly gentrifying. When it comes to the banlieue, however, such tourism has gone online or has been transferred to spaces where the banlieue permeates the city center (e.g., transit hubs, parks, shopping centers). This cross-class cruising is organized by spatial habits particular to the dynamic between the gay ghetto and the ethnic ghetto. The Paris *intramuros* prejudice (which causes Parisians to stay between its "walls") often plagues relationships between banlieue and city center residents: it nips online relationships in the bud because some Parisian may perceive the trip to the banlieues as either inconvenient, undesirable, or "dangerous." That real estate developers and property owners now count on a gentrification that proceeds by recourse to an acceptable degree of gay-friendliness,[71] has special implications for these queer banlieue spaces and communitarian enclaves. This state of affairs produces the irony that upwardly mobile gay expansion replaces the gay sexual expression of less moneyed Europeans of color, in public space.[72] Encouraging women and homosexuals to leave the banlieue for a more emancipated life in the city center is a narrative that can be summarized by the expression *il faut en sortir pour s'en sortir* (one must leave it [the banlieue] in order to make it [in life]). Often recycled in the French mainstream media, this narrative only exacerbates the blindness to the banlieue's queer cultures since the departing homosexuals vacate the banlieue spaces left behind.[73] This exhortation to leave impoverished, multiethnic areas has a literary corollary known as the "escape narrative" genre, which is immensely popular not only in Europe but also in the United States, with "get out of the ghetto" bestsellers and the proliferation of "misery lit."[74] The sometimes restrictive North African and Muslim cultural values that shore up the home or community may themselves provide forms of homoeroticism for banlieue residents familiar with them (see chapter 1). They create bonding sites of communal homosociality that may slide into homosexuality, illustrating how "a heteronormative home . . . unwittingly generates homoeroticism."[75] Spaces of "extreme gender conformity" that seem "fortified against queer incursions" from the outside,[76] show themselves to be hospitable to queer incursions from the inside. Against the prevailing representation of the banlieues as not queer enough, some cultural actors have been sensitive to the queer and erotic potential of clandestine banlieue spaces. The cover image chosen for this book features François Sagat, a non-Muslim, non-Arab French actor and artist who nonetheless adorns his body with an Islamic crescent tattoo, professes an admiration for Arab culture and men, and launched an illustrious career in gay pornography by playing an Arab homo-thug character named Azzedine. The studio that fostered his emergence profits from fantasies about concealed, dangerous, and underground sex in the banlieues, which are attractive not merely due to the draw of the taboo but also due to the novelty of the sexual cultures on display (see chapter 5). Sagat's financially successful ethnic drag and self-decoration indicate how Islam and Arabness have been eroticized and severed from Arab and Muslim bodies, becoming transferable in-demand commodities just as Islam and Arabs are deemed incompatible with homoeroticism. With his face turned away in the direction of a wall, Sagat channels the anonymity of ethnic fetish objects, as well as the anonymity of France's prison population, the majority of which is estimated to be Muslim and young. Sagat's rippling musculature clash with his nude vulnerability and obvious injury. This image encapsulates the complicated representation of the Arab man and his vacillating passage from powerful aggressor, to bloody martyr, to interchangeable sex fodder, to an easily seized incarcerated body, to an object of admiration and back again.

Exposing the Arab

It is a crisis at the level of sexual ontology and the perception of "foreign" sexualities that makes unintelligible the sexual practices of the other, or in France's case, those of the immigrant or *banlieusard*. The crisis is particularly noticeable in situations in which outside observers use the term *hypocritical* to describe the sexual fluidity of married immigrants when it concerns bisexuality (see chapters 3 and 4). At the same time, these observers approve of sexual fluidity when it comes to the outward appearance of androgyny and metrosexuality. This rejection of sexual difference happens in the name of sexual liberation or, as I argue, because of the imperative of sexual disclosure required in European "sexual modernity."

Joseph Massad details how sexual repudiation, or the rejection of what is not sexually normative, functions in the gay press's coverage of the Arab world. Studying gay journalists' reaction to Arab men who sleep with men and women, Massad underlines that it is not just the homosexual category that falls apart when presented with behavior that refuses its contours, but the category of the heterosexual as well:

> Rex Wockner, the author of an acutely othering article on "gays and lesbians" in the Arab world and Iran, which was reprinted in a large number of gay publications in the United States and Britain, wonders in bafflement about Arab and Iranian men who practice both "insertive" same-sex and different-sex contact and refuse the West's identification of gayness: "Is this hypocritical? Or a different world?" he marvels. "Are these 'straight' men really 'gays' who are overdue for liberation? Or are humans by nature bisexual, with Arab and Moslem men better tuned into reality than Westerners? Probably all the above."[77]

Both the French and the American media—and this comment is by no means restricted to the gay press—show a certain glee in exposing the sexual "hypocrisy" of Muslims, no matter the consequences for those Muslims who want to keep their sexuality private. When "unveiling" Muslim or Arab sexuality, journalists justify their gesture by portraying it as resistance to the patriarchal values perceived to suffuse Arab and Muslim cultures. When outing Muslim sex, flimsy analogies are made to the outings of conservative politicians in light of their homophobic votes, actions, or beliefs. Oftentimes, the practice of exposing Muslim homophobia falls into a homophobic pattern itself. When critics utter such phrases as "Muslim men are so macho, yet look at all the homosexuality behind closed doors," they depend on a tired equation between homosexuality and effeminacy, making the very existence of "macho" homosexuals an aberration. In this schema, effeminacy would supposedly be the "worst fear" of Arab and Muslim men, explaining its use as an injurious weapon by seemingly progressive commentators who might otherwise criticize such an amalgam of homosexuality and effeminacy if presented in plainer terms.

There is a further problem at the level of sexual perception and intelligibility when one reduces Arab and Muslim youth to a caricature of virilist violence by disconnecting them from "a rich and complex" North African heritage of homoaffectivity, homosociality, and love between men.[78] This heritage stands in polar opposition to their current status as purveyors of violent homophobia: in the recent past, affection, tenderness, and warm accolades between men characterized North African sociality and occasioned disapproving remarks when they manifested in diaspora.[79] These affective principles stood outside the homo-hetero binary, and managed to subsist in the first generations of immigration. While one view holds that, as a result of immigration, these homosocial cultures have been lost or transformed, others might argue that they remain, albeit mainly inside the North African community in question, sheltered from outside scrutiny so as not to be confused with more explicitly sexual gay cruising. Homoaffective North African practices, such as kissing and handholding, have been replaced in French-born generations with a harder, more Americanized etiquette that rejects old-world customs, according to Guénif-Souilamas. This hardening transpires due to a combination of social factors, some hypothetical and some averred: the less-than-warm welcome and occasional humiliations of these generations' immigrant parents in the host society, producing resentment in the children; the embarrassment their fathers felt when performing these affective gestures in front of French colleagues and bosses sometimes quick to judge this affectivity as perverse; and finally, these particular youths' failure to improve socioeconomically upon their parents' generation (which would result in the adoption of a contrarian posture). In French high schools and on stairwell landings, the "no homo" handshake of American minorities has replaced holding hands and kissing on the cheek, in Guénif-Souilamas's version.[80] When virility is isolated to sexual violence and hardness, cut off from any affective or socializing function, all that it can signify is criminality, streamlined into ideal fodder for political scapegoating. Foucault's idea that virility and perversion are often closely associated, has not only been reinforced by politicians condemning the banlieues but also by pornography producers (see chapter 5).

The televised war between the "macho" banlieusards and "macho" security-minded politicians threatens to dominate representations of urban France, eclipsing alternative virilities that have no stake in power or violence. Journalists and politicians too often have shored up the border between the banlieue using sexual vocabularies that invoke a sexual clash of civilizations.[81] This opposition structures Eric Fassin's concept of "sexual democracy" which, far from being an inclusive meritocracy, indexes inclusion on highly restricted and often very heterosexual concepts of gender equality and the free expression of public sexuality (saluting feminine women and metrosexual men only). These elements become new cornerstones of French identity even though they are demanded of others before being officially secured in France (as equal representation shortcomings and crackdowns on public cruising have shown).[82] An "end-of-history" telos drives sexual democracy: it articulates "modern" European identity through sexual vocabularies. Conversely, minorities lose the privilege of sexual citizenship when they exhibit "antimodern" behavior, like the intentional closeting of North African men or the veiling of Muslim women. In this way, the term *sexual modernity* becomes intelligible: it is an umbrella term, encompassing everything from the promotion of sexual diversity and gender equality, to a zero-tolerance policy regarding "excessive" virilities (banlieue machos) and "self-censoring" femininities (veiled women).

Once an obscure concept, sexual modernity has made it all the way into naturalization surveys and exams in a variety of European countries: these have elsewhere been called citizenship tests, as in the German province of Baden-Württemberg.[83] The province introduced a citizenship application in 2006 that principally contained two types of questions: one category surveyed attitudes about national security and terrorism, while the other surveyed attitudes about sexuality, asking gendered questions that seemed tailor-made for identifying Muslim sexists in order to deny citizenship: "What is your view of a man in Germany who has two wives at the same time?," or, "Imagine that your adult son comes to you and explains that he is homosexual and would like to live together with another man. How do you react?" However, when media outlets in Germany invited their general readership to weigh in on the same issues, the German-born scores indicated a surprising intolerance of sexual diversity. This result highlights the curious way in which immigrants are often expected to display a level of tolerance and progressivism above and beyond the level existing in the resident population, as a sign of their readiness to assimilate. It also echoes the way right-wing parties in a variety of countries have at times suddenly become defenders of women, and in some cases sexual minorities, when it comes to articulating anti-immigration or pro-war arguments. As opposed to the American picture depicted by Puar, in which the overseas wartime context colors the sexualized relationship to the other, in France the geographical parameters are more local: the "fight" against sexual intolerance is framed as a necessary war of "national defense" on home soil, aiming to protect the suddenly representative French values of "sexual modernity" from withering away in ethnic "ghettos."[84]

Ghetto is a loaded term that has become a site of controversy: ghettos would foster a kind of communitarian isolation that is anathema to the principle of republican indivisibility. Yet not every ghetto is treated or represented in the same way, because some seem less of a communitarian threat than others: there are rich ghettos, gourmet ghettos, yuppie ghettos, hipster ghettos, and gay ghettos, none of which imperil the French Republic.[85] Can ghettos be places where a given community comes together in rootedness and solidarity, or must ghettos always be sites of regression and retreat from national unity? Sexual and ethnic minorities are linked along this ghetto continuum. The "discreet" clandestinity once demanded of homosexuals in the Marais district of Paris is now reprehensible when incarnated by residents of the banlieue, who may prefer to mark their difference in the era of gay hypervisibility via communitarian insularity. One type of communitarianism (gay), once denigrated during an era of homophobia now forgotten, is valorized if it becomes a sanctuary from a more "dangerous" type of communitarianism (ethnic). This sanctuary, however, is not so much a freely chosen destination but rather a club one is required to belong to. In the process, minorities are asked to cut off family and social ties to the banlieue in order to be accepted into sexual modernity.

As recently as two decades ago, imperatives were placed on the gay ghetto to remain discreet.[86] Such forgetting of a past clandestinity that once united sexual and ethnic minorities in experience (see chapter 4) now contributes to their needless alienation from one another: it also leads to an altogether impossible situation for LGBT people of color who may not want to choose between their sexual and ethnic identities. This amnesia affects the way the different ghettos are conceptualized in today's France. It is no accident that one of the primary sources analyzed in my study, Franck Chaumont's investigative report into an exclusively banlieue homophobia (titled *Homo-ghetto*), is symptomatic in its very title of "ghetto" amnesia, of forgetfulness about past commonalities between ethnic and gay ghettos. This ahistoricism also drives the once stigmatized gay community to forget the marginalizing rhetoric of which it was once a victim, thus placing that community at risk of reproducing such language when it comes to other minorities. Dangerously opposed in this way, the ethnic ghetto's homophobia and the sexual ghetto's racism are destined for radicalization.

Sexagon Road Map

Chapter 1 explores how the sexism and homophobia of "problematic" male and female banlieue youths has been constructed in activist rhetoric by juxtaposing an indeterminate "sexual modernity," residing in the metrosexuality of the city center, to an ethnicized "sexual antimodernity" emanating from the periphery, including banlieues and hubs of immigration. Progressives determined to promote sexual diversity and tolerance have often shown themselves to be intolerant of masculine and feminine attributes deemed too communitarian or ethnocentric. In dismissing the banlieue's virility cultures, prominent journalists and politicians, such as Franck Chaumont and Fadela Amara, neglect the contemporary socioeconomic factors that frequently bond the expression of virility to working-class communities and minority groups.[87] In their rhetoric, virility is never admissible as a form of resistance, nor does it extend to the figure of the female "thug" or *racaille* type; instead, it is editorialized into a false consciousness. Such characterizations of banlieue gender expressions, however, have been met with criticism by activists, such as nightclub entrepreneur Fouad Zeraoui, who have challenged the all-too-familiar *miserabilist* rhetoric according to which sexual minorities of color are victims who will only find salvation within the borders of the tolerant city center; this rhetoric perpetuates the idea that staying in the periphery will only result in misery, solitude, and violence.[88] Instead of viewing banlieue sexual minorities as doubly oppressed, Zeraoui highlights their upward mobility and visibility in a French urban setting that may actually favor androgyny and metrosexuality.[89]

Chapter 2 examines the interventions of psychoanalysts and ethnopsychiatrists such as Fethi Benslama, Michel Schneider, Jalil Bennani, Malek Chebel, Tahar Ben Jelloun, and Tobie Nathan who, claiming an intimate knowledge of sexuality's relation to culture and politics, have weighed in on the "menace" of immigration to the "sexual peace" of the sociosymbolic order in France. The chapter details that some of these thinkers' conclusions emanate from the experimental Algiers School, a colonial-era group known for its experiments on the indigenous and its tendency to demonize Muslim and North African sexuality. This demonization extends to many current psychoanalytical commentaries on the "problem families" that are supposedly the product of immigration and communitarianism. What emerges is a "broken" family portrait, made up of the delinquent youth, the self-effacing mother, and the impotent immigrant father, all of whom enable one another.

Chapter 3 scrutinizes the literary figure of the delinquent or "troublesome" Franco-Arab youth which takes the form of an indigenous ephebe in the travel writing of European writers such as André Gide, Joe Orton, William Burroughs, Oscar Wilde, and, more recently, Frédéric Mitterrand and Roland Barthes. In their writings, the figure of the once exploited "Arab boy" breaches the Mediterranean barrier through immigration, posing an unknowable and threatening presence to metropolitan lives. Yet the literary "Arab boy" provides a complementary, albeit elusive, model of masculinity: in his outward self-confidence and physical splendor, he becomes a role model and object of fascination for writers, filmmakers, and artists accustomed to exploring the fragility of the self. These storytellers engage in a kind of self-fragmentation that can be productive in the artistic sphere but has a tendency to wear them down: the fragility they associate with "whiteness" causes them to seek (and at times create) the masculine rigidity of Arab boys. In addition to Barthes and Mitterrand, the novelists Abdellah Taïa, Rachid O., Renaud Camus, Nina Bouraoui, and playwright Bernard-Marie Koltès have detailed the various peregrinations of the "Arab boy" in and outside of France.

Chapter 4 looks at how cinema provides insight into the perception, surveillance, and policing of the "troublesome" figures on the periphery. Virility, a gender disposition normally characterized as aggressive, is shown on-screen to serve a protective, even chivalrous purpose for other wayward characters in need of orientation. The strategy of clandestinity, normally employed in the context of immigration and underground economies, becomes key to understanding how immigrant-issued sexualities negotiate and escape scrutiny on-screen. Protagonists are shown to deftly navigate the public-private distinction, carefully controlling sexual disclosure. This form of representation takes on culturalist overtones when it is suggested that these figures adopt a private persona, among family members or lovers, and a public persona when facing an open society expecting disclosure of sexuality. Select directors, evincing sympathy for minority subjectivities, show an appreciation for culturally informed sexualities that become "dissident" when relocated to Europe and compared to European norms. These directors have set out to illustrate why immigrants' attitudes about sexuality may go beyond mere hypocrisy and serve to instruct European observers in how to pass freely between communities, sexual and ethnic, without wearing one's sexual orientation on one's sleeve. New families and new communities are born, they suggest, of the "happy" meeting of sexual and ethnic minorities in an urban space enabled by this malleable understanding of the public and the private.

Chapter 5 explores the most unapologetically explicit medium for depicting the sexualization of immigration: pornography, both heterosexual and homosexual. Pornography presents a liberatory vantage point, less vexed by controversies about representation, but also carries within it certain dangers having to do with the distortion of ethnic images and the capitalist exploitation of bodies.

In the conclusion, I bring into relief my portrait of the sexualization of immigration and diversity in French culture in light of recent tragic events and controversies that have put pressure on European and American understandings of hospitality, asylum, and foreign policy, and have exacerbated the perception of Muslim (sexual) intolerance and the dangers of hypervirility. At the same time, these crises have provided a platform for those critiquing the sexual demonization of religion and ethnicity based on generalizations after violent incidents. These crises have allowed researchers, and especially queer Franco-Arabs, a greater role in counteracting the historical amnesia that depicts Muslims and the Islamic world as timelessly intolerant and the Euro-American world as always having been sexually progressive.

1 / The Banlieue Has a Gender:
Competing Visions of Sexual Diversity

You know what fascinates me with blacks and beurs? It's their way of always being strong even when nothing's going right. Even when they are in the worst shit they'll never let themselves sink . . . they are all super-physical, you see them at the gym, the way they walk. I want to be like that you see, hard as concrete . . . in any case it helps me. They are role models.

LAURENT IN SEBASTIEN LIFSHITZ'S *LES TERRES FROIDES*[1]

On September 29, 2010, the public ARTE television network aired the controversial documentary *La cité du mâle*, directed by Cathy Sanchez.[2] Set in the Cité Balzac—a housing project in Vitry-sur-Seine near Paris where in 2002 seventeen-year-old Sohane Benziane was burned alive by her former boyfriend—the documentary examines the alleged widespread nature of male violence against women and sexual minorities in suburban housing projects (*cités*). *La cité du mâle* consists of four disturbing vignettes that feature young men defending prisoners locked up for violence against women; an anonymous male homosexual who fled the banlieue for the purported safety of the city center; the female leader of a male gang who "sacrificed" her femininity in order to gain respect; and two girls talking about the constant pressure to maintain one's "good" reputation as chaste. Even before its scheduled airing, the film was engulfed in a controversy involving a crew member, Nabila Laïb, who demanded her name be removed from the production credits because she disagreed strongly with the film's final cut. Laïb insisted that Sanchez "only chose passages that corresponded to what she had already written in her report," and that the film's focus on the rampant sexual violence against and victimization of women was not always in line with the uncut interviews.[3] The controversy escalated even further when Laïb was sentenced to four months in prison for making phone threats against Sanchez.[4] Following the documentary's broadcast, filmmaker and community organizer Ladji Réal launched a *contre-enquête* (or counter-documentary) titled *La cité du mal* (The city of evil) in which he revisits the full testimonies of the interviewees and critiques Sanchez's editorializing by focusing on how the banlieues have been vilified as the locus of violence and evil.[5]

La cité du mâle is representative of the various ways journalists and activists who purport to fight for sexual diversity often end up reifying sexual conformism by demonizing the banlieue's racialized, nonnormative sexualities on the one hand, and denying the banlieue's queer potential on the other. In their reports and interventions, journalists and activists professing to represent gay and feminist interests have focused on an uncommonly sexist *banlieusard* virility with alleged roots in Islamic cultures. Indeed, some of the same commentators who suggest Muslim women are coerced into wearing headscarves by their communities also criticize immigrant women if they do not conform to traditional notions of femininity. Their rhetoric about "saving" banlieue women and homosexuals defines their subjects as victims while espousing "appropriate" expressions of their subject's identities or practices. If Western human rights groups have represented the Muslim world as a place inhospitable to women and sexual minorities, recent media coverage has characterized the banlieue and its prevailing attitudes toward gender and sexuality as a microcosm of the Muslim world inside France.

Réal's counter-documentary to *La cité du mâle* aims to establish a filmic rebuttal to stereotypical trends of banlieue representation. Changing the last word of the title from *mâle* to *mal*, he spells out the slippage from "male" to "evil" that the first documentary had only hinted at. It notably features an interview with Nacira Guénif-Souilamas, who has written extensively about the concept of sexual vilification which is variously observable in media, politics, and even academia. Sexual vilification takes the form of reproaching minorities and immigrants for allegedly regressive, patriarchal, or antimodern attitudes about sexuality in a way that stigmatizes their neighborhoods explicitly and their cultures of origin implicitly. The counter-documentary exercise is innovative, as it presents a creative reaction to banlieue residents' regrets about having engaged with the city-centric media. Many banlieue interviewees have cited negative experiences with journalists as a reason for disengagement and hostility to film crews who seem to land out of nowhere in their neighborhoods. They point to the recurrent experience of having their stories distorted or conveniently edited, of being subjected to the practices of suggestive questioning, and of being misled by journalists who need their consent for filming.[6]

Banlieue Girl Gangs and Muslima Soldiers

Although Sanchez's documentary focuses on men in its depiction of sexual violence and territorialism, its portrayal of women—and in particular "virile" women—is noteworthy. Narrator Daniel Leconte describes how Imèle and Melissa, two young women interviewed on the subject of Sohane Benziane's death, have fallen into a kind of "virility trap" despite their best intentions: "Imèle and Melissa are twenty years old. They know the projects by heart; they were born there. Sneakers, baggy jeans, and sweat suits—they dress in the manner of tomboys [à la bonhomme] as they say around here, to be at peace. Like most girls, Imèle and Melissa do better in school than the boys. Both have degrees and work. In short, they seem rather emancipated in the projects." A confusing sequence ensues, in which the camera cuts to the girls joking about how they would not want to be struck by any man or woman and how they would probably "punch back" if that were to transpire. The narrator's commentary raises a topic that has bothered more than one journalist: the substitution of feminine attire with a butch banlieue uniform made up of baggy, "gender-effacing" athletic wear. What the narrator fails to acknowledge is that athletic wear has become a marker of urban belonging rather than a dubious sign of masculinity or gang affiliation; in addition, he ignores the ways in which minority women—not just in the banlieues but in most multiethnic urban centers around the Western world—have feminized athletic wear by sporting tight sweatpants and hoodies or baggy clothes that show off, rather than hide, feminine curves. Two films have been instrumental in detailing how banlieue street fashion connects with female virility: *La squale* (2001; The squaw) and *Bande de filles* (2014; *Girlhood*).[7] Both films feature strong, black female protagonists who belong to banlieue girl gangs and have gained significant respect in their communities. In both films, they pass through cycles of butchness and effeminacy, and, although initially portrayed as heterosexual, express affection for other women, especially after they have achieved female virility. Moreover, both protagonists feature in love scenes where they dominate men and force them into vulnerable positions. And both films exploit the virile beauty of women's musculature, women in combat, and women sporting leather jackets, hoodies, and short hair. Such representations of repressed femininity culminated in the widely popular TV movie *La journée de la jupe* (2008; The day of the skirt).[8] In it, an on-edge Isabelle Adjani plays a French teacher who loses control over an especially insubordinate banlieue classroom and decides to take her students hostage until officials meet her demand to institute a "skirt day" during which female students would proudly wear skirts (an article of clothing the student characters no longer wear for fear of sexual harassment) in class as well as in their neighborhoods. One teenage student, portrayed as a female *caillera* (thug, delinquent), wears the familiar banlieue uniform of baggy athletic wear and is cross-examined by Adjani's incredulous character about her motivations for concealing her body. When the young woman finally reaches breaking point, and admits to being a victim of rape, Adjani halts her inquiry, suggesting that women wear loose-fitting clothes out of a desire to protect themselves and hide their desirability. In this film, butch minority women sport athletic wear to "veil" an essential shame about a deeply buried femininity that can only be unearthed by secular representatives of the French state.

Sanchez's documentary pursues its investigation of how banlieue women have internalized virility codes with another interview subject, Habiba. We first see her deftly handling a soccer ball, repeatedly bouncing it on one foot, as her gang mates look on in admiration:

> NARRATOR (LECONTE): Girls don't have it good [*mal barrées les filles*]. Yet, in the projects, there's another category of girl that doesn't get harassed. But this tranquility has a price—namely, erasing any trace of femininity, so as to resemble boys to the point that one can't tell boys and girls apart. This is the story of Habiba, nineteen years old. In her neighborhood, Habiba is the leader of a gang of boys.
>
> HABIBA: I don't like it when people call me "tomboy" [*bonhomme*], I've already fought with several people about this. I have a name.

Karidja Touré plays Marieme, aka "Vic," in Céline Sciamma's *Bande de filles* (2014; Girlhood). Here she prepares food in her apartment, after her "tomboy" transformation.

CATHY SANCHEZ: Still, we can all agree that you kind of look like a tomboy.

HABIBA: (*Smiles*) Yeah, I guess.

Sanchez is persistent in trying to get Habiba to admit to an elusive "feminine" vulnerability, to share an anecdote of suffering at the hands of boys. Unable to elicit such an admission, she later attempts to categorize Habiba as homosexual, despite her assertions of heterosexuality in the full interview. Instead of focusing on Habiba's mastery of virility codes and her refusal to be categorized, the filmmakers suggest that her social mobility is the mere result of not being an attractive target for men. In so doing, they display a startling adherence to gender conformity, disciplining virile women by suggesting their appearance is abnormal.

Of the many constituents of stigmatized banlieue life, virility and its more intense cousin machismo have been singled out as fundamental causes of sexual intolerance. For the filmmakers, it would seem, it is more important to condemn virility than to show concerns for women in general: Habiba is not worthy of feminist solidarity—even though she is a woman who has struggled to gain some level of emancipation and power —because she exhibits butch traits too evocative of a surrounding virility culture. The narration also ignores how Habiba distinguished herself through her soccer skills. This point of view represses the diversity of women's gender expressions by contending that women who adopt "virile" postures must necessarily be victims of false consciousness, of internalized machismo. According to this argument, "tough" banlieue women have internalized, despite themselves, an overpowering and nontransgressive virility that conventionally fits the dominant laws of the banlieue. Though the Latin root of *virility* (*vir*) denotes "man," I do not mean to interpret these women's practices as a mere appropriation of traits that fit men more "naturally." In the examples throughout this study, virility combines assertiveness, ambition, potency, and sometimes combativity, regardless of gender. Though one could find in these practices a projection of gender norms, I argue that these women (and, in a different way, banlieue sexual minorities) remove the gender component of "virility" to arrive at a gender-neutral concept that reflects urban belonging rather than gender belonging. Absent from the depictions in *La cité du mâle* is a sensitivity to how virility might constitute a manipulable tool that allows women who master it to deal in the currency of the environments in which they reside. Such mastery often helps them gain the respect of their peers and demonstrates their standing in their communities. Evidence for this mastery is found, paradoxically, in the very examples the filmmakers use to dismiss banlieue virilities. What is most startling, notwithstanding assertions of false consciousness, is the dismissal of a banlieue women's resistance to the perceived patterns of miserabilism that classify women (as well as sexual minorities) as victims. Such resistance—expressed in virile form—is deemed inadmissible by those purportedly fighting for, and in the process arguably reifying the victimized status of, women and sexual minorities in the banlieue.

The movement that perhaps most exemplifies how defenses of sexual tolerance can turn into attacks on diversity is Ni Putes Ni Soumises (NPNS).[9] Founded in 2003, the group advocates for better living conditions for women in impoverished banlieues. One of its former leaders and author of a book on the movement, Fadela Amara, was appointed secretary of state and urban planning (2007–2010) in President Sarkozy's government. Much has been written about Amara's place as a woman of color in a right-wing government, her views on Islam and Islamic feminism, and the effectiveness of the group at combating sexism in the banlieues and greater France;[10] here I want to draw attention to how Amara and the NPNS members talk about queer gender expressions.

Considering her characterization in the media as tenacious and resistant (*insoumise*), Amara's views on assertive female "virility" are somewhat surprising. In the first section of her book on the movement, *Breaking the Silence*, entitled "Social Breakdown of the Projects," Amara classifies banlieue women into three groups: "the submissive, the mannish, and the invisible," "those who wear the headscarf," and "those who offer daily resistance" (69–75).[11] This breakdown of anthropological types represents not so much diversity as a closed system, a limited horizon of possible gender expressions. Against these limited categories, the examples of the "tough girl" or the female gang member would seem to provide for an exception. Amara, however, interprets this toughness differently:

> [One] type of behavior involves young women who want to resemble men and force others to respect them. They adopt mannish attitudes, tactics, and gear. There are all-girl gangs in the projects, using violence as a means of expression, dressing in jogging clothes and sneakers, all-purpose unisex clothes that hide their femininity. These young women are violent in their language and behavior: they use extortion, they pick fights—even with young men—and they are quick to use insults or their fists. No tender gestures that might be perceived as a sign of weakness. They are sometimes worse than the young men, because they can be tougher or more sadistic than males. They think

and live like the worst machos, they act as if they were "putting their balls on the line." In order to exist and earn respect, they believe they've got to hit harder than the guys around them.[12]

Amara decries the virilization of banlieue life because it means the acceptance of patriarchal laws and the withdrawal of "femininity." Elsewhere in the book, she calls for the right to dress as one wishes, without pressure. What is striking, however, is that she in fact denies this freedom of choice to "virile women," whose preferences, in her view, are informed by a desire for patriarchal assimilation that expresses itself through imitation and compensates for a lack.

In Amara's description, it seems taboo to acknowledge the degree to which women could set a standard for virility, independently of men. The objective of "earning respect" would be achievable only by emulating the masculine, since, in this arrangement, women who earn respect do not do so in their own name but rather through victimized imitation. Respect would no longer be the ordinary goal of any and every individual, irrespective of gender, who seeks to stake out an advantageous position in a highly dense urban environment. While the dismissal of virile women's resistance might be justified in light of the destructive tactic of violence sometimes adopted by girl gangs, the fact that these gangs have targeted men in itself deserves to be commented on. Amara may be justified in criticizing violence; however, she problematically assumes its mimetic nature, insinuating that violence is essentially masculine. The creative adaptation of these women, in terms of sartorial choice and gender expression, also goes unnoticed, collapsed as it is with off-putting (gang) violence directed at both themselves and others. Though androgyny is considered desirable in banlieue men (according to norms of the new "sexual modernity" discussed in the introduction), it becomes undesirable in banlieue women.

When virility culture is the assumed status quo, men's androgyny can allow for great social mobility. Banlieue men may adopt shifting postures of gender that are comfortable, practical, or desirable depending on the context; for instance, trading hoodies and baseball caps for pastel chemises and tight pants at nightclub doors or for job interviews. The "threat" (real or imagined) of patriarchal force hidden in "virile" clothing can be tempered by recourse to androgynous stylings that demonstrate gender flexibility. All of this takes place in contemporary society in which mixing different gender traits is increasingly common. But when transposed to the banlieue feminine, androgyny is rid of its practical aspect and reduced to a lesser purpose: in tough women, androgyny is not the positive, voluntary expression of another gender but rather serves only to conceal feminine gender. This breakdown neglects the notion that athletic women, or those wearing athletic gear, could be considered attractive, or that athletic wear can be used to express femininity.

Pascal Duret—a sociologist of sports, youth, and the body—participates in this denial of queer banlieue cultures: he insists that virile and combative banlieue women incorporate a norm rather than create it themselves.[13] In the following passage he describes a fight among teenage girls that started when one criticized the other for dancing suggestively at a party:

> In the projects, the norm of virility is so urgent [*pressante*] that it can very well be coveted by girls. Thus, what changes in the projects is that, despite the spectacular domination of boys over girls, violence also becomes a girl's affair. Nora, the most manly of all the girls in her neighborhood, explains how in her class, she's the gang leader [*caïd*]. . . . Nora strikes without hesitation. The hits delivered have nothing to do with traditional catfights or hair-pulling [*crêpages de chignons*]. The confrontation occurred in a masculine mode of impact. Roughed up, the party pooper had to abandon combat, not without unleashing a broadside of insults (also virile: slut, *enculée* [someone who is anally penetrated]). This altercation is in total conformity with the heavily codified model of masculine brawls. They stage virility in order to claim it. After announcing herself in this way, she leaves no room for conciliation. . . .
>
> Nora is not the only one to incorporate these warrior values, she tells us how one of her friends, Salima, is even "harder" than she is.[14]

Here, Duret gives men first rights over violence; violence by women essentially must be imitative. In his comments about vulgarity, "hair-pulling," and "catfights," Duret reveals surprise at women's forcefulness that betrays conventional views on gender propriety. If female authority can only be derivative of the masculine, it becomes impossible to map out and give intrinsic meaning to the power hierarchies that organize women's spaces in the banlieues. Girl gangs could be said to participate in setting the standard for a nongendered virility; for Duret, however, unmooring virility from masculinity is read as an abnormal disturbance of gender conventions.

The condemnation of women's toughness and combativity is not limited to girl gangs. Here is what Amara says about the wearing of the hijab:

It is possible, in fact, to distinguish different categories of young women who wear the headscarf. First of all, there are those who wear it because they believe that the fact that they practice their religion affords them a legitimate existence. . . .

But there are many young women who, forbidden any outward display of femininity, wear the headscarf above all as armor, supposed to protect them from male aggression. . . .

Finally [another] category of women who wear the headscarf includes those whom I call "soldiers of green fascism." In general, these are women who attended university and who, behind this emblematic headscarf, fight for a social project that is dangerous for our democracy. These are not disturbed kids who are troubled or searching for an identity. . . . No, these are real (activists)! They often begin their justification of wearing the headscarf by explaining that, in their view, it is part of a process of emancipation. It bothers me to hear them talk about freedom of expression because behind this symbol is a project for a different society than our own: a fascist-like society that has nothing to do with democracy.[15]

This description encapsulates a point I made earlier in the introduction: that, through the lens of sexual modernity, Islam "virilizes" the women who adhere to it. Amara's classification—of women who opt for the hijab in its protective "armor" role—virilizes the hijab by associating it with violence and combat, predetermined as male.[16] That sartorial item would repress an essentialized, internal femininity thought to be inhibitive of Islamic piety. In such a view, there is no room for those who use the hijab to be conventionally "feminine": women who might accent their hijab with makeup, who play with textile color, draping, and transparency while respecting the laws they believe to be religiously mandated.

The use of the term *armor* contributes to the vilification of women who make the choice to be actively combative. Though Amara's use of armor evokes a defensive passivity, much testimony of veiled women, when interviewed by newspapers, has built up the positive and active connotation of their sartorial choice, which, many declare, affords them self-confidence and even greater social mobility.[17]

The assertiveness of women, valued when they are unveiled and feminine, is dismissed when that assertiveness is expressed through religious means. In media testimonials, veiled women are asked to address the gendering of the hijab via the question of a male gaze: because the hijab is portrayed as patriarchal body censorship, it is assumed that women would only wear it in response to a specifically male jealousy or posses-siveness. However, this gender component is often rendered irrelevant when Muslim women respond that they wear the veil in modesty before a genderless, unitary God, not any male mortal. Amara designated these women as soldiers with a sardonic tone, alluding to their deference to an assumedly male leader. Her remark also promotes the transatlantic concept of "Islamo-fascism," or green fascism (green symbolizing Is-lam). The routine insult of "ninja," designating Muslim women who wear the niqab—a cloth that covers the face in addition to the body—is not far removed from the rhetoric that sees a combative posture in Islamic dress. Having passed several emancipation "tests" (advanced degrees, ac-tive community engagement, leaving alleged home confinements), the women described fall crucially in Amara's understanding because their combativeness is of the "wrong," masculine nature, all the more danger-ous for having the appearance of being "sane."

Amara reiterated the idea that women who opt for the hijab must be mentally unbalanced in a public tiff with a female rapper who embod-ies both banlieue and Islamic butchness. Diam's, an ebullient wordsmith who had found a huge following among French youth upon the release of her 2006 hit "Jeune demoiselle recherche . . . " (Young Miss looking for . . .) which satirizes the world of heterosexual Internet personals and ISO ads.[18] Of Greek Cypriot origin, the rapper often broaches themes of injustice, immigration, discrimination, and abandonment by the state of the banlieues; it was her light-hearted, "girly" hit that first connected with a pop audience. The song and video were also important to her career trajectory because they provided a space to clearly assert her heterosexu-ality: as with many female rappers in the United States and the United Kingdom, Diam's faced constant questions about her supposed lesbian-ism, seemingly in light of her hip-hop attire (athletic wear, hoodies, and chains), her hairstyle (close-cropped), and voice (gravelly and loud). In this sense, Diam's resembles the butch banlieue girls whose repeated as-sertions of heterosexuality could not stop journalists from raising the specter of lesbianism. Around the release of "Jeune demoiselle," Fadela Amara initially declared herself a fan, but this changed when Diam's was photographed by tabloids wearing the hijab. When asked to explain Diam's conversion and donning of the veil, Amara attributed it to Diam's having reached a psychological breaking point due to her fame, saying that the only way for her "to regain her humility was to take a spiritual path" and that she wished Diam's would "take her headscarf off tomor-row." The press articles covering this spat underlined Diam's "violence" in each instance.[19] Diam's, once an ally of NPNS, later distanced herself from the group because she felt it had alienated banlieue residents. With her transition from a heterosexual materialist pop star to a Muslim, hoodie-wearing rapper with political grievances and a combative persona, Diam's fell out of favor with Amara, who now perceived her as too close to the reviled image of the girl gang members said to have internalized virilism, rather than mastered it.

In the representational economy of *La cité du mâle* as in Amara's book on the NPNS movement, female virility is reduced to an impoverished imitation of patriarchy. It loses its capacity to express the nonessentialist nature of virility, to divorce virility from the male sex. While viable examples of empowered female virility have been lacking in the French banlieue context, queer theorists elsewhere have had much to say about how "masculine women" have redefined gender hierarchies, from the butch/femme debates to biker gangs and female soldiers. See, for example, Judith (Jack) Halberstam's introduction to his *Female Masculinity*:

> I claim in this book that far from being an imitation of maleness, female masculinity actually affords us a glimpse of how masculinity is constructed as masculinity. In other words, female masculinities are framed as the rejected scraps of dominant masculinity in order that male masculinity may appear to be the real thing. . . . I detail the many ways in which female masculinity has been blatantly ignored both in the culture at large and within academic studies of masculinity. This widespread indifference to female masculinity, I suggest, has clearly ideological motivations and has sustained the complex social structures that wed masculinity to maleness and to power and domination. . . . If what we call "dominant masculinity" appears to be a naturalized relation between maleness and power, then it makes little sense to examine men for the contours of that masculinity's social construction. Masculinity, this book will claim, becomes legible as masculinity where and when it leaves the white male middle-class body. . . . My book refuses the futility long associated with the tomboy narrative and instead seizes on the opportunity to recognize and ratify differently gendered bodies and subjectivities.[20]

Halberstam considers the agency of unconventional women deprived of consciousness by commentators who are unable to imagine them in a leadership role. She also introduces a crucial race and class component, which shows how recourse to virility, and the very construction of virility, can be made intelligible through the consideration of factors other than gender: race and class. Virility surfacing in banlieue subjects, and especially female banlieue subjects, makes virility "legible" as a neutral, freestanding concept, one that is constructed rather than naturalized. Ethnic and class background in this case would constitute equally, if not more, important factors than sex in explaining the prevalence of virility, because virility becomes intelligible "when it leaves the white male middle-class body"; in the current context of the banlieue, it becomes intelligible through a female, brown, urban population. Halberstam rejects the futility of tomboys or in the French case *bonhommes* or *garçon manqués* (*La cité du mâle*'s odd, confused Habiba deriving masculinity from others) and instead highlights their case to clarify how power works. She shows, furthermore, how the dismissal of female "virility" reinforces masculine domination, the very thing Sanchez and company had set out to fight.

Ethnographic Obfuscation in the *Homo-ghetto*

Combative virility has also been condemned, in the discourse of prominent gay rights activists and gay-interest media, when adopted as a mode of resistance or coping by sexual minorities of color in the banlieues. In 2009, the former Beur FM editor-in-chief, Franck Chaumont (a colleague of Fadela Amara at NPNS), published *Homo-ghetto*, an investigative report on homosexual life in the banlieue.

Homo-ghetto features a cover image almost as grim as its content. A long-angle shot, looking up at a housing project façade in the bleak Brutalist style, the image dwells on a single window, similar to all the other gray windows except for a vivid pink blind that shields the inside from outside scrutiny. The immediate symbolism suggests pink to be the color of gay liberation but also privacy. The singular window provides an individualist spark against a crushing and monochromatic communitarianism (*communautarisme*), that is, the tendency of minority groups (sexual, ethnic, or religious) to stick together and thus form somewhat segregated or uniform communities. That outcome, however, can also be the result of decisions regarding the concentration of the urban poor in disconnected areas. Exceptions have been made for the case of sexual minorities, which have often been viewed more favorably, as studies on gay-friendliness and gentrification have argued.[21]

In the book's accompanying back jacket blurb, Chaumont describes his respondents, most of whom requested anonymity, as being *hauts en couleur*, an expression that figuratively means "of strong and memorable personality." More literally, just as the pink window cell on the upper floors suggests, it translates to "high in color." An alternative reading, however, might find this "gay" fluorescent hue—superimposed onto the black-and-white cover via color manipulation—to be an almost artificial addition, an out-of-place burst of character that would seem unnaturally grafted onto the banlieue. This would come despite the book's homosexual respondents' long-standing roots in such areas. The pink enhancement affirms homosexuality in working-class areas to be a kind of postmodern supplement—postmodern in the architectural sense of associating esoteric or anachronistic elements. Furthermore, the fleshy connotations of pink evoke a raw vulnerability that elicits the viewer's protective instincts.

The conflicting readings of this image underscore a "beleaguered" status of homosexuality in the banlieue. The first reading would do so in order to recover homosexuality from a hostile (yet native) environment, and the second would stigmatize it as foreign for the purposes of expulsion. Neither interpretation examines the extent to which sexual marginality and queerness has been "indigenously" produced in the banlieue. Nor do they entertain the possibility of a "queer" banlieue influence on the city center, a situation in which the city center would no longer be the sole source of alternative sexuality. Such an antagonism between structurally similar perspectives on homosexuality recalls Joseph Massad's argument in *Desiring Arabs*. Speaking of Egypt, he contended that LGBT international rights organizations and Islamist groups resembled each other insofar as they each sought to identify (and more importantly expose) homosexuals. The international gay rights groups sought to do so for the purposes of "saving" Arab homosexuals and retroactively, after positively identifying them, justifying the contentious presence of gay rights campaigns in Arab countries. The Islamist groups sought to do so for the purposes of stigmatization, exotifying homosexuality as a foreign "import" so they could condemn Western influence on local mores. To forge a parallel: in the banlieue as in Egypt, such readings reduce and revise a heritage of sexual diversity according to the intelligibility of the visible and public alone. These approaches neglect the less tangible, private, and communitarian ways—queer clandestinity—in which sexual marginality has presented itself in areas populated by the immigrant working classes, where visible individualization and "outness" might not be viable or might function in a nonemancipatory way.

While the book jacket seems to support an individualist, atomized sexual resistance when it comes to being visibly gay, it is ironic that Chaumont is less tolerant of other, perhaps more discreet forms of *droit à la différence* or "the right to be different." The title's alarmist subheading—"The Clandestines of the Republic"—makes it clear: "clandestines" designates homosexuals who opt for secrecy, who remain in the closet. It is this very clandestine sexuality that is deprived the *droit de cité* (or the right to stake out a position of citizenship) in Chaumont's restrictive sexual liberation. The desire to melt into the (sexual) republican fabric is assumed, and desires for sexual *non*assimilation are thus never entertained.

I use *Homo-ghetto* to show how gay media personalities use the figure of the clandestine, proudly *banlieusard*, male homosexual to warn of the dangerous influence of a culturally informed virilism over homosexual life in the banlieues. I show how, in condemning a virilism that would drive banlieue homosexuals underground, Chaumont misses the chance to glimpse the banlieue's queer content, often because he neglects inequalities of race and class that also explain the retreat into the clandestine. I do this by reading the ethnographic portraits Chaumont supplies against the grain and offer alternative interpretations informed by queer of color analysis. I find that the reporting of banlieue homophobia (including that attributed to gay men of color) reveals much about unacknowledged privilege of those doing the reporting. Though an undeniable sexism is traceable in the speech of *Homo-ghetto*'s interviewees, an even stronger element of both heterosexism and homonormativity appears in Chaumont's attempts to discount the legitimacy of homosexuals "happy" to reside in the banlieues. Gay establishment activists and journalists, I argue, use the alleged "sexual intolerance" of *banlieusard* homosexuals who have decided not to make the salvational escape to the city center, to distract from the gay elite's own communitarianism and cultural intolerance.

One of the portraits in particular stands out for its intolerance of Other homosexualities, a chapter entitled "Majid: Pédé et racaille?" (Majid: Faggot and Thug?). Majid is a twenty-seven-year-old resident of Toulouse, described as a professional jack-of-all-trades. Though he was then unemployed and on financial assistance, Chaumont portrays him as a young man who pays keen attention to his looks and dress. The question mark in the chapter title renders the conjunction *and* ambivalent, as if to point out the mutual exclusivity of being gay and of exhibiting the dominant sartorial codes of male banlieue groups in France, a style often described as "thuggish."

As the first subject in the series of interviews that make up *Homo-ghetto*, Majid's interview sets the tone for the book. Chaumont evidences a rhetorical desire to puncture banlieue subjects' "false" strategies of self-valorization—recalling the earlier, dismissive portrayals of virile women in NPNS. These strategies, created in often difficult circumstances, would seem to require an "unacceptable" compromise on sexual liberation, for example, avoiding outward displays of homosexuality. Especially for those banlieue subjects like Majid who lead embattled but nevertheless contented lives (by their own proclamation), this rhetorical campaign targets strategies of self-preservation, resistance, and negotiations of *libertés tempérées* ("tempered liberties," to borrow a term from Guénif-Souilamas), that put too great an emphasis on expressions of virility or, in a larger sense, toughness.

I cite at length the "writing-over" of Majid's words to show that, while Chaumont aims to do the work of the investigative journalist who owes it to his reading public to be critically vigilant at all times, he goes beyond his call of duty to deform the speech of his interlocutors, until he can draw forth a gaffe that would confirm his preestablished thesis of their sexual antimodernity:

> Homosexual and homophobic, sometimes a thug, sometimes a faggot; hostage of the projects, Majid incarnates the disarray of an idle [*désoeuvrée*] and disoriented youth generation, living within a closed jar. . . . Very relaxed, yet hyperactive (he can't stay still), he is very attentive to his looks and plays himself off as a "hottie," as he says [*se la joue "gossbo"*]. Our interview opened with one of his questions (rather than one of my own): "Did you see my Lacoste shirt?" Such is Majid: beneath his powerful but exaggerated gestures designed to impress the impressionable [*rouleur de mécaniques*] we see that he is still but a child.[22]

Reading *Homo-ghetto*'s impressionistic findings (often cited as an authoritative source in subsequent journalistic articles on homosexuality in the banlieues[23]), it is easy to pounce on faulty methodology, so inflected are the analyses with an uninterrogated class and cultural slant. Such a critique might explore, without excusing or justifying what is objectionable in Majid's speech, the conditions that lead virility to be read as juvenile and antimodern, rather than as an instrument formed by contemporary socioeconomic circumstances. The speech of virile sexual minorities has rarely (save for queer of color analysis) been read as anything other than the reification of a timeless patriarchy. Even more rarely has it been interpreted, in the banlieue case, as a possible response to gendered humiliation at school or the workplace, or a response to social injustice their parents' generation faced, as these youth might perceive it.[24] In the French gay press, commentators have often depoliticized virile homosexual identity by calling it a compensation technique, but few have interpreted virilism as politicized gender reaction to class and race conformism in the gay community. Such is the lens through which one can begin a critique of Chaumont's analyses, not to excuse or look charitably on virilist abuses where they do occur, but rather to consider the condemnation of virility in relation to a homonormativity rapidly consolidating around particular determinants of class, culture, and race.

Seen as a prisoner of his banlieue environment, what nevertheless transpires through Majid's account of himself (adjusted for the histrionic exaggeration youths are sometimes prone to) is a capacity for urban mobility and cross-class interactions, evident in his subsequent anecdotes about meeting men of all backgrounds in the city center. Chaumont's critical focus on Majid's inconsistencies—his refusal to stick to a single identity—repeats negative precedents in the history of homophobia, especially in regards to the medicalization of homosexuality. The way Chaumont mines contradiction in Majid ironically echoes the debilitating gestures of nineteenth-century Western European medicine, which, as recounted by Foucault, was in the habit of diagnosing homosexuals as alienated, their "performances" and coping mechanisms laughably transparent, greeted with nonapplause by peremptory doctors. Such dismissiveness recalls the following passage from Kenneth Lewes's history of the psychoanalytical treatment of male homosexuality. Here he describes the early analyst Bergler and his views of sexual alterity, alienating to the point of being humorous: "What is so extraordinary about Bergler's work on homosexuality is the intemperate and abusive tone he adopted when describing his patients. He was frequently annoyed and exasperated by their behavior, by their 'unique . . . megalomaniacal superciliousness' and their 'amazing degree of unreliability. . . . There are no happy homosexuals,' he claimed denying his patients' assertions to the contrary. . . . Claims of bisexual potency are spurious: 'Nobody can dance at two weddings at the same time, not even the wizard of a homosexual.'"[25] Under analytical attack in Majid are Bergler's concepts of homosexual "megalomania" (pride in his own looks and standing) and "bisexual potency" (Majid later admits to bisexual desire), of unique relevance in this case because bisexuality has long been associated with North African men in Orientalist and colonial representations as well as their modern extensions.[26] Most of all, Chaumont refuses to allow the figure of Majid's "homo thug" to get away with "passing" through more than one community (heterosexual, homosexual, banlieue, or city center), an ease of movement across borders facilitated by that figure's successful performance of virility. Conventional wisdom holds that "straight-acting" homosexuals would enjoy the easiest passage between straight and gay communities: however, even though homosexuals exhibiting a "virile" appearance may pass unnoticed in the banlieues, thus benefiting from increased mobility, the presence of "virile" banlieue men in gay centers has sometimes been met with apprehension and skepticism, culminating in some gay nightclubs instituting discriminating policies at the door.[27]

While Majid is but one figure in Chaumont's assortment of banlieue prototypes, he frequently plays the role of native informant, explaining the secret codes of banlieue cruising and giving glimpses of private Franco-Arab attitudes about sexuality. I am more interested in Majid as a perhaps unlikely sexual philosopher or ethicist, whose differing views prompt an examination of gay city center privilege. Though it is not my province here, the world of ethnic personal ads and GPS-enabled services such as Grindr offer a rich archive of the terms banlieue users similar in attitude to Majid employ to define their clandestinity, their discerning and occasionally discriminatory sexual preferences and tastes in men: among these are *scred* (back slang for "discreet"), *hors milieu* (outside the gayborhood), *pas de folles* (no "flamers"), *couz pour couz ou feuj* (Arab cousin for Arab cousin or Jewish man), or *pas de hallouf* (Arabic for "no pork," which can mean anything from no uncircumcised men to no white French men).[28] Those *banlieusards* who would seem to distance themselves from more effeminate men receive the brunt of Chaumont's critique:

> Majid prefers boys to girls, but hates faggots [*pédés*]. That's how he artlessly admitted to me that he had organized a punitive expedition to throw cans of beer at homosexuals, on l'île du Ramier, one of Toulouse's main cruising grounds. Like a real [security] guard from the projects, he violently rejects the social representation of homosexuality. In his hierarchy of values, the passive homosexual, is inexcusable. . . . That's the homosexual par excellence, the one who gets fucked, who is submissive. . . . In contrast, the active homosexual can be "pardoned" because his sexual practices remain dominant, he does not chip away at the sacrosanct myth of virility: "The (exlusively) passive homosexual, is a feeble guy. An active guy, that's power, he is very much solicited. I am both of those, but I feel more active. If I am passive with someone and it doesn't go well, I would feel swindled or tricked [*roulé*]. Imagine that tonight, I meet a guy and have sex, well the guy, if he wants to fuck me, I would fuck him first. I would have been the dominant one and not the submissive. That's how it is with guys from the hood [*des quartiers*]. When you're active, you dominate, you're stronger!" . . . Active or passive, Majid is not proud of his homosexuality.[29]

Majid's punitive expedition, while never recounted in his own words, is appropriately condemned and its gravity noted. Beyond this, however, what surfaces in Chaumont's description is a disavowal of multiple ways of being homosexual. Such a pluralism might be considered welcome, if it weren't for the regrettable fact that, in this case, the differentiation between types of gay identity becomes evident through the reported outbreak of violence between homosexuals with opposing views about self-presentation. Consider for a moment the vexed history of the argotic term *pédé*—linked at its origin to pedophilia, then evolving to include "faggot," and more recently reappropriated as a term of unapologetic gay self-definition. The word's pejorative charge still stings, its self-referential uses are quite narrow even today. The term, however, stands as code in Majid's argotic lexicon for a form of homosexual identity-affirming expression that he rejects, or at least doesn't recognize himself in; yet he fully admits to being homosexual himself, the difference has to do with disclosure, with the "social representation of homosexuality." This distinction hinges, of course, on whether one accepts that there may be different ways of being publically gay, an idea inadmissible in some gay universalist rhetoric. Could Majid's framing of homosexual differences, behind its exclusionary violence, mask an internecine conflict in the gay community? A conflict in which a working-class, multiethnic homosexual group has become estranged from the homosexual city center elite, to the point of coining vocabularies to differentiate one "type" of homosexual from another? Or are these self-declared homosexual "thugs" (in personal ads: *caillera*) merely reiterating a conventional heteronormativity and patriarchy? When such interhomosexual conflicts are subsumed under a general homophobia, and not a specific sexual intolerance according to which one section of the gay community rejects another, this dimension of class and race-based differentiation is lost.

In his description of banlieue homophobia as a system with its own categories of persons, Chaumont ascribes various roles to Majid, none of which seem to stick. By referring to Majid as a security guard, he takes Majid's rejection of public identity-affirming homosexuality and frames it as a form of policing.[30] In so doing, he reduces Majid to a status of social and professional immobility: the dead-end security guard jobs that many (often educated) youth of minority background interpret as the glass ceiling of their upward mobility, as seen in a recent documentary by filmmaker and former government minister Yamina Benguigui.[31] Instead of attributing Majid's rejections to a dispute about homosexual self-presentation, Chaumont provides an explanation that reflects the superficiality of many neo-Orientalist "gay travel guides" to sexuality in the Middle East: in Arab sexual mores, only the homosexual who appears "passive" would be devalorized, while the active party would be valorized (assuming of course a very dubious connection between appearance and preferred sexual role).[32]

Majid's inconsistencies make ascribing just one role to him so difficult: they also humanize him as someone with an evolving sexuality that shifts according to context and partner(s). This evolution appears within his changing views on casual sex and the question of sexual roles.[33] Majid clearly rejects the very principle that Chaumont declares to be at the foundation of his internalized homophobia—that only the passive partner in intercourse would be homosexual. Chaumont does not register the fact that Majid engages in insertive as well as receptive sexual relations, in this case within the same encounter. Glossing over the shifting strategy of self-presentation Majid engages in, Chaumont seems to abhor the erotic philosophy at the core of Majid's rhetoric. Majid's understanding posits that the "bout" to determine the passive partner might itself be erotic: such negotiations between two apparent "tops" (or insertive partners) erotically conceal the possibility, which might have reassured Chaumont if more explicitly disclosed, that both partners could "bottom." In contrast, Chaumont's dismissal would seem to recommend a philosophy of imperative sexual versatility and almost contractual exchange, a top-down enforcement of similitude. In this latter version, self-presentation is not distinguished from sexual practice: there is no room for the person who looks and acts like the stereotype of a "top" (insofar as such a thing can be entertained) but likes to "bottom," an occurrence that has come to be quite banal. Majid states, firstly, that he mostly now pursues other like-minded Franco-Arab sexual partners, and secondly, that his sexual relations involve penetration for both partners. Chaumont insinuates that Majid is a self-hating homosexual, because he supposedly does not proudly and publicly own up to "bottoming": thus, the avowal of passivity becomes a missing prerequisite for homosexual pride. Moreover, if pride in the active role becomes a barometer by which to measure homophobia, a significant portion of the mainstream gay community in Europe and the United States must also be declared homophobic.

An aversion to unapologetic virility thus emerges in *Homo-ghetto*'s culturalist analysis of sexual roles among Franco-Arab men. Such an aversion seems inconsistent, however, with images circulating in the gay mass media that valorize virility on the aesthetic level yet condemn it when asserted in identity-affirming fashion by banlieue subjects, who seem to embrace it too literally, without irony. Majid goes beyond the limits of the MSM (men who have sex with men) category, adopting an identity-affirming understanding of homosexuality ("I *am* both . . . active and passive"), in a way that would put to rest objections accusing Franco-Arab homosexuals of abrogating gay "responsibilities" (*Ils ne s'assument pas*: they don't "assume" themselves, or don't own up to every component of their homosexuality). When speaking of that night's hypothetical sexual encounter, instead of telling a story about unilaterally imposing his exclusively active sexuality on a passive recipient, Majid acknowledges that he could very well be perceived as someone who might attract active partners ("if he wants to fuck me"), and thus that his self-presentation suggests a possible separation between stated role and actual role. In addition, he acknowledges that whatever sexual relations transpire would be the result of negotiation (and not imposition), as are any of the everyday sexual relations contracted by "ordinary" people to the point of being absolutely banal, unrepresentative of anything suggesting a disconnect between banlieue and city center sexualities. Speaking of his hypothetical sexual encounter, Majid has evidently "amped himself up" in anticipation of a consensual sporting match between formidable opponents, a bout that will have to involve some form of passivity, even if it is elided in public speech.

A rich illustration of this clash of perspectives—about whether virilism constitutes internalized homophobia or is just a particular form of homosexual desire—can be found in the world of graphic arts. In the series Momosexuel—which combines the diminutive form of the name *Mohammed* and the French word for *homosexual*—illustrator Kim Roselier chronicles the life of a homo thug who passes freely between the projects and the Marais (the gay center of Paris).[34] Momosexuel captures the eroticization of banlieue homosexual sex as virile combat, while humorously mocking the protagonist's sexist nausea before what he considers to be too effeminate (a vast category that actually includes heterosexual sex). In a comic strip entitled "Lesson no. 2," the bearded and athletic Momo glares at the reader and proclaims in capital letters: "Making love to a woman is based on worthless kisses and caresses [*à deux balles*], it's a lady boy thing [*femmelette*], when I fuck with a guy, it's a kind of brawl [*baston*] except that we use our dicks, you see what I mean? I can tell you right now it's not something for faggots."

Though the illustrator derides Momo's aversion of the effeminate as irrational and comically extreme, he also seems to take great pleasure in having Momo speak provocatively, with virile enthusiasm of enjoying anal stimulation, a preference that has been historically feminized: one comic strip shows Momo being punished as a child for asking his father to repeatedly take his temperature with an anal thermometer. Roselier elsewhere casts Momo in flattering situations in which he appears to be

In "Lesson no. 2," Momo explains how gay intercourse is more "manly" than hetero sex. (Courtesy of Kim Roselier.)

sexist and physically threatening, only to have him "come out" in the last frame as a sensitive and misunderstood homo thug with a big mouth but also a soft heart. An illustrative vignette is "Raquéquette" (a play on racketeering and the slang diminutive of penis), in which Momo demands a twinkish homosexual teenager's phone—"give me your 06"—in what appears to be an attempt to steal it. This strip shows that Momo may lambast the "effeminacy" of heterosexual sex but desire and love effeminate male partners (as the illustrated hearts around Momo's head in one dating sequence makes clear). "Give me your 06" is another way of asking for a French cell phone number, as almost all cell numbers begin with those two digits. When the "twink" (a gay slang term for youngish-looking men without much body hair) nervously relinquishes the device, Momo says, "I only want your phone number, you idiot!" The startled teenager stutters an answer, and Momo leaves him standing there disoriented, walking away with an over-the-shoulder "I'll call you." Hearts appear in the teenager's eyes as he mutters to himself: "What a crazy guy." In the comic strip "Boulette," the illustrator depicts Momo with a *banlieusard* friend who has just been seriously roughed up. The friend begins to complain about having been mugged by a bunch of "faggots." Momo glares at him with the promise of an even worse beating and the friend quickly changes the designation to "*enculés* [passive sodomites] . . . I mean bastards! I mean bastards!" The pejorative *pédé* (faggot) is highly variable and unstable in the comic strip's usage, employed in one instance to reject the exhibition of sexual orientation, only to be used self-referentially in a later instance. The Momosexuel strips, beside bringing humor to a humorless subject,

"Raquéquette" showcases Momo's heavy-handed but effective flirting technique. (Courtesy of Kim Roselier.)

evidence the same extolling of combativity visible in the portraits of female gang members and virile banlieue girls seen earlier in this chapter.

Homo-ghetto explores the highly discriminating (in all senses) taste in men exemplified by Momosexuel, as well as its impact on race and class relations:

> Even while confirming that yes, logically, he only goes out with other Maghrebi guys [*rebeus*], Majid still maintains an ambiguous relationship with "whites." Although he's very conscious about representing an exotic sexual curiosity to them—a "street thug" [*racaille*]—his disgust about this only goes so far and he is not averse to taking advantage of the situation. . . . "In my case, when a European flirts with me in a bar, I milk him for whatever he's got [*je le gratte*]. The guy had better go up to the cash register and pay for some drinks. For some, we are their fantasy, they dream of being 'gang-banged.' A guy gave me 50 euros and asked me to put on some sneakers 'that really stink,' so that he could lick them while he jerked off. What I've got (at home), see, is not a wine cellar but a cellar full of old sneakers!," he concludes, bursting out with laughter.
>
> If Majid is to be believed, it's quite frequent for homos from the projects to sell their bodies. On the telephone personals networks, the formula for this purpose is "Arab hood guy for rent" [*rebeu à louer*]. "You have to hook them on the phone by using a deep voice," he explained to me. "You have to say stuff like: 'Arab hoodlum, hot, well-hung, top for rent.'"[35]

Chaumont underlines the evidently exclusionary logic of only going out with men of one's own ethnic background. However, he depicts as racial intolerance what could derive from other exclusions, based on class differences and feelings of nonbelonging relative to homonormative communities. That Majid prefers clandestinity and restricts himself to a known community, at the very moment when the telos of gay liberation was supposed to make such "restrictions" passé—is what particularly unnerves the interviewer. He sees in such voluntary community stricture the romanticization of once "regressive" homosexual living conditions: when gays did not have the option of the closet, but were forced into it. A charitable reading of Chaumont finds in his condemnation of clandestinity a critique of a youth generation that fails to appreciate the accomplishments of gay activists in removing obstacles to gay emancipation that formerly seemed implacable. Chaumont's condemnations however seem to misrecognize their target. He calls an erotic *passéisme* what is really a contemporary erotic "ideology" of willful clandestinity and virility conformism that emanates from urban cultures of minority-populated neighborhoods: one could find many parallels in non-Muslim neighborhoods of New York or London, where clandestine homosexuality exists as part of a "down low" culture. The French gay press often articulates the fear that such virilist ideology would hearken back to an Arab past of supposed masculine domination. If this idea can be entertained at all, it is only in so far as this ideology's young actors selectively emphasize aspects of heritage that serve their contemporary interests. For instance, in his attraction to Muslim men for whom homosexual sex must remain secret, Majid turns the values of religious modesty and avoidance of vice into a platform for erotic fantasy.[36] Thus Majid appreciates and isolates an essentialized "Arab" morality he finds erotic, while discarding tradition in other situations (drinking, going to clubs), showing that this heritage does not dominate him entirely.

With his techniques of convincing, of passing, of getting what he wants by other means, of adapting according to shifting contexts, of turning a stigmatized element (lower-class dress, swagger, aggressive posture) into one valorized and even eroticized, Majid introduces queer material to the interview. Majid's appropriation of country club attire (he turned up the collar of his polo shirt, imitating a popular street fashion) must be dismissed as a mistake of youthfulness rather than acknowledged as a class-defiant gesture. His queer potential is defused, passed off as yet another performance, something which one "plays at" (se la joue goss-bo). The interviewer is humorless in the face of Majid's refusal to greet the circumstances of his sexual and social life with anything other than laughter that shirks miserabilism.

Majid's ambivalent and vacillating relationship with whites is added to the list of contradictions that undermine the legitimacy of his speech. The racial designation "white"—quite unusual and a bit aggressive in casual French speech—emerges from Chaumont's mouth, and not Majid's, who uses national and regional designations that only secondarily have a racial component ("European"). Chaumont inserts the innuendo that Majid engages with whites through prostitution, and that his convictions about having sex only within his own community are not held any more powerfully than his attachment to money.

Receiving no comment is Majid's transformation of an exploitative erotics of class tourism into an opportunity for auto-eroticism, which is evident in his comments about the fetishized sneakers and the virilization of his voice. The way Majid conceives of the eroticized group he belongs to, the way he navigates within it, points to an ability to co-opt and manipulate the terms by which he is objectified. The playfulness of his many joking asides illustrates his defiant attitude in the face of an often dehumanizing sexual market that fetishizes the inner city. He notably addresses the class tension in the conversation by making a joke about how, instead of the wine cellars that are a staple of upper-class homes, he possesses a cellar of his own in the projects, filled with smelly sneakers that might thrill fetishists from the city center, as evidenced in the fantasy scenarios featured on many French ethnic pornography websites. While much of the academic conversation on this topic has focused on how ethnic subjects are sexualized, Majid aims to sexualize his own body in a way that brings it better within his control. In Chaumont's view, however, responding to objectification with economic hostility does not constitute a legitimate form of resistance to class tourism. The fact that Majid makes light of being literally reduced to a fetish object (through sneakers representing the sporty virility of banlieue men) counteracts his own exploitation by turning the "strangeness" of fetishization into a platform for comedy.[37]

While the hostile terms of exchange present in Majid's recorded phone ads are regrettable from the point of view of social estrangement, they nevertheless exemplify a relative agency, however small, for sexualized youth wishing to take advantage of the limited place for them in the homonormative imaginary. This produces an exploitation of the exploitation so to speak, which does not translate, in *Homo-ghetto*, to a behavioral art but rather further evidences Majid's subjugation to an economy of virility.

Expanding upon the "hypocrisy" of Majid's lifestyle, Chaumont turns to a story Majid recounts about a night spent squatting an abandoned apartment with friends, an anecdote that particularly annoys his interviewer:

> Homosexual and a prostitute on occasion, Majid has nevertheless so well "internalized" homophobia that he is able to deny his own homosexuality, just as many youths from the "hood" have. How many are there, around him, living within this permanent contradiction? "Often, with my buddies, we squat an apartment, we watch porno movies, we jerk off and watch each other, we stare from the corner of our eyes without daring to say anything," he tells me. "Because it's a group, nothing should happen. Sometimes it goes off-script because of alcohol or a joint. One evening, with one of my best friends, we were watching a hetero porn, we were alone in my room and we kissed. And then he pushed me away, saying he was bi. He kept his distance." Homosexual, homophobic, bisexual? From one phrase to the next, Majid never stops contradicting himself.

Chaumont emphasizes a supposed lack of sexual fulfillment among banlieue men, and the juvenile character of "thug" sexuality that always carries within it a certain futility, just as Halberstam underlined in regard
to portrayals of female masculinity. It is assumed that a sexuality that
forgoes penetration, stopping at kisses and masturbation, is "incomplete."
Majid and his friends fail to achieve dignified status because their behavior is nonpurposive, more like juvenile playing than mature sexuality. In
Majid's story, however, it is the stifling of a typically explicit outcome that
lends the scene the minimalist eroticism that suffuses his storytelling,
which Chaumont nevertheless deems worthy (or perhaps "titillating")
enough to cite in full. Furthermore, the element of "play" (present in this
and other erotic subcultures) has, in a different vein, been theorized as
a form of communication, intimacy, creativity, and therefore growth.[38]
In the "squat" scene, the young men hanging out together use play to
build up a formidable erotic charge when the young men boyishly explore
abandoned areas, erect their porno "treehouse" in the squat, and add the
sexual catalysts of alcohol and joints. The group sexuality they partake
in moreover exists within the homosocial group formation of the band
or sometimes gang, and is therefore integrated in preexisting banlieue
social formations, breaking with the exit imperative usually imposed on
banlieusards as the condition of their sexual fulfillment.

Gay filmmakers and pornography producers have mined just such scenarios for their erotic charge.[39] A plotline in which a homosocial gathering among "apparent" heterosexuals threatens to turn homosexual carries
obvious dramatic potential. Queer of color analysis offers an illustrative
parallel: some of the most intense forms of queer desire on the page and
on-screen can emerge from homosocial, sex-segregated spaces coded as
sexist.[40] The ways certain subjects have accommodated heterosexist strictures, while simultaneously eroticizing them, is formally interesting from
a number of academic and artistic perspectives. Majid's narrative of fleeting sexual pleasure, which exists within certain structures, is palpably
more exciting to him than the straightforward sexual release that can be
had in the visible gay marketplace. In Majid's eroticization of a night out
with the boys, Majid courts the red lines, keeping to one side so that he
may at the right time more deftly cross over to the other.

José Esteban Muñoz's concept of "disidentification" is useful here.
Muñoz describes how queers, people of color, and especially queers of
color maintain a relationship to normative or "oppressive" identities that
is more formally complex than mere rejection or embrace.[41] Through the
practice of disidentification, these subjects "recycle" the normative while
at the same moment renovating it, injecting into the normative a creative

commotion that both increases its longevity while altering its shape. The end result, while derived from norms, is no longer wholly normative. Applied to Majid, one could imagine the unpredictable changes a normative and heterosexist virility undergoes when eroticized and manipulated by men who have sex with men: for example, how does our concept of an urban gang (or other homosocial group) change when the fraternity at its center is eroticized by its own members? Though Majid's story ends upon a regrettable nipping in the bud of an opportunity for romantic fulfillment with a close friend, it is not clear whether that is what either party would have ultimately desired. The eroticism in such a scene is generated not so much by the hovering possibility of a monogamous relationship, as by the scene's sexual charge and time pressures. Majid dwells on the blurring of the line between homosociality and homosexuality—brought on by circumstances of group sexuality—which are not far removed, in action if not philosophy, from visions of sexual utopias once nurtured by gay French radical groups and intellectuals. While Majid's "limitation" of his own homosexuality to anonymous, casual sex and cruising may seem like an unacceptable failure in the homonormative lens, this reductive view can be criticized for its unquestioned privileging of individualism.[42] Majid may be sacrificing monogamous couplehood for something (to him) more expansive and exciting, for a way of life that does not demand he sacrifice homosocial attachments for sexual pleasure, since that sexual pleasure would already exist within those attachments.

As evidenced by Chaumont's frustration with his interview subject, Majid, together with the existence of willfully clandestine queers of color, presents a set of problems for mainstream gay coverage of the banlieues. Like Sanchez, Chaumont continually misses opportunities to recognize the queerings of homonormativity and heteronormativity at work in the banlieues, spaces predefined as never queer. Nevertheless, the queer does surface, producing moments of cognitive dissonance and palpable frustration in this journalist/activist community that cannot conceive of itself as restrictive of sexual liberty. The phenomena producing this queer discomfort must be passed off as pathology rather than allowed into the encyclopedia of sexual formations. Queer of color analysis has underlined that, in the American case, the "pathologizing" of nonheteronormative sexual customs not only works to repress these customs, but also prevents their "critical possibilities." In other words, such an approach prevents all attempts to theorize about or dignify the sexual diversity of queers of color on a more intellectual plane.[43] When commentators judge the banlieue to be a flattening, monochromatic wheel of communitarianism repressing all diversity and dissent, the "absence" of the queer in the banlieue becomes a self-fulfilling prophecy. In some serious ways, the French republican activists who advocate against sexism actually reinforce patriarchal strictures when they deny the sexual diversity of the banlieues, and pass off whoever resists this characterization as exceptions that confirm the rule.[44] The difficulty here of excavating Majid from the morass of Chaumont's pathologization is a case in point. Campaigns like that of *Homo-ghetto* take on a homonationalist character when they drum up the threat of a culturally informed banlieue homophobia to French republican values. In this account, Majid aberrantly appears as the only example in the book of a homosexual who does not express a wish to exit the banlieue.

The vicious circle of miserabiliom in representations of banlieue homosexuality remains a glaring unstudied territory in mainstream as well as academic publications.[45] On this point, the activism of NPNS members and that of Chaumont are similar: Chaumont was the communications director for the organization from 2003 to 2007. He has since continued a meteoric rise in the communications world, having entered government, just as his NPNS colleague Fadela Amara had done.[46] The promotions to government of various NPNS figures has led to the claim in the radical press that the NPNS organization acts as a recruiting ground for the Socialist Party. When the NPNS-seasoned Amara became secretary of state for urban planning, large swaths of the banlieue youth population her office was meant to aid rejected its severely underfunded initiatives.[47] The alienating rhetoric of her former colleague in *Homo-ghetto*, while not rejected on as massive a scale, was importantly criticized by an influential member of the Franco-Arab gay community who caters to banlieue youth. Fouad Zeraoui, a successful nightlife entrepreneur, had previously been an ally of Chaumont's but now takes a respectful distance, laying out his reasons for doing so in an exchange I consider next.

Capitalizing on *Banlieusard* Homosexualities

The media reception of *Homo-ghetto* was positive and most of its claims went uncontested, except for a rare critique that appeared in the popular gay monthly *Têtu*.[48] Giving his own critique of Chaumont's critique of virility-philia, Fouad Zeraoui pointed out that Franco-Arab and banlieue homosexuals should not be the sole parties reproached for this attitude, given that virility exhibition is exactly what has been requested of them by various gay markets (such as fashion photography, erotica, and personal ads). Prominent gay-interest magazines such as the now defunct *Têtu* and

PREF have eroticized virilist postures in photo spreads while condemning the attitudes that underpin them in editorials.[49] Zeraoui suggests that
antieffeminate prejudice—a potential consequence of virilism—is something that affects the mainstream gay community as a whole; the critique
of this prejudice, however, would seem to target ethnic sexual minorities
in particular. Zeraoui's take on the Marais "gayborhood" emphasizes this
point: he spreads the circle of virilism from the banlieues to the social
conventions of the gay ghettos: "The Marais symbolizes a young white
culture, buff and well-built, masculinist, almost fascistic, as if the gays
there had fantasies of joining aggressive heterosexuality."[50] In the late
1990s, Zeraoui filled a nightlife void by inaugurating the still popular
Black Blanc Beur (BBB) club nights.[51] The ethnically diverse soirées first
took place in Pigalle, Paris's red-light district, which is heavily populated
by families of immigrant origin as well as sex workers and easily acces-
sible from the city's northern banlieues.[52] In its catering to a previously
ignored nightlife audience of queer, (Muslim) youth of color, the BBB
resemble the Gayhane club nights in Berlin for the LGBT German Turkish community, an immensely popular and still ongoing soirée that also
surfaced in the mid-1990s and attracted an audience that over time grew
more diverse than its intended target.[53]

When Zeraoui launched his nightlife venture, the popular news weekly
Le Nouvel Observateur organized a panel discussion during which the
moderator asked him: "Is the avant-garde (still) soluble in the Marais?"—
with emphasis placed on the shifting meaning of *soluble*, between "that
which can be solved" and "that which can be dissolved." Would the Marais
dampen the gay avant-garde or provide a sanctuary for it? Zeraoui declared
his club to have restored a missing edge to a gay nightlife scene that had
grown too comfortable with its repetitive offerings. Nightclubs, according to Zeraoui, play a special role: they offer sheltered spaces of assembly
(where cameras are taboo) for clandestine *banlieusard* homosexualities,
where attendees can exhibit in a semi-public space what is normally practiced in private. Nightlife spaces constitute public-private cultures where
the queer phenomena that are sometimes the most fleeting and difficult
to document momentarily occur.[54] In these spaces, participants both play
with and affirm their ethnoreligious belonging, displaying Arab or Islamic clothing and facial grooming in a way that eroticizes them; at the
same time, they resist the sartorial conventions and body language of the
gay city center.[55] The BBB, Zeraoui stated, would welcome all those who
had been rejected or felt uncomfortable at Marais establishments, especially those of working-class, *banlieusard*, and multiethnic backgrounds

who are said to experience rejection or fetishization in mainstream environments. Business hours at the club observed the schedules of the Paris RER, the commuter trains that link the suburbs to the city center. The RER trains to the banlieues shut down earlier than the metro, which explains why Zeraoui initially opted for early evening "tea-dances" rather than all-night parties. He also launched the social networking website Kelma.org—which dubs itself "the ethnic and gay site" and counts over fifty thousand members mostly of North African, Antillean, and West African backgrounds—as well as the now defunct magazine *Baby Boy*, borrowing from American hip-hop terminology (i.e., the Beyoncé and Sean Paul 2003 hit song).[56] The club night, website, and magazine he promoted all positioned themselves as portals for an American hip-hop and homo thug culture, banking on its perfect intelligibility to banlieue youth, a bet that has reaped handsome rewards when one assesses his nightlife and Internet empire.

Zeraoui and Chaumont used to be creative collaborators (they had recorded a radio episode on homosexuality in the banlieue for Beur FM), but their friendship hit a snag when Chaumont released his investigative report. Taking note of the mixed reception of *Homo-ghetto*, the gay culture magazine *Têtu* set up a debate between Zeraoui and Chaumont. The fruitful and often testy exchange was reproduced in its entirety on the Kelma.org website in the Café Chicha section, with eighty-one lengthy commentaries from Kelma members. The published debate represents the most ample, some might say only, prominent media pushback against Chaumont's book and similar commentaries that present the banlieue as incompatible with homosexuality.[57]

The tone of the published debate is remarkable indeed. Zeraoui revealed an understanding of the evolution of *banlieusard* attitudes about sexuality that had been missing from studies that present these attitudes as antimodern and ahistorical. The *Têtu* debate directly interrogated homonormative ideas regarding "coming out," the meaning of personal independence, and what modernity means to gay men. During the sustained sparring between Zeraoui and Chaumont, the *Têtu* moderator only managed to raise two questions. Zeraoui speaks relentlessly as if wishing to get a long-suppressed message off his chest.

Chaumont asserts one of the more controversial theses from *Homo-ghetto*: that there are "two speeds" of evolution in regard to the viability and acceptance of homosexuality (slow in the banlieue, faster if not already complete in the city center, which Chaumont admits has not always been welcoming). In this schema, city center homosexuals have a salvational responsibility to extend a hand to banlieue gays:

CHAUMONT: There is no solidarity between the homos from the city center and the kids from the projects. . . . I say to the homos: do not shut the door behind you, you are acquiring rights, visibility, you set trends, you write communiqués against homophobia in Iran, but right here at home, there are also people in distress! These kids are victims of a double punishment: rejected in their neighborhoods, but also in the city center. They are victims of discrimination at the nightclubs, and don't necessarily have the means to lead a gay life in Paris, because it's expensive.

ZERAOUI: When I opened the door to ethnic gays, in 1997, it was really a no man's land. . . . I couldn't get in anywhere, there was no visibility for people like me . . . we were not at all federated. In fact, at that time, one could say that the gay *beurs* and the blacks were not at all in the same situation as today. As it stands, the new generation has had less difficulty as compared with mine, which took the first steps [*a essuyé les plâtres*]. Everything you say in the book was true ten years ago. For me, this book is ten years old. Because I see the evolution! I am not saying there aren't dramatic episodes, as there are everywhere, but how can you ask young people to have a certain courage in regard to their homosexuality, while in reality there is an incredible cowardice in the "gay white" establishment which doesn't at all lead by example, which acts in a careerist and opportunistic way? . . . As for myself, in the banlieues I also see happy people, young beur and black couples.

CHAUMONT: I feel they have a lot of courage, because the system constrains them to clandestinity. The people I met in my book, I didn't meet them ten years ago! . . . To be left in peace, they have to go elsewhere, but for me, modernity means being who you are in your own neighborhood.

By speaking of a missed opportunity for solidarity between homosexual subjects in the city center and banlieues, Chaumont is able to introduce a platform for human rights intervention. He makes a connection, if only by association, between the respective homophobias of Iran and the banlieue (presumably linked due to commonalities of Islamic "sexism").[58] It is not clear, however, whether Chaumont calls for a rights intervention out of sincere concern for a familiar "friend" (banlieue homosexuals), or whether the reference to Iran serves instead to exoticize the banlieue youth's alleged sexism, so as to reinforce the foreign danger of a homeland "enemy." Furthermore, although Chaumont acknowledges—which few commentators do—the existence of a dire gulf between homosexual communities due to lack of communication, class hierarchies, and disconnected agendas, his analysis of class does not go far enough. A telling article in the radical press, which postdates Chaumont's book, takes to task the contemporary rhetoric of gay-friendliness that almost never interrogates class. Entitled "Homosexualité des bobos, homophobie des prolos?" (Bobo homosexuality, proletarian homophobia?), it underlines the common association of homophobia with the working class, while demonstrating through police statistics that working-class people have constituted the majority of those accused and condemned for homosexual activities, prior to the decriminalization of homosexuality in 1981. Majid's working-class "machismo" would explain his avoidance of the gentrified gay ghetto.[59] If banlieue homosexuals are to be "saved," Chaumont's vision of what salvation might look like (i.e., leaving the banlieue) would have more to do with financial and cultural autonomy from family than with an improvement in the tolerance of sexual diversity. The Socialist Party within which Chaumont works has privileged anticommunitarianism in its outreach efforts to the banlieues. When the banlieue is constructed as a site permanently inhospitable to sexual diversity, this neoliberal aspect of the "imperative of flight," of the get-out-of-the-ghetto narrative, easily is overlooked. If he is convinced that the banlieue cannot host the queer, it makes sense that Chaumont can only grasp clandestinity's negative connotations, not its queer possibilities.

Zeraoui's (somewhat dramatized) retort establishes a contrasting version of events. He describes the historic stifling of minority visibility in the gay ghettos such that his club ventures could be heralded as unprecedented and much needed. Early on in the 1990s and 2000s, Zeraoui's activism arguably was responsible for a significant part of gay journalistic interest in Franco-Arabs, as well as the fashionable enthusiasm for *banlieusard* diversity in the worlds of fashion, gay cinema, and erotica: in almost every press report on race relations in the gay community at that time, he was asked for comment. Of note here is his subtle way of balancing clandestinity and visibility, allowing for the articulation of *libertés tempérées* at his discreet clubs located outside the gay centers where patrons can meet like-minded individuals without exposing their sexual preferences to outsiders. Zeraoui shows sensitivity to the public-private distinction in spatial considerations such as a discreet nightclub entrance that protects his patrons from outside scrutiny, manned by vigilant security guards, so as to give greater peace of mind to those inside. Zeraoui set up the club in an immigrant neighborhood instead of a gay ghetto, taking advantage of Pigalle's historic hospitality to new arrivals and the special, if ambivalent, coexistence that prevails there among sexual and ethnic minorities. Chaumont also pays attention to the desire for clandestinity among banlieue homosexuals, except that he sees in it only antimodern limitations. Zeraoui doesn't glorify clandestine homosexuality, but speaks of discreet and "happy" couples that might not have been intelligible to Chaumont, especially considering the heavy-handed method of homosexuality excavation he has brought to the task of identifying and saving sexual minorities in the banlieue. Thus Zeraoui recognizes that the purposefully (and not reluctantly) clandestine homosexual is the anthropological "type" missing from analysis in *Homo-ghetto*.

Ethnic sexual minorities, of course, have existed independently of Zeraoui's activism; but he can be credited for dramatically increasing discourse about them, and for politicizing the question of diversity in the nightlife scene. *Federation*, the term Zeraoui employs to describe the improvement in the banlieue homosexual condition, evokes a sudden crystallization into a recognizable shape that previously clandestine or dispersed ethnic sexual minorities underwent. These networks have not necessarily become publicly visible, but they have become privately visible to each other, evoking what cinema scholar Patricia Lange has called the "privately public": subjects make themselves available in online gay environments which, although public, require specialized interest and inside knowledge in order to be accessed.[60] Parallel to this, the banlieue, and to some degree contemporary immigration as a whole, have reactivated, I argue, "old" forms and spaces of cruising once commonplace in the Euro-American context, spaces vacated in the wake of cruising's move to online forums such as personal ads or GPS-based localization services like Grindr. Journalistic articles and the field work of geographer Stéphane Leroy have found that cruising grounds like Paris's Bois de Vincennes have become especially popular among men who identify as heterosexual or bisexual, and in particular among men of North African background, who reportedly prefer its anonymity, clandestine shelter, and unique homosocial character.[61] In this way, when *banlieusards* who avoid outness populate "old" cruising spaces such as forests and car parks—the "pro-regressions" discussed in the introduction—they are not hearkening back to a lost tradition, but injecting them with contemporary meanings. At the same time, the move to online has enabled "pro-regressions" of its own, with users creating a virtual clandestinity on the Internet that aims to duplicate and expand the clandestine spaces of the banlieues, using a (sometimes offensive) language of cultural exclusivity and filtering. As seen with Majid in *Homo-ghetto*, users on Zeraoui's Kelma personals platform have been known to write *cousin cherche cousin* (Arab "bro" in search of other "bros") in a way similar to members of "down-low" cultures in the United States. This gesture is notable because it is mostly, but not always, unintelligible to the very target group it is aiming to keep away: its primary purpose is to signal common tastes to other users (an aim that has not escaped accusations of communitarianism). Interestingly, this communitarianism is not exclusively Muslim, as many of those online ads exclaiming repulsion for uncircumcised men solicit sex from Jewish men as well. All of these rapid modifications of the cruising environment triggered by online communication add to what pornography scholar Tim Dean has called "a marked acceleration in the history of sexuality."[62]

In his assessment of the living conditions of banlieue homosexuals, Zeraoui offers an evolutionary timeline where Chaumont offers ahistoricism (things have been, and always will be, bad). This attention paid to chronology recalls a consistent criticism of the NPNS organization which Chaumont once belonged to: Eric Macé and Nacira Guénif-Souilamas stated in *The Feminists and the Arab Boy* that NPNS's brand of feminism was in some sense regressive—missing the third wave and its heightened considerations of race and class—and thus out of step with the banlieue's contemporary circumstances of gender performance coupled with ethnic affirmation. The same can be said of the failure of *Homo-ghetto* to recognize the ethnic affirmation of sexual minorities in the banlieues. It is in turn important for Zeraoui to play up "progressive" credentials in light of stereotypes of neotraditional patriarchy attributed to *banlieusards* who purportedly take pride in nonassimilation. This chronology helps establish the "evolution" Zeraoui touts: he suggests that aspersions of a homophobia "unique" to the banlieue might once have been well-founded, but are no longer pertinent today. In so doing, Zeraoui shifts the terms of the debate to Chaumont's nonacknowledgment of progress made in regard to combatting sexism. Zeraoui looks to convince the readers of *Têtu* that his argument is valid in light of his closer proximity to the newness of facts on the ground, of sexual diversity in its most current, "hip" form. In contrast, Zeraoui underlines Chaumont's inability to grasp "sexual modernity" in its most recent phase (that is, an inclusive rather than exclusive "sexual modernity": one does not reject *banlieusards* but sees them as contributing to the cultural avant-garde). In the introduction, I examined the ambivalence of the term *sexual modernity*: that it can conceal less than progressive politics (xenophobia) within a forward-thinking outlook. The sexual modernity delineated by Zeraoui would carry a more literal, fundamental meaning that has to do with the vanguard of critical thought about sexuality. Though Chaumont does employ the term *modernity*, its meaning, for him, has to do with obligations of public disclosure (outness) and sexual citizenship. Zeraoui's modernity, in contrast, plays on the versatile manipulations of the public-private distinction among ethnic sexual minorities, who have seized upon opportunities for selective disclosure offered by the Internet age.

Finally, it may seem trite to talk about happiness as a subject of academic inquiry, were happiness not so patently absent from the realm of possibility in *Homo-ghetto*. By emphasizing the existence of happy couples, Zeraoui fills in the glaring omission that occurs in most journalistic portrayals of banlieue society that take suffering as a given. Historian Gérard Noiriel's analyses in his history of immigration to France, *Le creuset français* (The French melting pot), are useful, as they underline a statistical prejudice toward collecting the dire and the miserable in studies of immigration. In the following passage, he critiques the often untested premises that underlie the study of immigration, stating: "[T]he first effect of this a priori is to identify immigration and unhappiness. . . . Within this logic, the criteria with which we define the object are outside of scientific thought because what counts above all, is to emphasize the 'exemplary' character of the studied case: it is always the most unhappy, the most exploited, the most pitiful, in brief the newest who are chosen as a matter of preference."[63] The recourse to happiness as counterargument seems an antidote to the diagnostic miserabilism found in *Homo-ghetto*. The rejection of miserabilism can be assimilated to a precedent in critical theory: it recalls how Michel Foucault spoke of the happiness of homosexual men as a killing-off of psychology, a resistance against diagnostic aggression. In Foucault's account of the "advent" of homosexuality during the nineteenth century, homosexuals came into being as an identity-affirming group by resisting the medical designations that sought to pathologize them (at the same time however, they assented to be identified as a group).[64] Foucault famously mentioned that it was not the fact that gay men engaged in sex that was intolerable to a judging society, but that they were "happy," as the scholar Leo Bersani retells it.[65]

Happiness is politicized when it is relevant to nightlife: for instance, in the practice, attributed to female and gay *banlieusards*, of changing into clothes on the metro they supposedly would never be able to wear in their own neighborhoods, when gathering for a night out in the city center. Is it everyday hedonism or caving in to the banlieue's alleged patriarchal and homogenizing dress code?

ZERAOUI: I see *beurs* and blacks in a completely different manner. You talk about *beurs* who go change at Les Halles, but they don't even have to change anymore because heterosexual *beurs* today dress exactly like them, with tight-fitting pink T-shirts; they go to shisha bars, they are devilishly sexy, they have mohawks, they have adopted the same sartorial look (as gays). Everything has changed, the trend is no longer set by thugs [*racailles*], they don't have anything to say anymore.

CHAUMONT: But, today, can someone come out as a homosexual in the projects just as they can in the city center?

ZERAOUI: One cannot, because it's a ghetto, but the struggle is individual. Live your own life, take some distance if you need to . . .

CHAUMONT: So you agree with me, in order to exist, one has to leave.

ZERAOUI: Just like it has occurred in all the other communities. Just like the white gays who have come up to Paris.

CHAUMONT: But I'm talking to you about freedom of choice!

ZERAOUI: But there is no freedom of choice, we are dealing with nonchoice. . . . This is the reality. With homos who all have the same look, it's all about being amongst one's own kind [*entre-soi*]: there's poverty at the level of intellectual debate and cultural production. Why would anyone want banlieue youth to identify with that? There's nothing there. So what do they do? They also opt for staying-amongst-your-own-kind [*ils font de l'entre-soi*], from the other side . . . it exists for homos just as well as heteros, and you know it very well.

Zeraoui displaces the terrain of this tense debate from the issue of fleeing sexual intolerance to the more innocuous topic of how fashion trends are instigated. He attempts to upend a legacy of representations, according to which banlieue homosexuals always defer to banlieue "thugs" and bullies, by reframing those homosexuals as intermediaries, communicators, and leaders who are now imitated by their former tormentors. Invoking the transit hub of Les Halles is no accident, as it constitutes a point of social and sexual intersectionality, a *banlieusard* entry point into central Paris immediately adjacent to the Marais's gay clubs, bars, shops, and museums. Rather than fleeing the banlieue for the refuge of the Marais, these youths take strands of the sartorial culture of the "gayborhood" and bring them back to the banlieue, and vice versa, mixing them with their own self-stylings. In so doing, they pluralize an ethnic, gay look which then appears within a more general metrosexual style adopted by society as a whole. Anecdotally, such an evolution is evident in the enthusiasm for manicured facial hair, diamond studs, soccer-style haircuts, flashy boxing shoes, tight leather jackets and form-fitting sweatpants now banalized among French male youth of all ethnic backgrounds.

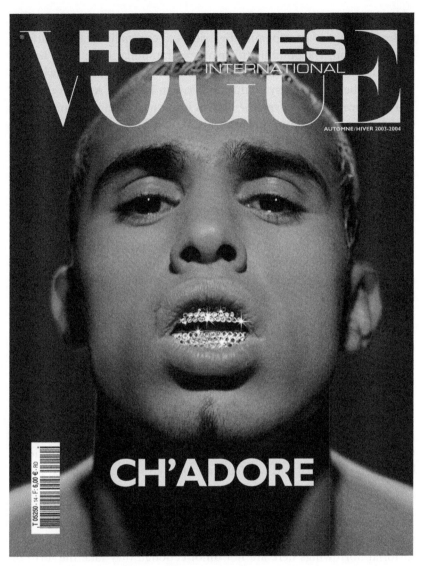

Olympic Gold Medalist boxer Brahim Asloum on the cover of *Vogue Hommes International* (Autumn 2003–Winter 2004). The title, "Ch'adore," expresses the European fashion industry's zeitgeist for Arab men, tinged with the taboo of the Iranian *tchador*. (Courtesy of Ali Mahdavi.)

The Fall 2003 issue of *Vogues Hommes*, titled "Ch'Adore," is devoted to the influence of postcolonial diversity, and especially Arab culture on French fashion. The punning title plays on the similarity between *J'adore* (I love it!) and *tchador* (the Iranian, full body cloak), which is awkward because it betrays a flimsy confusion between Iran, the Arab world, and North Africa. On the cover, the French boxer and Sydney Olympic gold medalist Brahim Asloum shows off his bleached blond hair and a flashy "grill" mouthpiece full of diamonds.[66] Inside the magazine, the athlete was androgenized with corsets and wrapped in body-size watches, as if trapped within an interminable S&M scenario. The issue's photo shoots —comprised entirely of Arab and black models, a rarity in fashion publication at the time—consistently blurs the line between homosexuality and homosociality in banlieue fashion, featuring embraces that were as much redolent of male-male affectionate displays, like public handholding in the Arab world, as they were hip-hop salutations or gay couples strolling in the Marais. Using models with stronger builds unusual for the runway, the photographer for the main spread featured: breakdancers in sweat suits; bouncer types in leather jackets; models with close-cropped hairstyles called *tribales* that etch atavistic patterns into the scalp, and eyebrows split in two so as to resemble boxer's injuries; and finally men holding their crotches menacingly and invitingly. The same models were then featured as upwardly mobile men in business suits and ski wear. Another photoshoot, set in Israel and Palestine, eroticized the encounter between Palestinian boys and Israeli policemen in uniform. As a whole, the issue showed not only how much fashion editors have eroticized Arab and North African cultures and populations, but how homosexual and banlieue fashions have cross-pollinated in the way Zeraoui describes.

This cross-pollination between communities illustrates a key concept in the analysis of fashion trends, according to which gay men have historically lifted sartorial and self-care cues from ethnic minorities. Such sartorial borrowings here are not unidirectional: they take the form of back-and-forth exchanges, leading to mutual enrichment. *Têtu* magazine founder and veteran of the AIDS activist group Act-Up Didier Lestrade elaborated on this concept in his musings on facial hair styling trends, wherein he speaks of the mustache traveling between gay ghettos and Latino barrios: "I think the main element that explains the young gay generation's attraction to the mustache is its place in Black and Latino (culture)."[67] Another instructive illustration of Zeraoui's claim is the French Tecktonik dance subculture, which reached the zenith of its popularity around 2008. At its origins, Tecktonik was a dance form combining el-

Also in the "Ch'adore" issue, Rankin's photo spread heralds new runway fashions that borrow freely from banlieue street style, homo-Orientalism, "tribales"
cuts, and luxury bling. (Courtesy of Rankin.)

ements of martial arts, modern dance, extreme flexibility, an emphasis
on upper-body movement, video games, mangas, and physical reenact-
ments of male personal toilette gestures such as running gel through one's
hair. Most of these elements are also to be found in the vogue subculture
engineered by New York's black and Puerto Rican gay youth (popularized
by Madonna in her video "Vogue" (1990) and before that Jennie Livingston in her documentary *Paris Is Burning*[68]).

Gay-interest publications picked up on these resemblances between homosexual and ethnic subcultures. *Têtu* devoted an issue to the Tecktonik trend, featuring a profile of the promoters at the Metropolis nightclub, a banlieue staple where the movement got its start. The article is accompanied by an action photospread of some of the most fashionable Tecktonik dancers (all hailing from the banlieues), all of whom are self-declared "straight" men who engage with androgyny in visually spectacular ways.[69] The editorial cover caption for the issue posed the following question, as if to call back to homonormative order the banlieue's sexual instability: "Is Tecktonik crypto-homo?" Notably, the article immediately preceding this feature is an interview with Fadela Amara, entitled "A banlieue plan for gays?" In it, Amara paints a picture of the banlieues as a place that would repress any and all gestures of effeminacy or androgyny. Yet the androgynous Tecktonik subculture did blossom in just such a place. The contrast between the two features within the same issue is striking, revealing contradictory views on the question of sexual tolerance in the banlieues.

Zeraoui relativizes the belief that there has been a unique exodus of banlieue homosexuals to the city center. He mentions other classes who have also made the trip from a culturally, sexually, or professionally stifling region of the country to the city, including gay men who continue to leave the countryside for the promise of a more "liberated" and individual life in Paris. The parallels between rural and sexual exodus merit a closer look, as do so many other blind spots of "sexual modernity": if "white," middle-class, rural or city center gay men also seek refuge and liberty in the gay ghettos, this would contradict the "sexual modernity" thesis, which states that Muslim or banlieue homosexuals most urgently flee homophobia.

Having dislodged the *banlieusard* monopoly on sexual backwardness, Zeraoui disputes the claim that *banlieusard* homosexuals are unique in suffering a "double oppression" in light of the discrimination stemming from both their ethnicity and sexual orientation:

CHAUMONT: Discrimination exists. When those kids get to the city center establishments, the fact they come from the projects is visible on their faces.

ZERAOUI: No, they are not discriminated against, they do better than their heterosexual elders. They are the crème de la crème, the elite even, of the Muslim and black community. All those people have choices. . . . Afterward, yes, there is a larger discrimination, based on looks, in hiring, in housing assignments.

Gay-interest mag *Têtu* featured Tecktonik dancers. With their irreverent hair-styles, extreme flexibility, and anime vogue, Tecktonik dancers announced that the banlieue was comfortable with androgyny. (Courtesy of Takao Oshima.)

CHAUMONT: Why was it that everyone asked to remain anonymous, when I came to your club nights for my investigative reporting?

ZERAOUI: They don't have the means [to refrain from being anonymous], and they have the right to be anonymous. They have other kinds of courage, namely that which involves posting their photos online, on their profiles. You don't realize it, but this didn't exist ten years ago. Today, they post their real photos, even though it's risky, they do it! Life is full of compromises, but at the end of the day: they meet each other, they have a sexuality. But they live with their parents, because they can't pay for rent on their own. Why do you ask them to come out loud and clear?

CHAUMONT: What I'm denouncing is the creation of ghetto cities where it's impossible to be oneself.

Here Zeraoui deviates from the narrative of double discrimination, of *double peine*, a term Chaumont employs elsewhere in this debate in reference to *banlieusard* homosexuals. *Double peine* means "double punishment"; it is more frequently used to describe those immigrant subjects raised in France from an early age who found themselves sent back to their parents' countries after a delinquent infraction: the term thus refers to receiving a double sentence for a single crime. Chaumont's usage is noteworthy because he refers to a practice that has historically affected the alleged oppressors of the homosexual victims he writes about (macho, delinquent, *banlieusards* of immigrant background). This rhetorical move eliminates the pity one might feel for possible victims of deportation by bringing up their victimization of others in another instance. This is not to say that Franco-Arab homosexuals have not also participated in delinquency, or been sent back to their parents' home countries because of an infraction.

Zeraoui presents the altogether opposite case of the *positive* discrimination that he believes favors homosexual, metrosexual, or androgynous men of color in greater French society. The point that androgynous or openly homosexual ethnic minorities and *banlieusards* might actually do better, or be more favored to do better—in the professional and educative spheres—than their heterosexual peers has rarely been broached. On the other hand, scholars such as Guénif-Souilamas have identified the kinds of "excessively virile" Franco-Arab subjects that have been presented as countermodels to sexual modernity, and how they are stigmatized for a lack of assimilation rooted in their "heterosexual excess."[70] Zeraoui—perhaps benefiting from the discursive freedom available to the nonacademic who replaces empirical evidence with personal experience—goes a step further by saying that it is the disclosure of homosexuality that pushes gay ethnic minorities into the elite sphere. Doing an informal survey of the French media sphere, Franco-Arabs who appear on the daily variety and news shows often demonstrate at least a metrosexual sensibility. This point echoes my argument in chapter 4 about how the homosexualization of Franco-Arab actors is a common step toward acceptance in the cinema world, a way of proving commitment and versatility, as well as a way to mitigate the introduction of cultural difference on-screen.[71]

After the allegation of double punishment has been rejected by Zeraoui, Chaumont targets a habit that is more difficult to deny: *banlieusard* homosexuals' frequent (though not unanimous) decision to remain anonymous. Zeraoui underlines that certain material and class conditions are required to pursue a life of individuality in the city center, notably the cutting off of ties to a family support system.[72] Chaumont himself wrote disparagingly of homosociality in *Homo-ghetto*, declaring that in the banlieue, what matters above all is the group, always the group. In contrast to these views, Zeraoui fills in the perspective of chosen anonymity, one that calls out the imperative of disclosure foisted on ethnic sexual minorities in order to then refuse it. Zeraoui, meanwhile, slowly assembles the argument that sexuality and the driving impulses behind it are what guarantee the social mobility that Chaumont declares lacking in the banlieues, the social mobility that would cancel out the ghettoization feared by the anti-communitarian camp.[73]

Summary

Gay and feminist activist journalism has contributed to the sexualization of discourse about the banlieues. Female virility seemingly poses problems for French feminists, who see in tough or tomboy women a lost cause rather than examples of successful coping strategies or resistance; girl gangs—with their sportswear and homosociality—are criticized for resorting to a culture of violence that allegedly saturates the banlieues, while those who harbor outwardly feminine gender expressions are celebrated for their courageous resistance. Women's combativeness is dismissed as illegitimate or aggressively editorialized into irrelevance (see *La cité du mâle*), when it too closely resembles the strategies adopted by virilist banlieue men. As such, women's issues are subordinated to men's in a newly alienating and misogynistic way. Even women wearing the hijab cannot escape judgement, as is evident in Amara's dismissal of the "soldiers of Green fascism."

Likewise, banlieue sexual minorities, especially male homosexuals, have been criticized for their recourse to virility. In his investigative report *Homo-ghetto*, Frank Chaumont frames homosexuality in the banlieue as beleaguered and uses an interventionist, human rights rhetoric to "save" homosexual *banlieusards* from their home environment. Gay happiness is judged according to an unspoken, homonormative telos that leans toward monogamous relationships; Majid's anecdotes about collective and homosocial banlieue homosexualities are dismissed as unfulfilled, locked in a juvenile state. The queer potential of the collective and gregarious banlieue homosociality incarnated by Majid (which many avant-garde filmmakers have exploited for aesthetic purposes) is left unexplored.

Chaumont's vilification of banlieue sexualities, however, has not gone unchallenged. The nightlife entrepreneur Fouad Zeraoui launched his immensely popular and hedonistic nightlife ventures to provide a gathering place for banlieusard ethnic and sexual minorities who experienced rejection elsewhere. A debate between Chaumont and Zeraoui, organized by the now defunct *Têtu* magazine upon the release of *Homo-ghetto*, reveals the gulf in perspectives often engendered by the controversial topic of banlieue homophobia: While Zeraoui accuses Chaumont of being out-of-step with how banlieue attitudes on sexuality had evolved within the last ten years, he doesn't contest the sexual modernity imperative set up by Chaumont, in which "thuggish" gender expressions must be discarded in favor of metrosexual ones. Chaumont, in turn, accuses Zeraoui of capitalizing on the willfully clandestine banlieusard, including the homo thug and his admirers. They cannot see eye to eye when it comes to the presence and meaning of sexual diversity and gender experimentation in the banlieues. In the end, Zeraoui surprisingly bests Chaumont's miserabilist narrative by stressing that banlieue homosexuals may "have it better" than their heterosexual counterparts in terms of social and professional mobility. What's at stake in such infighting over happiness and miserabilism is the capacity, known intimately by those in the artistic sphere, of transforming struggle or resistance into an opportunity for creation and innovation. As I explore in chapters 3, 4, and 5, cultural actors and artists are more likely than activists to recognize and work with the creativity that emerges from banlieue clandestinity, combativeness, and virile performance. First, however, I want to examine why psychoanalysts are drawn to Islam and North Africa in chapter 2.

2 /　Constructing the Broken Family:
The Draw for Psychoanalysis

Islam itself is grounded on a disavowed femininity, trying to get rid of the umbilical cord that links it to the feminine.

SLAVOJ ŽIŽEK AND JOHN MILLBANK[1]

From the early days of colonial ethnopsychiatry and the Algiers School to the current era of media interventions by French psychoanalysts, commentators with backgrounds in psychoanalysis have often been called upon to lend their expertise to the discussion of cultural and ethnic difference.[2] In this chapter, I look at how experts in these fields, with their particular attentiveness to sexuality, have approached issues of immigration, Islam, and the place of minorities in French domestic affairs. At the core of my reading is the argument that psychoanalytical commentators have conceptualized these issues through the lens of a (broken) family unit that updates, in dystopian fashion, the Freudian family unit of bourgeois Vienna for contemporary circumstances. United in their "pathologized" status, the "juvenile delinquent," the "veiled woman," and the "impotent father" are figures that together make up a symbolic family unit, constructed by psychoanalysts who write about urban France, immigration, or North Africa. Reading about this dysfunctional family unit, one quickly gains the sense that Muslims' continuing influx into Europe will have dire psychosexual consequences on the continent, due to their psychoanalytically aberrant views on the public-private distinction and patriarchal law. In fleshing out the individual "members" of this projected family unit, we come to understand how concepts such as "sexual terrorism," "female self-censorship," and "paternal failure" have been constructed and in turn condemned by prominent psychoanalytical opinion-makers. The recurrence of these tropes—and their associated psychological types—in political and cultural affairs has contributed to the estrangement of immigrant-based sexualities from sexual modernity. This overexposure, I argue, has also rendered assimilation more difficult for these minorities faulted by the psychoanalyst guardians of sexual modernity, in so far as some important thinkers have described psychoanalysis itself as a pathway toward French assimilation. I also unpack the intellectual family tree binding together the psychoanalytical community that participates in these processes of psychological othering that exists transnationally between North Africa and France.

First, some background on the historic engagement of the field of psychoanalysis with (North) Africa. Sigmund Freud once considered women's minds the underexplored "dark continent" or "Africa" of psychoanalysis, and Ranjana Khanna later problematized this phrasing and explored its colonial underpinnings.[3] Much of the French psychoanalytical writing on immigrants reveals a tendency to view in immigration a simple transposition of African mentalities into Europe. Because postcolonial urban France counts many African and North African immigrants, the psychological processes present among banlieue inhabitants and social phenomena, at times, have been conceived as more primal or unadulterated versions of psychological processes that were elevated to the symbolic plane when it came to contemporary bourgeois Europe. Full consideration of the novelty of the banlieue case requires us to shift this viewpoint, however: the sociopsychological discourse specific to the banlieues differs from both discourses at work within the Freudian bourgeois family unit (often presented as a universal case) and discourses that circulated in (North) Africa. Thus, the civilizational timeline that an officialized history of psychoanalysis provides must be updated, and insights related to this unit cannot be applied without alteration to banlieue subjects. Furthermore, I insist that projections about banlieue sexualities among prominent psychoanalysts are the logical outcome of a failure to recognize and grapple with immigration and its impact on what should be an evolving psychoanalysis. This failure to account for immigration psychoanalytically helps exclude French banlieue subjects nationally at a moment when psychoanalysis itself is gaining currency. This exclusion reinforces one of my main arguments, which is that the guardians of French culture can play a role in rejecting Muslims and banlieue subjects through cultural elitism by using the vocabulary of sexual enlightenment.

In this psychoanalytical field of thinkers, religions (especially Islam) have been established as particular targets for analysis. Islam is portrayed as an all-encompassing explanatory system, sometimes competing with mainstream psychoanalysis in its ability to account for everything. Other thinkers have resisted assertions of competition or incompatibility between Islam and psychoanalysis as all-encompassing systems. Psychoanalyst Jalil Bennani, describing his clinical practice in Morocco, insists that psychoanalysis ought to thrive in Islamic societies, because the "exterior censorship" that occurs in public "calls for a liberation in intimate space," that is, people expressing their feelings among friends, family, or in the psychoanalyst's office.[4] Even if responding to the psychoanalytic imperatives of confession might be difficult in a society to which he ascribes self-censorship, "such barriers fall once confidence is instilled between patient and therapist."[5] Instead of one eclipsing the other, Islam and psychoanalysis could coexist comfortably and even incorporate each other's symbolic vocabularies, depending on the negotiation of the public and private.

The penchant in some psychoanalytical literature for symbolism and interpretive excess is especially pronounced vis-à-vis Muslim patients. This is due to the multiplicity of exotifying projections upon the monolithic Arabic-Islamic heritage presented for analysis. In this sense, unstable and often mistranslated texts such as *The One Thousand and One Nights* can become representative of "Muslim psychology," as has already occurred in Malek Chebel's work on Arabic erotology.[6] Chebel, perhaps the most prolific francophone author on Arab sexuality, is himself an interesting example of how psychoanalysts, with their special expertise on matters of sexuality, are called upon to give a portrait of Islam, Muslims, and French Muslims to a French audience. Chebel is a frequent guest on French political and cultural talk shows, often as the sole "representative" of Islam and Muslims; he is also the author of many op-eds on the subject in leading newspapers.[7] Some critics have viewed his research into Islamic sexology and his overemphasis on narratives of transgression as at best a case of wishful thinking, and at worst a willful deformation of history designed to line up with a kind of French republican sexual nationalism. The latter nationalism would offer him a privileged place because he supplies an anticommunitarian history of transgressions of Islamic customs. Muslims that fell in line with this narrative would model the successful assimilation into French society, an assimilation that prioritizes individualist sexual liberation over ethnic or religious attachments: a consequence of "sexularism" to borrow a term from Joan Scott.[8]

Historically, North African as well as Franco-Arab attitudes toward psychoanalysis can be characterized by a deep ambivalence, especially during the colonial and decolonization eras. Whether seeking medical help, being processed by social services or dealing with the criminal justice system, France's Franco-Arab population has increasingly resorted to psychoanalytical and also ethnopsychiatric solutions, with some critics arguing that these populations have been directed or forced toward such therapies: they accuse certain branches of ethnopsychiatry of constantly returning patients to their ethnocultural origins. This last point has led to controversy, and has been contested in a very public debate between ethnopsychiatrist Tobie Nathan and critic Didier Fassin, who argued that ethnopsychiatry is a mere expedient solution with superficial "results" that has been privileged by certain social and judicial services over other, less "culturalist" options. Fassin disputes the notion that patients would seek out an ethnopsychiatric solution without being directed to do so.[9]

Before proceeding further with the question of politics in psychoanalysis, it is necessary to summarize a long-standing debate pitting contemporary ethnopsychiatry against mainstream psychoanalysis. The colonial ethnopsychiatry of old, practiced by the Algiers school, sought to define the psychological particularity of indigenous populations in an often unethical pursuit of "scientific" innovation. Openly racist and breaking with the idea of a universal subconscious, this experimental ethnopsychiatry sought to define and stigmatize a Muslim psychology considered "dangerous" and "perverse." This rhetoric occasionally informed French anti-immigration policy discussions, as I explain. This openly differentialist psychiatry, which seemed to die out with decolonization and other ruptures with colonial policies, has been called *ethnopsychiatry* by some, due to its focus on distinguishing ethnic categories in the field of mental health. The more well-known *modern ethnopsychiatry* that has emerged in France aims to assist populations of immigrant origin, filling in where traditional medical and psychological services have fallen short. Passionate arguments have erupted in the French media sphere—already accustomed to psychoanalysts weighing in on important social issues—about whether this new ethnopsychiatry is a continuation of the old one.[10]

Previous generations in France and in the former French colonies had ample reason to be wary of the psychoanalytical apparatus, as explained by Jalil Bennani, Abdelmalek Sayad, Richard Keller, Ranjana Khanna, and Tahar Ben Jelloun. Despite legitimate reservations about the colonial applications of these special sciences, numerous psychoanalysts and ethnopsychiatrists have shown themselves to be adept at commentary on the intersections between sexuality and immigration. Lending an inquisitive ear to the politically "incorrect," an active group of psychoanalytical thinkers has investigated some of the most politically and emotionally sensitive components of the French immigration debate. One could cite, for instance, Fethi Benslama's early writing on the Islamic symbolism of the veil, the work of Jean-Michel Hirt on religion in the clinic, and the journal *La Nouvelle Revue d'Ethnopsychiatrie*. Conservative French psychoanalysts, however, have been adept at finding the media spotlight, offering sweeping analyses and often prescriptive recommendations for dealing with the symbolic and sexual "violence" of Muslim immigration to France and European societies. As Ranjana Khanna observes, psychoanalysis, then and now, has been invested with a volatile political ambivalence, as it "embodies the violent inception of colonial being and reveals its colonial specters, which are at once the call of justice—the by-product of reading strife—and the forms of violence it engenders."[11] Thus the discipline, haunted by its colonial applications, contains within it the capacity to injure as well as knowledge of the cure, gleaned from the witnessing of those injuries. Richard Keller summarizes this alternating shift between tool and weapon in his book *Colonial Madness*, where he generally presents psychoanalysis as a battlefield far from being monolithic.[12] He also touches upon the ambivalence of experimental nature of ethnopsychiatry, predisposed to breakthroughs as well as highly culturalist readings (i.e., readings that ceaselessly view the analyzed person as an artifact of their ancestral culture rather than an individual capable of evolution, and, most crucially in the French context, integration within a foreign culture).

Tahar Ben Jelloun—now predominantly seen as a literary author—published his first major scholarly work as a psychiatrist. His 1975 doctoral thesis was published as *La plus haute des solitudes* (*The Highest of Solitudes*), in which he links clinical observations of sexual impotence among migrant workers to their feelings of social injustice and the mistreatment of workers in France. Ben Jelloun found that most of the patients coming to his service for treatment complained of sexual impotence, a phenomenon the book attempts to explain. Even though France evolves, for immigrants who have moved from a former country of domination to one of hospitality (*terre d'accueil*), the act of displacement and uprooting separates them from socially sanctioned outlets of sexual and affective fulfillment. This prevents both comfort and pleasure in the new land, cutting off the then largely male immigrant pool from "the capacity of *jouissance*" (a metaphorical term difficult to translate which includes elements of pleasure, orgasm, fulfillment, and thriving). This frustration emerged out of their difficulties finding "socially approved" sexual partners, as well as a more general affective alienation and solitude. The immigrant thus evinces through sexual symptoms a stifling social lack.[13]

Ben Jelloun spells out a double standard that clouds the reception of immigrants in France: immigrant bodies have been recruited for the purposes of meeting demands for manual labor, but the same bodies have been rejected as undesirable on the dating and marriage market, a process leading to great psychological frustration in his reading. By shutting down sexually, Ben Jelloun argues, the North African immigrant refuses the logic of social profiteering (*rentabilité sociale*) and the capitalist exploitation of bodies, suggesting through this reproductive refusal that he finds France inhospitable for his future progeny.[14] It should be mentioned that Ben Jelloun later riffed on this theme in his ironically titled *Hospitalité française*, on the perceived lack of hospitality inherent in France's immigration policies, measured against the more familiar concept of Arab hospitality.[15] Those with psychoanalytical backgrounds, Ben Jelloun explains, are ideally situated for contemplating such "no-future" horizons of sex and death.[16]

Some of the most far-reaching interventions on immigrant sexuality have been produced by thinkers with backgrounds in the humanities who employ psychoanalysis as a heuristic tool. Some of the more sensational writers in this community, like Michel Schneider, have deployed sexualizing explanations that use Freudian and Lacanian rhetoric in order to "understand" banlieue virilities and sexual violence. Elisabeth Badinter, a best-selling philosopher and writer whose specialty is a feminist reading of cultural affairs, states in her introduction to *XY*—a trans-historical meditation on masculine identity—that Europe has traversed in recent times many crises of masculinity, and that the discipline of psychoanalysis brings an essential clarity to their comprehension. A shared point between masculinity crises, in her view, is that "they are born in countries of refined civilization, where women enjoy a greater liberty than elsewhere."[17] The exception to her diagnosis, however, are men not "historically" French. Badinter establishes a separation, especially tenuous during the postimmigration era, between "national" masculinities, limiting her inquiry to the part of the national population of long-standing European origin, out-of-step with the diverse France of today.[18]

The Juvenile Delinquent

More than any other, the figure of the juvenile delinquent embodies the idea of a volatile banlieue virility, invoked by politicians campaigning on the issue of urban security. Usually male, phallocentric, and unassimilated—the juvenile delinquent is the first member of the family pathologized by the psychoanalysts of immigration examined here. Some critics question this process of pathologization by calling for greater recognition of the universality of the turbulent adolescent condition. Nevertheless, those working on issues related to psychoanalysis, the banlieues, and immigration accept the singular focus on adolescence in diagnosing banlieue "problems": violent teenagers would be the most visible symptom of social strife, if not necessarily representative of all sentiment in their neighborhoods. These writers still assert that adolescence carries unique importance as an age pivotal for the symbolic determination of the self, and thus a make-or-break moment of decision-making for the parents, social services, and judges concerned.

In the literature at hand, provocative parallels between the phenomena of migration and adolescence have often been drawn. Psychiatrist, psychoanalyst, and essayist Jalil Bennani—based in Rabat, Morocco, and recipient of the Sigmund Freud prize—declares these phenomena similar because of their triggering of *dépaysement* (a notion difficult to translate that combines elements of exile, unfamiliarity, and change of locale): adolescence is a kind of exile from childhood that triggers the disorientation one ordinarily feels upon leaving a familiar country for the first time. When considering *adolescent* migrants, or even youth immigrants who don't remember a life before France, the similarity between the conditions of migration and adolescence are that much more magnified. Hence, Bennani singles out these youth as *most* representative of the uprootedness all adolescents are said to feel.[19]

Adolescents are a revelatory object not just because they have been the focal point of media-driven anxieties about urban and sexual violence, but also because, as Bennani explains, they could reveal the role of the psychoanalyst. Adolescents are subjects that the latter would have to competently understand in order to anchor the relevance of his or her own analyses, because adolescents are said to be the "prime witnesses of their epoch."[20] Adolescence is also unique, he says, in its position as a kind of theoretical frontier, a vanguard that forces sedimented theories to evolve, since youth cultures have consistently brought with them contestations of the thinking of previous generations. Striking a tone that departs from the alarmist literature on the violence and destruction wrought by adolescents, Bennani describes how that growth phase can offer a platform for creativity.[21] The overconfidence often exhibited by male adolescents could, in one reading, constitute a precondition of self-expression, a form of creative resilience rather than an empty practice compensating for an original weakness or poverty. Drawing parallels between artists and teenagers, Bennani sheds light on how teenage suffering can oblige the subject to be creative, to take up, engage with, and transform their own psychological makeup with a reconstructive "force of desire (that) refuses weakness." Such a description refutes the miserabilist predictions of un-avoidable failure most often prescribed for banlieue adolescents, called "unsalvageable" social cases in media accounts.[22]

Bennani maintains that working on adolescence entails a "permanent questioning of our theoretical frames" and that "our practice (of psychia-try) changes as adolescents change."[23] However, psychoanalytical thinkers such as Tobie Nathan and Fethi Benslama are in rare agreement when they discount the capacity of youth to create stable, all-encompassing cultures on their own that could orient and ground subjects with the same degree of rootedness provided by more established value systems, whether emanating from one's parents, one's origins, or the state. At stake within this opposition is the possibility for a science to be changed by its object—for psychoanalysis to mirror and not just define adolescence—an outcome sometimes precluded by explanatory systems that are more interested in preserving the "symbolic order" than evolving to adapt to shifting subjectivities.

Bennani's profile of the adolescent enters the terrain of sexuality when he details at length just how adolescents confront us with simultaneous feelings of attraction and repulsion. Adolescents would recall an inner turbulence once felt intimately only to wane later—instincts that popu-lar culture has expressed and explored. Speaking of itinerant youth who haunt the streets as if they were a second home, Bennani says:

> A troubling phenomenon—visible in our streets, on a daily basis—it is something we sometimes prefer to see hidden away. We tend, at the same time, to reject and to be strongly engaged [interpellés] by these youth, so different from other people. The media and the cinema have given them a voice; not to exploit them as a fashion trend, but to por-tray them as a model of social trouble. A very current phenomenon, quite representative of our age and our society. . . . A phenomenon long hidden suddenly becomes very apparent. That's why it gives us a feeling of déjà-vu.[24]

Oftentimes, Bennani states, the same media that condemns adolescent violence alternately romanticizes danger, violence, and risk in other ven-ues (e.g., the increasingly popular televised depictions of the gangster life-style). Thus, the media misses an opportunity to deal with violence in a therapeutic way, psychologically assessing its motivations on an aesthetic level but not willing to go the same sympathetic distance at the level of social reality. The media does not contribute, Bennani says, "to the puri-fication of violence or make it play a cathartic role."[25]

Abdelfattah Kilito, one of Bennani's compatriots, has theorized the same universality of adolescence. Kilito tackles the question of the compatibility of the psychological concept of adolescence with Moroccan culture. He delves into Arabic letter roots to find the word that best approximates *adolescence*: the most literal translation, *mourahaqa*, is not part of common parlance, he finds; *irhaq*, from the same root, seems to him a better fit, signifying "exhaustion" or "overwork," joining with the idea expressed earlier that adolescence represents the psychological boiling point of society.[26] One concludes from this that adolescent turbulence and sometimes violence must be put in context as an integral part of a holistic social order, an outlet of tension (where volatile subjects can tire themselves out) that is crucial to the well-being of the whole. Bennani, on the other hand, claims that adolescence, a short time ago in the "Arab world," did not fully exist as a conceptual category, as youth in these societies passed directly from childhood to adulthood, he claims.[27]

In order to make symbolic sense of adolescent violence, including sexual violence, some psychoanalysts—often in collaboration with mainstream self-help or psychology magazines—have pointed the finger at Islamic patriarchy, and in some instances Mediterranean patriarchy. Discourses of absentee fathers (*pères démissionaires*) and single, overworked mothers have also proliferated, offering the explanation that parental disempowerment is the reason the banlieues lack an intimidating father principle: this has created a situation where Muslim fathers are simultaneously accused of being both too present and too absent. Bennani locates the emergence of adolescent violence not within patriarchy but rather its "fissuring and deconstruction" in contemporary times, with father figures no longer able to assure a controlling role over youths.[28] In his seventies-era output, Ben Jelloun offers a different take on the place of patriarchy in immigrant psychology: He opposes attempts to attribute an up-tick in sexual violence to the influx of Arab or Islamic attitudes about women. Instead, he describes an obsession, among his North African patients, with protecting the symbolic penis from hostile and unwelcome exterior conditions that cancel desire and give no hope for procreation.[29] Ben Jelloun depicts a surprisingly vulnerable phallocentrism that is sensitive to being endangered, which is a significant departure from the aggressive postures of phallocentrism that, according to the mainstream media, are rooted in Islamic patriarchy.

In an attempt to explain this gap in paternal authority (which some psychoanalysts call the root of delinquency), Bennani suggests that when it comes to adolescents of Arab or Muslim background, the death of the father—a requisite feature of the path to psychosexual maturity in

Freudian theory—seems to have come too easily, and thus ushered in a sense of disorientation. These rebellious figures initially see the collapse of parental patriarchy as their own "accomplishment, having finally vanquished their parents, but later they are said to feel regret and seek to distance themselves from this act," Bennani explains. "If parents cave in to teenage pressures too easily, [the adolescent in question] feels much more guilty than one might imagine."[30]

A former government official has given his own psychoanalytical reading of "problematic" banlieue youth and absentee fathers, albeit from a very different political perspective. Michel Schneider, former director of music and dance at the Ministère de la Culture (1988–1991), expounds upon the great absence of the Father principle in France in *Big mother: psychopathologie de la vie politique* (Big Mother: psychopathology of political life).[31] His case further demonstrates the proximity of "experts" and intellectuals with a background in psychoanalysis to political power. Camille Robcis mentions him prominently in an article discussing how a panoply of experts on kinship and the symbolic were commissioned to weigh in during the intense societal debate in the late 1990s surrounding the PACS (Pacte Civil de Solidarité), the French civil unions that preceded gay marriage. Along with Caroline Eliacheff and Irène Théry, Schneider was one of the most prominent voices describing how the prospect of officialized homosexual couplehood and especially parenthood (eventually excluded from the PACS law) would imperil society because of its scrambling of symbolic laws; for Schneider, the PACS was yet another attempt to "kill the father."[32] For its panels and commissions, the French political world has often turned to psychoanalyst writers for instruction on matters of society and kinship, especially when they relate to sexuality; the conversation has spilled over into newspapers, as Robcis shows.[33] In his larger oeuvre, Schneider extended his reproach of maternal forces in politics by critiquing feminist texts that suggest Nazism was a distinctly masculinist phenomenon. He also laments the increased confusion of the masculine and the feminine in the era of "sexual modernity": the provocative author's note in his book *La confusion des sexes* warns that, in our day and age, "each sex takes itself for the other, out of fear of penetrating the other. Do we really want moral and political socialism to deliver us from sexuality?"[34] He suggests that strong feminine and maternal preoccupations with power exist, despite a prevailing consensus that only patriarchy saturates the political world. He adds that principles such as equality of the sexes, if followed to the extreme, do create their own totalitarianism.

Closer to the subject matter at hand, Schneider has attempted to connect the "sexual terrorism" harming the banlieues with the terrorism of the

9/11 attacks. His sexual reading of that disaster, shock value notwithstanding, follows a path well-traveled by other writers and philosophers—from Jean Baudrillard to Michel Houellebecq and, more recently, Yann Moix—who have suggested that terrorism is a form of "revenge" against the West's sexual liberty, a form of sexual frustration in itself, or an attempt by the castrated to castrate (with a host of psychoanalytic associations arising in suit). Sensitive about criticisms of patriarchy and especially the place of the father in his adopted science, Schneider disparages feminist critiques of psychoanalysis by reducing them to mere fashion trends: "In the last few years, the symbolic has become no longer fashionable, and the father totally old hat."[35] He points to the peril of such symbolic negligence during times of catastrophe, and maintains that "one needs a father" (*il faut du père*) in order to traverse (national) identity crises.[36] Schneider is not the only commentator to diagnose a psychopathology of political life, nor are such diagnoses the exclusive domain of the political right.[37]

Going back to basics, Schneider reminds readers of the "symbolic order," often invoked but less often explained: "1. An order of language. 2. An order upon which the individual holds no sway. 3. An order derived from the rapport between the sexes. 4. An order founded upon the notion of time. 5. An order linked to the negative and to death. 6. An order of which the paternal function is the guarantee."[38] Schneider's reminder is important as it implies that the "symbolic order" was rigidly defined in the first place, something that critics of conservative psychoanalysis decry as being an instance of psychoanalysis falling into a prescriptive rather than descriptive role. The "symbolic order," as one can see, has been heavily gendered. It further functions as a term of choice in newspaper op-eds wherein psychoanalysts are asked to weigh in on controversially current topics with significant ramifications for gender norms: examples of topics include the PACS or civil unions debate, as well as *parité*, or legally sanctioned gender equality measures, as Eric Fassin has noted in his scholarship.[39] The symbolic order is a conceptual institution valued far more in the conservative reaches of French psychoanalytical commentary than in other less prescriptive French psychoanalytical guilds, where such timeless fixations on symbolic rigidity might be considered regressive. Though anchored in Freudian theory, the fixation with the symbolic order alone can be criticized for departing from the spirit of the Freudian formative period and the necessity to leave room for a plurality of explanatory systems.

In his attempt to rehabilitate Father *politik*, Schneider stresses the linguistic connection between *virtue* and *virility* (both stem from the Latin *vir*, or "man"). He adds that France, with its "over-mothering, welfare state" attitude, does not have the courage to admit to lacking the solution for dilemmas ailing society.[40] It is important to note however that Schneider does not want to expunge the maternal from political life, but rather to reduce its supposed domination and instill a greater complementarity between the maternal and the paternal. This is an offshoot of his larger project of (re)confirming the happy difference between the sexes, with complementarity of the sexes sometimes advanced as an especially French *virtue*. Schneider says he refuses "the dilemma between a totally devoted and infantilizing mother and a totally prohibitive, equally infantilizing father."[41]

Schneider's concept of Big Mother is a product of its political context. After 9/11, Schneider's enemy during French leftist rule was a Socialist Party *mollesse* (softness or weakness) that he believed had replaced swift, "paternal" decision-making, and left banlieue unrest to fester. Like many right-wing writers marketed as "courageous," Schneider takes upon himself the task of disclosing the politically incorrect truths on the tips of everyone's tongues, but which no one dares articulate. This doomsday-announcer personality goes hand in hand with the summoned images of a society tearing apart at the seams and political vacuums in need of intervention, in need of a male savior. For Schneider, one example of a courageous truth that needs to be stated, but has often been censored (because of political correctness), has it that what is psychoanalytically proper to the male is to rejoice in impropriety, and to never abandon the desire to hurt: thus he announces that politics will never be able to expunge the war of "all against all" and that there will always be "evil in delinquency" (a turn of phrase that recalls the documentary *La cité du mâle* and its equivocation of evil and male delinquents; see chapter 1).[42]

Commenting on the banlieue polemics of the day, Schneider positions himself in the curious role of sympathizer (juvenile delinquents are only doing what is in man's "nature") and stigmatizer (he reifies a violent nature presumed to be essential to their ancestral Arab culture). Schneider straddles these positions while also disputing the supposed immigrant monopoly on virilist violence, declaring that banlieue violence merely represents the visible symptom of what is latent in "good," city center society. His special interpretation of banlieue violence entails a reconsideration of sexual aggression and its sanction. Schneider claims that desire is something that "imposes itself on its object just as it does on the desiring subject," and warns of the danger of desexualizing human relations in favor of the "un-erotic" obligation of explicit consent. This idea naturally leads to the controversial matter of the *tournantes* (or gang rape) phenomenon, a matter he frequently revisits.

Schneider derives the title of his book from what he identifies as the neutering influence of politicians under the "illusion" that they can erase an integral part of the "symbolic order": the difference between the sexes. "Above regressive non-differentiation," Schneider says, "Big Mother hovers, a kind of psychoanalyst who cultivates the neutral in the name of the Good."[43] This generalized sameness joins with what memoirist and recent anti-immigration activist Renaud Camus has condemned as "the triumph of the same," stemming from the left-wing policies of diversity and multiculturalism (see chapter 3). Like Elisabeth Badinter, who has long been a critic of aspects of French feminism that emphasize victimhood, Schneider believes that classical patriarchy died over a century ago in a loosely defined Western society; vanquished "here" it would exist much more starkly "there." Despite being moribund, patriarchy remains the dead horse that criticism "erroneously" targets, all "while no one risks analyzing or depicting an evident matriarchy."[44]

In this scenario, any hopes of pacifying violence as a social problem are doomed to fail under Big Mother, who would actually run the additional risk of baiting the violence she is trying to quell. This is due to the "fact" that societies in which the mother dominates at the familial level (read, immigrant, and especially Mediterranean, Muslim, and Arab societies), are the most violent: to support this claim, Schneider calls upon several historians and anthropologists in his support without ever naming them. Schneider has dim hopes for prized state measures seeking to establish greater equality of the sexes of ever bringing a "sororal concord to the political arena or pacification in the banlieue."[45] Another accomplishment of a Big Mother approach to sexual rights at the state level—the PACS or French civil union—is an object of scorn for a "majority of psychoanalysts," he says.[46] This black-and-white arrangement of psychoanalytical majorities and minorities is misleading considering the fracturing and splintering of schools of thought on the psychoanalytical scene in France. Critics of the deployment of psychoanalysis in politics have claimed that only the most insensitive, polemical, conservative branches of psychoanalysis get media exposure. These branches depart from a crucial tenet of Freudian psychoanalysis: the restriction of judgment to the private, therapeutic sphere for curative and not stigmatizing purposes.

For Schneider, the peril of the Big Mother welfare state is the establishment of a body politic that takes no risks and at the same time fails to provide security. Its surveillance practices (i.e., over-mothering) would create frustration bound for release in violence. It is here that Schneider's line of argument turns to youth delinquency: "the return of *insécurité* (lack of security, increase in violence) appears as the socially repressed aspect of the welfare state."[47] This amalgam paves the way for perhaps the most controversial of Schneider's conclusions, in which he establishes a psychoanalytic causal chain between the sexual violence of juvenile delinquents, the supposed breakdown of relations between the sexes in the banlieues, 9/11 and the Iraq War, all in relation to Big Mother.[48]

This hasty association between the Islamist terror of 9/11 and the terrorizing of women and sexual minorities in France's banlieues is based upon a novel and highly tenuous concept—sexual terrorism: according to Schneider, sexual terrorism is a phenomenon that unites the Islamists in Afghanistan and the gangs in outer Paris, who both find unbearable the fact that women can equal, surpass, reject, or dominate them (as soldiers, policewomen, or competitors at school). This rhetoric has a direct echo in the Goncourt prize-winning novelist Yann Moix's meditation on the link between terrorism and sexual frustration: *Partouz* (Orgy). In the following passage, Moix ventriloquizes the voice of 9/11 mastermind Mohamed Atta, whose act, according to this reconstruction, was specifically motivated by one woman's rejection of him:

> We've come to help you, guys, dudes, all the men who've been scoffed at by women, yes, you, the little romantic puppies who've been humiliated all around. To tell you that you must stop filling your libraries with novels that speak of romantic suffering! That's enough. You shouldn't let those whores lead you on by the tip of your dick. . . .
> We're coming to bring order to your romantic disorder, to the surrounding sexual disorder, to the sexual disorder which has begun to invade the world and which debases [*avilir*] us men. . . . At present what's required is the subjugation of women all over the planet, in order to control lovesickness.[49]

Moix caricatures what he considers to be a casualty of sexual modernity—the vulnerable, feeble yet intelligent man whose only company is his library filled with novels about sublime and ultimately unobtainable love and sex. Moix introduces this figure to a natural "ally" in the Islamist terrorist who promises to restore a take-no-prisoners phallocentrism to its rightful place. Though this ventriloquizing could perhaps be explained as an exercise in experimental fiction, an exploration of societal tendencies pushed to their hypothetical extreme, Moix reserves little irony for the condemnation of a society that enforces, even at the level of fantasy, an egalitarian harmony in heterosexual relations. This same society promises pleasure just as it sexually incapacitates the attentive men who signed up for the West's modern sexual contract when they agreed to give up being "macho." It is in this sense that Moix has Mohamed Atta target the sex club (*boîte échangiste*) that occupies the novel's alternate hemisphere, and from which the book's title is derived.

Such loose amalgams between sexuality and Islamist terrorism are enabled in part by the symbolic free association common in psychoanalytical inquiry. Authorized in this way, Schneider claims that "religion, actually all religions, have as their unconscious center the question of sexuality."[50] We have elsewhere in this study interpreted the sexualization of religion as a symptom of a general incitement to discourse about Muslim immigrants—sexual hearsay being one of the ultimate forms of social gossip about other groups. Those who stress the sexualization of Muslims in the psychoanalytical understanding give scientific cover to this gossip, allowing for the public expression of sexual anxieties about Muslim immigration that were previously unutterable.

Schneider's proclamations about the importance of psychoanalysis in light of Islamic terrorism, both domestically and internationally, would seem marginal if not for their reiteration by actual world psychoanalytical organizations. In a statement following the attacks of 9/11, the International Psychoanalytical Organization asserted that "given the present terrorist assault on the United States, and the growing concern of the international community on the relationship between fundamentalist ideologies, terrorism, and the outbreak of primitive violence, psychoanalysis has an important role in contributing to understanding the psychodynamics of violence at the level of the individual and social groups."[51]

One hermeneutic tool in the psychoanalytical inventory that has consistently been used to analyze immigration, violence, and sexuality has been the notion of the "return of the repressed." Historian Benjamin Stora studies how the question of memory has been politicized in commemorations of French Algeria and the Algerian War of Independence. In *La gangrène et l'oubli* (The gangrene and forgetting), he describes a French society generally afflicted with colonial amnesia, save for two minority groups—Muslim Algerians and former *pieds-noirs* (French Algerians of European descent)—who continue to spar over the historical narrative of colonial entanglement.[52] The nation, Stora suggests, dismisses troublesome, unresolved, and violent historical episodes for the sake of idealizing an elusive golden age, at its own peril. Psychoanalysts such as Schneider have contributed to this understanding by adding a sexual component: they detail how the twin forces of Big Mother (repressor of male sexual expression) and colonial amnesia combine for a cataclysmic release in violence. They employ a vocabulary of impulses and outbursts, explaining the now banal incidence of the phrase "the return of the repressed" in the academic literature on banlieue violence and colonial memory.

Schneider relates sexual repression to historical repression. He states that the vilified Big Mother politic evokes, for example, the rapes that occurred during the Algerian War as a kind of screening tactic, "no doubt in order to avoid speaking of those which are taking place during the actual civil war ravaging this country," a civil war that, it is suggested but not spelled out, pits immigrant and *banlieusard* classes against an unspecified French national class.[53] With this connection to Algeria, Schneider implicitly ethnicizes sexual violence in France, an assumption not supported by statistics, as sociologist Laurent Mucchielli argues.[54] Schneider attributes the self-flagellating French reticence to counteract banlieue violence to a left-wing guilt that prompts those afflicted to sift through a blameworthy past rather than address alleged upturns in sexual violence in the present, especially if those committing today's violence turn out to share the ethnicity of the victims of yesterday's violence.

Eric Fassin pushes back against the idea that the banlieue would constitute a repository for the repressed sexual urges of a France whose home is in the city center. He warns that creating a divide between the city center and the banlieue is not only unwise and dangerous, it also repeats the past expulsion of "undesirables" to the periphery: "We voluntarily send back this embarrassing reality toward Others—yesterday, toward the rural world, today toward the banlieues . . . toward the strangeness of a different culture. Violence against women would be the product of 'youth' . . . of immigrants and proletarians, barbarous and retrograde."[55] This vision of domestic affairs has been echoed at the highest political levels. Socialist presidential candidate Ségolène Royal (who lost in the run-off to right-wing UMP candidate Sarkozy in 2007) once declared on the campaign trail that "the legitimacy of masculine impulses has been questioned what with laws against pedophilia, sexual tourism, the prostitution of minors, and sexual harassment. Society is evolving in the right direction."[56] Implicitly referring to controversies about sexual violence that have often been associated with the banlieues, she went on to call for the banishment of lingering societal impulses, virilist in character, that "incite one to take action" in terms of sexuality or criminality (*incite au passage à l'acte*). She described how one of the consequences of this virilist impulse, when given free reign, was the "degradation of relations between girls and boys . . . as if the pornographic counter-model could serve a sexual education purpose. Boys are also victims," she explained, "so we must extirpate from man's collective unconscious the idea according to which all masculine impulses would be legitimate."[57] Her rhetoric brings together recurrent motifs appearing in discourses on the banlieues without connecting them directly: journalists and politicians have often emphasized the perceived danger to public safety stemming from the alleged saturation of pornography in the minds of adolescents, and banlieue youth in particular. The Kriegel government report linked sexual harassment and violence against women to the consumption of pornography by adolescents.[58] The report focuses at one point on a gang rape incident involving a group of minors, following which the aggressors declared that they didn't know they were committing a crime because they thought the victim "liked it," a perspective enabled by the banality of rape scenarios in pornography, the report concludes.[59] Other controversies Royal touches upon in her speech include prostitution, sex trafficking, and finally sexual tourism in France's former colonies and protectorates. Her assertion that men are victims of their own unconscious and must therefore revise its violent contents constitutes the ideal target for Schneider's thesis of a neutering, maternal state bent on domesticating what "should" be, in his view, a spontaneous and natural element of male sexuality. Though opposed on the political spectrum, Royal and Schneider both politicize gender and wed it to the state in structurally similar ways.

The Mother-Enablers of a Male Islam

The very notion of a Big Mother disciplining the enterprise of her sons has strong precedents in other psychoanalytical literature as well; see, for example, Tania Modeski's explanation of how a male child situates himself in relation to his parents: "The male child allies himself with the mother against the law of the father, which it is the function of the mother to beat out of the son."[60] One might wonder, does she beat him to extirpate patriarchal laws (Schneider's neutering French government), or to instill patriarchal law in him through discipline (confirming those laws by subjecting the child to the force that it will later use against others)? The latter interpretation has often been extended to Muslim women, who belong to societies Schneider deems maternally driven, where patriarchal law nevertheless reigns. Some psychoanalytical studies center on women in traditional societies who strategically assert patriarchal power through the exploits of their sons; these studies trace a deferred Muslim women's agency in these practices, an agency that manipulates patriarchal structures to its advantage. Bennani touches upon this when he writes, "the mother, lacking social rights, never renounces her claim to her child— especially if it is a boy—as he would constitute for her the guarantee of social recognition."[61] This ambivalence about the mother and patriarchal law is crucial for judging Schneider's statements about Big Mother and the place of immigrants and Muslims relative to it. In his reading, Muslim mothers would be enablers and kingmakers: their son idolatry would give free reign to banlieue boys who fear no sanction. Would Muslim women's manipulations of patriarchy confirm Schneider's claim that the paternal is subjected to the maternal? Or would these manipulations affirm the opposite idea, according to which women make the most of a disadvantaged position by resorting to patriarchal tools for lack of better options?

Ben Jelloun, for his part, conceptualized the immigrant's relationship to a hypothetical Big Mother in marked contrast to Schneider's. The geographic displacement caused by immigration symbolizes for Ben Jelloun a difficult weaning from the mother, one that reactivates anxieties about the child's first separation and impairs the immigrant in his or her adaptation process. This image is a far cry from Schneider's violent immigrant virilism that resists an overbearing mother. This second weaning (from the motherland), in Ben Jelloun's reading, is chosen with much reluctance and affective suffering. Here, mother is not a claustrophobia one wants to escape from but a sentimental shelter one can't bear to leave behind: "French" Big Mother's passive-aggressive coercion is nowhere present. Ben Jelloun sets up an intriguing gender paradox when he states that the new French "fatherland" (*patrie*) is felt as at once a "bad, cruel mother," and the "absence of mother."[62] Ben Jelloun's statement echoes Schneider's language about parents standing in for the nation, but attributes blame differently—to more than one mother, and to a father resembling a bad mother—while Schneider caricatured an omnipresent but ultimately careless mother.

Though Ben Jelloun invests his mother with affective warmth, he also establishes her as an imposing figure with maternal expectations of her progeny's success in the host country. Unlike Schneider's mother, she has a friendly relationship with virility and knows how to wield it. The male immigrant encountered in Ben Jelloun's case studies, however, often suffers from a sexual impotence that pronounces itself due to immigration. The male subject then cannot bear the airing of his sexual humiliation and refuses out of shame to return to the now intimidating North African motherland, to avoid the risk of his emasculation (*dévirilisation*) being made public. Settling into exile, Ben Jelloun writes, "signifies an evasion from the mother, elevated to the rank of a moral and psychological authority concerned by the sexual becoming of her progeny."[63] It is before her that the male North African immigrant feels his impotence most acutely. When impotence is revealed, something is lost between mother and son, and a strong castration anxiety appears in the patient.[64] In this sense, the emergence of sexual impotence after immigration unleashes the same fear of returning home found in more familiar immigration anxieties—the fear that pronounces itself if the immigrant's material, living, or marriage situation has not significantly improved while away from the home country.

The Tunisian Fethi Benslama, who elsewhere offers a creative psychoanalytical reading of the politics of the veil in France, evokes in his writing something very similar to Schneider's mediating maternal force in politics. In the following decidedly abstract passage from his *Psychoanalysis and the Challenge of Islam,* he reflects on universalism, language, and controversies over how the universalist French state might prohibit certain forms of differentialist expression, like the hijab in public schools: "What would the universal speech that might come to interpose itself for all of humanity look like? . . . The universal prohibition would presume a position of INTER between every inter of human communities, incarnated by an absolute femininity, a Woman-world that would have no identity and would thwart all identities in order to dispense with the difference between truth and non-truth for all: a mother of humanity after the fact [*après coup*] whose language would be maternal at the interior of all languages."[65] Benslama here sets up a correlation between the feminine, the maternal, the universal, and the management and repression of identity-affirming assertion. He genders universalism as maternal in order to define it, perhaps misogynistically, as a mode of all-encompassing surveillance, micromanagement, and intermediation. The language here can be contextualized by attaching it to discourse among contemporary French intellectuals that seeks to locate the very concept of truth in the ability to make distinctions, starting with the sexual distinction between man and woman.[66] This discourse, perhaps not accidentally, emerged at the same time as the media sphere was debating the PACS, and especially the prospect, ultimately not included in the law, of gay adoption and parenting. Psychoanalysts against the PACS reasserted the importance of the symbolic, of sexual difference, in their attempts to explain how gay parenting would lead to confusion about the difference between men and women. Several of the same thinkers had located the origin of the symbolic in sexual difference, as Camille Robcis explains.[67] In a similar vein, Benslama calls "feminine" the capacity to distinguish between truth and nontruth. For this purpose, he uses the Islamic story of Khadija who helped her husband, the Prophet Muhammad, tell reality from illusion, as discussed later in this chapter, in "The Veiled Woman." This correlation between universalism and the repression of identity-affirming assertion is a crucial precondition to the claim, explored in this chapter, that submitting to psychoanalysis can constitute a form of assimilation for communities of immigrant origin in France.

Against Europe's progress toward a maternal destiny, Benslama posits an object, "Islam," with a special role to play as *masculine* obstacle: "What the West encounters through Islam is the interposition, the stone in its path, that keeps it from realizing its female identitarian destiny."[68] This point recalls one of Claude Lévi-Strauss's more controversial claims, namely, that Christian Europe was irrevocably transformed by its centuries-long imbroglio with Islam, such that it missed its "natural" encounter and rapprochement with Indian spirituality and society.[69] Lévi-Strauss concludes that the West lost its chance to "remain woman" because of Islam's interposition. More recently, Slavoj Žižek used Lévi-Strauss's notion (that Islam emasculates everything it comes in contact with) to ground his reflections on the original repression of femininity within Islam.[70]

These arguments suggesting the gendered nature of government mediation simultaneously posit Arab and Muslim men as unforeseen obstacles to a scheduled progress, and the derailers of natural complementarities between men and women, interposing themselves with a kind of phallic impoliteness. Yet, in the French psychoanalytic literature discussed here, this representation of Arab men—virile, still in touch with basic psychoanalytical impulses, which are firmly rooted in a symbolic order—seems to be "just what the doctor ordered." They would constitute the missing masculinist messiahs capable of reorienting the inhibited masculinities that Schneider describes as the victims of Big Mother. Instead of following his argument to the limit and embracing this conclusion, Schneider feels he must exclude immigrant masculinities from any possible national solution for problems stemming from the gendering of politics. This entails a host of contradictions and double standards, ultimately showing that while some androgynous sectors of the population may direly "need" a dose of virility, it shall not come from the very place Schneider has invested with a surplus of virility, the multiethnic banlieues. Like Badinter, Schneider would rather suppose nonintelligibility and noncommensurability between banlieue and *centre-ville* masculinities than imagine them on a continuum. By its very excesses, immigrant virility would make comparison unreasonable, if not impossible.

It falls to others to provide reasons for why the intimate mother-child relationship, in the imagined Arab's case, does not result in the expected outcome of neutering by Big Mother. In his study of the migrant body and healthcare institutions in France, Bennani delves into North African child psychology to speak of a special relationship between mother and son, a relation that departs importantly from Schneider's dystopian view. According to Bennani, the early childhood pattern of strong affective intimacy and physical proximity between mother and child lasts up until the age of sexual maturity in North Africa, and may result in the mental state of the King Baby (*enfant roi*), a complex usually represented by adored sons constantly celebrated, venerated, and spoiled. Often described in more general terms as masculine privilege, this state-of-mind has become a cause for concern among critics of immigration from North Africa, because, it is suggested, the King Baby phase instills in sons the roots of phallocentrism, encouraged to blossom by permissive mothers, for whom the infant son is an "absolute master."[71] In this scenario, if the King Baby is to be thwarted, the father arrives on the Oedipal scene with shocking suddenness, presenting his intimidating law. According to Bennani, the father's threats of castration are experienced as a painful tearing away from the mother world and can explain the "acuity of castration problems in Maghrebi patients."[72]

In Bennani, the maternal and the filial mingle inextricably, because, in his reading, the mother never renounces a psychological claim to her son. It would be in her interest to hold tight to her son because by his accomplishments he would determine her own social status. Present here is not the antivirile mother of Schneider's welfare state, but something more entrepreneurial: a system in which virility is not directly associated with sex, but instrumentalized. This instrumentalization is yet another component of the nongendered virility of girl gangs (see chapter 1), who also disassociate virility as a currency of power from the male body. Here, the prevailing attitude of the Arab youth is not hatred of the maternal but feelings of comfort and homeliness within it, as if returning in so far as it is possible to a paradise lost.

This alleged masculine favoritism, enabled rather than repressed by mothers in the Arab world, leads to exchanges among French psychoanalysts about the possibly violent consequences of encouraging phallocentrism in youth. Represented as masculinist identitarians who resist state attempts to pacify and "feminize" them, the banlieue delinquents depicted in sensational newscasts are the adversaries of the state's feminine *intermediating* entity, which strives to erase identitarian affirmation. Schneider, for his part, reins in the abstraction of the Big Mother discourse to focus on the specific example of banlieue youth: "The multiplication of gang rapes by minors is also the abominable response to the will to abolish violence and difference within sexuality."[73] In this way, banlieue youth in particular present the visible, violent symptoms of a general social malaise resulting from the repression of men's desires to express their masculinity. If the psychology of the nation could be represented spatially, banlieue youth would constitute the boiling points, at the periphery, in this centralist vision of a molten core whose inner turbulence remains

undiagnosed and invisible. In such a scenario, only the superficial ruptures of the surface (youth sexual violence in the banlieues) are detectable
and reducible to an object to be analyzed. In contrast, the more general
malaise at the city center is absorbed into the mass of the whole, pushing
at the edges but not exploding.

"Be Careful What You Wish For"

In one section of *Big mother*, memorable for its transitions between
seemingly disconnected elements, Schneider tries to stave off the unsayable—the notion that Islamic terrorists and the sexual terrorists of the
banlieue are the logical outcomes of his recommendations for conserv-
ing sexual difference and the symbolic order—by describing how Muslim
fundamentalists are actually not messiahs for the right to sexual difference, but rather . . . homosexuals: "Their phobia of women appeared as a
repressed homosexuality."[74] This follows a section attacking the prospect
of gay parenthood (*homoparentalité*) for its perilous scrambling of the
symbolic order. Such an aspersion belongs to a province not unfamiliar to
sensational tabloids in America and Europe, which in the past routinely
published stories stressing the homosexual aspects of Muslim terrorists'
clannish and tribal mentalities, the hidden innuendoes of their sex segregation. While Schneider previously connected the political influences of
the homosexual to the maternal—in the way the maternal recommends
androgyny, neutrality, and nondifferentiation—here he connects homosexuality to a sexual differentiation taken to the extreme.

One doesn't know, in this scenario, if banlieue youth are too heterosexual or too homosexual. Are they champions of sexual difference and
the potent productivity of the attraction of opposites, or dictators of phallocentrism and the reign of the masculine same? Such contradictions can
only be put to rest if one accepts the double standard that holds that nonminority French men's virile enterprise should be restored, but not that
stemming from immigrant or Islamic sources. The latter are relegated to
representing the extremist blowback against Big Mother policies that ideally require a softer response; they are the "bad apples" that have opted for
violence when civil disobedience would have sufficed, and as such they
must be rejected. Schneider's logical inconsistencies lead the argumentation to the point that potent heterosexuality is acceptable in some but
not others, especially if that other happens to be perceived as a Muslim
"competitor." Schneider seems to retract from the goal he had initially set
out to achieve, combating sexual nondifferentiation, when he mentions
Muslim terrorists who seek the same end. Instead of continuing in the

old vein, he takes brief ownership of a civic androgyny that he previously had reviled, saying "they want to destroy that part of *us* [my emphasis] which they fear might spread in their own countries: sexual nondifferentiation and a generalized symbolic non-differentiation."[75] During the PACS period of his activism, recourse to the symbolic became a vehicle for homophobia, while in the case of *banlieusard* minorities and Muslim immigrants, the symbolic has been used to sexually other entire ethnic and religious groups. Arab delinquents, Islamists, and homosexual parents are all said to have "perverse" relationships with the symbolic, with Schneider providing an unexpected bridge between these otherings.

One explanation for why this double standard occurs stems from the ambiguous way Schneider uses the evidence and examples supporting his case. He denies subjectivity to banlieue youth he accepts as symptoms of a problem but not as psychologies one can empathize with. The most flagrant denial occurs when they are not included in the centralized French social body Schneider diagnoses as suffering a crisis of masculinity. Khanna is useful here as a rejoinder to Schneider, because she speaks of just such a denial of subjectivity, and how expelling the non-European reifies by contrast the holistic integrity of a European psychoanalytical self: "The national self in Europe is structured in psychoanalysis as a modern counterpart to the primitive colonized. In its profoundly European constitution, it expresses the unsayable: the impossible achievement of selfhood for the colonized, who remain primitive and concealed, and the simultaneous tenuousness of the metropolitan colonizer's self once decolonization is in place and the strife that sustains the colonized as primitive is over."[76] Though Khanna's terrain is the transition from colonization to decolonization, the similarities in this passage regarding the tenuousness of the European self and the denials of the "primitive's" subjectivity have echoes in the present. They point perhaps to an undigested psychoanalytic heritage bequeathed by colonialism to multiethnic France. Schneider describes the fractured nature of the contemporary French/European ailing subject against the unfractured nature of immigrant and Muslim men. In so doing, he testifies to the world-changing event of decolonization, and how it has caused a crisis of masculine integrity in the abstracted European male. In the postdecolonization era, the former primitive has exited Khanna's "concealment," but only to be faced with a familiar situation by which the metropolitan French white man defines himself in counterpoint to the primitive (now residing in the banlieues) once again. In this schema, the most modern traits of masculinity (metrosexuality, androgyny) are those most inverse to the neoprimitive masculinity of the banlieue's decolonized youth. The corollary to making such a point, however, is the transformation of the decolonized other (and now the banlieue youth) into solid allegories of masculinity incapable of the psychological depth inherent in the very fact of having a mental complex or psychological crisis.[77] They are thus not democratically included in the modes of sociocultural expression available to the jaded, the sensitive, the mentally anguished, the blasés, the *ennuyés*, or other psychologically complex types so often at the representative edge of a culture.

Schneider must resolve what is an apparent contradiction: Muslims are the antithesis to Big Mother while also the ultimate symptoms of its presence. In doing so, he uses some gymnastic wordplay delving into Arabic philology: "Waging war against women is simultaneously a waging of war against the opposite sex and a waging of war against sexual difference. In the name of the Mother. Led by men who worry they might become women, this war gathers them together in the one-ness of the One, Unique and Eternal Mother, the Umma. This name, which designates the community of all Muslims, derives from "*Um*," meaning "mother." In societies centered on maternal love, hatred toward the mother takes the form of a fear of women."[78] Schneider establishes a scene in which Muslims privilege the mother over the wife or girlfriend in the symbolic organization of society. He pathologizes relations between mothers and sons and valorizes the heterosexual embrace of woman: horizontal relations toward women are healthier than vertical relations. In this scenario, an imagined Muslim mother makes an alliance with her son and pushes for the thwarting of other women beside herself. The French soft commerce of sexual complementarity is eclipsed by the mother-son dynamic. An inconsistency surfaces: over-mothering, the object of his criticism, would seem to exacerbate virility rather than pacify it, but only in the Muslim case. In Schneider's scheme, heterosexual embrace is the optimal French way for men to counteract the symbolic dilution of sexual difference that Big Mother causes. While banlieue youth seem to work toward the same goal, they do so in a pathologized way, namely, through the homosocial group violence of all-male bands, ambiguously homosexual. This differentiation between types of masculinity—measured versus excessive and perverse—recalls Todd Shepard's analysis of *pied-noir* masculinity and its representations in *The Invention of Decolonization*.[79]

Schneider denies psychological complexity to the very subjects, banlieue youth, that validate his thesis, because they have acted out his recommendations *too literally* as opposed to merely symbolically: "Several signs show that, banished from displayed models, [sexual difference] is making a comeback, one can make the case, in the sexual representations and practices of youth, notably those descended from immigrants, under the most violent of forms (murders, kidnappings, gang rapes, physical violence, a degraded image of all women, except the sister . . .). A sexual difference purely *imaginary and real* [my emphasis], not symbolized, leads to these perverse and contemporary pathologies afflicting sexual relations."[80] This view of Muslims as incapable of distinguishing between the symbolic and the literal, between representation and reality, has many ethnopsychiatric as well as literary parallels: this inability to distinguish would have special and at times dangerous consequences when it comes to flirting, consent, and seduction, relations in which partners must always be careful not to confuse the literal with the symbolic language of desire (i.e., "treat me like your slave," "eat me,"). In contrast, psychiatrist-turned-writer Ben Jelloun gave testimony about his clinical studies and the language North African immigrants used to describe physical pain and psychological suffering. He noted that they expressed themselves in highly metaphorical terms that would constitute proof of symbolic awareness, which would undermine the idea that North Africans could not think on the symbolic level, a view once held by colonial-era psychiatrists of the Algiers School. In Ben Jelloun's retelling, French medical doctors described these patients' language as evidencing delirium (*bouffées délirantes*), part of the reason they had given up on the patients, who were then directed to Ben Jelloun.[81] Richard Keller, more gravely, explores over the course of an entire book "the genealogy and development of the Muslim world as a space of madness from the beginnings of colonial expansion to the present."[82] Always already mad, Muslims are represented as constituting an ideal experimental terrain. In an Orientalist sense, they can be symbolized but not symbolize themselves, and thus supposedly present more stable, ideal "scientific conditions" for analysis. They would tend to obfuscate less while presenting naked impulses. Schneider, however, does not isolate madness to non-Europeans, but rather makes a distinction between the Muslim and the European ways of responding to the psychological imperative of recognizing sexual difference, central to the symbolic order. He opposes a Muslim willingness to act on impulse to a more European ability to turn violent impulses inward: "Against the terrorists' perverse rapport with the symbolic order, we must oppose our own neurotic rapport."[83] As Freudian psychoanalysts state, neurosis is the default position of civilized (European) society, a state of control over impulses that seems "mad" but which is opposed to the more extreme psychosis.

Historical Echoes of the Colonial Delinquent

In *Colonial Madness*, Keller gives historical context to the relationship between psychoanalysis, madness, and theories of North African sexual delinquency. He gestures toward the survival of such a relationship in the postdecolonization era of immigration. Keller maintains that it was during colonial psychiatry's experimental phase in Algeria that these theories were first elaborated. Stereotypes about sexual aggression formed then and were importantly already employed at that time to argue for the curtailing of North African immigration and migration to France. Antoine Porot, founder of the Algiers School of Psychiatry and recipient of Frantz Fanon's critiques in *The Wretched of the Earth*, sought to demonstrate the relative primitivism of North Africans. This intellectual inferiority supposedly manifested itself in what Keller paraphrased as "a capacity for violent criminal impulses—especially sexual violence."[84] Keller goes on to describe how these theories were already impacting the nascent immigration debate in 1950s France: "In France, mental health practitioners and criminologists cited works by the Algiers School to support their demand for an end to immigration which in their view threatened to overwhelm France with criminal lunatics from North Africa."[85] Links between ethnic background, sexuality, and criminality continued with Porot's son, Maurice, who specialized in youth studies and was president of the French Société Médico-Psychologique as late as 1991.[86] Keller writes: "A review of a 1950 article by . . . Maurice ascribed the greater frequency of delinquency among Muslim children (compared with Europeans) to congenital attributes of the Muslim family, especially the sexual segregation of the family, alcoholism, and amorality."[87] The Algiers School's influence extended all the way up to the Paris police prefect, Charles Hirsch, who used the school's work to analyze crime patterns in France. Writing in the late 1950s, Hirsch assimilated North Africans, who were for him "an endless source of conflicts," to the "Puerto Ricans in New York" and "wetbacks in Texas."[88]

When it became apparent the tide of history was in favor of Algerian independence, the Algiers School and its theories about North African inferiority fell into temporary disrepute. However, members of the school found other avenues of distinction in metropolitan France, Maurice Porot reestablishing himself in Clermont-Ferrand and Jean Sutter in Marseille. What is remarkable, considering the now discredited ideas about Arab criminality circulated by the school during the colonial era, is that its members successfully rebranded themselves as experts on delinquency in postdecolonization France.[89] The intellectual genealogy of Jean Sutter is revelatory in this respect. During the heyday of the school, he cowrote with Maurice Porot an article entitled "The primitivism of the North African indigenous and its repercussions on mental pathology," published in 1938.[90] With Henri Luccioni, Sutter elaborated a theoretical innovation—"The Lack of Authority Syndrome"—in 1959, an outcome of their collaborative creation of the medical organization Assistance to Unadapted Children, in Algiers. Today, Sutter has become an unavoidable reference in the literature on juvenile delinquents. Psychiatrist and author Jean-Claude Scotto writes that Sutter was the intellectual father of concepts like the Lack of Educational Authority Syndrome that "is of universal relevance today." Jean Sutter had been the head of the Blida-Joinville hospital from 1938 to 1958, the same hospital that had radicalized Fanon, who disclosed the ethical abuses he encountered there in *The Wretched of the Earth*. Sutter prolonged the chain of intellectual filiation that started with Antoine Porot, with Sutter's students finding appointments in Rouen, Reims, and three others in his adopted city of Marseille.[91]

Keller's findings support the idea that sexualization of North Africans historically had a place in anti-immigration politics. They also help put into context Schneider's prediction of a generalized sexual delinquency and violence taking over France in the aftermath of immigration. A range of programs in France have sought to improve the condition of women and bring more comprehensive sexual education to banlieue communities (see chapter 1). Schneider, however, rails against the welfare state in his condemnation of Big Mother, and seems opposed to any state that would intervene domestically. Keller notes the Algiers School's lasting effect on "the place of the Welfare State in the resource-poor post-colony."[92] Its influence, however, also extends to Western Europe, he contends, stating that in contemporary times "there are strong similarities between mental hygiene programs in French Algeria and the efforts of social workers in much of Europe and the United States, where the activities of a range of private and public agencies lay at the heart of an interventionist welfare state."[93] In this sense, Schneider's sexual delinquents of Muslim background, first seen in the theses of the Algiers School, are scrutinized and regulated by the welfare state. While Schneider and the Algiers School thinkers shared notions of Muslim sexual criminality, they find themselves opposed, when it comes to the question of regulation by the state, with the Algiers School for more robust social intervention.

One thinker who paved the way for the sexual demonization of Muslims and North Africans was Don Côme Arrii, a member of the Algiers School. Arrii, who defended the first formal thesis of the Algiers School, used court documents inculpating mentally ill North Africans to extrapolate criminal characteristics to all others.[94] He also was fond of calling the Prophet Muhammad a "rapist," explaining that other Muslims only followed in his example. "North African men therefore murdered in full sexual excitation," he wrote, "for erotic intoxication is an extra contribution to impulsion and aggravation, to the unleashing of this homicidal furor."[95] Other members of the Algiers School prolonged what can be called the climactic eugenics of colonial propaganda, making tenuous links between the Mediterranean climate and sexual delinquency. Adolphe Kocher's 1884 thesis on crime in Algeria's indigenous population suggested that violence among Arabs was chiefly a "matter of race," that Arab violence was a sexual and inhuman violence, that "like all Oriental peoples, the Arab is a sodomite," and that they have bestial relations with "goats, sheep, even mares," concluding that "as the native has the animal's instincts, he also takes on its habits."[96]

Sexual demonization was not restricted to colonial Algeria, from where it quickly crossed the sea and appeared in contemporary anti-immigration rhetoric. Historian Yvan Gastaut highlights a "wanted" poster displayed throughout France in the early 1980s: "Depicting a sneering, hook-nosed, mustachioed caricature of an Arab wearing a fez, the poster declared: 'WANTED: MOHAMED BEN ZOBI, born in Algeria, residing in France. THIS MAN IS DANGEROUS! Susceptible of: MURDER! RAPE! THEFT! BURGLARY! To find him do not go far: all around there are 700,000 just like him!'"[97] The fictitious name "Mohamed Ben Zobi" reveals a knowledge of Arabic: "Ben zobi" means "son of my penis," and evokes the special Arabized French argot first employed by French Algerians of "European" descent (pieds-noirs) before spreading to the metropolitan masses with the influx of immigration. The capitalized term "Wanted" echoes the ambivalent shifting between desire and incrimination that has characterized much representation of North African men surveyed thus far. Keller finds that this propagandistic rhetoric reappears in modern-day crime novels and media representations which drew on a lexicon established by the Algiers School: "The distance from Don Côme Arrii's indictment of the North African Muslim as rapist and murderer who could not escape the innate criminal impulsivity of his being to the popular image of the thieving fanatical Arab of the banlieue was miniscule."[98]

The Veiled Woman

After the violent adolescent, the second member of the figurative Muslim family most pathologized by psychoanalysts is the veiled woman, sister, wife, or mother. The figure of the veiled woman relates to the male virilist delinquent in two ways: first, because the veil would symbolize his dominion over the banlieues and the form of protective chastity he imposes on female relatives to ward off other (similarly) aggressive men, and second, because the veil has often been associated with armor, combat, and even aggression itself.[99] Fethi Benslama, the aforementioned Tunisian-born analyst practicing and writing in France, was instrumental in turning Islamism, and especially the figure of the veiled woman, into an object of psychoanalytical inquiry. He gave a psychoanalytical portrait of the veil, and Muslim attitudes toward it, in his 1997 essay "The Veil of Islam," later translated by the journal *S*.[100] Benslama's itinerary is strikingly similar to that of his intellectual adversary, ethnopsychiatrist Tobie Nathan.[101] They later took divergent paths in regard to the place of culture and ethnicity in the clinical arena. While Nathan has been accused of ethnocentrism and embracing cultural relativism,[102] Benslama's more recent work exhibits a hostility to Islam that approaches secular fundamentalism.[103]

In the initial version of his essay, Benslama is situated at a different point in his intellectual trajectory, before his critique of Islam and Islamism had fully taken shape.[104] He interrogates the term *conspicuous* (*ostentatoire*)—which politicians had increasingly been using to characterize the hijab, or veil—in his commentary on the veil controversies of the late 1980s and early 1990s. School principals suspended insubordinate girls from school, as in the Creil Affair of 1989.[105] The controversy culminated in two laws: the 2004 ban on "conspicuous" religious symbols at public schools and the 2010 ban of full-face veils anywhere in public.

Benslama's analysis at this stage of his career is notable for its imaginative qualities, his impressive knowledge of Islamic symbology, and the lucidity and nonjudgmental calm in regard to the politically explosive material he was engaged with: a marked contrast with his more explicit and trenchantly political later essays. Benslama's intervention fits into a particular political moment, falling between two contrasting argumentative campaigns against the veil in public schools. One campaign rested on *laïcité*, while another abandoned this tactic in order to emphasize equality of the sexes—and in a more implicit way, *complementarity* of the sexes—as a French value. This was visible in the tonal difference between the two veil "affairs": in the 1990s, concern for secularism was more often cited, while in the early 2000s, the issue was traversed by concerns for women's rights and perceptions of a regression on this front. Critics such as Christine Delphy, a radical feminist essayist who has lobbied against the various veil bans, have argued that the change was tactical, a causal substitution: the antiveil activists only adopted the women's equality argument once they realized how difficult it would be to reconcile the tenets of *laïcité* with the proposed law. Thus, she argues, equality of the sexes was retroactively rendered an "eternal" French value, when it had in actuality been chosen in strategic haste.[106] Such a shift from a secularism-based argument to a gender-based argument is not without consequences for the psycho-political readings carried about by psychoanalysts weighing in on the veil issue. It moves the matter from the territory of government policy on religion into a more uncertain territory influenced by sexual projection.

Benslama's critique of politics around the veil revisits a symbolic opposition fundamental in North African and Islamic symbology, between the hand and the eye, both of which are common motifs in jewelry and superstitious ornaments. According to Benslama, values such as protection, goodness, limitation, and asceticism govern the hand, while excessiveness, bad faith, bad luck, jealousy, and rumor govern the eye. The veil, Benslama says, lines up with the hand against the eye, and thus becomes an instrument that limits excessiveness: "While excess is thought of as essential to the (eye), the hand symbolizes the ethical organ par excellence, capable, or not, of standing the eye in its excessiveness."[107] Projecting further, the veil would seem at this stage to counter, not foment "ostentation": "From the Islamic theological perspective that prescribes it, the veil is not a sign. It is something through which the feminine body is partially or totally occulted, because this body would otherwise indicate too much [*ferait trop signe*]."[108] Benslama argues, however, that in the politicized French context, the veil's original purpose of "limiting excessiveness" (turning the hand against the eye) has been lost and replaced with its opposite (the eye trumping the hand, "ostentation"). This happens in two ways, which hopelessly confuse the question of whether wearing the veil is an act of exhibitionism or self-censorship. "Conspicuousness," for French officialdom at least, would be paradoxically apparent in the gesture of protecting oneself with one's hands—via the veil—against surrounding eyes. Muslims who believe the veil to be mandatory find that it achieves the opposite of conspicuousness, namely, modesty. To call a demonstration of modesty "conspicuous" may seem paradoxical, according to Benslama, in light of what he has proposed about the veil limiting excess, but it is in exactly this paradoxical sense that veiled subjects are assessed in France. In other words, not wanting to show is showy, to paraphrase historian Joan Scott's critical take on French antiveil sentiment.[109] Anthropological investigations into what the niqab means to French Muslim women as a whole uncovered similar understandings: the "original purpose" of modesty, according to some respondents, would not be assured by the niqab, since in a French context it actually attracts attention.[110]

Show and *demonstrate* are terms that Benslama returns to repeatedly. He opens the essay with a provocative turn of phrase, calling veiled women "monstrating monsters" because of their high symbolic charge. He links the roots of *monster* and *demonstration*—*montrer* (to show) and *démontrer* (to prove)—in order to argue for the interconnectedness of the veil's dual actions: both attesting to faith and being a monstrosity for those barred access to the woman (who is said to signify polymorphously). This is due to the veil inhabiting the ambiguity between showing and not showing. The same veil called "conspicuous" in France functions as an antisign for Muslims, in Benslama's rendition. The veiled woman and signification itself are overcharged: she *means* too much, and the veil would act as a filter against what Benslama calls her "monstration," or outward radiation of signs. "The veil is not a sign," Benslama explains, "but that which makes the woman into a sign. It shields her body, which emits a multiplicity of signs, in order to envelop it as a unique sign," a limitation that would "cease the monstration of woman as a swarming monster of signs" and that "effects a de-monstration of how a woman becomes an obscure sign."[111] This nuance provides an exit from the contradiction of the veil's showiness and nonshowiness mentioned earlier, for we now have a distinction between exhibitionist signs and inhibitionist signs. Still, for both the French state and the Muslim subject as presented by Benslama, woman is taken as a nexus of meaning and signs, recalling the sexist consideration of women as symbols that must be defended, protected, or managed. In this economy, disagreement only regards whether the veil, or the woman under the veil, is the source of signing, and which kind of signing is appropriate: the unfiltered kind (France's ideal unveiled woman) or the restricted kind (Benslama's understanding of the veil for Muslims). Thus, the French politicians wishing to manage the signage of the veil have to face a conceptual contradiction: how can they support equality of the sexes as a historically French republican value, while objectifying women's bodies as they are instrumentalized into signs, meaning, when they are seen not as women but simply as veils?

French politicians and journalists did sometimes take note of these volatile contradictions, as well as the politicized stakes of the symbolism being attributed to women's bodies in the veil debate. Philosopher Jean-Jacques Delfour criticized François Bayrou—a centrist politician and prominent opponent of the veil—in an op-ed published in *Le Monde*: he aligned Bayrou's willingness to regulate sartorial choices with regulating free speech. Delfour entitled his intervention: "François Bayrou, semiological censor."[112] In 1994, Bayrou, who was minister of education at the time, had said: "According to whether we will have defended our ideal or renounced it, the face of France, in ten, twenty years, as well as the place of Islam and that of the Muslim woman, will not be the same."[113] Working against Muslims who supposedly thought her "too significant" in her unveiled state, French political actors were falling into a conceptual trap by assenting to the idea that women's bodies were signifiers in need of control, albeit only when veiled. The figure of the veiled woman was considered uncontrollably significant by those French politicians who were ostensibly lobbying for her liberation: reproducing Benslama's story of Muslims censoring woman as sign. Indeed, Bayrou claims that an increasingly loose attachment to the ideal of *laïcité* would jeopardize the meaning and especially the face of eternally feminine France, objectified into allegorical form. The choice of a corporeal and, in particular, a facial analogy seems no accident. The "changing face" of France also carries demographic undertones: letting Muslims get the better of *laïcité* would go hand in hand with a France whose demographic "face" is changing as a result of immigration.

The veil had become an object of French psychoanalytical debate long before the controversies of the 1980s and 1990s. As historian Keller shows, earlier commentaries by colonial-era psychiatrists practicing in North Africa have influenced French policy-making on policing and immigration.[114] While those influences affected mostly men, colonial psychiatrists did speak of the Muslim woman, seemingly always in the shadow of the Muslim man, when assessing the veil as an instrument of antimodern patriarchal control of women. In the contemporary period, psychiatrists working with Muslim immigrants and their descendants in France have instead critiqued this phallocentric reading of the veil. For Keller, the difference between the past and present ethnopsychiatrists—a difference that some critics of ethnopsychiatry dispute—is that political orientations have shifted to the antiracist Left, while previously ethnopsychiatrists in colonial North Africa made arguments for curtailing immigration.[115] Keller underlines that the veil controversies, as well as other flashpoints in the immigration debate, helped implant the new ethnopsychiatry, which criticized the stigmatization of the veil.[116] These intellectuals switched the tenor of ethnopsychiatric commentary from colonial stigmatization of Arab and Islamic culture to the postcolonial defense of cultural and ethnic affirmation. They were involved in what Keller calls a "recasting of the debate over the administrative ideologies of assimilation and association for a post-colonial context."[117] Within this movement, the veil (among other symbols of cultural belonging) became an analytical tool, part of an

ethnopsychiatric lexicon helping to illuminate the psychological itineraries of immigrants, rather than a barrier to analysis.

For Benslama, like many psychoanalytic observers, the veil is primarily a marker of sexual difference and also a site of eroticism, considered
through the male gaze.[118] He speaks of the veil as the "hymen of truth"
and asks what would happen if "the extremity of men's desire was to want
to enjoy this place where the truth and the non-truth communicate with
each other?"[119] Expressions like the "hymen of truth" and references to the
veil as a truth condition may seem perplexing when taken out of context,
but begin to make sense when the story of Khadija, the Prophet's wife,
is analyzed by Benslama. When the Prophet began to receive spiritual
visits from the Angel Gabriel and to hear the voice of inspiration, he did
not know whether he was receiving an angel or a demon (*djinn*). Khadija
used her knowledge of spirits—a knowledge here considered specific to
women—to help answer the question. During a subsequent visitation she
removed her veil and the Prophet noted the absence of the spiritual presence. Since the revelation stopped, she explained to her husband that he
was dealing not with a demon but with an angel who fled out of modesty when presented with an unveiled woman. Thus Khadija, and veiled
women, become a "condition of truth," because they clarify the answers to
questions that men cannot answer alone. Interestingly enough, this story
actually shows how the relationship of Muslim woman to Muslim man
might mirror the complementarity of the sexes enshrined as an enduring
French value, despite portrayals of Muslims as having repressed heterosexual desire.

In explaining his reasoning for approaching the question of the veil,
Benslama says: "This question of modesty vis-à-vis God demands that we
explain it."[120] To better explain the urgency of the explanation, we must
return to the story of Khadija. Muhammad's wife had dispelled his doubts
about whether the spiritual presence he felt surrounding him was that
of an angel or a demon, by removing her veil and thus causing the angel
Gabriel to flee out of modesty. Khadija, Benslama concludes, acted as a
"veil of truth" for Muhammad, helping him to distinguish between di-
vine illumination and its impostor. He thus conditions access to God on
understanding the synergy between man and woman: "Whereas woman
believes what she does not see, man does not believe what he sees. He
must thus pass through her in order to believe."[121]

Benslama prefaced this essay by acknowledging that he was incited
to speak by France's veil controversies and the possibility of women's
subjugation. Nevertheless, his reading, which resembles an explanation
of a controversial practice rather than a justification of that practice,

resubjugates women just as it seemed to recover them. While describing itself as an analysis of Islamic symbology, Benslama's critique reifies women as symbolic canvasses and instruments, dangerously polyvalent, intimate with magical underworlds, and able to communicate with spirits by virtue (fault?) of what is assumed to be a morally different nature. Complementarity of the sexes here becomes instrumentality of the sexes, which are separated into morally unequal roles, with women's signs more uncontrollable than men's. The veil is the condition of faith for an additional reason: concealing one's "signage," all while emphasizing the existence of that signification, produces a spiritual exhortation for men to believe in the unseen. The imperative "not to look" becomes the imperative "to believe." This process is contingent in the story upon the harmony between husband and wife.

The Veil, the Clandestine, and the Public-Private Distinction

The psychoanalytic commentaries on immigration surveyed here consistently return to the public-private distinction in their "diagnoses." Benslama suggests that the most erotic thing possible for a man's desire is to enjoy the place where truth and nontruth communicate with each other, that place being marked by the veil. This reflects an underlying perception that the public-private distinction can be eroticized. Benslama also sheds light on how the notion of clandestinity (which plays on the private and public, the inside and outside, the veiled and unveiled) can be a locus for the most important of values: truth. French critiques of ethnic communitarianism have often focused on clandestinity, whether in immigrant enclaves with underground mosques, private marriage arrangements, or local economies that shy away from scrutiny. The root word *private* takes on different shades of meaning in Benslama's argument, which plays on the confusion of privacy and privation. The veil, and the privacy it conceals, become an intolerable privation (in the sense of inhibited access) for the barred party.

In the era of immigration and implantation in France, psychotherapy has moved from being a private practice, most often sought by individuals of a certain social standing, to one that can be partly or entirely covered by state health insurance.[122] Ethnopsychiatry stands somewhere in between: Nathan has spoken of numerous case studies in which youths that had run afoul of the law were addressed to his university service. Moving from the private to the public in this way significantly impacts the issue of confidentiality. In the case of low-income immigrants and their families, this opens the door for increased psychological scrutiny for a population already exposed to state services, with consequences for the public-private distinction, the right to privacy and also intimacy, and finally the increased publication of mental illness studies focusing on populations of color. Critics such as Didier Fassin warn against the echoes of colonial ethnopsychiatry in the new ethnopsychiatry.[123] He points to the "alarming" number of cases addressed to ethnopsychiatrists by the state, as if by habit, alleging that populations of immigrant origin may be subject to the unchecked experimentation and highly culturalist analyses he has reproached ethnopsychiatrists of engaging in.

The public-private distinction, and navigation through it, are impacted when the immigrant encounters the medical apparatus, of which the psychotherapeutic wing is a part. Bennani, Sayad, and Ben Jelloun concur that psychological health can be impacted by the potentially devastating and very public traumas triggered by immigration. These authors describe immigrants who, with mixed results, turn to the medical and psychiatric fields to have a private "problem" recognized by an outside authority, in the hopes of having their subjectivity validated. Bennani points to a significant risk at the center of this recourse to medicine for recognition: he finds that the disclosure (and the ensuing exit from the private) may be harmful in the long term, because although the subject's difference can finally appear and possibly lead to more personalized solutions, that difference has in the past emerged only to be stigmatized as problematic by the medical community.[124] As far as the project of detailing an "immigrant psychology" is concerned, such potential medical alienation runs the risk of making the private more private, with immigrant patients and their families avoiding psychotherapeutic options and discussions of the "private" in light of possible abuses.

Keller echoes the potential for the state psychiatric apparatus to engage in abuses of power, addressed here by Bennani. Though Keller starts with colonial medicine, he connects to the contemporary period as he surveys the new ethnopsychiatry that has thrived in postcolonial France treating ailing immigrants and their descendants.[125] "Colonial medicine," writes Keller, "can amass data about the population because it can demand any form of information in exchange for its services. It can establish truth about patients because it exploits their vulnerability. It is a unique form of totalitarian power because it is one to which we willingly submit."[126]

This Foucauldian language surrounding the admission of vulnerability is crucial to the question of clandestinity. It is worth noting that the confessionalism and incitement to discourse that have characterized many minority and immigrant accounts that express sexual suffering have emerged through the framework of cooperation with psychoanalysts or psychiatrists. I think, for instance, of Samira Bellil's *Dans l'enfer des tour-nantes*, which Marie-Hélène Bourcier has characterized as an act of psy-chological ventriloquism,[127] in addition to the aforementioned works by Ben Jelloun and Bennani. It is this private, intimate space of bartered, necessary confession that allows for the exposure of sexual secrets that might have otherwise remained clandestine. What's more, confessions carry a higher "truth value" as they emerge from what is suggested to be vulnerability, a mode of relinquished control in which manipulation or deceit is thought to be impossible.

Khanna examines such abuses of power in regard to the public-private distinction in her reflections on psychoanalysis and colonialism. This occurs within a discussion of the Heideggerian neologism "worlding," which she explains in the following way: "Worlding, for me, is the pro-cess of understanding the violence of the production of psychoanalysis in the world. . . . Worlding is the understanding of global strife in the production of textuality. It understands history as an utterance projected into the world and understands the world, and not only the local context, as profoundly shaped into unconcealment through the event of saying."[128] The special, linguistic violence Khanna roots in colonial omnipotence—central to the action of unveiling and "naming things into being"—has ramifications for postcolonial psychoanalysis. To extend Khanna's analy-sis to the present subject matter, one such ramification affects the notion of clandestinity. If the clandestine, as I have suggested here and in other chapters, is a consistent factor in portrayals of postcolonial immigrant societies in Europe, then psychoanalysis—as an "uttering," disclosing medium—"worlds" those societies out of clandestinity. Psychoanalysis would mold immigrant experience into an exploitable shape that bears the imprint of the hierarchies of power that have produced psychoanaly-sis, arguably the same hierarchies that contribute to the inequality be-tween immigrant and native. The process can at times terminate in the production of an immigrant entity that can be seized, analyzed, and, as has been suggested, stigmatized.

Jean-Michel Hirt touches upon the cultural ramifications of stamping out the clandestine. He explains that the "invisible is no longer recog-nized, in the West, as a dimension of existence valuable in itself, a dimen-sion in no need of being converted into the visible. Worse, the invisible has become synonymous with the occult, or in other words, that which is reluctant to appear in the open."[129] Respect for the invisible, Hirt concurs, is the casualty of a European cultural evolution toward confessionalism. It is a loss that the immigrant, attesting to this change of affairs, suffers intimately. For Hirt, the "visible" becomes a key theme in his reading of

Muslim psychology—central also to the frustration of Muslims in Europe: "The interiorization of the 'Western' visible can provoke a conflict in the exile that opposes the invisible, collapsed henceforth with the abandoned and then idealized origin, and the visible, understood as a permanent visual solicitation incarnated by the land of exile."[130] Hirt reveals how the immigrant might think of his rapport to the visible in national terms, as well as sexual terms. Ben Jelloun explored this idea of "permanent visual solicitation," describing in *La plus haute des solitudes* how the single immigrant worker's sexual isolation was made all the more unbearable in a foreign society in which women were thought of as more visually available than in the home country.

As the notion of the clandestine gains a national connotation it can also obtain a political one. Respect for the clandestine could be considered leftist in a multicultural sense of respect for private customs. Respect for the secret, however, gains a rightest orientation in Western political affairs according to Michel Schneider, who finds this left-right splitting unfair, as he reveals in his characteristic mocking tone: "Transparency is of the Left, the secret is of the Right. Don't ask me why . . . I would like for someone to explain why the secret is always vicious and nudity virtuous, an idea which in its generality is as false as its contrary. . . . When will we see a secretary of state for outing, a ministry of transparency?"[131] When immigrant cultural attitudes about the private and public are introduced, established political compasses can be momentarily scrambled, with the Right and the Left aligned: for example, leftists who might criticize the secrecy of the French business elite would not criticize underground economies of necessity established by immigrants, and thus find themselves in partial agreement with free market policies. Does an alignment between the Right and the Left "across cultures" point to a political inconsistency? Or rather, has the Left compromised its values of visibility and transparency in its "misguided" attempts at being multicultural? This ambiguity could explain in part why the persistence of immigrant subjects retreating into the clandestine so unsettles the mainstream Left, which finds itself unable to support two conflicting principles. Such instances occur frequently in the gay press (which ordinarily supports the Socialist Party), as in an investigative report on homosexual men of North African descent who were criticized for preferring a clandestine life in the banlieues to the more "open" gay meccas of Paris.[132] The editorial line could not find a comfortable balance between the principles of homosexual liberation and the right to privacy. However, a distinction could be articulated showing that respect for the secret need not be akin to deception or inconsistency, but rather a consequence of freedom of expression and the right to determine the private and public. Oftentimes, recourses to the clandestine, the private, or the secret have been portrayed as stemming from schizophrenia or stubborn nonassimilation in much literature spanning the social sciences, the media, and even feminist and LGBT interventions. It remains a challenge, for the section of the French Left concerned about immigration's impact on sexual mores, to philosophically articulate within its immigrant outreach an understanding of the *sexually* clandestine, just as it had with the politically clandestine (as seen with the *sans-papiers* support movement).[133]

The Impotent Father

After the turbulent adolescent and the veiled woman, the figure of the "impotent," formerly employed, immigrant father rounds out the family constellation pathologized by this group of thinkers. The impotent father, by his very weakness, "enables" the rise of the adolescent, who replaces him. The French mass media, as well as some republican activists, have often attributed a supposed rise in youth violence to the vacuum of authority left by absentee fathers. Fadela Amara, the former government minister and founder of the group Ni Putes Ni Soumises profiled in chapter 1, echoes Schneider's genealogy about the absence of the father by underlining what happens when paternal authority falters. In her banlieue storyline, a generational malaise triggered the rise of the *grands frères* (Big Brothers), replacing "fathers [who] are absent . . . Now the eldest son has taken over; he rules the family. He has physically replaced the father in his protective and repressive roles."[134] Bennani speaks of the dire consequences of a replacement of the father by the male adolescent. He warns that an adolescent must not replace his father in the household as this might provoke the return of incestuous sexual impulses, incestuous because the newly patriarchal adolescent would compete with the father in his husband role, as head of household.[135] This role replacement has psychoanalytical ramifications when considered in light of the Freudian idea of "killing the father," a point often revisited by Bennani and other psychoanalysts. He contends that one of the singular aspects of his case studies with North African youth is the problematic ease with which the father has been eliminated.

This point impacts the notion of Big Mother in the sense that the withering away of parental authority enabled the entrance of the "Big Brothers," introducing a "perverted," less responsible patriarchy (fratriarchy?) in its place. In Schneider's reading, brothers, and not fathers, are the foot soldiers contesting Big Mother, the residual blowback after the disappearance of Big Father. He describes the distinction between the types of discipline enforced by a fraternal and maternal state respectively: "Big Brother has you under surveillance. Big Mother watches over you [*Big Mother veille sur vous*]."[136] Though Big Brother resides in the land of Orwell, this point directly pertains to the ambivalence about surveillance— between protection and intimidation—that often clouds the representation of Franco-Arab young men: are the (Muslim) Big Brothers watching over their sisters in a dangerous place, or asserting control over their lives so as to better anchor a macho reputation?

One must question, however, the onus placed on the absence or presence of a father figure in analyses of Muslim psychology. Hirt focuses on the Freudian understanding of the primal father in monotheistic religions, commenting specifically on Freud's idea in *Moses and Monotheism* that the Islamic civilization enjoyed splendor only when it recovered the concept of the unique, great primal father.[137] In this history, Muslims briefly enjoyed a Golden Age but missed the opportunity to prolong and deepen the interior development of the new religion because they did not duplicate or repeatedly commemorate the murder/death of the founder of the religion, as it occurred in varying forms in Christianity. Hirt, however, says this reasoning cannot encompass Islam's historical arc because it fails to acknowledge that the concept of God in Islam explicitly does not include paternal, male, or any gender attributes.[138] Other thinkers, like Ben Jelloun, who have weighed in on this issue claim that the symbolic murder of the father happens without enough resistance in Arabo-Islamic culture, putting to rest the idea that "killing the father"—a required phase of universal psychological development for young men—would somehow be absent in patriarchal North African cultures.

Schneider nevertheless reproaches Muslim youth of immigrant origin of not properly internalizing the Freudian killing of the father, of not learning from the guilt this phase entails. This lack of guilt can occur in the case of an absentee father, or a father powerless to face his own son. Fear of authority dissipates when the subject bypasses this essential phase, and the father's authoritative law cannot be reproduced in subsequent generations, who no longer respect their elders. For Schneider, something has gone off the "normative" Oedipal track in the case of French youth delinquency, which he repeatedly attaches to immigration. He stresses that leaving an essential Oedipal itinerary untraveled translates into psychological superficiality and a lack of moral intelligence.[139]

While some psychoanalysts writing about immigration have sourced delinquency back to paternal failure, others suggest that immigrant fathers have been infantilized, turned back into sons, creating a generational confusion. Ben Jelloun speaks of how France can represent a punitive Big Father that prevents these men from asserting their maturity in a new society. Since their countries of origin in North Africa are coded as motherlands, their surroundings undergo a change in symbolic gender through immigration to France, which can be experienced as traumatic: "This host society (which doesn't offer an image of the mother) presents itself to the immigrant via perpetual phallic aggression: it's the repressive and foreign father who imposes himself on the [immigrant's] imaginary faculties in the form of a cop, a boss, a foreman, of unreadable technology [*technique illisible*], hence the 'deculturizing' process they have been subjected to."[140] It was Ben Jelloun who arguably first depicted the portrait of the faltering immigrant father, so dispirited by his unaffectionate welcome in France that he expresses no interest in continuing a line of filiation there. According to Keller, Ben Jelloun, better known for his novelistic output, occupies a pivotal role in regard to increasing awareness about sexual anomie among immigrants. His *La plus haute des solitudes*, a project rooted in the social psychiatry research he performed at Université Paris VII, "explored the psychological tensions of the immigrant worker from the perspectives of sexuality, isolation, and the political economy of desire, and in so doing radically interrogated French attitudes toward immigration and the dangers of the immigrant body."[141] The book, a best seller for its genre, was published as part of Seuil's series *Combats* (lending it a certain sense of social mission), caused a critical splash and set the tone for the sexual themes featured in Ben Jelloun's later novels.[142]

Keller attributes the concept of the "deracination of desire" to Ben Jelloun, crediting him with explaining how the severing of affective roots triggered by immigration can break the reproductive cycle. Single men, or husbands who had left their wives behind, came to France in the 1960s and 1970s to work in factories and construction jobs: they often felt rejected by the host society and bereft of romantic or family options. As such, the male immigrant was no longer able to project himself into a kind future involving love or children in France. He subsequently is overcome with an acute sexual "homelessness" at a time when only immigrant men were traveling to France on worker's visas. They discovered through sudden lack what a "sexual home"—and the comfort of filiation—was and is. The physical outcome of these feelings was sexual impotence, an ailment Ben Jelloun repeatedly found in his immigrant worker patients. However, Ben Jelloun's conclusions about impotence triggered by affective isolation are time-specific, his research occurring shortly before the introduction of family reunification laws in 1976. In recent interviews, he has acknowledged that the policy significantly alleviated the isolation he described in *La plus haute des solitudes*.

Jalil Bennani has described, like Ben Jelloun, how the affective suffering brought on by immigration often expresses itself through a language of sexual impotence. Affectivity is lost further when immigrants confronted with the scientific facts of medicine and industry begin to increasingly speak of their bodies in mechanical rather than affective terms. In *Les féministes et le garçon arabe*, sociologist Nacira Guénif-Souilamas makes a similar statement in her historical narrative about an atrophying immigrant affectivity worn down by factory life, with consequences for the gestures of warm homosociality like kissing salutations and men holding hands, often associated with North African culture.[143] Such "mechanical outlooks" inhibit the talking cure because, as Bennani explains, "it is striking to see that the sexually impotent speak little and ask for a medical or surgical solution . . . when I would propose that we speak more, the most frequent response was: 'I've already told you everything.'"[144]

The male immigrant worker's body becomes sexualized when psychoanalytical writers conceive of him in active and passive terms. Strapping and hopeful, the body starts out active on the immigration journey, but this quickly changes once the cycle of work begins. The passive body, Bennani explains, is "frequently that of a subject working on the construction site or at the factory." With the sexual connotations of passivity present in the background, this reading could contribute to the idea that virility is perceived to deteriorate when one speaks of suffering. This deterioration, according to Bennani, is part of a vicious cycle that keeps getting worse "the longer the body has followed the medical circuits, the more it presents itself in a passive way to the institutions it meets."[145] The reason why presenting one's body passively to the medical apparatus is conceived as a "failure," is because that body, "linked to a certain social condition" of working life, "finds itself in France to insure an active role from the start. . . a patriarchal role."[146] As if describing an insurance policy that failed in its protective function, Bennani frames the narrative of immigrant workers in France as one of abrogated responsibilities and botched ventures, devastating for what was supposed to be an entrepreneurial virility. "We leave healthy, we return broken" is a phrase Bennani frequently heard in the clinical arena, a phrase that touches upon themes of integrity and dissolution. Within these case studies, the act of immigration becomes less of a venture and approaches the risky terrain of symbolic castration, which plunges the subject ever deeper into an isolated silence. Recourse to family and the possibility of a collective cure are then inhibited for reasons of shame.

Ben Jelloun echoes this idea of a "talking animal" rendered silent. His *La plus haute des solitudes* bore witness to a great affective exclusion from the host society, one that expressed itself in sexual impotence at a statistical level too high to remain ignored. Ben Jelloun described impotence as the outcome of a "subversive silence" that passes through the passive-aggressive phase of "death within life." The latter is the sole remaining tool of resistance when the hopes raised by the immigration project are dashed.[147] When asked at a talk in 2010 about the origins of this project, Ben Jelloun noted a startling lack of enthusiasm at the institutional level for treating the rise in immigrant complaints of sexual impotence in a manner befitting its scale.[148] Ben Jelloun found himself stranded, at an uncharted juncture between psychotherapy and social work, wherein the remedies proposed for what seemed like a basic social problem of affective isolation were disproportionally psychiatric or chemical. In the same talk, Ben Jelloun discussed affective separation and, he said sarcastically, the "generous" proposal of family reunification, which postdated his clinical work. Speaking with some irony, he added that French officials may have thought family reunification "was very nice, but they may have thought immigrants didn't have sex with their wives. They had children, their kids grew up, and in 2005, they were thirty years old. They were French, they went out and burned cars. In the media they said immigrants rebelled, but it was their kids."[149] Such an interpretation brings us full circle back to the image of fathers powerless to restrain adolescents, who then replace them as authorities.

Pioneering sociologists such as the late Abdelmalek Sayad had already described how the stakes of "becoming sick" have dire consequences for the immigrant. In *The Suffering of the Immigrant*, Sayad explained that the immigrant couldn't afford to get sick, either physically or psychologically, because this would imperil his working status and negate his entire immigration project by bringing about the dreaded final stop, unemployment.[150] If the immigration project—that is, providing for one's family back home or reuniting its members in the host country—were to fail, this would entail consequences for the provider's sense of virility. This theme is developed at length in the documentary film *Welcome Europa*, which presents a masculinity broken by unemployment: the interviewee's eventually fruitless search for jobs becomes the catalyst for what is depicted as their final "emasculation": homosexual prostitution (see chapter 4).

Sociological work on immigrant suffering often states that the immigrant uses illness to settle a dispute of a social nature. Similarly, Ben Jelloun's case studies of immigrant impotence reveal a strong correlation between sexual satisfaction and the possibility of work: the second would seem imperiled by the loss of the first. Unseasoned doctors for whom this immigrant complaint of impotence was hard to decipher linguistically were quick to counsel drug remedies instead of examining the socioaffective foundations of the problem. One patient explains that, without the accompaniment of a woman, work is impossible, because one no longer has enough "character," but with the drugs prescribed, he is fine because he no longer thinks of women and just sleeps.[151] Thus, in the case studies collected by Bennani, Ben Jelloun, and, to a certain extent, Sayad, a complex etiology of impotence passes from the affective to the professional to the psychiatric. This multiphase storyline often confounded the analysts treating the immigrants and caused them to lose sight of the social origins of their patients' afflictions along the way.

Psychoanalysis, Assimilation, and Community Attachment

In composing the broken family portrait of absent father, self-effacing mother, and delinquent child, commentators with backgrounds in psychoanalysis have developed a pathology of nonassimilation, in which these figures stick out as sexual miscreants. This pathological family story contrasts with a psychological path toward symbolic republican citizenship, recently made normative with the increasing currency psychoanalysis has gained in French society. In some instances, scholars have indicated how familiarity with psychoanalysis and psychoanalytic therapy itself can be markers of successful assimilation to French values when consented to by immigration-issued subjects. Camille Robcis, who has endeavored to explain "how the symbolic became French," supplies many examples of how psychoanalysts with rigid conceptions of the symbolic order have been asked to serve on government commissions and panels, or weigh in as experts in opinion-forming news dailies; some even have occupied political office.[152]

A key dimension of the idea that psychoanalysis can provide a gateway to successful assimilation is the underlying principle of individualization. Individualization, I argue, is seen as a necessary condition of the successful transition from a communitarian to a republican model of self-affirmation. A crucial consequence of individualization, however, is potential alienation from family and social bonds left behind in the community. Psychoanalytical critiques of communitarianism bring sexuality into the equation when they call for ruptures of filiation (with the family, group, or community), which then impact a host of orienting psychoanalytical episodes like confrontation with the incest taboo and the reproduction of the parent's law, to name but the most obvious.

Discussions of psychoanalysis and assimilation have often revolved around links to the parents' or ancestors' country, and whether they should be severed for the purposes of better integration into French society. The works of Benslama and Nathan illustrate the wide range of responses offered to this question. Their positions diverge notably in regard to the psychosexual question of filiation: Nathan posits that psychological well-being can only be the result of a coming to terms with filiation and roots, whereas Benslama maintains that well-being often comes about in spite of those attachments, by replacing parental or cultural filiations with filiation to the French nation.

Republican values do not always play a positive role in the psychoanalytic discourse around immigration. Nathan, like Benslama, revisits the Oedipus myth in the context of immigration, but comes to a different conclusion: against assimilation for reasons of symbolic violence, Nathan argues that the republican values underpinning the encouragement of assimilation reinforce a sedimented and conservative psychoanalytical practice in France. He questions the relevance of the Oedipus myth, as well as Greek mythology, for assessing the particular networks of filiations that he believes govern the immigrant psychological experience in France:

> Oedipus does resolve an enigma, but in the Greek style. He is definitely a founder, a civilizing hero, but of a city that opted for the secularization [*laïcisation*] of thought . . . a city where the son knows more than the father. On the other hand, he initiates a world of equals where, politically, the son is identical to the father, suppressing with the same stroke all extra-territorial niches and exceptional status. In this, Oedipus does belong to the modern West; and as a result one understands why psychoanalysts, unconscious priests of a forgotten religion, continue to honor him with their prayers and to offer in sacrifice the children of "*métèques*" who have made the mistake of being born into other myths.[153]

The term *métèque* is ambiguous: on the one hand its meaning in Greek etymology suggests a person who resides in a foreign city and does not enjoy full rights, while its contemporary, pejorative French use refers xenophobically to immigrants, and in particular, Arabs. In this passage, Nathan connects *laïcité* to the Oedipus myth, and assimilation to submission and sacrifice. Nathan republicanizes traditional psychoanalysis and contests its appropriateness for populations in which filial piety is assumed to be stronger. These contestations of the relevance of the Oedipus myth for ethnic minority populations recall Fanon's *Black Skin,*

White Masks, in which he explains that the colonial situation changes the traditional outcome (of identifying with the father and thus desiring the mother), which is disrupted by the father's social exclusion. For Nathan, the sons and daughters stigmatized in secular France will have to look outside of republican structures for an anchoring principle of psychosexual organization.

Other critics have parodied what they see as an unquestioned imperative to submit to officialized psychoanalysis in order to prove civic worth. Responding to criticism from Elisabeth Roudinesco, herself a great defender of psychoanalysis's place in society, Nathan mockingly announced: "Immigrants, go seek psychoanalysis and you will finally become republicans!"[154] Joseph Massad, in his critique of Benslama, suggests, similarly to Nathan, that Benslama's insistent attachment to liberal principles in his critique of Islam resembles religious observance in its lack of interrogation of those venerated values. Psychoanalysis again functions as a tool establishing the liberal West, which is receptive to the science, as evolved and a suddenly non-European Islam, which rejects the science, as backward:

> For [Benslama] the only tolerable Islam is a liberal form of Islam that
> upholds all the liberal values of European maturity and is intolerant
> of the Islam of the Islamists whose values are said to oppose liberal
> values *even when they do not*. He also wants to fix the meaning of
> Islamism as one that upholds the illiberal Islam, which he cannot tolerate. In Benslama's hands, psychoanalysis becomes the handmaiden
> of European liberalism that shows no ambivalence about itself or its
> projected other. On the contrary, the certainty with which "Islam"
> is *christened* the other of liberalism and the West aligns it with the
> figure of the primitive and the pre-Oedipal child in the cosmology
> of Freudian psychoanalysis.[155]

Massad recognizes the infantilization at work in the psychological portrait of the Islamic faith. Like the figure of the Arab youth, Islam has been rendered delinquent in its (sexual) intolerance, with commentators like Benslama brushing aside aspects of Islamic cultures that are indeed liberal, expressive, or emancipatory in regard to sexuality.

This move—of removing all sexually alternative material from figures associated with Islam or the banlieues—is a familiar operation (see chapter 1). Marie-Hélène Bourcier, author of the provocative and popular *Sexpolitiques* series of books, sees in officialized psychoanalysis itself an enemy that represses both sexual and ethnic minorities' demands for affirmation. She created, along with her collaborators, a form of direct action called *zapping*. Often comical but also quite serious, zappings turn the tables on the psychiatrists and psychoanalysts who have pathologized minorities (especially trans people) and violated their right to privacy, by analyzing these analysts in unflattering and invasive ways in public.[156]

Bourcier has turned the table (or rather couch) on the psychoanalytic establishment by condemning the type of officialized psychoanalysis that forcibly assimilates what she calls "sexual outlaws"; in fact, she is one of the few who has pushed back against the demonization of virile girl gang members. In *Sexpolitiques: Queer Zones 2*, she highlights the case of the late Samira Bellil—whom she sees as a tough *caillera* (thug) from the banlieue whose memoir, co-written with Josée Stoquart, details the horrors of gang rape—in order to underline psychoanalytical abuses in France, as well as a republican sexual conformism. Bourcier recounts with regret Bellil's unforgettable story: her short life was tragic, Bourcier says, not only due to the traumas she experienced (multiple gang rapes at home and abroad in Algeria, life-ending cancer) but also because of how psychologists ventriloquized her victimized body during her life. Stoquart declared that "it is a great honor and privilege to take part in the liberation of a human being," and that Bellil's real "truth" emerged through the expression of suffering.[157] In so doing her counselors removed all resistance from her formerly embattled self, taking special care to remove all traces of the (strategic) virility she had mastered as a female *caillera*, who had mostly gained respect in her neighborhood. To Bourcier:

> [Bellil's memoir] seems like it was written so that one might read it like the story of Samira writing a book after a long therapy. Exit Sam, as well as her autobiographical resources and her powers of self-nomination. Too bad. . . . There were also slaps and some *fight back* [English in the original]. . . . Sam dealt blows to the tibias, to family members. The aggressive masculinity of Sam the butch thug protected her from the boys' aggression. But Sam became Samira the day where the construction of her identity as French victim was set in motion by psy-discourse, proposing to her, in the most French of traditions, a writing cure. . . . This is what was needed to get rid of the *caillera* [scum or thug]: a psychologist and a *ghost writer* [English in the original].[158]

Bourcier describes how Sam's initial performative force and her capacity to be multiple are slain in a kind of gender policing, by what she calls "positive pathologization." Bourcier adds that Stoquart, Bellil's collaborator, is an acquaintance of Bellil's psychoanalyst. Stoquart prefaced the book to assure the reader that, with Samira, "we have passed from disintegration to integration." In this context, "integration" is not a neutral turn of phrase, as it suggests both conformity with the nation as well as mental integrity. Bourcier quotes Stoquart, who seems to judge the success of Bellil's recovery on her integration to an almost geometric degree: "When the violence of her story was extirpated from her memory, printed, read and reread, she started to distance herself from her past and to pacify herself. All had been said, shouted, cried. All had been reflected on, understood, integrated. She had put the pieces of her life back in their right places. Everything had been sorted, arranged, consigned."[159] Bourcier then connects Samira's story and the experience of "psychologized depoliticization" to the Stasi commission, a body of experts authorized by legislators to elaborate recommendations for the 2004 laïcité law, which culminated in a ban on conspicuous religious symbols in public schools. She describes the committee members' attempts to create an "instruction manual on laïcité" and mentions a Le Monde article that described the Stasi process as a "psychoanalysis of French consciousness."[160] From the psychological ventriloquism of one of France's urban others to the commission that pathologized wearing the veil, Bourcier details an emerging republican psychoanalysis that demands assimilation with its gender normativity.

In her sociological study Des beurettes, Guénif-Souilamas speaks of young Arab girls—some of whom, like the occasionally delinquent Bellil —do not fit the ideal "child of immigrants" model. Guénif-Souilamas highlights the "variable but real alienation that assimilation can implicate" when young Arab women are pressured into it.[161] Assimilation, considered by popular opinion to be a positive process of inclusion, is rarely considered for the cultural violence it can entail, with the exception of fringe sources perhaps. Often, it involves renouncing ties to family, community, and especially men of the same cultural background, in order to seek individual distinction outside the banlieue. Psychoanalysis as a heuristic tool remains uniquely positioned, with its theorization of interpersonal bonds, to study the consequences of these ruptures of filiation from family and community members that appear to be holding these women back.

In her reaction to the reception of Dans l'enfer des tournantes, Bourcier argues that Bellil's sexual and cultural marginality were censored. She attaches Bellil's experience at the hands of analysts and coauthors to that of others who have been declared victims of alienation and false consciousness. Veiled women, virilist youth, prostitutes, homosexuals, and trans people have all combatted psychoanalytical repression at different historical junctures, some even devising instruction manuals for how to speak to psychoanalysts seeking to pathologize them.[162] Bourcier explains how an officialized psychoanalysis can successfully provoke a rallying together of active ethnic and sexual minorities that are rarely thought of in conjunction and are sometimes posited as openly hostile to each other. Mainstream feminist groups, and writers on feminism, have not always accepted the connection between these communities, or have accepted that psychological stigmatization be removed for one community but not the other (Elisabeth Badinter, for instance, allows psychological maturity for prostitutes, but not for veiled women). As with many populations previously pathologized by the medical field, some of these minorities have redeployed the scientific language used to disqualify them toward positive, self-fashioning purposes, deriving psychic enrichment from the process.

Officialized psychoanalysis comes to resemble a conservative religion that opposes nonnormative subjects, especially when it comes to ethnic and sexual minorities, who may rally together against it. In the following passage, *Nouvel Observateur* journalist Jean-Claude Guillebaud, collaborating with Bennani, reflects on the "symbolic order" and asks: "Is it not . . . an old belief that we would do best to emancipate ourselves from? (Psychoanalysis) today has become the guardian of the idea of the limit. . . . From this perspective, we can say that psychoanalysis has become the nurse of social desperation, the depositary of collective representations. . . . This is why sexual minorities and gender studies activists have laid siege to it. For them, psychoanalysts have become the new parish priests, the last defenders of genital normality, of morality, of moralism, even obscurantism."[163] Guillebaud echoes Bourcier's insistence that an officialized psychoanalysis has departed from the critical stance of its founders, who always kept theoretical space for psychoanalysis to be remade by cultural evolution. The "science" has in certain hands become a conservative limiter, prescriber, and dictator of psychological itineraries. Yet, perhaps this ambivalence was always a tendency of psychoanalysis, as Foucault's work suggests.

The individual emancipation that officialized psychoanalysis calls for has one very important casualty when it comes to immigrant psychology: North African homosociality. Fanon recognized this long ago, at the same moment he was famously ejected from French Algeria after declaring that psychiatry as it was practiced locally made a mockery of medicine. After renouncing French citizenship, he transplanted his practice to Tunisia, where he developed what can arguably be called a precursor to the new ethnopsychiatry, a practice that preserved community bonds between men as part of the cure. He elaborated forms of game and group therapy, instituting a "Moorish café" that recreated the North African homosocial environment familiar to his patients, who had been shocked by the isolation of patients in Western medicine.[164] It is this homosociality that Bennani identifies as a lost instrument in postcolonial psychiatry in France. He cites a case study in which one patient, who already had difficulty accepting outside help, announced that he preferred the plural care of his friends, rather than the dependency on a nurse which he found "humiliating." Bennani went on to say that "what appears here is the inversion of the classic cultural behavior in Maghrebi societies . . . male accompaniment . . . is not forbidden but valorized."[165] It is this emphasis on collectivity that practitioners like Bennani insist should be implemented in French psychiatric practice, to reduce the alienation sometimes felt by immigrant populations.[166] The reason, I argue, that republican psychoanalysts call for the enforced isolation of the individual members of the pathologized *banlieusard* immigrant family, is due to the fact that their culturally informed bond (i.e., their inability to exist outside a group) is seen as the root of their pathology.

Sickness triggered by immigration disconnects the male immigrant worker from his social constellation in multiple ways. Sayad has explained that once given the official status of "sick person," the immigrant finds himself separated from the able-bodied group. Remedies gravitate around the self rather than the community. No sooner has the immigrant discovered the individuation of his body than he is dispossessed of it, Sayad explains. Keller reprises Sayad in order to speak about the isolating, individuating effects that occur when the patient assimilates into the medical field. That event would exactly mirror the process by which the immigrant is reduced to his body for the labor market: "conceived as part of the social and familial group in the country of origin, the body becomes individuated through social functions of capitalism and the specific forms of alienation that apply to the immigrant."[167] This violence of individuation has been touched upon more recently in Guénif-Souilamas, who maintains, when speaking of the figures of the *garçon arabe* and the *beurette*, that the passage from family to individuality often requires a certain material-class foundation not always evident in immigrant itineraries: "An adhesion to the individualist model becomes, when deprived of material and cultural support systems [*assises*], a negative model."[168] In a similar vein, a certain imperative in gay liberation narratives requires a dissolution of family bonds, an escape toward the city center, and the embrace of individualism, as so many documentaries and news reports about the "conflict" between cultural belonging and homosexuality show (see chapter 1).

Nathan has given a psychological voice to a certain backlash against individualization. Because of this, Nathan has come under attack, in the press and within academia, for promoting ghettoization and ethnic separatism. Fethi Benslama himself criticized Nathan in the pages of *Le Monde* for trying to "send [immigrants and their descendants] back on a flying carpet in the direction of their culture."[169] At stake in this intellectual debate is the question of how the immigrant struggle should be conceptualized psychologically: as a story about the individual (experiencing exile and alienation) or as a story about the group (striving to hold on to cultural links). Keller cites the importance, however, of placing this debate within a context of rising xenophobia that brought increased scrutiny of communitarianism.[170]

In its emphasis on homosocial and collective solutions, one of the most pragmatic innovations of modern ethnopsychiatry has been to interview all "love objects" together, in the hope of providing a group cure. This technique also serves to confront the subject with other family members (to whom one can usually trace the origins of psychological suffering as seen in many case studies). The choice of setting also proves important, as the ethnopsychiatric clinical theater is most often crowded by a varying assortment of doctors, relations, social workers, and traditional healers, creating a decidedly un-private space (a far cry from the typical psychotherapist's chair and divan) in which doctor-patient confidentiality is abandoned for a cure that happens not in spite of a suffocating family presence, but because of it. This approach has its detractors, however, who warn of the potential of cultural imprisonment. In contrast, Benslama mocks this unusual, multidisciplinary gathering of "experts" for its supposed regression toward the mystical, even if it resembles the Moorish Café innovated by Fanon: "The layout consists of a cultural dramatization of the migrants' symptoms, in front of a heterogeneous assembly that is supposed to represent the group or village one belongs to."[171] Nathan, for his part, often describes how the tensions the individual hosts in his or her body—born of being torn in two by family conflict—are evacuated by this approach into the room itself, where the love objects who began the conflict in the subject's mind must come to a long-delayed resolution. This was the case in a memorable case study published in the *Nouvelle Revue d'Ethnopsychiatrie*, wherein a Franco-Arab young male patient complained of bodily pain that was later revealed to be psychosomatic. It had been triggered by an enduring and unspoken conflict between his French wife and his Arab mother in regards to the couple's mixed marriage. As the two love objects were forced to think through their differences, the patient adopted a more relieving role: the "one who waits."[172]

Summary

These ethnopsychiatric commentaries show how officialized psychoanalysis can sometimes constitute a form of assimilation, with the prerequisite that the Franco-Arab subject divorce him- or herself from the obstacles of family filiations and cultural attachments. In sketching the portrait of the pathologized family of immigrant ancestry, I explained how the figures of the delinquent youth, the veiled woman, and the impotent father cause alarm among certain psychoanalysts, who—instead of calling for family reconciliation as is traditionally the case in psychotherapeutic remedies—call for family divorce and atomization. This is due to a combination of traits associated with these figures: the excessive virility of the delinquent youth who eventually eclipses his father and acts out his subconscious desires too literally; the showy inhibition of veiled women which causes confusion about gender norms; and the absenteeism of fathers defeated by manual labor who cannot assure the subsistence of the father principle. Pathologized in this way, this family retreats from medical scrutiny—which here tends to stigmatize rather than help—into the shelter of clandestinity and alternative therapies called "mystical." This defensive move against pathologization is then further pathologized, as an inability to deliver oneself for analysis, that is, to engage in a confessionalism upon which officialized psychoanalysis depends.

In the next chapter, I examine this imaginary family's "black sheep": the troublesome Arab boy. This figure has ventured outside the spheres of journalism and the social sciences, taking robust shape in French literature as a recurrent and almost always problematic character. The psychosexual projections explored in this chapter continue in much of francophone literature I will examine, especially as regards gender rigidity and sexually informed miseducation. The expressive mode of literature, however, also offers the possibility of bypassing the confines of media and psychoanalytical representations in order to access, through aesthetic consideration, the missing or undervalued dimensions of Franco-Arab masculinity.

3 / Uncultured Yet Seductive: The Trope of the Difficult Arab Boy

Ever since my return from Morocco, it's been a problem for me: what is it, to be French? People reproach me for being too French. I'm hurt each time that people exclude me from the beuritude so in vogue today. The gays [les pédés] fixate on the archetype of the beur thug [racaille], with good reason I might add. These bodies are sexualized quite a bit. But I can't reconcile myself with the idea that any beur that has not turned thug is a well-integrated beur.

FARID TALI[1]

In this chapter, I survey representations of the Arab male in contemporary French and francophone literature. Arab men, especially those who show signs of ethnic affirmation, I argue, are cast outside the privileged circles of a "gay" space just as often as they are eroticized. This can happen in narratives about sex tourism, about the mixing of classes and ethnicities in metropolitan France, or in the mixing of classes and ethnicities that concern the French cultural elite, wherein Arab men are posited as threats and nuisances to gay cultural, aesthetic, and philosophical sensibilities. This is especially the case at moments of literary collaboration between Arab and white authors, or when Arab partners try to assert themselves in a literary or intellectual sense. There is, of course, a backlash against this intellectual belittling, both from a new generation of white gay writers as well as from emergent Franco-Arab voices. In my discussion, I pay attention to how postcolonial resentment about past interethnic belittling is portrayed via the historical motif of the "Arab boy," transplanted from an exploited status in colonial settings to an unassimilated status in contemporary France.

First, I consider how two gay-identified North African authors (Rachid O. and Abdellah Taïa), who write from France, have responded to calls for sexual disclosure as "native informants." These writers both contest and in other ways reify a tradition of literary and sexual collaboration that has existed ever since Paul Bowles fostered the emergence of Moroccan voices. Then, I introduce two modern-day collaborators, Renaud Camus and Frédéric Mitterrand, who have pursued forms of collaboration with North African writers that recall those of their predecessors. Between then and now, however, their young Arab interlocutors have gone from being available and servile to being difficult and resentful. The trope of the difficult Arab boy has been taken up more recently by Nina Bouraoui, who importantly offers a lesbian perspective on the phenomenon of non-Arab youth imitating Franco-Arab models of masculinity. The playwrights Bernard-Marie Koltès and Jean-Marie Besset drop the ambivalence toward ethnic virility and instead valorize it in plays which dramatize interethnic and interclass conflict. This heterogeneous group of authors all participate in either the demonization and recuperation of the so-called difficult Arab boy. I explain how the Arab boy is constructed by prominent French writers as an intellectual void made only of confidence and physical presence. This figure would carry within his "impenetrable" male envelope a cultural threat: the "dumbing down" of the French language and civilization.

Sexuality, Ethnography, and Literature

What has come to be known, for better or worse, as *beur* literature still bears the traces of a debate concerning the connection between fiction and the social sciences that has accompanied this genre ever since its emergence. A central question has been whether immigrant and *banlieusard* writers focus on social questions more than other types of authors, and whether readings of these works overemphasize this dimension. Such questions have arisen before in considerations of francophone writers from the former colonies, who were often commissioned to play the role of "native informant" or ethnographic guide. The debate has recently taken a new direction with regard to works that explore sexuality, especially those that seem to offer anthropological insight into the sexual codes of the banlieue or what appear to be closed immigrant circles.

Franco-Arab writers have generally been characterized as treading a difficult path between wanting to claim a voice as members of a minority group and having their work defined by this ethnic identity. This dynamic is especially acute in the case of LGBT Franco-Arab authors who experience conflicting impulses with regard to the question of whether to privilege cultural over sexual identity or vice versa. This double-bind is in a sense falsely restrictive, as some of these authors have moved beyond these choices and achieved distinction largely due to aesthetic merit, as is the case with Nina Bouraoui.

A number of contemporary Franco-Arab authors have resisted being looked at as "representative" or being read anthropologically, while others have embraced that reading and taken advantage of the role of native informant. Still others adopt the posture of the native informant in order to effect change from within by supplying narratives designed to thwart a knowledge or power complex.[2] A central factor enabling the continuation of the native informant trope has been the contemporary success and proliferation of literary works based on the disclosure of Franco-Arab and, to a greater degree, Muslim sexuality, as indicated in the works of Tahar Ben Jelloun, Abdellah Taïa, and Bouraoui. Some journalists and editors in the *monde des lettres*—Paris's international publishing world—have tasked themselves with amplifying the homosexual voices of the Oriental world, so that they may be as loud in the West as they are supposedly quiet in the East.[3]

It is important to acknowledge, however, that "ethnic" or minority literature has not always settled for merely being an impoverished substitution of the sociopolitical for the aesthetic, a charge leveled by many French literary commentators of *beur lit*. Neither does that literature have to be grittily attached to social realism to be of critical interest. The surreal or fantastical sequences of a Taïa or a Ben Jelloun speak volumes about real social and cultural issues. In important ways, an alternative literature exists both to correct or adjust such insistently realist representations and introduce another kind—less judgmental, more stylistically adventurous, and amenable to what cannot be easily explained or categorized— in its place. In *Desiring Arabs*, Joseph Massad speaks not only of distorted political and journalistic representations of Arab sexuality that dwell exclusively on regression, violence, intolerance, and phallocentrism, he also presents the potential of Arabic literature (and the cinema based upon it) to offer a nonjudgmental and nonfearmongering view more attuned to local vocabularies of the sexual. Literature sometimes succeeds in representing a fuller scope of sexual diversity where a heavy-handed ethnography obsessed with classification and truth claims fails. This is shown in the work of Bernard-Marie Koltès and Nina Bouraoui, who arguably create a more detailed and instructive world in their fictional and metaphorical accounts, which dwell on sexual and ethnic difference, than the often reductive ethnographic accounts that treat the same subjects from which such fiction was inspired.

When the criterion of sexuality clouds the border between *beur* literature and the ethnographic mission, a preexisting tendency in ethnographic fiction is exacerbated. The element of ethnography that pries into fields resistant to inquiry takes on a new layer of meaning. Immigrant sexuality would seem to constitute an ethnographic target par excellence, because of the way it has been represented: occurring in secrecy, animated by specialized and uncharted codes and in need of excavation. Thus a knowledge battle is set up between the writer and a nonconsenting partner—practitioners of clandestine sexualities who may shy away from exposure, as in the case of closeted bisexuals or sex workers. It is against this challenge that writers of ethnographic fiction can demonstrate their excavating skills, unpinning the Orientalist knot of old.

However, a significant difference exists between literature that stands in for social science and literature that seeks to dismantle the very platforms of scientificity that permit the rush to judgment. Where do we place sexually dissident Franco-Arab writers when it comes to this epistemological conflict? The dilemma often pits the desire to divulge Arab "alternative" sexuality against a reticent instinct, one that cautions against the airing of experiences that could result in the disappearance of clandestine sexualities or their appropriation for other agendas. Such appropriation has occurred with interventions in the *banlieues* in the name of LGBT rights (see chapter 1): in order to combat sexism, activists excavate what is purported to be a generalized sexual misery, and in the process attach a new stigma to the communities they are trying to save. Gay-identified Franco-Arab writers have special access to worlds often separated by class, ethnicity, gender, and sexual orientation, and can thus act as intermediaries (in addition to native informants) between them. They have a crucial role to play in regard to the intelligibility and translation of local sexual cultures for outside readers, and can sometimes act as the bellwether of human rights intervention. Uniquely positioned, these writers can also serve as peacemakers by acknowledging symbolic and physical violence against sexual minorities where it does occur, while at the same time questioning the always problematic nature of immigrant sexuality. This diplomatic tone is often absent from the sensational and judgmental media treatments of homosexual life in the banlieues, which often recommend that sexual minorities leave those areas for good. The stories they tell evince a respect for difference and a kind of communitarian right to privacy, as well as a respect for the accommodation of family obligations *and* individualist desires. Such authors often effect a rehabilitation of an otherwise vilified Franco-Arab virility, presenting the rarely discussed ways in which this "problematic" masculinity could instead serve a welcome, productive, or ethical purpose.

Sexual Informants of Bad News

One criticism leveled against authors such as Taïa and Rachid O., whose novels often tell "secret" stories about North African sexuality, alleges that their literature perpetuates the Orientalist trope of the native informant. It is worth noting, however, that the terrain (straddling Morocco and urban France) upon which such native information is collected has shifted significantly since decolonization. Territories become "uncharted" not only due to overseas distance but also because of domestic barriers of class, race, and culture. In this way, a Parisian suburb only ten minutes away by train can become exotically worthy of exploration, its "novel" mores—sexual and otherwise—conducive to surprise. A hushed, surreptitious tone haunts Nina Bouraoui and Taïa's prose especially, both of them voyeuristically portraying their respective milieus, populated by residents from the most disparate of origins. Taïa documents the lives of neighbors spied on from his window in Le rouge du tarbouche, while Bouraoui surveys and scrutinizes the nocturnal residents that haunt the city's clubs and bars in Poupée Bella. They both describe the ways in which the "clandestine secrets" prized by an exotifying ethnography, assumed to exist only in distant countries, can be found under one's nose in the metropolis.

Authors writing in this vein bring Arabic cultural mores into European settings, and often these mores are subject to pressure and undergo significant change. When it comes to sexuality, these writers neither mourn a dying, nativist Arab "authenticity" left in the country of origin nor allude to a golden age of irretrievable Arab sexuality. They accept that such attitudes toward sexuality may have changed in immigration as well as in North Africa itself; and they often find the changes as worthy of exploration and study as what has been "conserved." Their literature of sexual dissidence embraces transnational promise, relating a certain "Arab" nomadism to, for example, stories of immigrant wanderlust in Europe. Characters intoxicated at first by narrative and sexual freedoms no longer lament the points of no return that separate their preimmigration from their postimmigration identities. At the same time, the Franco-Arab characters they create challenge the idea that Arabs do not share in sexual modernity: in search of romantic and erotic fulfilment, characters move across cultures, races, and borders, establishing a romantic transnationalism of sorts. Françoise Lionnet and Shu-mei Shih have elsewhere described how a certain kind of transnationalism (a "transnationalism from above") tends to idealize a writerly homelessness of the intentional kind, a world citizen attitude that dwells on a "free-flowing subjectivity rooted only in language." While Lionnet and Shih describe the "utopian impulse of postcolonial intellectual approaches" that have led "to a romanticized view of the seductive power of geographical displacement,"[4] I argue that one can expand upon this and say that the market for immigrant sexual confession also encourages a rootlessness, built upon the disavowal of ancestral origins, family, and language in favor of a modern sexual enlightenment. This is visible in such instances as the preponderance of narratives that present the family home as a place of backwardness from which one must escape, the choice of French as the default language for expressing sexuality, or an avoidance of rooting sexual alterity in an Arab context and speaking of salvation only in a Western one.

A casual visit to any major French bookstore confirms the prominent marketing of testimonial works about gender and sexuality authored by immigrants, populations of immigrant origin, or Muslims. As far as scholarly work is concerned, Kathryn Kleppinger has conducted an interview-based study of the journalism and public relations maneuvers projecting *beur* authors into media relevance, with special attention paid to gender dynamics in this arena. In one section, she profiles Faïza Guène, a precocious literary talent who resisted having her work portrayed as ethnography or victimized sexual confession. In a TV appearance, she responded to a journalist attempting such a reading by complaining: "Everyone wants me to talk about subjects that sometimes I don't want to talk about. I'm not there for that. I come from a poor neighborhood, I'm of undetermined heritage, I'm a girl as well, so I have to apologize for not being a victim of gang rapes at the age of nine."[5]

Perhaps the most famous and celebrated of authors writing in the vein of sexual confessionalism, Abdellah Taïa and his unique portraits of North African sexual dissidents have found a wide European audience. The pages of mainstream French magazines have often singled out the Paris-based Taïa, hailing him as a courageous gay rights pioneer for his Moroccan homeland.[6] His "coming out"—in a 2006 interview in the Moroccan francophone monthly *Tel Quel*—was the subject of much fanfare, yielding many declarations of historic events because he was heralded as the first "out" gay writer from the Arab world.[7] This declaration comes in spite of the historical precedents of Arabic and Persian literary production celebrating nonidentity-affirming homosexual practices.[8]

French and, more recently, American publications have tended to present Taïa's literary project as an extension of a Stonewall liberation narrative—an inexorable march toward greater visibility and freedom of sexual disclosure. Much of the extant scholarship on Taïa does not engage with his work critically. This has much to do with Taïa's reception in French and Anglo-American circles, where his work has mostly been analyzed in a celebratory mode, heralding him as an innovator. My treatment of his work is different in that I acknowledge, on the one hand, that Taïa's words sometimes contribute to a reductive civilizational divide in which Arab sexual intolerance stands in opposition to Western sexual liberation, and on the other hand, that Taïa supplies a critique of the North's sexual consumption of the South in form of (sex) tourism and suggests how Moroccan understandings of the sexual could queer Western liberal notions of sexuality. My work diverges from extant scholarship by emphasizing that Taïa's oeuvre is in many ways a double-edged sword: focusing solely on the celebratory plays into the divide that Taïa's work elsewhere seeks to dismantle.[9]

The transnational informant position of authors who write from France about North Africa has been harshly criticized by the Morocco-based former *Le Monde* journalist Jean-Pierre Péroncel-Hugoz: "Today, north of the Mediterranean, a small handful of pen-pushing Maghrebis—without any inspiration besides pimping themselves or 'sword-crossing' [*partie de touche-pipi*] in public bathrooms—have calculated that, by posing as victims in their home countries while in the Marais . . . or on the Ramblas of Barcelona, they might find the ideal means to flatter their ego, their misplaced vanity, and spur to fruition the sale numbers of their repetitive autobiographical booklets."[10] Péroncel-Hugoz has professed royalist sympathies and anti-Islamist stances that make him far from a neutral source. However, such a comment goes to show just how much Franco-Arab writing about sexuality can become embroiled in conflicts about authenticity and "the right to represent others." He alleges that writers such as Taïa and O., who are never explicitly named, write for a Western audience and that their French-language works do not resonate in the Moroccan literary market. These disagreements about "authenticity" are difficult, if not impossible, to settle in an age when transnational exchanges obfuscate the borders between supposedly impermeable national cultures, let alone literary markets, Moroccan or French. Taïa felt the critique was addressed to him and responded with a polemic of his own, lambasting the Orientalist privilege of such figures as Péroncel-Hugoz, expatriates living the good life in a former protectorate, who benefit from keeping Morocco locked in a frozen-in-the-past age of authenticity, Taïa says. The writer believes that this nostalgic possessiveness, impeding the country's "progress," also produces a kind of sexual exploitation:

> Make no mistake, the Morocco Péroncel-Hugoz is talking about was invented by Orientalists in the nineteenth century, and frozen by Marshall Lyautey at the beginning of the twentieth. A Morocco that has never really existed and that nevertheless continues to inform the

fantasies of a large number of the French (and not only the French). A Morocco where privileged westerners can sample the *dolce vita* in full tranquility, with eyes firmly shut. Where they can have Fatima as a cook, Mohamed as a gardener, Saïd as a chauffeur, and Rachid or Meryem as a sexual object. All this for but a few dirhams.[11]

In his response entitled "The Return of Marshall Lyautey," Taïa underlines Péroncel-Hugoz's attempts to regulate Moroccan behavior, sexual or otherwise. He compares Péroncel-Hugoz to a military figure at the heart of French imperialism (Lyautey), who first occupied Morocco in 1907 and laid the foundation for the protectorate. This spat between Taïa and his critic can be read not just as a fight over authenticity or privilege, but as a struggle over who has the right to represent North African sexual dissidence, a struggle that changes with the advent of the sexual refugee as immigrant (from France, Taïa has strongly called out Morocco and especially his own family's treatment of homosexuality). On the one hand, immigrant sexual dissidents act as intermediaries between communities, between spaces segregated by gender, sexual preference (if not identity), and often class. On the other hand, their status as immigrants in Europe positions them as conduits between cultures, in perpetual transit, ideally situated for a commentary on globalization (as well as the globalization of sexuality) and its destabilizing but also enabling components. This versatile status reflects the myriad connotations of *clandestinité*—in both the sexual and immigrant senses. Being an immigrant sexual dissident means being exposed to how sexual and ethnic "undergrounds" intersect, armed with unique capacities for explaining what they have in common. Such commonalities are plainly visible in transitional neighborhoods in the French metropolis where immigrants and sexual "refugees" of all types find that they meet at the same levels, in the same spaces. The term *dissident* also changes meaning when the immigrant passes from a country where his or her sexual practices, if openly confessed, might clash with social norms, to a country where such practices are protected from sanction, at least in privileged spaces. One cannot forget, however, that such immigrants still remain dissident after immigration, in the way their sexual practices or identities clash with convention in European homosexual communities.

Péroncel-Hugoz criticizes gay Morroccan authors for overlooking this subtlety of *clandestinité*, that is, of a sexual life whose discretion permits encounters between populations that might otherwise never interact. Though one must consider the source, Péroncel-Hugoz pinpoints a fundamental disagreement on the question of whether clandestinity actually represses or nurtures sexual diversity. Discreet, closeted, or clandestine homosexuality is often overlooked in accounts of sexual diversity, perhaps due to its lack of openness. In the following passage, Péroncel-Hugoz takes issue with what he describes as the sexual overexposure and oversharing that suffuses the works of gay Moroccan authors:

> Indeed, Morocco does not have to slip down this slippery and ridiculous slope. Why? Simply because it is an Islamic land, and the [Islamic] civilization settled the issue of pederasty (or homosexuality or inversion etc.) once and for all fifteen centuries ago. The thing is practiced here just like it has been under each and every sky since the beginning of time, because, just as the 1947 Nobel Laureate André Gide said, in substance: if pederasty is against nature, it is nevertheless in Nature. Exactly. And Islam, a realist system, has responded to the question, has taken it into account with modesty and discretion. Neither seen nor known. Neither display nor disturbance. And no one has complained after smartening up to it at the initiative of an older cousin or schoolmate, just as they themselves were introduced to it by those more experienced . . . and the cycle continues. This invisible erotic strand between boys has notably allowed most Muslim girls to reach marriageable age while still virgins, for some fifteen hundred years. This Eastern Eros has been dignified for ages, by everyone from the Mesopotamian poet Abu Nawas to the Tunisian chronicler Ahmed Tifachi, via some Persian or Mughal miniaturist or other.[12]

In addition to Abu Nawas and Tifachi, Michel Foucault sang the praises of the *ars erotica*, the often secret art of pleasure grounded in learnedness at the hands of a teacher and initiations of all sorts: Foucault located this *ars* in vaguely (Middle) Eastern sources. He opposed it to the *scientia sexualis*, rooted in extracted confessions, disclosure, and categorization. Péroncel-Hugoz stresses that homosexuality has always been practiced in Morocco, unremarkably, and that it follows the structure of knowledge discreetly acquired from elders. He underlines a distinguishing feature of Moroccan sexual customs whose existence is difficult to prove (since the clandestine cannot be exposed, measured, or documented). However, Péroncel-Hugoz also locks it up in timelessness and near-ancient sources, giving validity to Taïa's critique about nostalgic Frenchmen freezing into place their favorite version of Morocco. In Péroncel-Hugoz's vision, discreet homosexuality remains a by-product of male homosocial privilege, a circle of knowledge of which women are ignorant and protected from for their own supposed benefit. Though Péroncel-Hugoz brings up the oft-ignored issue of differences in attitude surrounding clandestinity, his perhaps valid point is wrapped up in language phobic about men who do not, and indeed may not be able to, pass publically as "straight." Their spat is most notable in my reading for the way Taïa, as an Arab author, is cast as someone unfamiliar with his country's (sexual heritage) because of a lack of learnedness, and is thus deemed unworthy of representing it. This operation is carried out not by a heterosexist Moroccan compatriot, but rather by a European critic claiming more authentic knowledge.

Exposure in the world literature market inevitably affects this distinction between such Eastern and Western understandings of sexuality, however essentialist. If the demand for sexual revelation can be said to exist in this market, it would epistemologically influence what surfaces as North African sexuality. It can be argued that sexually dissident literature written in a confessional mode (for a mostly diaspora and European audience) discloses clandestine practices that might otherwise remain silent. However, the Franco-Arab writers who respond to this call are significantly able to alter or redeploy the incitement to discourse in directions they find more respectful of sexual and cultural particularity. Accepting their place at the receiving end of a demand, some Franco-Arab writers have seized upon the invitation to speak to circumvent and deconstruct such demands, as well as send off demands of their own in response.

Rachid O. is one such author who supplies the titillating material many readers are looking for, only to leave them with a guilty conscience, unsettled by what they have read. The early output of O., in the fictional narrative *Chocolat chaud*, or in the autobiographical *L'enfant ébloui*, featured stories of an intergenerational sexuality articulated by adolescent agents who narrate, retrospectively, their underage sexual experiences with mostly older men (for example, married French diplomats or teachers more than twice their age).[13] The narrator of one vignette in *L'enfant ébloui* laments that, once beyond adolescence, he has passed a stage of no return, no longer possessing the ephebic appeal that once attracted older men. He meets a group of French homosexual tourists visiting Morocco who are fascinated by his tales of child sexuality. They beg him for stories with a kind of Scheherazadian insistence for continuity, reveling openly in the idea that they can engage in a subject of conversation that would be considered out of place in France. The visitors' excitement aggravates the narrator's disappointment, as they strain to see past his mature physical envelope into his childhood affair with Antoine, an older, married French diplomat:

> We went to a restaurant in Marrakesh owned by a French homosexual. And that's when we started talking. The only thing that interested Julien was my life with Antoine. It was unusual in Morocco for a twenty-year-old boy to live with a forty-five-year-old for five years. He was curious, he asked questions so that I would continue the tale. . . . Telling this story, I saw Julien marveling at me, he was happy to hear this. . . . It was then I understood that he was a man suited for very young boys and that I would have no chance with him. And then I told myself, on the spot, because I had a vicious side: "Since I have no chance, I will tell an even more extravagant story, I will go back even further, to when I was thirteen and had experienced a love story with thirty year-old man, my professor."[14]

O. realizes that a market and audience exist for this type of sexual storytelling just as his narrative self is banished from it. Like Taïa, O. exposes a homosexual tourism that might have otherwise remained shrouded. This authorial act provides an almost vengeful rejoinder to "outings" of North African sexual proclivities in past European literature, flipping the script on the European travelers who spoke of a pederasty supposedly rampant in Moroccan society. Although Taïa, compared to O., is much less explicit about adolescent sexuality, the theme suffuses his novels in an intense but understated form, with the eroticization of cousins, brothers, and opportunities to share beds with relatives, as well as the celebration of senior female family members and their sexual eccentricities.

Taïa's work, if read closely, actually offers a critique of the globalization of homonormative discourses and the way they might obscure the specificity of Moroccan sexual practices and attitudes. Some of Taïa's short stories can be read as a critique of a homonormativity that carries within it latent class and racial privilege. For example, the chapter "Terminus des Anges" in Le rouge du tarbouche stages a confrontation between a privileged position of (sexual) tourism and the grievances resulting from economic disparities inherent in tourism.[15] Some would call this reckoning overdue as there has been very little published in the way of pushback, very little "writing against" European and American authors who practiced and wrote about sex tourism, and certainly none from North African writers identifying as gay before O. and Taïa.[16] This confrontation is developed through a civil, alternatively stern and emotional conversation between a Moroccan protagonist, M'hamed, and the genteel French tourist René, who, despite the best of intentions, is firmly entrenched in the dynamics of economic injury. The chapter's opening sequence includes a morbid invocation of homosexual authors past who sought, in North Africa, a type of sexual and personal release unavailable in Europe: "Paul Bowles is dead."¹⁷ This sentence seems to signify the literal, historical closing of a chapter perhaps momentous and productive for those European and American authors, yet less emancipatory for their Moroccan interlocutors, causing worry amongst those later readers who, like Taïa, became concerned about the objects of these writers' sexual conquests and their treatment of the indigenous population. Taïa's return-to-sender framework, in which he turns a seduction into an interrogation scene, forthrightly answers publication trends in international LGBT publishing which favor first-person, Western narrators giving softcore accounts of sexual dalliance in the "lands of Islam"—from the spotty scholarship/sex tourism literature edited by Arno Schmitt and Jehoeda Sofer to the recent collection *Gay Travels in the Muslim World* edited by Michael Luongo.¹⁸

In Taïa's version, we witness a sudden transition from the romantic, depoliticized alignment of two men in a foreign country to one of frank economic necessity. M'Hamed meets René, whose attraction for the young Moroccan is obvious, and slowly proceeds to seduce him, inviting him to his mother's house. Once there, M'Hamed changes tone and pleads for help in getting papers to go to Europe, replacing touristic insouciance with nonerotic realpolitik. However, this occurs only after M'Hamed has given himself sexually to René, his gift of bodily intimacy presented as the most precious thing he has to offer, deserving at the very least of papers. The encounter, which takes place in M'Hamed's family home, is also inscribed within the dynamics of hospitality, making a potential refusal of reciprocation an even greater affront:

René: You don't find your country beautiful?
M'Hamed: No.
—Nothing pleases you here?
—Nothing. I don't have anything here, no luck, no future. Only rich people can really live in this country. For me, for the others, it's an everyday combat, and we are never the winners. . . . So why would Morocco be beautiful? I don't see anything done for our sakes, everything is done for you, for tourists. . . . I have to enter Europe . . . and for that I need you. You have to help me. Only you can. You see, I'm a nice guy, a poor person, I don't hurt anyone. . . . Do you hear me? Only with your help will I be able to enter. . . . It's the only present

you can offer me in exchange for what I have just given you . . . my
body . . . do you hear me?

René wondered where he had just landed, he was starting to get
scared. M'hamed's eyes, as he was speaking, were becoming ever
more red. He was speaking in utter seriousness. . . .

M'hamed was crying and screaming. All of his anguish, all
of his demons were assaulting him without respite. Desperation
transfigured him. René was paralyzed, incapable of reacting, to say
a word, to be compassionate.[19]

The cold water splashed upon the tourist's excitement is not merely a gratuitous, vindictive gesture, but also serves to mark a definite break with
the sexual tourism literature of the past. The novels of Moroccan writers Mohammed Mrabet and Mohammed Choukri frequently dwelled
on the resentment of male protagonists against unwilling participation
in homosexual prostitution or relationships of convenience with European sugar daddies. Taïa evokes inequality but also refuses to demonize
René, to whom he affords the capacity of ethical reaction when faced with
his interlocutor's socioeconomic misery and dependency. The Tangiers
generation of French, British, and American Beat writers—for whom
Morocco was a place of experimentation in every sense of the word—
ignored or avoided grappling with these class disparities.[20] In the scene at
M'Hamed's family home, it is the plaintive voice of M'Hamed's mother,
concerned after hearing the sound of her son crying from her upstairs
bedroom, that moves René. The sudden reminder of familial attachment
and corresponding humanity causes him to embrace M'hamed with an
implicit, if not verbalized pledge to assist him. The chapter ends on this
unresolved note, with only affective comfort promised. Taïa leaves the
reader to contemplate the uncertain fate of subjects similar to M'hamed,
to reflect on the ambiguous dynamics of tourism, after drawing them in
with erotic promise.

This scene's location and the theme of exchange raise the issue of hospitality, often saluted in charitable readings of North African culture as
a kind of ethnographic, precapitalist counterpart to systems of exchange
in the West. Expectations of hospitality are significantly impacted here
by economic and political strictures that have implications for reciprocity. These "difficult circumstances" cause evolution toward a much less
spontaneous, more planned model compared to the type of hospitality
that goes without saying: the encounter in "Terminus" morphs from
smiling overtures and offerings to contractual exchange and demands for
nonfinancial payment. Taïa's reflection on hospitality follows a vogue for

hospitality in recent French philosophical writing—something Mireille Rosello has explored in *Postcolonial Hospitality*—a wave of prohospitality interventions precipitated by increasingly stringent French immigration laws.[21]

The Guardians of French Letters

Outside his novel writing, Taïa developed a substantive literary relationship with a figure who, in 2010, appeared at the center of a controversy touching upon youth sexuality and tourism: Frédéric Mitterrand, former minister of culture and communications. Prior to fulfilling his ministerial role, Mitterrand enjoyed a successful career in television, directed the French Academy in Rome, launched an international arthouse cinema in Paris, and produced the work of aspiring filmmakers, several of them hailing from North Africa. A media storm erupted in 2009 around his "autobiographical novel" *La mauvaise vie*—which describes past trysts with "immediately available boys" in South East Asia.[22] After he publicly defended filmmaker Roman Polanski, who was arrested in Switzerland for having had sexual relations with a thirteen-year-old girl and later released, Mitterrand faced renewed and somewhat confrontational interest in *La mauvaise vie*. The binational nephew of former President François Mitterrand, Frédéric was accorded honorary Tunisian citizenship and often declares a great affinity for North Africa. It was deposed Tunisian president Ben Ali who granted Mitterrand citizenship in the 1990s after Mitterrand organized a cultural "Week of Tunisia," a fact that proved embarrassing during the Arab revolutions of 2011. During the uprising, Mitterrand dismissed claims of Ben Ali's tyranny, admitting only after his demise that Ben Ali had perhaps accorded him nationality for political reasons.[23] The *affaire* Mitterrand problematized the encounter between sexuality, politics, ethics, and aesthetics in a way that has ramifications for the representation of Franco-Arab youth sexualities.

Mitterrand was criticized both by the Left and the Right. First, from conservative politicians who found in his writings worrisome indications of pedophiliac sex tourism (under cover of sexual liberation and aesthetic "explorations"), and second, from the leftist LGBT wing which, although it did defend his explorations of sexual marginality and diversity, highlighted his lack of reflection on the power differentials of race and class inhabiting the sexual tourism exchange. However, few critics mentioned the prevalent ageism in the gay community that indirectly causes some men to turn to sex tourism. In their critique of contemporary gay fascinations with exoticism in France, *Homo Exoticus*, Maxime Cervulle and

Nick-Rees Roberts concluded that the Mitterrand scandal was a missed opportunity for self-criticism in regard to the gay community's ambiguous relationship with sex tourism, Orientalism, and colonial nostalgia.[24]

Mitterrand shows up relatively often in works on French homosexuality in the postcolonial context. He cowrote with Taïa the ode to Morocco *Maroc, 1900–1960: un certain regard*.[25] In 1987, he produced the film *Avril brisé*, which fostered the career of Liria Bégéja who later filmed Franco-Arab actors Sami Bouajila and Roschdy Zem as transvestite prostitutes in *Change-moi ma vie*.[26] He also had a role in the Philippe Barassat's *Mon copain Rachid*,[27] a short film about children's sexuality, in which he reads an Albert Camus citation in the film's prologue about "sin" being a relative notion. The short film explores the perspective of a young boy named Eric, who doubles as narrator, as he contemplates his slightly older Arab friend Rachid, with the main object of the boy's fascination being his well-endowed companion's genitals. The film dwells on the metonymy of the penis standing in for the human being, with Eric wondering aloud about what irresistibly draws him to Rachid's member, while at the same time acknowledging that "it wasn't what [he] truly wanted." Their friendship becomes slightly exploitative when the younger Eric starts paying Rachid to look at his genitals, after Rachid had initially stated that to touch it would be impossible as both boys agree "they are not faggots." Rachid's "alpha teen" unavailability and distracting interest in girls grate on Eric, who nevertheless views him as a masculine role model in the formation of his eventual heterosexuality. The film ends with Eric getting a classist "revenge" of sorts on the virilist antihero: many years later, we see Eric married and content while the thuggish-looking Rachid seems socially static, stuck in a rut professionally, during a chance encounter between the former friends in the street. Uneducated Rachid remains unaccompanied while Eric, thought to be less virile, has clear cultural capital in terms of fashion, speech, and mannerisms, and eventually "gets the girl." Such a film, and Mitterrand's participation in it, are notable for the links made between an interest in children's sexuality, and the interplay of sexual and ethnic difference.[28] Filmmaker Barassat and writer Mitterrand echo what was already found in Taïa and O., with their focus on the fascination of children for their sexually mature peers or even family members.[29] The film, which had been shown primarily to LGBT audiences at film festivals, was unearthed again by the media during the Mitterrand scandal and examined for possible clues leading to other charges of pedophilia, this time in regard to North African youth.[30]

Franco-Arab male figures in Barassat and Mitterrand's film seem to provide an orienting anchor for masculinities in formation. They also puncture the egos, intentionally or not, of those who admire them; despite their efforts of *rapprochement*, these wounded admirers seem to be kept always at a distance. In *La mauvaise vie*, Mitterrand reminisced about an emotionally unavailable Moroccan man he met one day in a French gay sauna; the sexual "brutishness" Mitterrand attributed to him was made even more injurious by his own reluctant attraction to the man. In the following passage, Mitterrand ridicules the man's attempts to "fuck the oppressor":

> There are some things that I no longer accept ever since I had a bad experience with a Moroccan, thirty years ago in a sauna. He was an immigrant worker, kind of good-looking, who thought only of his own pleasure and took revenge for everything else, like a good old macho, with class struggle on the tip of his *zob* [French-Arabic argot for penis] stuffed to the hilt inside young bourgeois ass. He had injured and infected me with a disease, a persistent and secret suffering that took me months to recover from.[31]

Mitterrand concludes that it was the experience with this man that provided a watershed moment along his own path toward sexual enlightenment. The notion of "sexual vengeance" for injustices related to class underlies the disparaging narration, which suggests that class struggle loses in righteousness when it enters the sexual arena. Though a victim of consensual sauna sex gone terribly wrong, Mitterrand persists in the same belittling of the class dimensions of interracial encounters that characterized the insouciance of tourists in North Africa. As mentioned earlier, Abdellah Taïa addressed this insouciance in his literary portrayal of global sex tourism, as did the scholar Joseph Boone in his examination of gay writers and class privilege in North Africa.[32] Mitterrand regrets his partner's unwillingness to "share" pleasure across class and ethnic lines; yet, the experience seems to provide a unique opportunity for poetic lament about lust and sometimes love unrequited because of a presumed "civilization" gap. In *La mauvaise vie*, Mitterrand expands on this theme when speaking about paid sex closer to home (France) as part of what he calls the "Maghreb Solution" (i.e., tourism in Morocco, Algeria, or Tunisia), which is less a "solution" than a source of frustration: "The exchange seems easy . . . one's [the visitor's] role is to play replacement wife and savings account . . . good-looking young guys arrive as if at a sporting event in order to finance appliance purchases for their future marriage to the cousin chosen by their mother. . . . The families are in on it and are the winners at the end of the day. . . . And then all of a sudden the boys disappear . . . fatigue [stemming from Mitterrand's role in these transactions] almost makes one want to stop."[33] Mitterrand disparages the economic hardship that would cause young men to resort to sex work in order to finance what may be the biggest expense (weddings) of their young lives, pausing to ridicule the inbred quality of Arab cousin marriages, all while pointing to a greater source of exploitation than sexual tourism: the Moroccan family. Mitterrand builds up the imagery of a sexual marketplace and its rotating supply of interchangeable boys: when they "disappear" after achieving some degree of financial solvency, the author again speaks in the tonality of lament and exhaustion at having to deal with boys who do not do as they are told. Mitterrand concludes this section by saying that "in any case, one can never bring any of these boys home, the airlines do not grant visas, and just try to convince a consular agent: even if you make a good impression, the twink won't get to immigrate."[34] Journalist Jérôme Dupuis highlighted Mitterrand's frustration at his chosen boys' fleeting unreliability in his critique of Mitterrand's opening chapter from *La mauvaise vie*, where Mitterrand describes his arrangement with a Tunisian family to serve as a foster parent of sorts for their sons while they pursue educational opportunities abroad: "Mitterrand recounts, in a devastating scene, how he brought a boyish Tunisian kid home to live with him in Paris, tearing him away from an obviously consenting but tearful mother. The minister spends generously where his 'adoptive' son's education is concerned and gives up his worldly life. [Yet] the turbulent child gives him a hard time."[35] In contrast with Taïa's tourist, who was ethically moved by the spectacle of a mother and son's fragile bond, Dupuis describes a character who relativizes a mother's exploitation of a child against his own. Mitterrand's sacrifice of time and money causes him to wonder, in lamentation, if "he would have gone through so much trouble if it had been a young girl."[36] This lament, which generates poetry in Mitterrand's aesthetic economy, originates in the contrast between a "turbulent" Franco-Arab masculinity that cannot adequately be seized, and the authors' literary attempts to grasp it.

The "difficult Arab boy" is a trope that extends from precedents in the travel literature of Gide and Wilde—now legend in the gay tourism canon—all the way to modern examples such as the thuggish yet attractive types that show up and steal the show (and women) in an annoyed Michel Houellebecq. One recent literary meeting of minds situates this trope in an unexpected venue, the Parisian world of publishing, in the form of a collaboration between the famed journal writer Renaud Camus and the young Franco-Arab author Farid Tali. Both openly gay, Tali and Camus first met at the screening of a 1997 film (directed by Pascale Bouhénic) about one of Camus's writing workshops. As they recount, a tense but finally amicable relationship developed, special enough that they decided to publish a cowritten journal about their encounter, entitled *Incomparable*.[37] The journal entries, they agree, are to be placed one after the other, with Camus's appearing first. Such a structure echoes the long-standing tradition, in gay European literature about North Africa, of collaborative writing as an at once literary and implicitly sexual inauguration (cf. Paul Bowles).[38] Slowly evolving in tone from hopes of intergenerational love (Camus is much older than Tali) to the mute bitterness of dashed expectations (resulting in the abrupt end of Camus's section), the journal then shifts, with Tali's contribution, to a much shorter, sparer, and arguably more "innocent" account of a young author's impressions upon meeting an admired pioneer, and his ensuing hopes of one day getting published.[39] Tali and Camus's interaction is arguably more noteworthy for its sociocultural ramifications, rather than its literary impact.

Camus has been celebrated as a gay literary icon, famed for his journals, art histories, and especially his chronicle of sexual encounters, *Tricks*:[40] while *Tricks* remained largely a-political and even utopian in the way the gay cruising culture described seemed to evoke a society absent of racial and economic strife, *Incomparable* featured commentaries about immigration and cultural assimilation. When collaborating with Tali, Camus flattered his protégé's immaculate French, and made a point of saluting his level of "integration" within republican France. Camus later founded a political party, Le Parti de L'In-nocence, whose mission statement underlines that the party "is constituted around values of civicness, civility, civilization, urbanity, respect for speech and 'in-nocence.'"[41] It goes on to announce that *in-nocence* is a virtue; as such it consists in never ceasing to increase in virtue. It is, by its nature, political.[42] The statement makes a distinction between *in-nocence* (non-harm) and *innocence* (innocence). The former is a doctrine against *nocence*, easier to assimilate in French to *nuisance* (harm), with the imperiled object being French culture.[43] Camus rings the alarm bells warning of an endangered French civilization, alleging that a gradual process of cultural impoverishment has been fomented by waves of immigrants whose daughters and especially sons lack respect for the French language.

Camus's recent career has seen him take an increasingly political drift toward the xenophobic right.[44] Camus was one of the official signatories behind the controversial "Apéro Géant de la Goutte d'Or: Saucisson et Pinard." The Goutte d'Or neighborhood counts a large number of Muslim residents; the Apéro event was a cultural provocation of sorts whereby participants would ostentatiously savor prized French gastronomical symbols that practicing Muslims abstain from (pork sausage and spirits) in an area which they declared in danger of succumbing to Islam, where Sharia law, it was said, could one day be imposed.[45] Camus published *L'abécédaire de l'in-nocence*, an instruction manual crossed with an introductory encyclopedia of terms, whose objective is to keep an insufficiently aware French public (Muslim or not) informed about a threatening religion presented as a novel arrival.[46] The party has attracted attention in a section of the media that takes seriously threats of cultural endangerment and possible Islamization. The far-right Front National Party popularized these notions, which in turn resulted in their proliferation online by xenophobic sites such as Bloc-identitaire.com and Fdesouche.com (which stands for *français de souche*, or "Frenchman of 'pure' French stock").[47]

In his political organizing, Camus has made explicit links between the increase of ethnic diversity and the impoverishment of French Culture. Raising alarm about the alleged threat of Islamization, Camus, in 2010, convened the "Assises internationales sur l'islamisation de nos pays" (Seated international meeting on the Islamization of our country), where he bemoaned the increasing banality of threats to the French language and culture. He alleged that the French media would not recognize (and perhaps even euphemize) these threats: "And hence we have the language that [the political-media complex] has invented in order to *not say*, to *not show*, to hide what is happening and what has already happened: *youth* for delinquents, *popular neighborhoods* for the neighborhoods that the indigenous popular classes have had to flee, *sensitive neighborhoods* for zones of violence and lack of rights, *multiculturalism* for the great 'deculturation,' *diversity* for the triumph of the same, for the disappearance of identities, for the universalization of the *banlieue*."[48] That Camus would locate the homogenization of identities in response to a policy of multiculturalism—arguably a strategy of tolerating limited assertions of cultural identity—is telling. Camus's complaint appears strangely similar in structure to that of the very constituency—minorities descended from immigrants—he is criticizing: in mainstream media representations, they both seem to assert strongly their identities and feel impeded in that task. Camus's use of the word *indigenous* is also historically controversial, as he inserts a colonial category in order to refer to a France untouched by colonial experience and the ensuing diversification of the populace. In interviews, Camus has spoken of a "counter-colonization" of replacement with deleterious effects on French civilization, a process engineered by immigrants as well as their descendants and their politician enablers; in fact, Camus theorized this notion in his book *Le grand remplacement* (The great replacement).[49] Theories of demographic replacement have been widely disseminated on the far right, although Marine le Pen has distanced herself from what she calls a "conspiracy."[50]

Renaud Camus neatly exemplifies the rapprochement of prominent homosexuals and the right-wing parties that used to reject them (prior to the era of African immigration). Some critiques emanating from the LGBT activist community have pointed to the "rightward" drift of homosexual elites which include personalities such as Camus, Frédéric Mitterrand, and Caroline Fourest. Cultural commentator Didier Lestrade, cofounder of *Têtu* magazine and the AIDS prevention group Act-Up, wrote a book entitled *Why Gays Have Moved to the Right*, in which he points to the ever-increasing trend of apocalyptic writing that mourns the "inevitable" loss of cultural *and* sexual liberty, often placing blame on an excessive accommodation of immigrants and Muslims.[51]

Camus is not the only celebrated gay French writer to make connections between the Arab world and the degradation of French letters. Roland Barthes, who was a close acquaintance of Camus's and wrote the preface to Camus's *Tricks*, filled the impressionistically named *Incidents* with mostly regretful stories of encounters with boys called "Mohammed (of course)" he met during a teaching engagement in Morocco, boys he finds depressingly dull and interchangeable. He makes light of the aspirations of one such "Mohammed": "Mohammed (of course), a policeman's son, wants (later on, when he's through with the *lycée*), to be a police inspector: that's his vocation. Moreover (he says): he likes football (right guard), pinball, and girls."[52] Here Barthes notes—regarding the same "incident" that the "Mohammed (of course)" citation was culled from—the over-abundance of "Mohammeds" in Morocco, and the simplicity of their literary ambitions: "Mohammed L., encountered one morning around ten, is still half-asleep; he just got up, he says, because last night he composed some verses for a play he's writing—'no characters, no plot,' etc.—and stayed up very late. Another Mohammed, the little one, told me he wrote poetry 'to keep from (getting) bored.' In this country poetry allows you to go to bed too late."[53] Camus explicitly refers to Barthes and his experience in Morocco when describing his relationship with Farid Tali. Camus sees in it an exact echo of the intergenerational rapport he had established with Barthes earlier in North Africa, with the elements of age disparity, Morocco, and regrettably platonic admiration conserved: "Everything makes me think of Barthes, in this story, *this non-story*—starting with Morocco of course. There was, between Barthes and I, the same age difference, give or take, as between myself and this boy. And not once did I consider, despite the veneration I had for Barthes, that anything on a sentimental or sexual level might transpire."[54] Camus inscribes himself in the recreation of Barthes's itinerary, almost as a sort of filiation ritual connecting homosexual mentorships past and present. Like Barthes, Camus makes light of his Arab interlocutor's intellectual stature. In *Incomparable*, Camus states that literature, the subject Tali most wanted to discuss with him, must take second stage to erotics in the dynamic between sage mentor and handsome apprentice: "[Farid] softly reproached me for not wanting to speak of literature with him. . . . I abstain from telling him that I'll only be able to speak of literature with him, potentially, *after* love, within the heightening of satisfied desire."[55]

Perhaps the most extreme example of a French gay author incited to both discourse and displeasure on the subject of Franco-Arab sexual partners, is Patrick Cardon, one the most "remarkable figures in French LGBT activism" according to *Télérama*.[56] He wrote the ostensibly literary but monotonously pornographic *Le grand écart ou tous les garçons s'appellent Ali (vignettes post-coloniales)* (The splits, or, all the boys are named Ali [postcolonial vignettes]), a novel that in its very title repeats the gesture of interchanging all Arab boys for one another.[57] Cardon, who has been a guest of Frédéric Mitterrand's on Pink TV, entitled one chapter of the book "Mohamed (bis)," the use of *bis* indicating a "second time" or a "second boy" and thus reinforcing anonymity.[58] Cardon concludes the three-page chapter with: "I would like to be rich to conserve my boys, so that they'd never again tell me, when they have to leave, that they have to go to work."[59] "*Boys*," which appears in English in the text, is an expression that formerly carried manservant associations in the French colonies, as illustrated in Cameroonian writer Ferdinand Oyono's novel *Houseboy*.[60] In *Incomparable*, Camus had confused not "Arab tricks" but rather Moroccan writers with one another, mistaking Tali for Rachid O. at first: "I also remember that I had envisioned that he was Rachid O. . . . of whom I had seen only one photograph, quite impressive, in the *Nouvel Observateur*, two or three years ago. But he, not without some emphasis, like someone irked that one would compare his beauty with that of any other, denies all resemblance with Rachid O., whom he says he knows well and who he says belongs to an entirely other physical, or even ethnic type. Nevertheless they are compatriots, both are Moroccan."[61] Camus brushes off Tali's dismay at being taken for another gay Moroccan writer as an overreaction that has more to do with Tali's own vanity than racism.

Joseph Boone has documented how the presence of such gestures produces an effacing anonymity of Arab boys in the highbrow gay travel literature of Joe Orton, among many other writers.[62] Boone's analysis of Orton in the following passage is worth citing in full as it pinpoints the symbolic and affective violence—which can also be found in Barthes, Cardon, and Mitterrand—of ridiculing Arab boys and their romantic or professional ambitions as intellectual voids. It also connects the dots that indicate a persistent interest in adolescents:

> A corollary of the occidental tourist's fantasy that all boys are available for the right price is the assumption that they represent interchangeable versions of the same commodity: (nearly) under-age sex. The number of identically named Mohammeds that Orton meets thus becomes a running joke in his diary ("His name, inevitably, was Mohammed"), and to keep his schedule of assignations from becoming hopelessly muddled, Orton assigns the boys farcical surnames: Mohammed (I), Mohammed Yellow-jersey, Mohammed Goldtooth. What may be humorous in the abstract is of course dehumanizing in reality, for such type-casting only reinforces the boys' anonymity and dispensability. Tellingly, Orton not only turns against the one Mohammed who attempts to assert his individuality—proudly declaring to Joe and company that he is off to Gibraltar to make a life for himself, with a legitimate job—but also belittles this ambition as bourgeois careerism and then claims, to top it off, that Mohammed is a bad lay. Not coincidentally, it is also this Mohammed who has asserted his subjectivity by complaining to Orton, "You give me money, yes—but me want *l'amour*. Me like you. Me want *l'amour*." *L'amour*, of course, is the one item missing from the vacation cruise package Orton has signed up for.[63]

Just as in Boone's anglophone context, it seems that the French writers profiled here ridicule their Arab (sexual) partners when they try to be taken seriously outside a purely physical sense. What this group of authors shares with the "forefathers" of literary gay tourism, is a common agreement about an irresistible yet exasperated attraction to "dim-witted" Arab boys. This results in pronouncements about the "difficulty," that is, brittleness or one-dimensionality of such boys, who seem propped up as cultural vacuums unreceptive to their "poignant," aesthetic appeals. Barthes and later Cardon complain that they can't find a suitable Arab boy with whom to talk literature. Boone and others have pointed out that in privileging sexual discovery and liberation above all else, such writers have turned blind eyes to the power differentials of class and race, the very factors that may have produced the educational discrepancies lamented by Barthes and others, as well as the writers' blindness to forms of learnedness other than their own. Scholar Jonathan Dollimore, on the other hand, has sought to nuance the exploitative aspect of sex tourism, asking of the critic more appreciation for the homosexual's historic "engagement with difference" both cultural and racial.[64] Whether between the colony and the mainland, or between the *banlieue* and the *centre-ville*, these writers have implicitly constructed an incompatibility between an enlightened homosexual aesthetics of *belles lettres* and a brutish, ethnic, male bisexuality, which must remain essentially dumb if it is to be properly virile and attractive. To what extent their representations trap (Franco-) Arab men in postures of mute virility because of the very demand for that virility, has not been interrogated much in their literature.

Such connections between virility and education pervade contemporary media representations of banlieue and Arab youth in contemporary times: these accounts declare the disruptive, "hyperactive," and "hypersexual" boys in French classrooms to be beyond educational salvation, because, it is suggested, for these boys succeeding in school degrades their masculinity (see chapter 1). Hopes of salvation are sustained, however, for their female counterparts who, because of a belief that young women fare better academically, ultimately have the potential to escape a deadening, sexually informed ignorance.[65]

Camus's collaborator, Farid Tali, departs from these limitations on learnedness courtesy of his adventurous style, through which he experiments with form and abstraction and abandons the socially realist fiction often expected of first-time Franco-Arab novelists. Though Tali is, in terms of linguistic sophistication if not storytelling ability, more advanced than Taïa and O., he is still much less elaborate than Camus, his prose being both much more austere and shorter (his section consists of less than half the length of Camus's). Considered side by side, Camus seems to eclipse Tali in volume and presence, making Tali's literary entrance appear almost meek in its restraint. This is not the "split writing" among peers seen with Derrida and Anne Dufourmantelle in their meditation on guests and hosts in *De l'hospitalité*, with columns placed side by side. Reciprocity has often been a key concept in philosophical reflections on hospitality: would hospitality rest upon a presumed reciprocity, or upon selfless overtures that assume no reciprocity? By being so generous in his prose offerings, does Camus honor Tali or eclipse him? Conversely, by being so humble in his literary stature does Tali honor Camus or deny him? What seems apparent most of all in their collaboration—as occurs often in love stories about disproportional expectations and misunderstood intentions—is a communication gap. However, when considered against a heritage of collaborations between France and North Africa that toe the line between the literary and the sexual, Tali's stylistic reticence stands out for its unwillingness to perpetuate that heritage of cooperation.

Even though the collaboration appears to offer an opportunity for Tali to demonstrate literary skill and gain notice, the contrast in verbosity between himself and Camus reinforces the stereotype of relative intellectual dullness. Taken by itself, Tali's contribution might have been evaluated on its own merits; compared to Camus, however, the text appears almost as a timid withdrawal. Camus, like Barthes, takes near-sarcastic tones in *Incomparable* when his Franco-Moroccan interlocutor takes an interest in the formal questions of literature and asks for advice from an established author: Camus suggests that his protégé's requests for literary guidance are misguided because Tali is already late to the game. With some insecurity, Tali recounts being taken aback by the offer to publish journals in parallel, and mentions his feelings of being predetermined to muster a lesser offering:

> First I thought he was being ironic. But he was serious. He said, since I was already writing a journal, it would be a good idea. Maybe. But spontaneously, in my identificatory rage [*rage identificatoire*], I told myself I could not write as much as him, that it couldn't be as interesting, that he is well-versed in that technique, uninhibited due to his years of practice, as opposed to myself. . . . I thought he would clarify [literature] for me, offer for my discovery the already traced path toward the literature to come. . . . That was my obsession, thinking that I could bypass the need for experience and avoid years of work.[66]

One incident, touched upon by both authors in *Incomparable*, is especially revealing, as it offers two radically different interpretations of the same event, a dinner party with the artist Flatters (a nickname for Jean-Paul Marcheschi). That evening Tali committed a striking breach of etiquette—according to Camus's reproach—guilty of disrespecting the food and being difficult during conversation. The latter circulated around the topics of whether soccer player Zinedine Zidane is a *harki* (traitor),[67] and how Moroccan compatriot Rachid O. is a "graceful" writer. Tali, on the other hand, detected a hint of the politically objectionable, as well as condescension, in the speech of Camus's dinner party guests (what's next, Tali, wonders, will we call Rachid O. "pure," or "authentic"?).[68] "We spoke of Zidane, of Monaco royalty and very rarely of literature," Tali remembers, "and here I was thinking that intellectuals spent all their time talking about it."[69]

Tali and his generation of Franco-Arab gay writers are acutely aware of the heritage of European and Arab homosexual encounters, embodied by

Burroughs, Gide, Wilde, Barthes, Orton, and Bowles.[70] When the dynamics of these encounters resurfaces in postcolonial relations between European and Franco-Arab men, it can create both nostalgia and resentment, depending on the party. In their writings in the 1960s and 1970s, which was inspired by their life stories, Mohammed Choukri and Mohammed Mrabet turned a critical eye toward the (sexual) tourists they worked for or had relationships of interest with in Morocco. Some postcolonial literature penned by gay European authors reveals a hyperawareness of the politicized stakes of such encounters, as evident in stories of self-declared "revenge fucking," which is sometimes happily encouraged by the European party. This becomes an at times sincere and at times mock therapeutic exercise that voluntarily delivers the suddenly national, "pristine" European body to the injured colonial party for a subversive penetration, as the radical gay activist and artistic group Front Homosexuel d'Action Révolutionnaire (FHAR) demonstrated in their manifesto: "We are more than 343 sluts. We've been fucked by Arabs. We're proud of it and we'll do it again. Sign and circulate this petition."[71] Cardon, the author of *Le grand écart ou tous les garçons s'appellent Ali*, was a founding member of the group.

The site of these encounters between North Africans and Europeans was in the process of shifting, as early as the sixties and seventies, to the European mainland and its metropolises. The sheltering distance between North Africa and France grew narrower, and could no longer permit the temporary, affectively careless sexual contacts that characterized the sex tourism exchange. In France, (Franco)-Arab partners could not so easily be abandoned and forgotten behind impermeable borders, sexual relations could no longer remain inconsequential, without the possibility of a jilted party acting on resentment. At the same time, metropolitan gay writing on the subject of (French) Arabs could no longer issue uncontested statements about Arab sexuality, as more and more (French) Arabs gained access to this topic and used their own experience to challenge the claims by French writers, as Taïa's and Tali's "correctives" have indicated. These demands of reckoning and reciprocity have occurred at sites of postcolonial encounters between Arabs and whites. These sites include not only the public spaces, parks and cruising grounds of the city limits of Paris, but also the banlieue, where a certain gay consumer interested in the domestic-exotic has increasingly turned to a populace previously separated by economic segregation. In the banlieue, this consumer encounters a sexuality often described as "other": this is the *beuritude* Tali refers to in the citation that opened this chapter. The Internet facilitated these previously difficult encounters between banlieue and *centre-ville*, ensuring discreet contact via the clandestinity of personal ad sites and forums that require users to sign up. Such a change of circumstances has only recently been attested to in gay Franco-Arab autobiography, as in Ilmann Bel's *Un mauvais fils*, wherein the male sex worker and former porn star gives a short history of Arab-white cruising techniques and the changing technologies that facilitate it.[72]

Looking Hard

The trope of the difficult Arab boy is taken up by the Algerian-born Nina Bouraoui, an author who offers a fascinating meditation on how white male subjects can sometimes covet Arab masculinity. She is perhaps the only prominent female North African author to write in-depth about male homosexuality, depicting it, in one novel especially, from a lesbian perspective. Much scholarship that analyzes North African and *beur* literary works on homosexuality fails to acknowledge Bouraoui's contribution to the construction of Franco-Arab sexual dissidence. I am most interested in detailing her gender-bending explorations of French gay male subjectivity, in which Arab men play a key orienting role as both models of virility and unenlightened counter-models when it comes to homonormative sexual liberation. In *Avant les hommes*, Bouraoui echoes elements of Mitterrand, Cardon, and Barthes in the way she portrays Arab youth as confident, spontaneous, physically splendid pillars insensitive to the fragilities of their European interlocutors, an unbearable contrast that provides the continued spark for the narrative lament over fractured masculinity to proceed.[73] This is not without irony, because in the literature of the literary forefathers, such narrators assert their cultural superiority over Arab boys just as they state their victimhood at their hands. Bouraoui however departs from the familiar tone of oral testimony and storytelling often found in francophone novels on North Africa or immigration, as well as the sexual subgenre incarnated by Taïa and O., both in terms of literary experimentation, as her stream-of-consciousness style demonstrates, and in terms of the opacity of the text which attracts readers who seek narrative challenges rather than immediate literary gratification.[74] Bouraoui's more recent output seems less concerned with presenting nativist credentials for the sake of striking a tone of ethnic "authenticity," at least in comparison with her first offering, *La voyeuse interdite*—a tale centering on a Muslim Algerian woman's claustrophobia at being sequestered and her ensuing street voyeurism—which received accolades, including the Inter Book Prize in 1991.[75] Addressed later in her oeuvre, the issue of homosexuality and the question of reconciling cultural roots and sexual orientation seem much less vexing to her than, for example, Tali (who declared such a reconciliation impossible in the faux documentary *Tarik el Hob*).[76]

Her 2007 novel *Avant les hommes* marks a turning point in her writing as she forgoes her stream-of-consciousness style and mostly lesbian themes in favor of exploring a desire to match and duplicate Franco-Arab masculinity from a white male teenage perspective. Like Rachid O., she writes critically of the gay communitarian enclaves of the Marais neighborhood and other identity-affirming gathering points available to the LGBT population in Paris. This is explored in the nightlife diary *Poupée Bella*, which can be read as a scorecard of the breaches of etiquette that occur in Paris's nightlife scene: there, the "savage" laws of base natures routinely take precedence over the gentility of daytime life and commerce.[77] Her picture of savagery applies not just to the gay world with its discriminating door policies toward female patrons, but also to the lesbian milieu and its internecine cruelties. The novel depicts in stark colors the lesbian and gay divide, both spatially (in terms of nightclubs and bars) and interpersonally, as expressed in the female narrator's testy friendship with a gay male friend chided for his vanity, antifemininity, and carnivorous consumption of men. The theme of a sometimes misogynistic male homosexuality extends into *Avant les hommes*, where the teenage protagonist's resentment against his mother—often absent as a flight attendant—provides a "justification" for his later obsession with a Franco-Arab teenager who might replace this void. Bouraoui effects, like Taïa, certain postmodern shatterings of the gendered self which allow her to adopt an opposite-sex perspective in *Avant les hommes*, or label as autobiographical fiction a novel that takes a male perspective.[78] Such interrogation of the barriers between sexual perspectives makes her portrayals of virility much more charitable than those of most Franco-Arab novels under the LGBT/feminist rubric which refuse to explore or entertain the possibility of a useful or ethical virility. One such confusion of gay male and female perspectives is evident in the words of *Poupée Bella*'s female narrator: "I am searching, like the men search . . . in the women's milieu."[79]

The hybridity of perspective developed in that novel helps illuminate Bouraoui's own genealogy of sexuality in two of her novels. In the semi-autobiographical *Garçon manqué* (Tomboy), the female protagonist's childhood friendship with the effeminately beautiful character Amine provides the conditions for her own desire for women to emerge.[80] Bouraoui goes beyond the usual cultural treatments of Franco-Arab masculinity, seeking out the poetic and the nonnormative in a domain often avoided for its phallocentrism. She does this by detailing how Franco-Arab virility is sometimes taken as an orienting compass for non-Arab men with identity crises, and by underlining solidarities between men and women from a lesbian perspective. Though she describes the rationale behind sexual and ethnic communitarian tendencies (i.e., what draws people of the same ethnic background or sexual orientation together), she just as often has characters break out of the enclaves that seem to define them, illuminating the parallels that might exist between communities. This process is evident in *Avant les hommes*, whose teenage protagonist Jérémie hails from a broken home. His mother is a flight attendant prone to sexual promiscuity, and his father is a retiree living in a separate town near the sea. Strongly disassociating himself from his mother and becoming vaguely misogynistic as a result, Jérémie identifies instead with a boy at school, the Franco-Arab teenager Sami. Jérémie gravitates toward him as an archetype of a more potent and self-confident masculinity. Sami's ability to "keep it together" is perceived as an antidote to the broken home and shattered self from which the narrator's voice emerges.

The psychocorporeal integrity of North African men—and the envy that integrity engenders—harken back to themes explored by previous generations of French gay writers. Much in the same way that a sickly André Gide attempted, in his desire for convalescence, to "absorb" (or be dissolved into) the energetic fabric of North Africa by surrounding himself with vital young boys, Jérémie searches for a similar self-dissolution in Sami. He wishes to take a vacation from himself in a sense by confusing their identities to the greatest extent possible. The parallel is perhaps most evident in the following quote: "I want Sami, I want his saliva, I want his sweat, I want his sperm, I want my blood to circulate already, I want a man in me to know who I am."[81] The idea of learning to become a man through homosexual exposure to a mentor has many precedents in Greco-Roman, Arab, and Persian heritage to name only the most obvious.[82] The trope of self-dissolution also evokes another theoretical framework: that of literary "transnationalism" as defined by Françoise Lionnet, wherein the self-shattering of subjectivity helps the writer surpass outdated models of monolithic national and heroic narratives. In Sami, in contrast to Jérémie, one notices a kind of neotraditional resurgence of rigid masculinities that seem to have bypassed this European "crisis of masculinity." Sami belongs to a pattern increasingly apparent in literature set in urban France and written by white male authors: that of masculine competition and feelings of sexual inferiority in the face of ethnic virility. Anti-Islam shock artist and best-selling author Michel Houellebecq has often detailed the hatred for new Europeans that characterizes his middle-aged white protagonists. This hatred is born of a sense of inadequacy inversely proportional to their inflated sense of the other's virility, and especially what they perceive as its appeal to the women they themselves covet but cannot obtain: in this scenario, the ethnic competitor becomes a scapegoat for the white protagonist's initial lack of confidence and appeal to women.[83] These masculine figures of immigration in France, often found in teenage form, are alleged to have no interest in a postmodern exploration of vulnerability or the fissures within masculinity that might be mined for art's sake. Jérémie's quest for virile personal integrity is notable in light of its departure from the requirements of sexual modernity, defined by gender experimentation and the intentional shattering of rigid gender identities. Nacira Guénif-Souilamas explains how Franco-Arab men and especially youth came to represent the rigid masculinity that the rest of French society had supposedly surpassed (see the introduction). In her account, the figure of the Arab boy is cast in the role of foil to the male cultivation of effeminacy, despite a North African social heritage often mocked for that very effeminacy in French travel accounts.[84] It is precisely this stigmatized, macho counterexample that Bouraoui's Jérémie invests with a value and dynamism unappreciated by others. He feels that such a fundamental masculinity constitutes his missed birthright, something he may have been destined for but must recover after losing it in the first part of his life. Thus, in his desire to "return" to masculinity, Jérémie often iterates almost redundant assertions of self-identity: "With all men, I feel I am myself, I feel true, I feel myself exist too, even if it's with men who prefer women. It's like being inside a closed circle, I feel accepted." This solidified sense of personal identity is anchored in a homo-social sense of community and comes in contrast to the persona of his distant father, a "loner" who, according to Jérémie, exists "outside the circle of men."[85]

In *Avant les hommes*, Sami is taken as the blueprint of a confident masculinity "without complexes" (*décomplexé*) that Jérémie would like to embody himself. That masculinity constitutes both an ideal and a "lost" model—lost by his father, and a lost opportunity during his childhood: "I saw (Sami) as a double and then later as the boy I could have become if I had had another history/story [*histoire*]. He sometimes seemed to slip off my body as if my desire had fashioned him in my image."[86] It is revealing then that in the next sentence after Jérémie first declares he "wants Sami," he suddenly announces a desire "to call my father, to hear his voice and then to slumber in his silences like an animal in the countryside's tall grass."[87] Bouraoui paints Jérémie's mother's world as fragile, inconsistent, and disorienting, while Sami in contrast provides a solid bridge to Jérémie's father, if only from a distance. Though Bouraoui stops short of providing a psychological "genealogy" of Jérémie's homosexuality,

Jérémie's idealism in regard to Sami indicates a strong attraction for models of masculinity that have gone from the role of eroticized object to one of parental substitution. Sami becomes the erotic model according to which Jérémie evaluates all other men, seeing fragments of Sami in all the men he subsequently finds attractive, as with one of his mother's boyfriends, Alex: "When I walk near Alex, I can fantasize about his looks [*son image*], but I know that at the end of my dream Sami will appear, pointing his finger at me. . . . I feel like I'm stealing my mother's man, it's almost as good as imagining myself naked against Sami's body. I want to take revenge against her, I want to reclaim from her what was mine, what she led astray from me [*ce qu'elle a égaré de moi*]."[88] Bouraoui gives a sympathetic, albeit also pathologizing, explanation for Jérémie's attraction to Sami. She illustrates how Franco-Arab virility, often mocked as outdated and caricatural, does not appear "fake" to the fragile protagonist who finds in it a structuring comfort. A different reading might designate Jérémie's interest as an instance of "slumming it with the lower classes," as in the upper classes' patronizing interest in working-class or street cultures, an interest that actually serves to bring the upper classes even more distinction. Pierre Bourdieu describes this process in *Les héritiers*, while playwright Bernard-Marie Koltès gives literary illustrations of "class slumming" (discussed later in this chapter).[89] Jérémie, however, would seem to escape this designation of class tourism because he belongs to the same dreary suburban landscape as Sami and seems largely undifferentiated if not inferior to him in terms of class.

Jérémie cannot satiate his desire because Sami has clearly stated his preference for women, a "distraction" that proves frustrating for Jérémie. Thus Sami's masculinity cannot be transformed into a commodity for consumption—contrary to the "always available" and interchangeable Arab boys of yore—Sami's masculinity is always beyond Jérémie's reach, and thus appears to him as unique, ideal, and interchangeable with no other. Bouraoui's character exemplifies the literary evolution of the Arab boy figure I have traced, from servile to unavailable. Jérémie agonizes over Sami, famished for moments of attention and communication. Jérémie registers even the most insignificant instances of physical contact with an earth-shattering intensity. All while his Franco-Arab friend seems most concerned by teenage endeavors such as finding marijuana and bedding members of the opposite sex. Yet, even as Sami is constructed as a "solid" young man of elusive integrity, Bouraoui does not dignify him with a robust subjectivity, as his expressions are limited to the simple and adolescent while all soul-searching and inner torment is concentrated in Jérémie.

While Bouraoui gives a detailed account of the erotic genealogy that guides Jérémie toward Franco-Arab virility, it comes at the expense of the maternal and the effeminate. A negative reading might posit Jérémie's story as a cautionary tale that depicts what happens when estrangements between mother and son progress unchecked, venturing into the demonization of motherhood and femininity. Bouraoui's presentation of degraded filial relations between mother and son recalls certain philosophical manifestos on parenting.[90] One cannot ignore the parallels Bouraoui establishes between *Avant les hommes* and her novel *Poupée Bella*—in which she discusses male homosexuality as loosely narcissistic, childish, and misogynistic through the character of Julien—because a similar homosexual misogyny is explored through Jérémie. He can be likened to an allegorical figure of resentment against a banalized 1960s sexual liberation said to weigh negatively on motherhood and the parental unit. Jérémie's mother is described as an aging flight attendant still relying on her fading powers of seduction, distinctly unready for motherhood. Such associations recall more extreme portraits in Michel Houellebecq's work, for instance the sections of *Les particules élémentaires* that wax philosophical about how Western European society has lost its parental integrity as well as any remaining control over its disgruntled youth, an error that is rooted in the abandonment of rigor and the privileging of comfort and tolerance.[91] It is suggested that this lax upbringing drives Jérémie toward misogynistic homosexuality. Amidst the homosociality provided by Sami and others, he longs to find an orienting principle that evacuates the feminine, which is for him a source of discontent that he amalgamates with failure.

Sami plays a crucial role in getting Jérémie to reinscribe himself in male filiation with his father. Only toward the end of his adolescent rapport with Sami does Jérémie become conscious of his estrangement from his father, and feel the need to reconvene with him. When he finally does so, visiting his father's home near the sea, away from his urbanized wasteland, Jérémie meditates on the type of relationship he would like to have with his father: "I want to tell him that I'm his son, that I come from his blood and that makes him my father, but my mother's hand still retains me."[92] Thus a homosexual rapport (with Sami), even if only imaginary, renews traditional principles of filiation that have become outmoded in a sexually "enlightened" society wherein family relations are always resignified, and some alarmist authors suggest, weakened. As if to make a connection between single mothers and urban decay, Bouraoui writes, of Jérémie's final reunion with his father at sea, that "the waves against the rocks imitate the sound of the housing projects crumbling."[93]

Bouraoui has explored attractions toward pillars of masculinity in several novels. In *Avant les hommes*, Sami harbors teenage aspirations of sexual domination, telling Jérémie that he wants to "screw" as many girls as possible before getting married (exciting Jérémie but also making him "want to cry"); in Bouraoui's earlier novel *Poupée Bella*, the male protagonist Julien revels in a similar erotic of hardness that rejects the "feminine." The novel's female narrator—a nightlife companion and close friend to Julien—describes in trenchant terms the effect of Julien's sexual proclivities on their tender but tenuous relationship: "boys are sexual, girls sentimental. I hold myself to that line. . . . Julien likes thuggish boys [*garçons voyous*]. . . . I like girls older than me. . . . Julien has never fallen in love . . . in the bathroom, he says: I want to look mean."[94] Bouraoui later describes Julien shaving his head in order to resemble a prisoner in the sun.[95] In Bouraoui's *Avant les hommes*, a violent "look" or appearance becomes a point of aesthetic and also moral divisiveness. Bouraoui's female narrator describes the difficulties of chaperoning the thuggish Julien into lesbian space (in light of his sartorial decisions) as well as the barriers facing women in gay nightclubs described as hostile to female patrons. These obstacles threaten their increasingly fragile friendship, which is notable for its complementarity between sexual minorities often segregated in public space.

Bouraoui does not take the judgmental tone of most commentators on the subject of Franco-Arab virility. Her vignettes illustrate how virility remains desired and in demand despite outward condemnations. Opting for description instead of directives, she delegates final judgment to the reader, concentrating instead on fleshing out a virility complex that is as interesting as it is problematic. Next, I turn to authors who stake out a trenchant position in favor of virility's place in society.

The Rehabilitation of Ethnic Virility

Bernard-Marie Koltès—a prodigy playwright prematurely lost to AIDS in 1989—explored the sexual dynamics of ethnic relations in highly sophisticated and abstract ways. Koltès took it upon himself to document in literary form the cultural contribution of ethnic others to French society, culture, and language, as explained in his interviews. Deeming himself a perpetual traveler happily stricken with wanderlust, the xenophile Koltès always stated the importance of including characters and actors of color in his plays. When his directives were not followed, with white actors cast in black or brown roles, he often disassociated himself from the play productions.

Koltès sought to valorize an abstracted posture of ethnic virility no-where more prominently than in his play *Dans la solitude des champs de coton*, which he completed a few years before his death.[96] In contrast to the dismissal of popular masculinities and their potential to produce any lasting cultural contributions, Koltès takes up a counterposition. He casts a vaguely ethnic hustler type in the role of a street poet who speaks in a richly symbolic, surrealist dream vocabulary in *La nuit juste avant les forêts*.[97] In *Dans la solitude des champs de coton*, he has a character named "dealer" make a lengthy case for his offerings—sexual, narcotic, or platonic, one doesn't know—to the reluctant "client" character. In the lat-ter play, Koltès takes an anonymous after-hours encounter between two shady figures in a park and turns it into a literary and theoretical frame-work for evaluating many of the sexualized dynamics that flare up within postcolonial ethnic relations in France.

Koltès's narrative talent lies in staging dramatic encounters between ghosts of colonization past and actors of decolonization present. These encounters take place in a fluctuating in-between space wherein power dynamics are uncertain and contested, shifting in favor of the formerly colonized (as in *Dans la solitude des champs de coton*, *La nuit juste avant les forêts*, or the meltdown of a colonial family transplanted to France in *Le retour au désert*).[98]

Koltès occupies a central place in the works examined here, because he so often politicized issues of class, race, and colonial memory in pro-foundly sexual ways. *Le retour au désert* chronicles an epic reckoning be-tween brother and sister for the family fortune in a sleepy country town, against the backdrop of the Algerian *événements* (a euphemism for the "events" of the Algerian War of Independence). In that play, Koltès articu-lates colonial and *pied-noir* anxieties about the fate of the settler popula-tion in contemporary France through intrigues involving the war of the sexes, the mixing of races, and finally political arguments between parents and children. In *La nuit juste avant les forêts*, he depicts the suffering and gendered humiliation of an aging, immigrant hustler through the latter's plaintive monologues about how life in urban France has made him hard-up and desperate. These monologues are addressed to a mystery figure that becomes, in the play's staging, a stand-in for the French audience and French society in general. The protagonist accosts this unnamed man on the street and does not let him go until his story has been told, providing for the kind of public transport annoyance that the everyday citizen late for work strives to avoid. Koltès seems rather to take the principled posi-tion that such "inconveniences" should be part of a required confronta-tion with an ethnicized poverty, too often skipped when possible. Finally, in *Dans la solitude des champs de coton*, Koltès treats us to a breakdown in relations—explored through breaches of politeness and etiquette—between the ethnicized "dealer" character and the gentrified "client." The unlikely companions cross paths at night in what could be a park, a dark alley, or a cruising ground, with Koltès building a dramatic patchwork out of social impasses and extended hands left unshaken. In Koltès's philosophical dramatization, most social overtures for exchange originate with the ethnicized party only to be repelled by a materially comfortable mainstream. Such a frame counteracts media representations that portray immigrants and ethnic minorities as closed-in, communitarian, hostile, defensive, and unwilling to take assimilative steps.

Not only does Koltès break with established patterns of demonizing ethnic virilities, he also details an alternative history in interviews describing how immigrants have made France a better country. Granted, he aired these views in interviews that took place within a 1980s sociopolitical context, before the recent declarations of "the failure of multiculturalism," the banalization of the extreme right in European politics, and the worst economic crisis since the 1930s. He presents the demographic waves of West and North African immigrants as fortunate arrivals saving a stale or aging society from itself. Thus, as with Jean Genet, the alliance with ethnic virility often takes the form of an eroticized solidarity, disclosed in Koltès's quotes detailing the perceived magnificence of black and brown peoples. In *Une part de ma vie*, a collection of interviews, Koltès speaks of his admiration for immigration's aesthetic impact on the host society's language: "I find language beautiful when it is handled by foreigners."[99] In saying so, he strikes an opposition with Renaud Camus who states that the greatest threat to the French language, besides Anglicization, is its mistreatment by the youth generation, especially those of immigrant descent.

Koltès has not shied away from an uncensored, even vulgar commentary on race relations in France, freely employing the racial designation "white" in a way that departs from the still pervasive caution among French intellectuals around this term. He has gone so far as to evaluate and compare races, as in one of his most celebrated plays, *Combats de nègres et de chiens*, the story of a fading French industrial installation located somewhere undisclosed in sub-Saharan Africa, of which he said: "I've made an emotional and at the same time radical choice by calling blacks 'good' and whites 'dogs' . . . but once the choice was made, I was able to begin to like whites."[100] Thus, a stark vocabulary—literally black and white—functions as a therapeutic airing of grievances, an initial shout that evacuates resentment and allows for reconciliation, marking the strange transition from tragedy to comedy. Koltès once said that his only self-imposed writing requirement, no matter the play's genre, was to make people laugh. In contrast to writers who strike a more pessimistic and reproachful tone on the possibility of racial harmony in France, Koltès does not exclusively demonize his white characters. While not letting them off the hook for their privilege and colonial legacy, he invests them with eccentricities and vulnerabilities that ultimately humanize them. Commenting on *Le retour au désert* and his frame of mind while writing it, Koltès said, "I understood very quickly that foreigners are Frenchmen's 'new blood,'" and that were it not for immigration, France would be transformed into a "nightmare, something like Switzerland, total sterility on the artistic as well as every other plane."[101] While insisting that he did not "despise" the provinces of France—the deep countryside—calling it the site of popular memory and also that which prevents the world from exploding—Koltès also claimed that: "Deep France . . . is a desert . . . a place where nothing thrives and, if something at all were to happen, it would be because of immigrants. If we speak of Marseille, we won't be talking about the whites. . . . The presence of immigrants is what keeps us at an intellectual level that is more or less proper."[102] Such positive verdicts on the worth of immigration to Marseille come in contrast to countless tabloid headlines that have disparagingly dubbed the ancient and historically diverse port city of Marseille as a lost "Arab city."

Koltès places his examination of interracial relations within a larger French meditation on hospitality. In *Dans la solitude des champs de coton* and *La nuit juste avant les forêts*, Koltès details the almost chic draw of risky hospitality. Risk is inherent when, in order to be polite, a host refrains from asking the intrusive questions that might reassure him or her in offering hospitality ("How long are you staying? Who are you? Will you steal from me?"). In Koltès, as well as other works examined in this chapter, reticence about hospitality is shown to be unfounded, concealing opportunities for the kind of cross-class, cross-cultural contact and reckoning that can be auspicious for social harmony. As we have seen in French gay postcolonial literature, literary revenge for "crimes of hospitality" can take the form of switching the figures of the victim and the oppressor, as when the practitioners of literary sex tourism are made to suffer by immigrants from the visited countries. It can also take a sly, rhetorical form, when it consists of the inconvenience of being forced to listen to forms of speech one could have previously ignored. Koltès perfected the rhetorical device of subjecting audiences to a monologue that "no one wants to hear," of inconveniencing them with (immigrant) speech that solicits attention in public spaces. A subsequent generation of

gay Franco-Arab authors produced similar scenes in which captive audiences cannot but listen to the demands of previously servile Arab lovers.
Instead of the failed cross-cultural communication found in the gay literary tourism of old, and more recently in Camus and Tali's *Incomparable*,
what occurs in Koltès is forced communication and forced listening. Not
only does Koltès's Arab hustler in *La nuit juste avant les forêts* accost the
reader/bystander in the first lines of the play, he also pulls the latter inside his own complexes about being a minority in France. In this way,
Koltès envelops the audience in the hustler's subjectivity by creating an
atmosphere of claustrophobic intimacy. The hustler, as he tells the story,
is down on his luck, defeated from all sides, not only by a hostile urban
climate but also by his own "cousins" on the metro: young, good-looking
kids of North African descent whom he initially wanted to resemble and
approach, but who rejected him as a loser and relic of an outmoded generation, before proceeding to steal his wallet and harangue him with an
assortment of homophobic epithets. Here, the protagonist speaks to the
accosted mystery man, who doubles as the audience, about the trauma:

> Don't take me for a queer . . . just because I am holding your arm. . . .
> I will tell you about a girl on a bridge, do you think a queer would
> have the guts to? . . . I can't really manage to say what I should say to
> you, it has to be somewhere else with nobody around, no question
> of money anymore. . . . [I was looking] at the well turned-out yobs
> who keep fit . . . maybe we could grab a beer together. Yobs so well
> turned-out that I always want to run after them to say to one or the
> other: give me your clothes, your shoes, your hair, your walk and
> your face without changing a thing. . . . (They steal my wallet. Then
> they said) we'll throw this queer off at the next station and smash his
> face in. . . . No one reacts, no one believes about the cash, everyone
> believes about the queer.[103]

Here the desperation of immigrant life in the metropolis provokes the
hustler's incessant solicitation. His situation becomes more desperate
when the pleas of a distraught immigrant are confused for solicitation of
the homosexual or prostitutional kind: this collapse of different kinds of
solicitation rejoins one of this book's main arguments, that sexual and immigrant clandestinities are connected and similarly vulnerable to exposure.[104] In *Les féministes et le garçon arabe*, Nacira Guénif-Souilamas tells
the story of how metropolitan and factory life managed to partly stamp
out North African affective customs, such as one man amicably clutching
another's arm, for fear of being suspected of homosexuality.[105] In *La nuit
juste avant les forêts* the *complexé* (someone ailing from psychological

complexes) finds no solidarity in his *décomplexés* compatriots—the "cousins" whom he sees on the metro and wants to imitate, to absorb their slick
good looks, body language, and absence of overthinking, much in the
same way Jérémie admired Sami in Bouraoui's *Avant les hommes*.

Koltès often uses the opportunity of serendipitous contact to force a
therapeutic conversation that would otherwise not occur. In *Dans la solitude des champs de coton*, he initiates such therapy by setting the drama
against the backdrop of a banal nocturnal exchange—as common as asking a stranger for a cigarette or directions. In this way, the Dealer presents a counter-portrait to the overly solicitous and sometimes sexually
aggressive Franco-Arab man described by Mitterrand, Cardon, and Barthes. Here the Dealer reminds the Client that he intends kindness but
must be respected in return: because he both poses a threat (due to his
stated physical advantage) and makes a conscious choice not to exploit
his superiority:

> DEALER: I could release my self-control and have all the violence of
> an Arab horse . . . the condition that I be humble and you arrogant
> is dusk, the hour when correctness is no longer obligatory and thus
> becomes indispensable. . . . I would have been able to fall upon you
> like a cloth on a candle flame . . . this correctness that I've offered
> you, indispensable, but for free, does bind you to me, if only because
> I would have been able, just out of pride, to loot you . . . because I
> know that the first difference between us is size.[106]

If the protagonist of *La nuit juste avant les forêts* represented the desperate side of solicitation, the Dealer represents its self-confident side. Koltès
produces a dynamic of productive ambivalence between the Dealer and
Client in which the Dealer's presence can shift from threatening to chivalrous; the ambivalence surfaces because Koltès avoids explicitness as a
point of style. Thus the Dealer who accosts the Client is invested with a
genteel politeness founded precisely on renouncing the overly explicit,
which is especially important in practices like flirting or negotiation. This
allows the Dealer to use, without getting caught, the gray area between
sexual and platonic solicitation, a crucial tool for those trying to find
out whether a rapport between men can pass from banter to eroticism,
from homosocial to homosexual. The Dealer's nonavowal of intention,
his subtle hinting and roundabout overtures, all characterize the ongoing
portrait of the ethnic other in Koltès. The playwright employs soft vocabularies to circle around desire in a clandestine way, sketching a courteous
etiquette, whose codes posit that the too explicit avowal of desire spells
the end of it. Such minimal language, reveling in what is left out, touches

upon the eroticization of the clandestine, that is, the unspoken and the secret. This code, attached to the Dealer, comes in contrast to the Client's impatient exhortations in *Dans la solitude des champs de coton* to just get to the point already. The Client refuses outright a familiarity that might signify getting close enough to bargain a personal exchange. In response to the Dealer's first overtures, he announces: "the immediate want I have is to see you drop the humility and keep the arrogance . . . if I do have some weakness for arrogance, I loathe humility."[107] This attitude parallels that of authors Camus and Barthes, who seemed to diminish ethnic virility just as they admitted a helpless attraction to it, all while cutting short the attempts of ethnic partners to assert their subjectivities in humanizing ways.

The scenes Koltès stages of interethnic contact in public space are especially notable because, at the moment Koltès was writing, segregation as a result of urban planning concealed the demographic significance of immigration to France more than it does today. While in many ways important aspects of the immigrant presence continue to remain concealed, demographic changes have increased the urban visibility of ethnic minorities in undeniable ways. Koltès was writing at a time when the banlieues were especially cut off from the city center. With the aid of an impatient Koltès, that population surfaces in public spaces and demands human relations. The hustler in *La nuit juste avant les forêts* stands in as an allegory for social blight, the casualty of an economy in which immigrants are interchangeable. In the following passage he demands recognition, an exit from anonymity, resisting the precipitous spiral by which each failed overture, each failed job search, renders new overtures more desperate and less likely to be acknowledged. "I dream the secret song of the Arabs, comrades," the hustler says, "I find you and I pull your arm, I want a room so much. . . . I love you. . . . I've looked for someone who would be like an angel in the middle of this shit hole, and you are there, and I love you."[108] As the hustler's overtures and pleas increase in pitch, so do his chances of rejection. The hustler's bitterness seems to stem from the notion that such overtures were routine, and routinely reciprocated in his community of origin. His old love of humanity becomes desperately confused with his need for shelter, and in this way his love becomes suspicious, even sexually suspect, like the sugar offered to sugar daddies. Economic necessity thus compromises a sacred cornerstone of Arab hospitality, poisoning the possibility of exchange.

In Koltès, the breakdown of hospitality is triggered by a harsh urban setting in which injuries are masculinist. Tahar Ben Jelloun explained with regard to the psychiatric case studies in *The Highest of Solitudes* that the male immigrant—when unable to provide for his family for lack of work, when mocked by men younger and stronger than he, when having to ask for help—suffers a deterioration of his masculinity, the integrity of which is sustained on being self-sufficient (a point echoed by renowned sociologist of immigration Abdelmalek Sayad).[109] This emasculation is reified by the hustler's pleas for a caretaker, a gentleman provider coming to meet a male prostitute. This portrait of the hustler closely resembles the sociological portraits of immigrant male prostitutes developed by sociologist Malika Amaouche who range from runaway youth to recent immigrants and include cultural illustrations that can be found in films such as *Wild Side*, *Un fils*, and *Miss Mona*, and the documentary *Welcome Europa*.[110]

Further exploring the issue of solicitation and its ambiguity, *La nuit juste avant les forêts* constantly tests the line that separates homosociality from homosexuality. The "hustler's" *blédard* ("fresh off the boat") mannerisms, which involve free-flowing displays of affection, are ridiculed by a younger generation of Franco-Arabs, portrayed as homophobic. These children of immigrants have no place in their social etiquette for traces of *blédard* behavior that could be mistaken for homosexuality. Thus the old Orientalist tendency of always confusing homosociality for homosexuality is transferred with sad irony to the younger generation, incarnated by the "hustler's" tormentors. These Franco-Arab boys would now represent the flag bearers of the same sexism that used to be directed against their fathers when they first arrived in France. Guénif-Souilamas speaks of this transfer of homophobia, as she attempts to make sense of young Franco-Arabs' rejection of parental mannerisms and the failure of inheritance on the level of affective mores.[111] She proposes that some have internalized shame in regards to their fathers' "ambiguous" homoaffective practices like holding hands and more facile physical contact.[112] These young men resemble, in their distaste for too much male familiarity, the metro tormentors of Koltès's hustler in *La nuit juste avant les forêts*. The idea that homosociality and homosexuality are the same thing is a judgment enabled by contemporary social and economic conditions, in particular, by the encounter between North African immigrants and European observers in urban settings, such as cafés and workplaces. This perception can occur in factory life, as described by Guénif-Souilamas, or in Koltès's literary reflections via the aspersion that an especially friendly and affectionate man is a homosexual man, an aspersion that can lead to depressed reflection and bitterness in the "hustler" character.

However, Koltès departs from this gloomy verdict on social overtures and the survival of male homoaffectivity, as he describes what seem to be French rejections of immigrant or ethnic male solicitation that actually do not reject it entirely. In *Dans la solitude des champs de coton*, Koltès describes how something as ordinarily unwanted as an overeager pick-up line can sometimes be in demand, regardless of barriers of class, race, and even sexual orientation. Koltès illustrates this point through the abstract nocturnal encounter between the enthusiastic Dealer and initially reluctant Client. Their meeting takes place in a minimally defined, semiconcealed space of what looks like the seedy corner of a park, where actives and passives of different sorts linger in search for a narcotic or sexual fix. Koltès said the plot could very well be a story about "fags" just as much as it could be an encounter between a "punk" and "a bluesman," or a face-off between a cat and a dog.[113] Intensely symbolic of both sexual and class-driven hierarchies of power, the play illustrates how bartering and deal-making play a central role as the Client and Dealer argue over who needs whom more and why. The Dealer character seems to thrive in a clandestine environment of privacy and nonjudgment, pushing the Client to try the risky and racy exchanges he has been avoiding. The Client seems uncomfortable in his shared environment, but nevertheless stays fixed in place. He remains drawn to the Dealer by an ineffable force, never turning his back and going on his way. The Client ostensibly wants to preserve the conventions of social hostility that oppose the Dealer to himself. He actually appreciates the barriers of what may be class and race that segregate the two characters: they offer an antisocial comfort. Consequently, the Client resists the Dealer's attempts to breach the gap in familiarity. The Dealer claims a superior physical expertise and stature, reading the "truth" of the client's desire through the latter's shifty body language. The Dealer pushes the Client to admit to his own desire, and the possibility that the Dealer might be able to satisfy it. This has the effect of disgusting the Client, who hates the idea of his desire being visible. The tone of bitterness and intransigence Koltès lends the elitist Client, which contrasts with the flowing speech of the suave yet maligned Dealer, shows the author's lack of sympathy for those who would refuse to engage in conversation with a stranger. If the play is indeed a "story about fags" and the cotton fields of the play's title represent a gay cruising space such as a park or forest, these would be strange places to not "be looking for something," as the Client repeatedly insists. Read in another way, Koltès can be said to critique the upper-class attitude of minding one's own business and repelling the solicitations of the talkative poor, who nevertheless read into the frigid faces of the isolated elite an obvious but unacknowledged desire for sociality.

Mireille Rosello, in *Postcolonial Hospitality*, examines this war of attrition between partners who refuse to acknowledge their need for one another, at a theoretical level. In a meditation on what hospitality might mean in postcolonial circumstances, she states that "the very precondition of hospitality may require that, in some ways, both the host and guest accept . . . the uncomfortable and sometimes painful possibility of being changed by the other."[114] In this light, the interaction between the Dealer and Client can be seen as a failure of hospitality, not just on the side of the Client who refuses overtures, but also in the posture of the Dealer who aims to escape social isolation unsuccessfully.[115] In Koltès, the breakdown of hospitality affects everyone: resident, immigrant, man, woman, giver, receiver, and even different generations of immigrants who squabble with each other. This is a departure from the representations of men of immigrant origin examined in media discourse (see chapter 1), in that such men cannot so easily be defined by a rigid and invulnerable masculinity that avoids being tied down in sentiment and human relationships: they too would suffer from stifled desires for hospitality.

Quite consistently, Koltès blames an elitist gay antisociality for the breakdowns of hospitality he dramatizes. The Client's initial hostility toward the Dealer evokes Leo Bersani's concept of gay antisociality outlined in *Homos*. This antisociality was incarnated, Bersani writes, in figures like Jean Genet who illustrated how queer desire could position itself against imperatives for community or solidarity. This is of course applicable to the early Genet, not so much the politically and internationally active later Genet, who formed solidarities with Palestinians and the Black Panthers. Bersani writes that "we may want to cultivate the anti-communitarian impulses inherent in homo-ness . . . to look at the dangers of our exhilaration in being a community."[116] In Koltès, an ethnicized homosociality—with its "easy" contact between men—is refused by the radically individualist Client, who embodies a type of *queer* antisociality. Koltès, in interviews, acknowledged that sexual dissidence could foster antisociality: "There is a form of rootlessness that belongs to homosexuality."[117] Yet Koltès also allowed for entrenched positions to be broken, by indicating what happens when substantive discussions between willing and unwilling partners are forced, when each party can no longer hold onto the stereotype they have of the other. Thus, the Dealer allows himself to be searched for weapons, rhetorical or sexual, and the Client's defenses are worn down as he starts to reveal his fear but also his desire for serendipitous human contact.

These ambivalent desires bring up the notion of class tourism, explored throughout Koltès's work, a process by which one can eroticize or aestheticize that which one finds repulsive on other levels. One wonders if the Client is curious about a socially exotic area, because his presence in what seems like the Dealer's territory is unexplained. The Client admits he has "come here for a reason," but evades disclosing it, save for one revelatory analogy found at the end of the following exchange, in which the Client shifts from disgust to need and back again:

> DEALER: If you believe I've got violent designs upon you . . . don't jump to conclusions about the kind of violence. . . . My dream was that I would know snow and ice, know the cold which is your pain. . . . It is easier to catch a man passing by than it is a chicken in a backyard. . . . If I might say so without giving offense, I hoped, in covering your shoulders with my jacket, to make you seem more familiar to me. Too much strangeness can make me shy. . . .
> CLIENT: What do you hope to get from me? Every move I think will be a blow ends up as a caress; it's very unnerving to be caressed when one expects to be hit. . . . I've not come here for gentleness; gentleness works bit by bit, cuts up piece by piece . . . at least malice will keep me in one piece. So come on, get angry: or where will I draw my strength from? . . . What if I could not help approaching you? . . . by the same sort of attraction as draws princes to slum it in taverns.[118]

The Client explains how his fear of the Dealer and his expectation of violence allows him to stay "in one piece"; in other words, stereotypes of aggression attributed to ethnic men allow the observer to derive a sense of personal integrity and superiority in counterpoint to this portrait. This process, through which the other's imagined roughness helps anchor the observer's cultural advantage, is a common thread connecting Mitterrand with Barthes. The integrity of personhood and intellect are reinforced by an opposition to the other's brute physicality: this was visible, for instance, in the Mitterrand sauna anecdote wherein he had set higher standards for himself ("there are certain things I won't do, anymore") after a sexual encounter with a Moroccan man described as angry and violent. In the play, Koltès introduces what can be termed an "erotics of poverty" when the client admits to touristic desire, acknowledging that he might have succumbed to the draw of "slumming it in taverns."[119]

Atonement for Cross-Cultural Injury

Whereas Koltès opts for abstraction, playwright Jean-Marie Besset offers a more explicit portrayal of hospitality conflicts involving male Arab guests. His work, which has often been adapted for the screen, gives a sophisticated account of the class and racial tensions that politicize the proverbial French bedroom. In his plays, Besset explores the client-like desire to resort to class tourism for sexual satisfaction. Characters with elite backgrounds briefly engage with minorities from across the class divide, only to sweep their desire under the rug when peers from the same class cohort approach. In *Les Grecs*, Besset profiles Alain, a sarcastic and misanthropic gay literary type—the epitome of Bersani's antisocial homosexual—who has had too much to drink at his friends Henri and Lena's dinner party. He lectures his friends condescendingly about their bourgeois insularity and the empty rebellion of their faux bohemianism, only to have his working-class lover Osman show up at their door in search of his absentee boyfriend: Osman then proceeds to give his own lecture about class, which proves embarrassing for Alain. When the Arab interloper enthusiastically shares that he and Alain live together, it prompts the husband Henri to conclude that Osman is Alain's man. Alain reacts explosively by rejecting the aspersion not of homosexuality but of hospitality, a greater affront to his class sensibilities. "You don't live with me, you live at my house," he tells Osman, adding that he doesn't "have a man," because he is "not married," thus rejecting the cohabitation Osman speaks warmly of.

Besset's play is notable for the way it modifies understandings of the "closet" in regard to race and class in France. His depiction of Osman contrasts sharply with preexisting stereotypes of Arab bisexual secrecy. While Osman is not reticent about speaking publicly of his homosexual union, Alain feels shame about the disclosure of his ethnic rather than sexual preferences, and the implication that he might be a sugar daddy. When revealed to be in a relationship with a Franco-Arab man from "the other side of the tracks," Alain experiences this as an unbearable assault on the self-critical bourgeois persona he has carved out for himself, a persona that would ruthlessly criticize any gesture that might come across as class tourism. Besset shows how class shame flips the script on the tropes of clandestinity and reticence to speak about sexuality that one usually finds associated with Franco-Arab characters in this literature: Alain is the one who leads a double life. Osman hints to hetero Henri that he knows Alain's "real nature"—hospitable and couple oriented—and that his antisocial harshness is merely a masquerade designed to impress his bourgeois peers. This turns out to be true when the alcohol wears off and Alain accepts that Osman take him home, when his friends are out of earshot. Besset mocks Alain's antisociality as being just as bourgeois as everything he criticizes, his posture critiqued instead for its misanthropic individualism.

Xavier Gallais (Alain) and Salim Kechiouche (Osman) face off in Jean-Marie Besset's play *Les Grecs* as a cynical intellectual and his secret Arab lover.

Besset's play *Grande école* (later adapted to the screen[120]) presents the Franco-Arab character Mécir, as an object of class tourism. Incidentally, the same actor plays both Mécir and Osman (Salim Kechiouche), a veteran of gay roles and former French kickboxing champion. Mécir is far from naïve, fully aware of the power dynamics involved in cross-class relationships, which he contracts anyway. The white protagonist Paul, an incoming student at an idyllic business school, enters a phase of sexual experimentation, and in this way beds Mécir, whose mother worked as a janitor at the same school: she eventually died after a life of back-breaking work. In the following dialogue we pick up on the strong influence of Koltès, through the development of several themes: the erotics of poverty, class resentment, the sparring around conflicting desires, even the figures of the Dealer and Client:

MÉCIR: She [my mother] would get up early in the morning, to do the floors, the toilets, vacuum the carpets, clean the tables and the chairs. She would wipe each chair, she said. It hurt her kidneys.
PAUL: There are several women I think.
MÉCIR: Several women breaking their backs so that all of you can put your butts on chairs that are always clean.
PAUL: At least you'll have had your revenge. [*A beat.*]
MÉCIR: You like that, do you?

PAUL: I don't know. . . . As it's my first time.
MÉCIR: Oh really? It didn't seem that way . . .
PAUL: Well . . . It must mean that I like it. And you? . . . Do you like it?
MÉCIR: Me? . . . That's not the question.
PAUL: No?
MÉCIR: Well, no. [A beat.]
PAUL: I recommend you leave, if you want.
[Mean smile from Mécir, who exits.]
MÉCIR: I'm out of here, don't worry. I'm out.[121]

This passage provides the first mention of Mécir and Paul's homosexuality in the play. The scene is notable for how homosexual desire operates in it: for Paul homosexuality acts as a bridge that makes possible cross-class and cross-ethnic contact in a way that might eventually erase such barriers, whereas for Mécir the bridge provides a rare opportunity to address and reckon with class and ethnic injuries that have always been swept under the rug in the heterosexist world.[122] With the cinematic adaptation, which departs significantly from the play in terms of its optimism, Paul's class tourism graduates to full-fledged political solidarity. Instead of exemplifying his class by bedding and disposing of working-class lovers, Paul commits an act of defiance against his bourgeois peers and against the cycle of class reproduction at the grandes écoles, France's elite group of colleges. In the play, Paul's progressive political solidarities do not extend to his romantic life, while in the film adaptation they do, at least until the final scenes. In the play, Mécir's initial callousness is justified by the exclusivity and insularity of the elite that rejects him: here, Besset seems more interested in detailing a cross-class injury than spelling out a cure. In the film version, Paul heroically intervenes when Mécir, who works as a painter at the school, finds himself the object of a racist barrage of insults because of an unintentional worksite blunder. Paul "comes out" as the only bystander speaking up in the name of antiracist values while his school colleagues look on passively. Thus Paul wins the esteem of Mécir, who intends to thank him, it turns out, by inviting him out for a date.

Paul's class anxieties are activated by sexual contact with Mécir. These anxieties are more deeply explored in the film adaptation: a recurring flashback shows Paul's developer father shouting at his young son for socializing with the Arab and black workers at one of the family's construction sites. Film director Robert Salis intersperses these flashbacks within Paul's cathartic love scene with Mécir, suggesting the paving over of a childhood trauma, and perhaps more controversially, atonement for being complicit with racism. Rather than falling into sexual warfare, Paul and Mécir's relationship turns into a reciprocal love story, culminating in a tender sex scene set at a romantic retreat near the ocean, a more natural and minimal space that seems absent of class resentments and cultural hang-ups.[123] Instead of the play's difficult delinquent who wants to touch and steal everything in Paul's room, we have in actor Kechiouche's Mécir an upstanding man with manners, a financially solvent owner of a car and credit card, commendable for his solid working-class ethic. He is eventually abandoned, with much pathos, by the experiment-minded Paul, whose eye has wandered toward the winning example of aristocratic masculinity incarnated by his colleague Louis-Arnault, a sort of Polo alpha male, whose lifestyle and body language both repel and attract Paul.

Arab characters, both in Besset's plays and their film adaptations, cause sudden reflection about various privileges: interactions with Arab characters often mark the first time that white protagonists have had their own class positionings revealed to them, sometimes aggressively. In the following scene from the film adaptation of *Grande école*, Paul and Mécir are out on their first date, at a Paris restaurant animated by the musicians of a *soirée orientale* (Arabic-themed party or club night). Mécir delivers the following with a beaming smile that indicates his reproachful remarks come partly in jest:

> MÉCIR: Should I have sent out an invite? That's done in your milieu, right?
> PAUL: What would you know?
> MÉCIR: What I can see. You all seem so sure of yourselves and at the same time so uptight. "Well-dressed, but just as soon out of style" [*bien sapés, déjà démodés*]. Arrogant and proud. Outside of reality. As a result, how can we be surprised the world is headed in the wrong direction?
> PAUL: Oh really?
> MÉCIR: If it's people like you pulling the strings. Insensitive and unscrupulous.
> PAUL: You're speaking without knowing, based on appearances. You're schematizing everything.
> MÉCIR: But I'm not talking about you. You're not like them. Albeit, at the beginning. . . . When you defended me, let's just say I was pleasantly shocked. That's the whole story!
> PAUL: It reminded me of my father and his mania for barking at people.

At this point, Mécir gets up to dance in front of Paul, as if to express his joy at their understanding. Director Salis provides an opportunity for the bourgeois Paul to redeem himself by righting the wrong when presented with a racist incident. In much the same way, Abdellah Taïa provided his French protagonist with a window of moral opportunity, giving the tourist René a chance to react to his Moroccan lover's socioeconomic lament in *Le rouge du tarbouche*. Most importantly, Salis grants possibilities to mixed-race and mixed-class relationships, by allowing the once isolated Mécir to be won over by overtures that attempt to reverse the course of injustice.

In *Les Grecs*, Besset revisits a similar triangulation of desire between social classes. A pivotal scene in *Les Grecs* occurs with Osman's unannounced arrival at the dinner party: as Alain's secret working-class lover, his discovery by Lena and Henri provokes much interest. The dinner party turns a dramatic corner when Alain, who openly tells Osman that he has always wanted to bed Henri, finally gets the green light. As in *Grande école*, the white gay protagonist's desire for an upper-class heterosexual eclipses his former desire for a working-class (and importantly, available) Arab bisexual, with much drama around the injury this entails. In the following excerpt, Osman speaks to Lena of the unflattering way Alain described her, her husband, and their social status, as if to take revenge for Alain's intended infidelity. He is uniquely positioned as a secret lover at the clandestine juncture of Alain's public and private worlds, and thus he can disclose information that causes the collapse of Alain's public reputation:

> OSMAN: [*Speaking to Lena.*] I know you, you leave messages on the machine sometimes . . . and [*looking at Alain*] I'm not allowed to answer. Tonight, he told me: I'm going to have dinner at a female friend's. You don't know her. They are not your kind of people [*c'est pas des gens pour toi*], you'll get bored. [*Alain nods his head vigorously. And then he said, while leaving*] With some luck, I'll bed her husband [*je vais me taper son mari*].
> LENA: He told you that?
> OSMAN: Just as I'm telling you now. [*Alain sighs and covers face.*] I found the address, I made an itinerary, the street, the RER [train], I spied, I jumped the fence, I was circling the house, I heard your voices, then a female voice, well, your voice, and then nothing. You had gone to sleep and them two, they were going to screw like dogs.

The scene delves into the awkwardness of two social circles intersecting where they shouldn't, a breach of social segregation that is made possible by the gay character's class tourism. Alain's social and affective hostility—he snaps his fingers at Osman, tells him that he will fuck other men, finds it shameful that they are living together and tries to deny it—surfaces when clandestine relations are aired publicly, and most importantly, when visible to the bourgeois heterosexual couple. Husband and wife in turn criticize Alain's impoliteness, his behavior finding censure for the first time because of the serendipitous way Osman has exposed the infidelity. Osman's arrival on the scene causes the breakdown of polite façades and sets a kind of sexual anarchy in motion: as Alain attempts to bed Henri, Lena invites Osman to bed, taking advantage of her husband and friend's infidelity to commit her own, almost as a form of justice. With this breakdown, Besset indicates the unsustainability of a "schizophrenic," classist, homosexual double life—one that allows for certain moral indiscretions in a clandestine mode—by orchestrating an embarrassing breach in the neat separation of worlds which serves as a lesson. This scene can initially be read as a critique of homosexual clandestinity itself. But within a field of representations where clandestinity is most often associated with immigrant classes, it is the French bourgeois who leads the truly duplicitous life, not the Franco-Arab Osman. The scene more implicitly stresses that those, like Alain, for whom outness is possible can also seek clandestinity, that is, outness might not just be about cultural readiness for sexual liberation but also conditioned on social status (which explains, for instance, the widespread closetedness of the well-to-do in France, underlined by Fouad Zeraoui in chapter 1). Alain stays closeted not out of sexual shame but rather class shame, as he may be seen by his peers to incarnate a bourgeois class tourism he elsewhere criticizes.

Besset cleverly uses the variable of Arab bisexuality to unsettle the stability of both bourgeois heterosexuality and homosexuality:[124] this comes due to the perception that Arab sexuality rejects the homo-hetero binary (as discussed in the introduction). Osman's Arab bisexuality is coded as common knowledge in Lena's mind:

> LENA: You also like women, right?
> OSMAN: Of course, I'm a man, after all.
> LENA: Fuck me. Fuck me in front of these two faggots.

Here, Lena and Osman form an alliance against the metrosexual husband and the urbane gay man. They point out, with pejorative violence, the masculine and arguably white privilege that encourages clandestine homosexuality behind the wife's back and out of reach of the working-class Arab. Lena and Osman then make a spectacle of their heterosexuality, which in contrast does not need clandestine cover in order to express itself. This dialogue establishes a contrast between the duplicitous and

Osman's bisexuality, suggested as a trait common to all Arab men, makes the flimsy walls of bourgeois monogamy fall down.

elitist sexuality of the city center, and the free-form bisexuality of the encounter with those on the periphery. It is notable that Lena chooses to belittle the masculinity of the men who have used their homosocial discretion to arrange for homosexual infidelity, comparing them unfavorably to the bisexual Osman as if to hit them where it hurts. At the same time, however, the zing of Lena's gesture depends on the idea that sleeping with a working class Franco-Arab man would constitute the ultimate breach of her class conventions, a willing sacrifice of her body as rebellion against social hypocrisy. In this way, Lena's intentional "sullying" resembles that of the FHAR activists who said they had been fucked by Arab men (always tops and always bisexual) and would do it again, as a form of social protest against the social conventions which hold that such actions are unfathomable.

Summary

The literary figure of the Arab boy alternatively inspires desire, admiration, and resentment. This figure has transitioned from being a servile accessory to white sexual fulfilment in colonial and sex tourism contexts, to being an object of frustration when he asserts himself in France postcolonially by thwarting his white admirers through denials of bodily access or sexual reciprocity. This dynamic translates the crisis of hospitality that has affected French social relations overall, in the age of immigration.

Readers bear witness to a succession of injuries and hostilities: the exploitation (sexual and otherwise) of North African boys in a colonial time frame, the postcolonial "revenge" exacted against privileged men in the metropole, and finally, the imposed sentence of cultural ignorance on North African boys thought to be trapped in a macho envelope. What seems to some observers like ignorance and nonengagement can be read in other contexts as a strategy of silent self-protection.

Not all French contemporary writers abide by this storyline, which can only end terribly for all involved. Taïa gives his white tourist protagonist the capacity for ethical reflection and raises the issues of privilege and economic disparities within the sex tourism exchange, issues so often brushed aside in gay hedonist fiction. Bouraoui explains how Arab masculinities may provide models to imitate, rather than countermodels from which enlightened gay men need to distinguish themselves. Koltès and Besset firmly take the side of the underprivileged in their dramatizations of conflicts between the bourgeoisie and the ethnic masculinities they covet, consume, and discard. These four authors, each in their own way, answer the literary demand for the disclosure of ethnic sexuality, but take advantage of the opportunity to offer moralizing lessons about social etiquette, or the lack thereof, in relationships that cross barriers of class and race. Koltès and Besset especially have found ways of sensitively depicting the clandestine spaces ethnic homosexualities occupy. In the next chapter, I explain how cinema conveys the clandestine sexual subcultures of minorities and immigrants, a process sometimes complicated by the medium's determination to visually expose.

4 / Sexual Undergrounds: Cinema, Performance, and Ethnic Surveillance

That's your life, Mehdi. A shitty little life with a recipe for success, but where does that lead you? Will you fuck everyone? You don't respect anything. You married Sarah because she comes from a moneyed family. You sleep with men but you spit on gays. . . . You're a predator, Mehdi, a little vengeful man who wants to consume everything.

ADRIEN IN ANDRÉ TECHINE'S *LES TÉMOINS*

This chapter focuses on filmic depictions of Franco-Arab and *banlieusard* sexualities. Against the backdrop of an overwhelming vilification of Arab, immigrant, and *banlieusard* masculinities on-screen, I show how a selection of innovative films have sought to rehabilitate that masculinity as well as demonstrate its unexpected importance, if not necessity, in French society.[1] Far from being possessive, ethnocentric sexists jealously guarding their community borders, Arab men are shown to stand at the center of social constellations that include sexual minorities and a high degree of sexual experimentation. Through films directed by Jacques Audiard (*Un prophète*) and Jean-François Richet (*Ma 6-T va crack-er*), we gain an understanding of the way conventions of virility hold together various homosocial orders by bringing together groups such as the police, delinquents, soldiers, criminals, and prisoners. In *Les témoins*, director André Téchiné meditates on these dynamics through the depiction of a singular character: a Franco-Arab policeman who polices sexuality just as he explores it. In Sébastien Lifshitz's films (*Wild Side, Les corps ouverts*), we come to understand the interconnectedness and mutual attractions between the sexual and ethnic minorities who have historically been the objects of political, cultural, and police scrutiny.[2] Recurrent throughout this chapter are the commonalities between the French policing of both ethnic and sexual "outlaws," which can take symbolic or literal form or come from unexpected perspectives. In this way, the policed sexualities of minority characters become socially delinquent, shifting in and out of a "French-ness" confused with orderly, bourgeois sexuality. In connection with my argument about the rehabilitation of ethnic virilities and homosocialities on-screen, I show how the concept of the urban sexual underground (populated by a variety of sexual minorities including sex workers and transsexuals) has crucially hosted Arab masculinities and offered them spaces to nurture and bear witness to their own social utility.

Exposing the Clandestine, Intimately

Arguably more "private" than film in terms of its audience and impact, the literature of immigrant sexuality has created a semiprivate space for the secret, the intimate, and the clandestine, a space where authors feel more comfortable sharing anecdotes about intimacy than they perhaps would on-screen. Cinematic explorations have been much less sensitive to the possibility that clandestine sexuality may be irrevocably impacted by overexposure, that it may be changed in its very nature once visually expressed: one has only to measure the impact of reportages depicting gay cruising areas to grasp the initial disappearance of those areas. Most French films that describe the private lives of French minorities expose the sexual activities of *banlieusard* or immigrant populations in a tell-all documentary mode. These films do not shy away from performing a sexual ethnography of the *banlieue*. The visual, however, does not necessarily need to exist in opposition to the clandestine, as demonstrated by the exceptional offerings of directors André Téchiné, Jacques Audiard, and Sébastien Lifshitz, all of whom have found subtle ways of representing the public-private distinction on screen. This distinction can at times take on a political character when directors suggest that ethnicity and culture may determine one's obsession with keeping a private life private, with Arab or Muslim minorities especially interested in controlling disclosure, whether heterosexual or homosexual. Characters of (North) African descent have often been portrayed as hypocritically saying (and doing) one thing in private and another in public in regard to sexuality. This simplified portrayal often comes at the expense of interrogating the very notion of sexual disclosure and the idea that exhaustive disclosure has become imperative in the era of sexual modernity. Though the word *clandestinité* is usually employed in a context of immigration, here it branches from that usage to describe sexual practices and sometimes identities that insist on remaining unspoken, even taking pleasure in silence and noninformation. The representation of *sexualité clandestine* in film—a medium that has the capacity to speak in images, through dialogue, or a combination of both—prompts us to interrogate how one might speak the unspoken, how one signifies by withholding, and how this slow-release game feeds into another structurally similar game, that of generating eroticism. A further question always emerges when the subject is a sexual discourse that is antithetical to publicity: where exactly is clandestine sexuality spoken, in what kinds of spaces? When contemporary sexual enlightenment calls for hypervisibility in the city center, the decision to avoid disclosure often causes directors to turn to the peripheries: the banlieues and the transitional districts of Paris populated by a diverse cross-section of ethnic and sexual minorities. Ironically, a cultural medium such as cinema that operates at the level of visual exposure can sensitively explore the way minorities and immigrants navigate the invisible and the underground.

Homosexualization and Acceptance

The films surveyed in this chapter deal with all of the hot-button scandals concerning immigration, diversity, and sexuality that have seized the French media, from sexual violence to homophobia to polygamy. In many cases they have not just reflected but also contributed to debates and controversies. One of the most recurrent targets of vilification has been Franco-Arab and *banlieusard* virility, deemed sexist, violent, and out of touch with contemporary French understandings of gender relations. Within the representations of that virility on-screen, many directors have resorted to a peculiar process of homosexualization in order to critique that virility: for example, some directors indicate the various ways in which macho immigrant men, far from being pillars of heterosexuality, are somewhat homosexual in their preference for exclusive male company, whether in gangs or cafés. While this has been a feature of films that demonize such virilities, homosexualization has also occurred in avant-garde, gay auteur cinema that seeks to rehabilitate the image of such men. The veteran trans journalist Hélène Hazera once joked that an Arab actor in French film has a 99 percent chance of his first (breakout) role being a gay one.[3] This casting of gayness, I argue, is an element of a cinematic ritual that permits the introduction of cultural difference on-screen, a way of attenuating expressions of ethnic affirmation seen as overly emphatic. The casting of gayness reflects, in some instances, a backlash against a "macho Arab virility" that is perceived to be hurtful, with ethnic machismo depicted as foreign, regressive, and intrusive. This generates representations in which Arab protagonists are invariably shown to suffer on their own from a kind of solitary punishment on-screen. This occurs most often through confusion about their bisexual feelings, paranoia about their private lives being revealed, schizophrenic attitudes in regard to being homophobic or homophile, and a general inability to reconcile their sexuality with their cultural origins.

More interestingly, in certain films the casting of gayness occurs not through the imposition of Western sexual identities on Arabs who may resist them, but rather through the eroticization of cross-cultural or interethnic contact. In films ranging from Richet's *Ma 6-T va crack-er* to Robert Salis's *Grande école*,[4] otherwise "straight" white male protagonists dally in homosexuality only under certain circumstances—when they are faced with Arab men. The accompanying table provides a more concrete overview of the place of gay roles in Franco-Arab male actors' careers; it lists the most prominent Franco-Arab actors in French show-business and identifies whether they have played homosexuals, bisexuals, or trans characters, and whether these parts were played in the early stages of their careers (a plus sign indicates that the actors have played additional roles whose homosexual character was ambiguous or merely suggested). Not included in this table is Jamel Debbouze, who did not have film roles, but produced the one-man show of a gay Arab stand-up comedian and is portrayed on the cover of the December 2011 issue of *Têtu* magazine and in its cover story on gay-friendliness.[5]

Prominent Franco-Arab Actors and Their Roles

Name	Roles as Homosexuals	Stage in Career
Malik Zidi	2+ homosexual roles	early in career
Yasmine Belmadi	2+ homosexual roles	early in career
Sami Bouajila	3+ homosexual roles	early in career
Abdellatif Kechiche	1 homosexual role	early in career
Salim Kechiouche	4+ homosexual roles	early in career
Jalil Lespert	1+ homosexual roles	early in career
Smaïn	1 homosexual role	middle of career
Roschdy Zem	1 homosexual role	middle of career

In this selection of popular actors, eight have taken up LGBT roles, five multiple times, and six early in their careers. Add Tahar Rahim as prospective fellatio giver in *Un prophète*, Dany Boon (born Daniel Hamidou to an Algerian father and French mother) as a gay nightclub owner in *Pédale dure*,[6] the often homoeroticized Nicolas Cazalé (with Algerian ancestry on his grandmother's side) in *Three Dancing Slaves*, and finally the trans and homosexual roles played by Gad El Maleh (of Moroccan Jewish heritage) in his one-man show later adapted to the screen as *Chouchou*, and the number of Franco-Arab actors who have played LGBT roles increases to twelve.[7] Auteur directors who often visit sexual themes—including André Téchiné, François Ozon, and Gaël Morel—have repeatedly cast Franco-Arab actors in LGBT roles.[8]

Rehabilitating Virility

In contemporary France, a group of critically respected filmmakers have broken with the general condemnation of Franco-Arab virility by offering alternative interpretations, which valorize that which once appeared threatening. They also question the depiction of virility as a regressive trait no longer necessary in society in the age of sexual enlightenment. In their attempts to recuperate ethnic virility, these directors interrogate stereotypes while simultaneously indicating that "atypical" castings of Franco-Arabs as artists, writers, or homosexuals should not be seen as such.

One director who performs this operation time and time again is André Téchiné. In *Les témoins* (2007; *The Witnesses*), Téchiné casts the Franco-Arab Sami Bouajila as Mehdi, a character that challenges the stereotype that French Arabs hate the police.[9] Téchiné invests Mehdi with many traits that dispel media assumptions about Franco-Arabs—Mehdi idolizes police work and reveres the military—to the degree that Mehdi seems to embody, at first glance, an ideal countertype rather than a character on a human scale. He plays an agent of Paris's *brigade des moeurs*, a sort of morality police in charge of combating prostitution and public "indecency." A newly minted father, he is married to the blond, moneyed, Jewish children's novelist Sarah (played by Emmanuelle Béart), whose father often takes Mehdi out on ritzy excursions at the local aviation club. Téchiné goes to great lengths to show that Mehdi's deference to his wife and accommodation of responsibilities relating to their baby actually stem from his virility—portrayed as a sense of chivalrous responsibility. Whereas Sarah distinctly lacks mothering instincts, which is "ironic" in light of her profession, Mehdi fills the void of unperformed diaper-changes and formula preparation, berating her all the while to care more about her offspring. He also accepts his wife's proposition of an open marriage without any real trace of jealousy. Outwardly, he shows few signs of machismo, other than perhaps his choice of profession.

While this singular character outwardly embodies a conservative masculinity of law and order, at home and in private Mehdi breaks with gender conventions. He seems to take up an androgynous role in relation to his somewhat absentee wife. Téchiné, however, manages to visually explain how what might be considered in Mehdi a form of effeminacy amounts instead to the unacknowledged underside of his specific culture of virility. Such a hybrid virility shows up in positively connoted values such as prioritizing the family and rule-based homosocial systems (like the police). Mehdi's upstanding character at first contrasts with the image of the macho Franco-Arab delinquent resisting assimilation—at polar opposites from the mature policeman: it represents, however, but another side of Franco-Arab masculinity as evidenced throughout this book. On the one hand, Mehdi's policing of public mores expresses a controlling virility; on the other hand, his surveillance of his wife's caretaking arises out of worry for their child. The lack of jealousy in regards to his wife expresses not a neutered virility but rather a confident heterosexuality, in which Sarah's trust and disarming beauty bring him to accept whatever open arrangement she requests.

This hybrid character stems from the fact that Mehdi, a policeman after all, exists on the pivot of the public-private distinction: virility appears one way on the "outside" (during work hours) but carries an alternative meaning on the "inside" (at home with his wife or in private during extramarital affairs). The distinction also applies to his police work: Mehdi's aggressive methods of regulating sexual delinquency (prostitution, cruising) only apply to violations that occur in public; acts in the private sphere never face the same scrutiny. The fact that the burden of proof for prosecuting a morality crime remains very high and requires, as the film's title suggests, witnesses, subtly evokes Islamic laws regarding prosecutions of proscribed sexuality, which must display a degree of public flagrancy to warrant punishment. This comes in addition to Mehdi's stubborn unwillingness to investigate the private realm, to let pass what doesn't disturb the public peace, an attitude stereotypically associated with Islamic forms of governance.

This motif—of depicting ethnic virility by inverting expectations about it—appears in yet another film by Téchiné, La fille du RER (2009; The Girl on the Train),[10] which he adapted from Jean-Marie Besset's play RER (see chapter 3). The film's plot is based upon a scandalous news story: in July 2004, a young Marie-Léonie Leblanc was reported to have been attacked, partially undressed, and marked with a swastika at knifepoint by a gang of boys of black and Arab descent. The allegedly anti-Semitic act was later exposed as fabricated: however, the corrections and apologies, often buried in the back pages of newspapers, made less of a public impact than the blaring headlines in the early days of the story.[11] The images of the delinquent youth were readily consumed by the media, ready to believe the "believable." These images contrast sharply with the film's lone representation of a North African man: after the protagonist has put her plan into effect, a soft-spoken Samaritan, also waiting for an RER train, approaches her, seeking to assist the visibly distressed young woman. He asks about the self-inflicted cuts on her face and asks whether she might require medical assistance; she remains silent, conflicted, unable to make eye contact with him. To follow the code-switching logic outlined earlier, such gentlemanly inquiry as to an unknown woman's state is itself the flip side of a commonplace motif, which has it that single women at train stations are constantly harassed by gangs of young Arab and black men. In *La fille du RER*, solicitation of the opposite sex is not condemned but rather transformed into an element of chivalrous virility.

Jacques Audiard's award-winning *Un prophète* (2009; *A Prophet*), written by Abdel Raouf Zifri, rehabilitates ethnic and especially Islamic cultures of male homosociality. This coming-of-age tale is set in a prison, a place that outwardly seems to foster survival-of-the-fittest attitudes, but which reveals itself to be a laboratory for moral instruction between men. The protagonist Malik (Tahar Rahim), a young and uneducated delinquent, arrives in prison as a naive newcomer and must quickly learn the ropes: in the first half of the film Corsican prisoners exploit him while in the second half he makes inroads with the Muslim inmates, educates himself, and aims to turn the tables on his oppressors. The storyline of *Un prophète* puts pressure on a dominant grid of representations according to which Muslims are socially reclusive outsiders and Franco-Arab youth are more often than not criminally inclined. These views reify Muslim difference by stressing and stigmatizing what are assumed to be deep-seated criminal virilities and homophobia: *Un prophète* significantly tests these preconceived ideas by detailing homosocial systems of emotional support and also revealing a subcultural economy of homosexual "favors."

The film describes the way in which the "homophobic" environment of the French prison system—in which Muslim men as well as regional minorities (Corsicans) are overrepresented—morphs into a world strongly structured by homoaffective, and occasionally homosexual allegiances. Reyeb (Hichem Yacoubi), an incarcerated drug kingpin of North African background incarnates the homosexual side of prison. He seems well-respected and connected in the prison community, and his purported sexual preferences (if not his sexual identity) are indicated only by his occasional search for a fellatio partner. Instead of feeding into the stereotype of the imprisoned and isolated effeminate type who invariably becomes *l'homo de service* (the token gay), Audiard and Zifri portray the kingpin as a pillar of the prison community who maintains powerful connections to outside gangsters. Reyeb has enough sway with the prison guards to ornately decorate his cell and receive personal visits, possibly sexual, from other inmates (and, most crucially, from the protagonist). A panoply of visual codifications including tweezed eyebrows, blonde highlights, and taste in fine literature cast him as a character who might seem effete, but who also constitutes an educated leader type threatening enough to alarm a competing faction in the prison, the Corsicans, who put a hit out on him.

Un prophète fleshes out the subtle principles organizing the homosocial and homosexual prison order and more importantly assesses their value to advancement within and outside the prison. This value is ironically heightened when director Audiard very brusquely kills it off in one of the film's initial scenes. Malik, an unseasoned, aimless young man as yet unprepared for the harshness and politicking of prison life, falls into the trap set up by César, an incarcerated Corsican crime boss (Niels Arestrup). César pulls the strings of both the prison guards and criminals on the outside: he coerces Malik into working for him as an *arabe de service* (a token Arab), cleaning up after him, serving him food, by presenting him with an ultimatum: either you kill Reyeb the adversary and competing drug-lord, or you yourself will be killed. This state of affairs plunges Malik into distress: his fear eventually overshadows any bond he might have sustained with other inmates from the Arab community, in a prison system where allegiances are heavily determined by ethnic and religious background.[12] Corsicans appear to lack a sense of homoaffective solidarity (incarnated by the Muslim inmates) that eventually proves their undoing.

Prisons are unique settings in that they allow for the thin line between homosociality and homosexuality to be explored. As discussed in the introduction, Orientalists had historically blurred this line when it came to Muslims, establishing neat equivalencies between sex segregation and same sex love. In discourses surrounding French prisons whose population, according to sociological studies, are overwhelmingly Muslim, this heritage has a special resonance.[13] Malik has access to the Franco-Arab homosexual target, because, in a previous scene taking place in the showers, Reyeb revealed his desire for him. The seduction attempt is at first unsuccessful: Reyeb solicits sexual services from Malik, who reacts with shock and anger in his refusal. Unfazed, during the same conversation Reyeb proposes that Malik request cell block B with the other *cousins* (Muslims) and offers hashish in exchange for sexual favors. Malik remembers this exchange when devising a plan to kill Reyeb, and agrees to perform fellatio on the target in order to gain access to his cell. At their next meeting in the showers, Reyeb asks Malik to step back, turn around, and remove his hands from his crotch area so Reyeb can examine his genitalia, introducing the notion that Reyeb's is not merely a substitutive prison homosexuality. For his part, Malik feels threatened at the core of his sexuality by what he has been asked to do: in a subsequent scene, he flips through a hetero porn magazine with what seems like frustration. With tension building, he beats up a fellow inmate in the prison sewing shop so as to let off steam; another interpretation has it that he does so to be punished and placed in solitary confinement with the aim of escaping his mission. This plan fails, however, and Malik has no choice but to prepare for the moment of truth.

The relationship between these men recalls centuries-old precedents in both Greco-Roman and Islamic cultures wherein homosociality, philosophical education, and sexual education are often blurred; the French prison circumstances, however, derail this classical proximity between teacher and student. Reyeb receives Malik's clandestine visit with effusive hospitality; the encounter is framed as a warm, brotherly, inter-Arab house call, rather than an explicit exchange of sex for money or favors. Malik, whose thoughts are elsewhere, cannot contribute to the warm tenor of their conversation, unresponsive to the man's overtures of hospitality and a mentoring relationship that would have plausibly gained him as many advantages as his tenuous alliance with César. Reyeb offers Malik beverages, shows him books, speaks of religion, and stresses the importance of reading and education, in a way that instills the sense that this man, despite his criminal background, is a relative force for "good," a possible provider of sanctuary, and an intergenerational educator in the classical sense, standing apart from the overall harshness that reigns in the prison. Importantly, this generosity is depicted as originating in both his homosexuality and his sense of Arab hospitality—both acting as homosocial connectors—in a way that remains ambiguous about their possibly overlapping nature. Such questions are suspended, for a time, with Reyeb's brutal murder by concealed razorblade.

Extending upon this overlap, the *arabe de service* (embodied by Malik) here encounters a situation in which he becomes the *homo de service*, participating in the homosexual service economy instrumental to power hierarchies in the prison system. The circumstances themselves seemed designed to illuminate a parallel between types of servitude. There are additional layers of meaning to these two expressions however: *homo de service* also includes the idea of "the homosexual who serves others in all senses of the word": I emphasize this meaning over the more figurative and accepted use of the term, in order to show the parallel between the expressions *arabe de service* and *homo de service* in the context of the prison. *Arabe de service* can mean the token Arab, but also the sycophantic employee who serves his bosses or masters in any way they wish, and in this sense has a service role to play. In the prison context, the main character Malik is both an *arabe de service* and in some ways a *homo de service*, in the sense that both figures occupy a servile position in the prison hierarchy as fresh recruits. Malik is used as a pion by the Corsicans who have blackmailed him under threat of death into cooking for them and cleaning up after them. Though he does not actively practice homosexuality on-screen, Malik does manage to gain access to a target the Corsicans have asked him to assassinate by agreeing to perform sexual favors for a high value Arab inmate, a form of access assured by Arab homosocial networks that here contain homosexual possibilities.

What is notable in a media landscape that portrays French Muslims of color as most homophobic in society, is that Malik finds a kind of queer emancipation with Islamic homosocial networks, with Islamic instruction from a decidedly queer mentor. Yet at this early point in the film, the nascent bond between Muslim prisoners meets a premature end with Reyeb's assassination, a "brown-on-brown" crime engineered by a rival Corsican brotherhood invested with a stereotypical racism against Arabs. This crime crucially occurs before Reyeb could transfer this sexualized Islamic instruction to Malik. The Corsicans seem happy to witness the internal collapse of a competing order just as two Franco-Arab inmates seemed to be building an alliance. One gains the impression that Malik grasped much too late the possibilities of collaboration and complicity with Reyeb, losing out on opportunities for social promotion; a situation he miraculously rectifies later in the film. After this initial trauma, Malik adjusts course and spends the rest of his screen time trying to atone for a bad and spiritually haunting decision made under duress. He takes advantage of his situation as a Corsican "slave" to better subvert his masters, finally destroying them from within just as they had him tear at the fabric of internecine Arab solidarity.[14] Such a gesture has echoes in the realm of queer theory, with ostensibly weak or stereotypical positions inhabited intentionally, in order to better profit from the situation by turning a defensive position into an offensive one, using one's sexuality along the way. The relevance for *Un prophète* concerns the way that one can sincerely occupy a role that ostensibly contradicts other actions and identities integral to the self, all while deriving cultural and even material capital in one's ambition to fulfill that role: this happens in *Un prophète* when the protagonist, who has a delinquent past, commits violence and treachery in order to finally join a Muslim prison group that renounces violence and treachery, when he agrees to Arab servility while plotting his future domination over the Corsicans. The hero's servitude turns out to be only surface level because, in a play on the master-slave relationship, the young Malik goes from being a blank slate to learning the mechanisms of the mafia trade, absorbing their language (Italian) and mannerisms. In a *mise-en-abîme* or mirror-effect of method acting, Tahar Rahim's Malik gives a lesson in naive immersion through his character, whose survivalist talent consists in being able to improvise, mimic his superiors, and adapt to any situation. This queer ability magnifies his success in inverse proportion to how "dumb" or uninformed he initially makes himself appear, an impression the Corsicans have of him that proves fatal.

It is this malleability of character that also is formed into the shape of a Muslim conscience, via the later phantomatic apparitions of the murdered Reyeb. Like the angel Gabriel in the Qur'an, Reyeb exhorts Malik at night to "read!" ("Iqra!")—building up an escapist mysticism that will eventually help Malik "escape" prison in the film's reality.[15] Importantly, Malik is illiterate as well; after receiving encouragement from his guardian angel Reyeb, he begins literacy classes along with other incarcerated Muslims. The respective homosocialities of the incarcerated Corsicans and the Muslims clash once again when it comes to their differing moral codes. Audiard and Zifri's film adds to the politicized conversation about the dangers of minority virility in France, dramatized in the media, by asserting that not all virilities are equal. On the one hand, there is a first school of virility in which spectacular and memorable displays of violence constitute the common currency leading to the making and breaking of reputations, embodied by the Corsicans. A second school of virility, regimented and restrained by constant reference to Islamic principles, avoids drugs, dirty money, and needless violence: it appears here as an antidote to the unfocused virility of the first type, from which solidarity can rapidly disappear. The sinful, anything-goes crime world of the Corsicans stands in opposition to the defensive, minimal virility of Muslim brotherhoods.

That the secret agent (Reyeb) behind Malik's transition between the two worlds is coded as homosexually inclined, coupled with the fact the he is nevertheless integrated in the Muslim community, can all be taken as an argument against the notion that Franco-Arab masculinity unequivocally rejects homosexuality. Through the character of Reyeb, homosexuality appears as an intermediary glue permitting transitions and unusual contacts. His apparitions evoke something mystical, a permissive Sufi Islam (supported by his later apparition as a whirling dervish

Reyeb appears beyond the grave as a Sufi angel guiding his murderer, Malik, along the straight and narrow path in Jacques Audiard's prison epic *Un prophète* (2006; *A Prophet*).

For Malik, Islamic homosociality proves the eventual key to his survival in prison.

whose shoulders are on fire) where Reyeb's flamboyance and eccentricity find a home. In the end, his premature martyrdom magnifies his spiritual, haunting character. As discussed in chapter 3, homosocially and homosexually inclined figures fuse worlds thought to be discrete or segregated according to moral codes, progressively moving beyond what seem like intractable antinomies.

The Sexualization of Authority

Like the incarcerated communities in *Un prophète*, the French police constitutes another school of virility in competition with others for dominance. The police as virility school is a theme explored especially in the films of Richet and, to a lesser extent, Téchiné. Like the prison's Islamic homosocial order, the police structure is shown to also commerce in homosexuality. The police-criminal dynamic that suffuses these films exposes forms of sexual policing that stem from these predominantly male, homosocial institutions. These directors also dramatize the relationship between (and contestations of) homosociality, homosexuality, and authority.

In *Les témoins*, Téchiné emphasizes that the surfacing of character Mehdi's homosexuality does not clash with the structure of his day-to-day life as a police officer; rather, police work provides the secretive conditions necessary for clandestine sexuality to thrive. This is evident in the film's depiction of the homosexual affair between Mehdi and Manu, a handsome recent arrival to Paris originally from a faraway mountainous province. In the voice-over narration, Mehdi's wife Sarah finds herself explaining—at each juncture where Mehdi and Manu find a moment to escape into a secretive intimacy—just how they have managed to assure the clandestine nature of their encounters. Such meetings seemingly always involve agreements between men; first via the flying club privileges handed down from Sarah's father to Mehdi and then to Manu; and then via an under-the-table arrangement between Mehdi's police division and a *centre de loisirs* (camping resort) hidden away in the countryside, where Mehdi has found a job and a mobile home for Manu that act as cover for their trysts.

It is due to the fact of the police being an order built on mostly male partnership that the sexual nature of bonds within it escapes scrutiny. Some of the central tenets of Mehdi's morality brigade are secrecy (raids kept undisclosed until the last minute) and irreproachability (it is difficult to scrutinize policemen, as many ordinary people wishing to contest their actions have found). The impermeable nature of the male order set in place by police structures becomes all too apparent when Manu's sister pays a surprise visit to see her brother at the vacation resort. While on her way to Manu's cabin, another policeman intercedes and declares that Manu is busy, offering that she wait in the mixed-gender family area, far away from what is implied to be a homosexual tryst hidden behind a police barrier. We witness a privileging of the homosocial that speaks to the power and paradoxical "publicness" of an unapologetic clandestinity. The nature of Mehdi's relationship with Manu is public knowledge to a restricted group of policemen, but remains concealed behind a screen when it comes to the general public. Thus Téchiné shows that what at first seemed to be unrealistically novel—a Franco-Arab officer who polices homosexuals yet also engages in homosexual sex—is not a directorial indulgence but rather an extension of the character's virilist profession, part and parcel of Téchiné's meditation on fraternal orders in both heterosexual and homosexual space.

One of the defining films of banlieue cinema, Richet's *Ma 6-T va crack-er* (1997; My 'hood is about to blow), also explores the way sexual regulation and police behavior intersect.[16] Like *Les témoins*, Richet's film recounts at length the dangers of an impenetrable police order accountable to no one. The film also stresses the homosexual undercurrents of police work, propping up yet another "boys club," and explains in a somewhat sexist sense that these homosexual currents are indicative of its internal corruption. Furthermore, the film explores aspects of banlieue sexuality that contribute to the demonization of ethnic delinquents, detailing their romantic failings and often apocryphal stories of sexual conquest as a precursor to their frustrated violence. In one revealing scene, Richet mines the sexual component of conflicts with the police, a component magnified during interrogations, imprisonment, and ID checks. Richet's later film *De l'amour* crystallizes these dynamics by featuring the story of the rape of a female petty delinquent in police custody.[17]

The storyline of *Ma 6-T va crack-er* follows the goings-on of a Parisian suburb on the verge of a popular insurrection, focusing on various members of the community while they react to a fatal incident of police brutality. In the films battle scenes, the director develops an aesthetics of *banlieusard* homosocial solidarity almost universally male. Richet seeks out violent but righteous subjects, depicting their antics with a gleeful emphasis on the aesthetic side of their carnage, an aesthetics of delinquency so to speak. This dramatically recalls the work of Jean Genet—who nurtured a sexualized political solidarity with various guerrilla groups. For him, the beauty of fighters could not be divorced from the righteousness of their cause. Richet's film explores the aesthetics of protest, giving brief profiles of exuberant young men in the community of Meaux, a banlieue in the Seine-et-Marne region France, men so numerous that it becomes difficult to associate names with faces. We discover during the closing credits that nearly all actors played themselves or kept their first names. This powerful anonymity of collectivity culminates at the apex of the film into a general riot: all of the featured young actors (as well as many others showing up on-screen for the first time), faces hidden under hoodies, seem gloriously indistinguishable as if showing the cohesiveness of their resistance unit.

In contrast, the police force in Richet's films is consistently depicted as white, male, right-wing, perverse, and willing to use homosexuality as a weapon against Muslim subjects who are presumed to abhor it. In the film's opening sequence, infused with the soundtrack of combat rap, Richet presents a female allegorical heroine who incarnates values in perfect counterpoint to those of the police. The famed French actress Virginie Ledoyen stands in mother-of-the-revolution mode, positioned next to her mixed-race daughter, who is helping mom load a gun, against a backdrop of international images of insurrection. Richet inscribes the daughter in a filiation that will reproduce the mother's revolt. By juxtaposing images of general revolt with those of *métissage* (racial mixture and diversity), Richet sets the theme of banlieue unity through diversity: in contrast, the banlieue's perverse enemy is racially homogenous and coded as repressive of multiethnic heterosexual reproduction.

Policemen, however, do not have the monopoly on sexual repression in the film. In one of the film's first scenes, a female undercover cop approaches two loitering youth from behind and demands their papers. The two were not committing a crime at the moment of interrogation but one of the men turns out to be carrying a pistol, for protection he says, of which the cop is skeptical. This escalates the charges against the men, already too familiar to the police. Thus, on a calm night in Meaux, the police erupt into the banlieue community as if to claim it, prompting remarks from the young man about how the police feel perfectly at home in their neighborhood, easing into their occupation in a dual sense. The female cop punctures any pretense of the youths' virile territorialism by handcuffing the men and threatening: "This is no longer your 'hood, you're gonna walk on the other side of the sidewalk, OK?"[18] The arrested party happens to be black, his phallic pistol confiscated by a Caucasian female cop, who barks at him from behind while he is bent over and pressed against a car, in a scene that is heavily racialized and sexualized; the cop is depicted as enjoying the chance to flip the male's physical advantage via her officialized superiority.

Ma 6-T va crack-er reflects on the dearth of private and especially intimate spaces in the banlieues. The film relates this idea to the fact that residents have converted many public spaces in the banlieues into semi-private spaces where one pursues activities normally more intimate, because truly private venues are so often in short supply in these high-surveillance areas of vertical living. Thus, when public space becomes private space, police intrusions and arrests of "loitering" youth take on a new meaning—the word *loitering* becomes illogical when the young men's sense of "home" is extended to the street. "Here, I am in my own home [*chez moi*]," says a teenager sitting on the sidewalk, complaining of the police presence. In this vein, one scene features an unnamed character from the town of Garges-lès-Gonesses (played by rapper Stomy Bugsy) recounting the tale of a date that was going smoothly until cops interrupted the courtship, demanding papers. The complaint evokes a certain sexual deprivation, ever present as long as the police continually violate a right to intimacy. Richet uniformly represents the police as interventionist, intoxicated by surveillance and asserting control through sexual humiliation over black and Arab subjects.[19]

Richet points out the myriad sexual undercurrents present in interactions between the police and banlieue youth. One memorable scene suggests that relations between the two orders are animated by a desire for homosexual domination over the adversary. The sequence in question depicts an aesthetically glamorized police chase, during which the pursued banlieue men display model teamwork and balletic grace, while the police seem inept and easily outmaneuvered, a chase scene that betrays the admiration of the directorial gaze. Three policemen finally catch one of the rebellious Arab young men and shove him into their van, getting in beside him. The ensuing dialogue is worth citing in full for its racialized and sexualized language, as well as for its exposure of a dynamic that usually remains secret outside of cultural representations, because of the police's ability to shelter itself from scrutiny:

ARRESTED MAN: Does it turn you on to put handcuffs on me? Does it give you a hard-on that you've caught a guy and it's three on one?

POLICEMAN 1: You're the excitable, jumpy type [*nerveux*], aren't you? You have nice skin, *enculé* [someone who gets fucked].

POLICEMAN 2: Do you have a sister? Slip us a little wog pussy [*chatte de bougnoule*] to calm things down. You upset me earlier. And you want us to refrain from being racist when it comes to brown sons of bitches like yourself [*fils de putain de ta race comme tu es*]? I'll put you on a boat and send you back to where you came from. You're breaking my balls; do you understand?!

At this point, the speaking officer slaps the arrestee, while the other officers crowd around him, holding him in place. Although the director sites the scene in Meaux (part of periurban Paris), all three officers have noticeable Southern French accents. In addition, their attitudes and assumptions in regard to North Africans strongly code them as either racist southerners, connoisseurs of French Algeria or *pieds-noirs* (former settler inhabitants of French Algeria of European origin). The teen resists for the duration of their trip, deflecting questions and advances, which serves only to further rile up the officers, already excitable after having participated in a high-adrenaline chase. The officers alternatively slap and caress the young man's cheek, a gesture full of sexual ambivalence. Suddenly, one officer grabs the young man's crotch, seemingly to provoke a reaction in the otherwise unresponsive prisoner, which finally results in him crying out. The other officers do not object to their colleague's homosexual grope, implying that this behavior is perfectly normal in their day-to-day police work.

> ARRESTED MAN: Aah! Get your hands off of there! What are you doing!?
> POLICEMAN 2: I heard that you guys fuck asses in your country, isn't that right? Have you been checked out by a man before? [He repeats this twice, while the young man looks at him in a kind of shock mixing repulsion and recognition.] Don't you want to suck me off too?

At this last provocation (or invitation?) the speaking officer kisses the arrestee on the mouth. The other officers still do not intervene, as the kissing officer gets even more excited.

> POLICEMAN 2: Don't you ever do what you did to me again! [He slaps him hard across the face, before kissing him yet again.]

Though speculation about the homoerotic nature of police violence has been rampant in many fantasy contexts (see, for example, the work of illustrator Tom of Finland[20]), Richet renders it explicit. Ethnocultural enmity, brought to a boil, here takes on a sexual dimension. The ensuing homosexual dynamic is not so much an essential as a circumstantial one, occasioned by the racist southerners' opportunity for long-sought domination over the Arab competitor, which in turn causes sexual excitement.

In this situation, homosexuality is weaponized as a way to break a recalcitrant prisoner; both the Franco-Arab arrestee and the police recognize the sexual component of their conflict, a component at first unexpected but finally intelligible when taking into consideration colonial and postcolonial forms of tension.

This sexualized war of attrition—in which the figures of a Franco-Arab *banlieusard* and the racist cops are surreally translated into North Africans and *pieds-noirs* competing for domination—echoes another war from the not-too-distant past: the Algerian War. In *The Invention of Decolonization*, Todd Shepard argues that French propaganda and media discourse at the eve of Algerian independence often spoke of colonial relations and the ongoing conflict in sexual, especially homosexual terms.[21] To illustrate, Shepard discusses how New Left journalists such as Philippe Hernandez, who advocated for Algerian independence, participated in the escalation of a machismo challenge by provoking the *pieds-noirs'* manhood and making light of the Mediterranean value system in which virilities are in constant competition: "The *pied noir* is convinced that he is, by nature, the Arab's male."[22] Shepard adds that in this specific context, "the pro-French Algeria struggle . . . should be understood as an attempt to maintain dominance in this homosexual economy." Richet's film, in turn, has the policemen occupy the role of *pieds-noirs* and the Franco-Arab that of the North African *indigène*. The cops employ homosexual advances as a weapon in order to designate the enemy as the passive, effeminate homosexual. Interestingly however, Richet depicts the cops as eventually more interested in the Arab's cultural affinity for active sodomy, and homosexuality of a more egalitarian nature (kissing), than they are interested in dominating him.

Shepard unpacks the homosexual aspersions once cast on *pieds-noirs* by journalists and other commentators. He demonstrates that when it became necessary, after then President de Gaulle's exhortations, to find reasons to separate once and for all from Algeria, the *pieds-noirs* (most of whom, it was assumed at the time, would stay) were suddenly invested with perverse penchants that underlined the fact that they were indeed "not French," thus making separation easier. Shepard discusses in particular Pierre Nora's *Les Français d'Algérie*, a journalistic, highly personal intervention that passed itself off as a historical account, in which "Nora fantasizes that the French(men) of Algeria 'with the purest masculine intuition' recognized the competition the Arab posed was as 'a man more than as a social or religious being,' which drove them to assault Arab women, who used the veil and the harem to protect themselves and their families."[23] The great irony, in Richet's mise-en-scène that pits *pieds-noirs* against Arabs in a war of sexual violence, is that both groups have been historically stigmatized as sexually aggressive.[24] Shepard writes, "pied noirs stood accused of embodying abnormal masculinity in ways that recalled charges that Orientalist writers and apologists of colonialism had leveled at 'Arabs' and 'Muslims.'"[25]

In Richet's film, the homosexualization of the encounter between white policemen and Arab delinquent functions as an extreme measure, taken in private, to assert control using a language that would be uniquely intelligible to the symbolic representatives of Algeria in France and French European Algeria, embroiled as they are in a postcolonial conflict that concerns only them. Thus the clandestinity of the police car functions as a "between us" space where postcolonial reckonings may occur. The Franco-Arab arrestee immediately recognizes the sexual tenor of the dynamic between himself and the policemen and is the first to cast the aspersion of homosexuality on his aggressors, with references to sadomasochistic handcuffs and orgiastic rape fantasies. However, it is the policemen who answer the aspersion of active homosexuality by turning homosexuality into a weapon, under the assumption that sexual humiliation and especially passive homosexuality are what "Arabs" fear most and thus represent the appropriate idiom in which to assert domination. It is the desire for domination that erupts here; the homosexual nature of the desire is secondary, merely the form it takes. Playing off the stereotype that Arab men always defend the honor of their female relations above and beyond their own, the policemen tell the arrestee that a *beurette* (his hypothetical sister) could replace him as their victim, especially if she "belongs" to the Arab male—according to the Orientalist notion of the harem, or the banlieue stereotypes of the possessive *grands frères* (Big Brothers).

Once the homosexual tenor is established, the scene takes on an almost clichéd pornographic character, with motifs of imprisonment, interracial rape, uniforms, handcuffs, and automobiles. The feminization of the otherwise virile Franco-Arab delinquent is the policemen's desired goal, with the pinning down and collective taunting in the scene reminiscent of *tournantes* or gang rapes. Richet interestingly casts a crime contemporarily attributed to *banlieue* youth onto their right-wing police adversaries, for Richet a more alarming source of sexual violence (notably, only sexual violence against men is represented in this film). Because the police force is itself coded as a homosocial closed network, full of right-wingers nostalgic for colonial domination, the homosexual abuse on display in the privacy of the police car will not face punishment or interrogation should the Franco-Arab victim choose to complain, since the investigation, as official protocol requires, would also be carried out by a police agency trusted to be self-regulating, a fact that arguably causes the expression of alarm on the arrestee's face: he seems to expect "homosexual" torture, bracing himself for it. The policemen wax anthropological about the supposedly rampant sodomy practiced by North Africans as if already very well-informed: they associate the Arab prisoner with a kind of civilizational inferiority rooted in exotic and "primitive" bisexual tendencies. Yet there also transpires a palpable excitement at getting the seized Franco-Arab to recognize this state of affairs, to recognize that he is the "pervert" they have projected him to be. In De l'amour, which follows a white female delinquent abused in prison by a guard before her Arab boyfriend rescues her, Richet also explores the perils of police custody. In that film, the prison cell symbolizes an unchecked laboratory for the expression of "perversion," enabled by the mixture of ethnic hatred, jealousy, imbalances of power, helplessness, and opportunities to exact revenge. A corrupt older cop, angered by the protagonist Maria's relationship with a Franco-Arab man and her rejection of the former's advances, rapes her in her cell after provocatively asking her, "What does he have that I don't?"

Richet's homosexualization of the police force, however, warrants a closer examination, especially when one considers the ideological components of his communist-leaning filmmaking. One strand of communist thought, not necessarily representative but present all the same, framed homosexuality as an "excess," an element of bourgeois decadence and a negative counterpoint to the working-class heterosexuality that Richet idealizes in his films.[26] Richet casts a nonreproductive homosexuality onto "perverted" and all-white forces like the French police that are purported to restrict the "positive" heterosexual reproduction of banlieue communities. Banlieusards, in Richet's depiction, are a population group that finds force in numbers, whose beauty comes in collectivity, as they harness the generative powers of métissage. In this way, Richet sexualizes race just as he does class. This point supports Roderick Ferguson's analysis of Marxism and heterosexuality,[27] wherein "capitalist property relations represent the ultimate obstacle to heteropatriarchal practice and being." Ferguson offers another version of what happens when the policemen thwart the "natural" progression of the banlieue's heterosexual multiplicity: "In disrupting heteropatriarchy, capital disrupted man's fundamental essence."[28] Richet's policemen and -women stand in for the capitalist forces of regulation (private property must be defended) which repress the banlieue's natural growth, sometimes with a "no future" horizon of a homosexuality symbolized as nonreproductive. This takes us back to the opening scenes of Ma 6-T va crack-er, wherein Virginie Ledoyen appears in allegorical form as Mother of the Banlieue insurrection next to her mixed-race child, encouraging workers and young people to battle the police and resist with fist in the air.

Richet occasionally intersperses the self-destructive violence of banlieue riots with sudden (also sexualized) departures into ideological territory. A conversation between concerned community organizers and rioting youth about reprisals and the cycle of violence turns into a call for mass class struggle: "We need to screw the pigs/the prize hen [*il faut niquer la volaille*[29]]! There needs to be a revolution! We must all unite!" Yet the call to "screw" a right-wing capitalist order indicates a convergence Richet wishes to highlight between seemingly aimless, sexually frustrated youth violence and the more "dignified" struggle to overthrow an oppressive capitalist order. Such a convergence presents penetrative masculinity as a point of unity between two orders (the police and rioting *banlieusards*) with ostensibly little in common. Overall, two types of homosocialities (or homosocieties) are opposed. On the one hand, the banlieue youth who mount a collective resistance to the police in fraternal harmony demonstrate an affectionate, nonsexual solidarity, while on the other hand, the police are coded as homosexual, cold, and pornographic, as if the turn toward sexual explicitness was necessarily a violation of a fraternal code.

Echoes of the decolonization era can thus be heard in *Ma 6-T va cracker*, as in the scene of forced confession at the hands of police. To fully contextualize this scene, however, it is necessary to return to some important historical precedents from French Algeria. Henri Alleg gave one of the most prominent accounts of his own sexualized torture at the hands of *pied-noir* officers during the Algerian war of Independence.[30] Citing the once-banned torture exposé *The Gangrene*, historian Todd Shepard explains how some French commentators at the time suggested that "colonial domination of Algeria transformed French officials and soldiers into homosexual sadists, excited by the suffering they inflicted on 'Muslim Algerian men.'"[31] In his preface to Alleg's *The Question*, Jean-Paul Sartre described how political relations of domination had been gendered and then also racialized: the colonial context sexualizes the color line, and this operation becomes the root of sexual torture, as the war between colonizer and colonized makes these sexual power relations more explicit than they normally would be.[32] Alleg consistently described the relationship between torturer and tortured as that of a bitter "couple": with its emasculating methods targeting genitals and nipples, the purpose of his torture was to turn him into a passive recipient. When he had mastered his nerves and successfully concealed his suffering, the torturers declared that he must have "liked it," attempting to elicit the same bodily confession of homosexuality found in the *Ma 6-T va cracker* scene. Frantz Fanon—meditating on the links between sexuality, violence, and vigilante punishment—had wondered in *Black Skin, White Masks*, if "the lynching of the Negro [is] not a sexual revenge? We know how much of sexuality there is in all cruelties, tortures, beatings. One has only to reread a few pages of the Marquis de Sade to be easily convinced of the fact."[33] New Left journalist Philippe Hernandez describes how for some, a symbolic wartime victory could be acquired by painting the enemy as homosexually passive (an operation frequent in torture). Here, Hernandez throws a virility challenge to other *pieds-noirs*, in "Lettre d'un pied-noir à un pied-noir" he writes: "'We're no faggots,' you tell me? Ok, comrades, this is the moment to prove it. The faggot is someone to whom things happen and things right now are happening to you."[34] Fanon recognized the sexual tenor of the war of decolonization, describing in highly masculinist and sometimes controversial terms an indigenous will to possess and penetrate "white" fortresses: "The look that the native turns on the settler's town is a look of lust, a look of envy; it expresses his dreams of possession—all manner of possession: to sit at the settler's table, to sleep in the settler's bed, with his wife if possible. The colonized man is an envious man."[35]

In *Les témoins*, Téchiné reflects on similarly unsettling undercurrents in homosocial orders of authority that are faced with an ethnic or cultural other. Though he explores this theme most obviously with the police, who often regulate ethnic and sexual minorities, he also exposes these undercurrents in the French military. The scene following policeman Mehdi's first on-screen homosexual experience shows him watching a televised Bastille Day (July 14) parade. The TV camera dwells on shots of the Arc de Triomphe, the soldiers' rigid salutes, and spectators rising from their seats as the president's motorcade passes. Téchiné highlights the phallic symbolism of the military pageant, with its weapons and tanks with long cylindrical canons passing by the Obelisk—an erect artifact lifted from its original Arab context—in a way that suggests an intersection between military power, virile displays, French expansionism, and a homosocial order that is at once homophobic and homosexually dominant. Mehdi watches somewhat worriedly, as if the homosexuality he had just engaged in with his lover Manu, even though clandestine and unexposed, separates him from an order he once belonged to. Téchiné explored this motif—the fallback on the military after sexual penetration—in an earlier film, *J'embrasse pas* (1991; I don't kiss), where the protagonist Romain, a country boy turned Paris hustler, joins the foreign legion after being revenge-raped by the pimp of a female prostitute he had seduced and fallen in love with.[36] In *Les témoins*, we are privy to the strange self-consciousness, at once ethnic and sexual, Mehdi feels when observing a celebration of colonialism. Téchiné makes an on-screen connection between Mehdi's othering as a Franco-Arab and his being made to feel other as a practitioner of homosexuality, in love for the first time with another man.[37] Both figures (Arab Mehdi and nonheteronormative Mehdi) stand on the receiving end of military or police scrutiny. The voice of the TV reporter announces that "this look back on history reminds us of the price of liberty," a liberty Mehdi might be interpreting in a manner different from patriotic fervor.

The juxtaposition of sexual and military scenes establishes an opposition between two homosocialities: one is private, homosexual, and bound to hide; the other is heterosexual, bombastic, and prone to outward displays. Meditating on the comparison of the two in this way acts as a call to conscience for Mehdi, a call back to the order of his chosen profession. However, the juxtaposition also establishes a link of intelligibility showing that, from a nonheteronormative perspective, masculinist institutions such as the army and police easily lend themselves to a sexual reading: such a change in perception is visible on Mehdi's anguished face when watching the parade. Mehdi's recent homosexual adventure, about which he seems to feel some apprehension, could possibly constitute a betrayal of an army or police code of homosociality: it renders explicit homosexual undercurrents that are unbearable for institutions dependent on their silencing. The flamboyancy of this display is evident in the phallic imagery and bragging about past colonial penetrations. That Mehdi himself belongs to this order creates cognitive dissonance, especially when we are reminded by the TV reporter that French liberty comes at a price. One might first think of the lives lost during both World Wars as the implied price, but the visible price is the colonial bounty (of the Obelisk), or in other words, the liberty to go beyond borders, to penetrate, explore, and collect. This occupation is not too distant from Mehdi's vice brigade intrusions into red-light districts and cruising grounds. Caught between penetrations, Mehdi is momentarily disoriented, cognizant that, from the perspective of the military or police, he may have partaken in a "disadvantageous" penetration. It is important to note that Mehdi does not disclose his role in sexual relations with Manu at this point in the film; he does, at a later point, take on the passive role. Full of doubt and in need of reassurance after his homosexual experiment, he turns to his wife, naked in the shower, and gazes upon her with a look full of longing. Somewhat spooked by his own thoughts, he asks his wife if they can shore up their heterosexual couplehood by abandoning the "open" part of their relationship, an opening that carried within it the threat of homosexuality.

Big Brother Is Watching You

Les témoins persistently questions stereotypes about macho Arab surveillance. Watching Mehdi watch protectively over his wife, he recalls the figure of the *grand frère*, the figurative or literal older brother who jealously watches over his daughters and sisters, just as he watches benevolently over the community. One can seize the ambivalence between the possessive and protective functions of male surveillance, an ambivalence that naturally manifests in Mehdi's police work. What appeared to be a form of caretaking when applied to his wife becomes intolerant surveillance in regard to prostitution and sex in public. In the words of the character Sandra, a sex worker who loves her job, Mehdi's supposed concern for the plight of women in her profession is itself sexist, as it activates notions of masculine involvement that assume women are unfit to defend themselves. Sandra describes her relationship with her male pimp in proprietary, almost loving terms: it seems that Mehdi is attempting to provoke divorce in a stable marriage, vying with another man over a woman, rather than looking out for her best citizen interests as a neutral peace officer. As in Richet's films, this representation importantly flips one of the aforementioned tropes that postcolonial theory criticizes: "white man frees brown woman from brown man." Here, the assimilated Arab man occupies power and attempts to free a white woman against her will from another man not racially specified. With assimilation as a police officer, the Franco-Arab inherits the right to intervene universally in the name of the law and human rights, and the culturalist, negative connotation of his surveillance disappears. At one point in *Les témoins*, the aforementioned sex worker Sandra calls Mehdi's aggressive approach a "revolution," a word choice that attributes novelty to his abolitionist approach (it is not purely abolitionist, in so far as it punishes sex workers who refuse to give police the names of pimps, while abolitionism aims to protect sex workers as victims and criminalize their pimps). The "revolution" seems to be the creative endeavor of one man who happens to belong to an ethnic background often stereotypically connected to the regulation of women's bodies.[38] A stereotype about Arab male sexism here invigorates and revolutionizes a state authority when it is assimilated into it: when channeled into state professions where force is called for, elsewhere reviled stereotypes about ethnic masculinity become palatable. Despite this success in the workplace, Mehdi still seems caught between a rock and a hard place. He assimilates through his membership in the police where regulation is encouraged, while his regulationist attitudes cause a culture clash with another segment of society, that of his wife and her educated gay friends, who disapprove of his invasive methods.

As *Les témoins* shows, however, both sex positivity and regulation will be altered by the advent of AIDS: this event offers a "way out" of the ethnicized dilemma in which Mehdi finds himself, between encouragement and disdain for his surveillance. In the era of AIDS, the repression of prostitution and homosexual cruising becomes a losing hand in the battle against new infections, because it has the limiting effect of driving such activities further underground, out of the public eye of medical professionals scrambling to contain the outbreak. At one point Mehdi fears he himself may have been infected; he turns to his wife's homosexual friend Adrien, a doctor and also one of the first anti-AIDS activists in the film's adaptation of history. Adrien sets a firm condition for his helping Mehdi in regard to his anxieties about AIDS: an end to raids on gay and red-light bars, and the acknowledgment of a *droit de cité* (right to exist in the city) for sex workers and homosexuals. This right—in the classical, Greek sense—thematically underscores the entirety of the film. It is part of the coming together of diversity that will allow the city to overcome the epidemic with which it has been tragically cursed.

However, Mehdi's surveillance tendencies—under pressure from various sides—do not remain negatively coded. Téchiné reassesses a normally vilified aspect of virility in order to explore its other, beneficial side: the strongest example being how surveillance can save lives. This is shown in what is perhaps the film's most memorably homoerotic scene, wherein the opportunity to play "lifeguard" allows for the construction of social bonds normally improbable. It begins during a sunny vacation scene at the Mediterranean family home of Mehdi's wife. Adrien has come up to join Sarah and Mehdi with Manu, whom he had just recently met. At one point, Manu and Mehdi leave the guests to go for a swim in a cove. Manu admits to Mehdi that he's not much of a swimmer, and asks if he can swim near him; Mehdi obliges and offers a swimming lesson. Manu tries swimming underwater, but ventures too deep and cannot make it back to the surface in time. Realizing the scope of the emergency, Mehdi plunges downward and grasps Manu's body: their first physical contact. The play of underwater light on their athletic bodies renders the skin color contrast less obvious, creating a kind of rapprochement between lifesaver and life saved through a homoerotic aesthetic of sameness. Graceful in their underwater ballet scene, their porcelain bodies are coded with a classical, almost Renaissance artistry, reminiscent of frescos depicting contact between Gods and men. Mehdi swims backward, cradling Manu's neck like a trained lifeguard, pulling him onto a pebbled beach in the isolated cove. The ensuing CPR might seem clinical if not for its resemblance to the famous kissing scene in *From Here to Eternity*.[39] Mehdi protectively cradles Manu's limp body as the waves crash nearby, looking up at the sky while taking deep breaths in an almost supplicating gesture, before resuming the erotic resuscitation. On the third attempt, Manu comes coughing back to life, spewing out the water inside his lungs while Mehdi holds him.

With a poetically elemental style, Téchiné meditates here on the relationship between life, death, and desire in an era defined by AIDS. The scene is pivotal because the saving of life causes Manu to fall in love with his savior (they previously had expressed no desire for each other, revulsion even). Mehdi, who seemed to take pride in a kind of upstanding moral rigidity, experiences for the first time some malleability of sexual orientation via the accident of physical contact with Manu. That such contact requires incredible serendipity in order to occur is a testament to just how estranged the police and sexual minorities were at the time.

In this scene, Téchiné inverts negative stereotypes about Franco-Arab virility (e.g., homophobia, big brother) when Mehdi's previously disparaged police techniques turn into a lifesaving, and homoerotic gesture: surveillance and caretaking here constitute two sides of the same coin. The scene also showcases a versatility of roles in which the two worlds that seemed to diverge in the film's initial scenes—the homosexual and the police networks—converge due to a state of emergency. Mehdi's resuscitative actions are perfunctory and parental as well as full of longing for communion. The film delivers a message that the AIDS era has changed the way bodies and, to a larger extent, communities relate to one another—independently of anything each says about sexuality. A love bond is born from this involuntary magnetism between bodies, which is all the starker because of the stakes of life and death.

Téchiné offers a genesis of unexpected homosexuality from the starting point of body contact that only policing could offer. Manu, driven by a powerful sense of obligation and, implicitly, desire, later tracks Mehdi down at the police headquarters to signify just how thankful he is. When later pressed by his wife—avid for material for her forthcoming novel— about his relationship with Manu, Mehdi evokes the cove episode as evidence of his first feelings for Manu, revealing that he had been repeatedly chiding himself in his head for having an erection "against his will" while pulling Manu's body out of the water. Manu's eventual death from AIDS proves to be especially painful for Mehdi, because it contradicts the life-saving experience that caused him to fall in love with Manu in the first place. Manu's sexual philosophy is changed on the very night his life is saved: he abandons promiscuous homosexuality, which saw him haunt Paris's public parks, in favor of exclusivity with Mehdi.

In Téchiné's film, it is an established generation of gay men who most ardently oppose Arab attempts at virile control (see chapter 1). Roles are switched with the character of Adrien, a tenacious, combative doctor who seems to police attitudes rather than bodies. Téchiné upends the status quo of power relations in the film—which holds that the police wield an uninterrogated power and that homosexuals can always be subject to interrogation. He does so by developing the notion of a gay community that had recently gained symbolic capital, leverage, and respect, such that the community could begin to criticize institutions of various sorts for their heterosexism. In the following exchange, at Sarah's family beach house, the openly gay Manu and Adrien interrogate what they see as an institution of virility in the form of Mehdi, both a policeman and a Franco-Arab family man:

SARAH: It's delicious [biting into a cake prepared by Manu].
ADRIEN: Which is normal, considering that Manu is our *maître queue* [a play on *maître queux*, accomplished chef, and *queue*, slang for "penis"].
MEHDI: Your sexual jokes are getting tiresome.
ADRIEN: If I want to be flamboyant, I will be flamboyant.
MEHDI: Yes, by all means, be flamboyant.
MANU: I've always wondered if gay cops exist.
MEHDI: Not to my knowledge.
MANU: Isn't it in all professions?
MEHDI: Come on guys, leave me alone. You guys don't know much about cops. What are you reproaching them for exactly?
ADRIEN: Their intolerance.
MEHDI: Come on now, they are very tolerant, they even let me grow out my sideburns. Honey, I am going for a dive [*piquer une tête*], watch the teapot OK? [He throws off his red shirt revealing his torso.]
SARAH: That's Mehdi for you, he gets out of sticky situations with a pirouette. He's very proud of his profession so we must not chide him about it. When I first met him, he told me he was a student, but he hid the fact that it was at the police academy. He waited until I was in deep before coming clean.

SEXUAL UNDERGROUNDS / 207

With power in numbers, Manu and Adrien give Mehdi a taste of his own interrogative medicine. They use their openness about sexuality as a tool for prying into what are construed as clandestine subjectivities resistant to penetration, that of the police officer as well as the Arab man. Mehdi, who establishes here a barrier preventing others from accessing the intimate world of the police, seems to have missed the teaching moment that might have caused him to see the parallels between his discomfort at being interrogated and his own prying work. Mehdi's mantra of clandestinity—repeated throughout the film: that sex is performed but not talked about—here begins its slow collapse. Manu and Adrien push what was implicitly sexual in the framework of interrogation to the limit, because they themselves do not have to abide by the terms of sexual clandestinity. After Mehdi's agile escape, the trio comments on his physical prowess and how he escapes scrutiny because of it. Mehdi's word choice (*piquer une tête*) takes on importance because it translates to "taking the plunge," or diving headfirst, an expression that can easily be read sexually as a willingness to enter homosexuality, when one considers the lifesaving scene with Manu that follows. The location of this scene importantly is an isolated, secret cove where sexuality, in clandestine reclusion, can be appropriately explored.

During the beach-side interrogation scene, Manu, Adrien, and Sarah seem to form a caricatural council of sexual modernity, wherein homosexuals and their heterosexual allies are the permanent members and the confession of sexuality is a duty. Mehdi and his police profession, far from being considered lawful and upstanding, here appear dishonest and contrarian, and are thus excluded. Sarah speaks of his profession as a kind of crime, a shameful secret (necessitating a later confession and "coming out"): it might have been a deal breaker had she known about it before her seduction. In so doing, Téchiné plays with another common trope in French cinema portraying mixed-race couples: the Arab male partner at first conceals his ethnicity by replacing his name with a name of different ethnic origin, usually Italian or Spanish.[40] Such refashionings of ethnic identity stem from the unfortunate fear of rejection among minority men, which sometimes provokes clandestinity and dissimulation. Here, in a further confusion of Mehdi's professional and ethnic memberships, it is the police rather than the ethnic origin that generates shame before a judgmental audience.

In many ways, Mehdi's evolution from repressor to enabler of homosexuality reflects changes in society as a whole. Mehdi is made to realize that his repression tactics against sex workers and homosexuals are perhaps vulnerable to judgment in light of his own lifestyle changes. Téchiné has Franco-Arab actor Sami Bouajila undergo a painful trial (falling in love with a man killed by AIDS) that becomes the price of his assimilation both on-screen (where his character Mehdi is finally accepted by his judgmental peers) and off-screen (where he was finally rewarded with his first César, the French Oscar equivalent, for Best Actor). Mehdi's puritan attitude and naive trust in justice and the letter of the law are revised by a wave of sexual reeducation that triggered changes in attitudes across French society in the 1980s. These changes saw homosexuality (and to a lesser extent prostitution) cease to be contentious, prosecutable phenomena and tolerance become the bellwether of a new sexual modernity.

The Interpenetration of Communities

As depicted in *Les témoins* and *Ma 6-T va cracker*, when the gamut of police activities consisting of raids, surveillance, and interrogation consistently penetrates minority spaces, parallels and overlaps between ethnic profiling and sexual profiling are revealed. The lasting impression after watching *Les témoins* is a conviction that the police seeks, at first, to eliminate a delicate harmony of sexual and ethnic minorities that has gently coalesced over time in Parisian neighborhoods such as Pigalle or Barbès: we get the sense that the increasing proximity between sex workers, gay men cruising for sex, and Arab immigrants endangers public hygiene as far as the police is considered. In its portrayal of prostitution and cruising sites in 1980s Paris, *Les témoins* insists on the diversity of the population inhabiting those spaces, suggesting in its nightlife scenes that prostitution may be firmly intertwined with the immigrant condition. Film critic Jean-Marc Lalanne, when asked to justify the merits of the film in the supplemental interviews that accompanied the DVD release, pointed to its ability to represent the intersection of various minority conditions at that point in history: "There was really a movement toward embracing all the elements, all the ages of life, all social categories, and it's that dimension of *métissage* that gives the film a very ample feeling of universality which gathers within it a whole sum of diverse experiences. At the end of the film we experience a strong sense of plenitude."[41] Lalanne makes a strong connection between *métissage* and universalism—but not in the way one might expect *métissage* to be employed in this case, as a facilitator of integration. Rather, one can use his remarks to derive a criticism of official universalism as incomplete, unlike Téchiné's universalism which is inclusive and respectful of the difference of the various social strands that lend the film its holistic realism, focusing on different communities' synergistic "embrace." Official universalism, on the contrary, seems to encourage the disappearance of the individuality of the single strands as they melt into one mass. When Téchiné depicts the delicate harmony of sexual and ethnic minorities as a vulnerable target of police prosecution, he shows how a republican goal (a *mixité* leading toward universalism) is subverted by another wing of officialdom (the police) that doesn't share the same set of goals, an error in the synchronization of official values across institutions.

Téchiné visually develops this sexual and ethnic *mixité* throughout *Les témoins*. Many of the patrons at the red-light bar opposite the hotel Beauséjour (where Manu and his sister are long-term guests) are visibly of North African background: a state-of-affairs that turns Mehdi's job as a Franco-Arab man enforcing the antiprostitution laws against other (Franco-)Arab men only a generation removed from himself all the more complex. This scene offers a commentary on the place of sexual expression in regard to immigrant adaptation and well-being in the host country: in the red-light bar, which provides some of the film's most jovial scenes, these immigrants' happiness and sense of rightful place is palpable in a space where their undervalued (and sometimes abused) workers' bodies are capable of freer expression. The police appear to be breaking the mood, intruding upon a singular phenomenon, a salvational social remedy that could be clipped in the bud at any moment. The patrons of the bar seem happily surprised to meet each other, celebrating with the glee that transience encourages. The preponderance of immigrant workers at the red-light bar reflects the findings of many sociologists and psychiatrists, who note that, with their wives often remaining in the country of origin at the early stages of their husbands' immigration, even after the era of family reunification, migrant workers often looked for sexual release by patronizing sex workers or engaging in (a sometimes) "substitutive" homosexuality. When police actions repress immigrant attempts at sexual satisfaction to the clandestine margins, they also endanger public health in the age of AIDS, wherein sexual practices forced into invisibility often carry higher risks of STD transmission. Eric Fassin, a French sociologist who has written widely on the politicization of sexuality in the media and public political discourse, describes how anxieties about prostitution often conceal more acute anxieties about immigration, regarding the sex workers but also their patrons.[42] Men of North African descent are also heavily represented on the cruising grounds where Manu and Adrien first meet. We learn that Mehdi's vice brigade has been harassing homosexuals at cruising spots and shutting down gay bars: this becomes a point of contention when Mehdi and Adrien reluctantly cooperate in their joint effort at controlling the spread of the AIDS epidemic. As mentioned before, the film makes the point that the worlds of prostitution, cruising, immigration, public health, and the police together constitute a continuum in public space: their collaboration becomes crucial when an epidemic strikes. Outside of cinema, the success of operations against the spread of AIDS (in Brazil, for instance) has often depended on attempts by the police and medical establishments to reach out to sex workers or homosexuals that previously may have been criminalized or excluded.[43] At stake when the police raid such establishments is a modern *mixité* specific to the European metropolis that collects "refugees" of various types: those fleeing financial or cultural poverty, rural domestic regions, or sexual or political oppression may all converge in these semi-clandestine spaces. However different their origins and reasons for migration, the refugees converging on such sites come to realize the similarities of their respective conditions when confronted with a sometimes hostile urban environment. What emerges in these films finally is a portrait of the *quartier* (neighborhood) as a site of social overlap but also historical transition between various groups who populate the area—immigrants of different origins, homosexuals, and sex workers. Narratives of gentrification have often spelled out this point: *Les témoins*, however, importantly isolates a moment in time when sexual minorities did not symbolize the winds of gentrification, but were themselves part and parcel of an undomesticated neighborhood that instead warded off gentrification.

Within these liminal spaces unifying different sectors of society, trans figures play an especially revelatory role as intermediaries in unique contact with Arab men. Films depicting relationships between trans women and Arab men dismantle stereotypes about Arab sexual intolerance: at the same time, they flesh out special complementarities that unite immigrants, *banlieusards*, and trans women that emerge within the conditions of postcolonial urban life. Transsexual women and transgender sex workers act as intermediaries between mobile populations that might rarely interact in their home societies. Liria Bégéja's *Change-moi ma vie* (2000; Change my life) is a Franco-Arab star vehicle featuring Sami Bouajila and Roschdy Zem in the roles of transgender sex workers who create an atmosphere of support around a struggling actress, played by Fanny Ardant, who looks to them for inspiration to set herself right.[44] Like Téchiné's *Les témoins* and Lifshitz's *Wild Side*,[45] the film exposes nightlife spaces of sexual clandestinity that outwardly seem seedy but are imbued with an ecstatic happiness. These bars and clubs are depicted as a treasured space invisible to the outside, uninformed observer. Whether or not the alcohol-induced glee the Arab transgender characters display is merely the after-work fix of a thankless immigrant life is an ambivalence the film leaves open. For Ardant's character, however, exposure to the world of Franco-Arab trans prostitution leads to a serendipitous discovery of immigrant entrepreneurial vitality that will help her get back on her feet, a vitality whose force she can latch onto. The director's affectionate camera work suggests that such trans spaces are "precious"—the film's only non-*misérabiliste* scenes in this very grim film take place at the trans bar—spaces worthy of encouragement and protection rather than shutting down, a point also underscored by the loving attention to nightlife spaces in *Les témoins*.

Films such as *Change-moi ma vie* and *Wild Side* stress the jovial, multiethnic, inclusive and sanctuary-like qualities of trans space, contrasting sharply with prevailing representations of trans women and sex work that insist on the vulgar and the seedy. Lifshitz's *Wild Side* reserves the highest dignity of representation and some of the only moments of comic relief for the scenes depicting the sociability of immigrant trans sex workers. In one scene, an international gathering of elegantly dressed trans women listen attentively to an emotive performance by trans singer Anohni (of Antony and the Johnsons band fame) in an upscale restaurant that resembles a cabaret. In another scene, trans protagonist Stéphanie plays *pétanque* (bocce ball) alongside the Canal St. Martin with a few talkative Latina trans coworkers and a group of ostensibly straight men (a handsome black man with whom they amiably flirt, and some white seniors). It is a scene of infectiously happy *mixité* both ethnic and sexual.

Jacques Nolot's *La chatte à deux têtes* (2002; *Porn Theater*) depicts a serendipitous and mostly harmonious *mixité* of trans women and ethnic minorities, focusing on their sexual and social complementarity in a pornographic theatre.[46] Most of the sexual exchanges between trans women and the male clients are depicted as nonremunerated, pursued only for their own pleasure, thus taking representation outside the usual scope of sex work. The police occasionally surveil the scene, but their interventions in the theater target the patrons for their irregular immigration status rather than their sexual behavior. This detail makes comparisons of the respective plights of sexual and ethnic minorities unavoidable: the police seem to have latched on to trans women in order to access and arrest undocumented immigrants, mostly men of color, turning a blind eye to public sex in order to better target border crossings. A central point of irony in the films at hand is that "criminal activities" such as public sex and sex work actually help achieve the goal of *mixité* so often pursued by a French republican agenda. Trans women uniquely facilitate this reunion of various clandestine populations—immigrant, prostitute, and gay—all of which have been the focus of past government crackdowns.

Porn Theater is perhaps one of the most comically irreverent reflections on *mixité* and ethnic masculinity ever produced. Scenes depict the comings and goings of patrons at the decrepit yet busy adult theater, where eyes seem to stick less to the screen and more to fellow spectators, most of whom are young, virile men of immigrant origin. Over the course of the film, the theater slowly becomes a theater of society exhibiting the novel social and economic circumstances of metropolitan life at the French margins. With keen entrepreneurial spirit, a group of trans women have capitalized on the potential of the space, some to derive a profit from prostitution but most others to engage in personal sexual fantasies. In a casting decision symbolic on multiple levels, promoter Fouad Zeraoui—the man behind the still ongoing Black Blanc Beur (BBB) gay club nights in Paris (see chapter 1)—plays a nymphomaniac trans woman with a loyal male following. As a nightlife entrepreneur, Zeraoui incidentally also has capitalized on the immigrant and *banlieusard* market for trans women: for several years, Zeraoui hosted the trans soirée Escuelita on the same night as his BBB parties[47]—the former beginning at midnight and the latter a tea dance—so that the respective clienteles inevitably mingled, many choosing to stay beyond the BBB hour. Both Nolot and Zeraoui show the inner workings of this sexual market on different levels, indicating the undramatic way in which ethnic, often *banlieusard* "straight" men engage with trans women and vice versa, without the feared outcomes of violence or sexual intolerance.[48]

Director Gaël Morel, Téchiné's protégé, explores the supposed openness of Franco-Arab men to sex with trans women in *Le clan* (2004; *Three Dancing Slaves*), a tale of three half-Algerian brothers coming of age in Southern France. The emotionally intense middle brother, played by Nicolas Cazalé, exorcizes his inner turbulence via acts of delinquency. He hangs out with a rough crowd, makes enemies, and in one scene, has group sex with an Arab trans sex worker. Though relations between the sex worker and the group are far from affectionate, their rapport seems commonplace, necessitating no justifying commentary about a possibly substitutive sexuality, one that occurs for lack of cis-female partners (i.e., assigned female at birth and identifying as female). One Franco-Arab youth in the gang asks the sex worker to turn around and face him during sex, her genitals exposed. This comes in contrast to the other young men who want to face her back, with all reminders of transexuality hidden away. The open-minded male character in question is played by Salim Kechiouche, a French champion kickboxer and veteran of gay roles in French cinema. Morel visually suggests that the homosocial hypersexuality of gangs, which here permits group sex with a trans sex worker, may

After his fellow gang members leave, Salim Kechiouche gets intimate with a trans sex worker, as her butch lesbian pimp looks on, in Gaël Morel's *Le clan* (2004; *Three Dancing Slaves*).

also by the same token be open to homosexuality, or at least a nonsubstitutive attraction to trans women. The evolution of Kechiouche's character supports this idea of a sexual continuum, when he eventually reveals his love and desire for the youngest brother of the titular clan. In the *Wild Side*, Lifshitz feels no need to explain the bisexual hustler Djamel's relationship with the trans sex worker Stéphanie, painting his loving desire for her as nonsubstitutive, also on a continuum with homosexuality. Lifshitz portrays Stéphanie as the conduit for the homosexual rapprochement of Djamel and Mikhail—Stéphanie's Russian, clandestine immigrant boyfriend—illustrating the idea that trans women can act as social intermediaries in the transitional spaces of the city described earlier.

Sex Work, Immigrant Work, *Travail d'Arabe*

A startling number of the most notable films reflecting on immigration, diversity, and sexuality have explored those themes through the trope of sex work: they weave together a portrait of Arab and immigrant sexual entrepreneurship that dwells in clandestine spaces away from official scrutiny. This group of films is one that explicitly relates economic necessity and sexual visibility, such that immigrant sexuality can be considered a "problem" afflicting public space, or a clandestine problem when driven underground and made invisible. Within this group of films, many of the most prominent examples have focused on trans women and transgender sex workers: Lifshitz's *Wild Side*, Bégéja's *Change-moi ma vie*, Zakia and Ahmed Bouchaala's *Origine contrôlée* (2001; *Made in France*), Merzak Allouache's *Chouchou*, and Mehdi Charef's *Miss Mona*.[49] Female North African prostitution in France was humorously explored in the outlandish comedy *Rue des figuiers* (cowritten by French-born novelist Soraya Nini), which dramatizes how a hardworking Algerian madam takes over a Southern French town from the rule and influence of the town barber.[50] Self-described feminist director Coline Serreau delivered perhaps the most famous portrait of an Arab female sex worker in *Chaos*,[51] in which the protagonist also turns the tables on male enemies: the film launched the career of Rachida Brakni, earning her a César for most-promising actress. Male North African prostitution received its first large-scale documentary treatment in Bruno Ulmer's *Welcome Europa*.[52]

An underground exploration of male immigrant hustling in Europe, *Welcome Europa* reflects on the links between immigrant and sexual clandestinity by drawing parallels between ethnic and homosexual underground societies. Ulmer follows young men from North Africa, Western Asia, and Eastern Europe who initially seek to make an honest living and send remittances to their families, but eventually fall into sex work as a last resort. Showing how immigrant sexuality can generate both desire and repulsion in public, the film offers that these immigrants' homosexual paths begin where their economic hopes end. Sex work is presented as a last resort for immigrants trying to get on their feet after their first attempts fail, bringing them face to face with the limits of their immigration project. The young men in Ulmer's documentary are reduced to the commodity value of their bodies, merely switching from manual to sexual labor. *Le Monde*, in its review of the film, encouraged greater awareness of this clandestine traffic in bodies: "This reality—because it was born from desires emanating from our societies, because it was perpetuated by prohibitions (against clandestine immigration) in the self-same society—deserves to be confronted head-on. *Welcome Europa* turns this exercise in contemplation into a task that approaches penitence."[53] In this way, Ulmer was able to create a sense of responsibility, even guilt, within European viewers of the film, who may have suddenly become more aware of the prostitution market in their countries and the potentially fatal dangers of forcing immigrant sex workers underground.

In his director's notes accompanying the film's release, Ulmer describes how the film made him realize just how much the erosion of bodily and gender integrity had colored the lives of his interview subjects: "I would have never thought, on the eve of filming, that death would be so present. . . . The death of the soul as well, long before that of the body, when, after having had to make unbearable choices between theft, begging, or prostitution, one's identity withers away, and brings these youths to ask the question: 'Am I still a man?' It's upon this essential question, about the shocks to identities, to masculinities, that I traced the narrative thread of *Welcome Europa*."[54] Ulmer correlates economic failure with an assumed sexual passivity that entails the loss of manhood. He alludes to the immigrants' inability to sustain themselves financially on their European ventures and how it is akin to sexual impotence. With many close-ups of truly anguished faces, Ulmer films young men from Morocco, Romania, and Kurdistan as they come to grips with the realization that they may have to resort to homosexual prostitution to survive in Europe. Far from their dreams of economic ascension and family planning, the boys find there is "nothing to write home about," severing bonds of familial communication rather than disclose their sexual shame. The migrants struggle to constitute a family away from home, finding some fraternal support in other migrants of similar age and experience, or, in one memorable scene, with older trans women who "act as mother and father." The novelist and former psychiatrist Tahar Ben Jelloun has used a similar language of fractured masculinity to describe homosexual prostitution arising out of a failed immigration project, in his recent novel *Leaving Tangier* (which recounts the story of a Moroccan immigrant in Spain who engages in reluctant homosexual prostitution),[55] as well as in his psychosexual study, *The Highest of Solitudes* (see chapter 2).

Two of the most tragic representations of Franco-Arab homosexual prostitution, Amal Bedjaoui's *Un fils*[56] and Charef's *Miss Mona*, have their protagonists meet grisly ends when their attempts to stabilize their financial and immigration statuses fail. In *Un fils*, Selim, the Franco-Arab son of a retired taxi driver, can't bear to tell his father of his failure to find a decent job and instead pursues much more lucrative sex work, splitting his time between a cheap hotel and a fellow sex worker's flat (who may also be his girlfriend). When Selim tries to pay for his father's much-needed back surgery with his earnings, his father stubbornly refuses the money, since he cannot determine its source. After a particularly difficult day in which Selim is both dumped by a client he developed feelings for, and then gay-bashed on his way home by a gang of Franco-Arab young men after refusing to perform sexual favors for them, Selim commits suicide in his hotel room. His father, disconsolate after losing his son on top of his wife's earlier death, must piece together Selim's life and discovers what he has long ignored about his son. Bedjaoui's film makes strong links between financial and sexual shame, exposing the ultimate consequences of giving in to them. As with nearly all films examining North African male homosexual prostitution in France, recourse to sex work is presented as the final mark of a failure to integrate oneself economically, to become part of a "normal" work force: after opting for it, the young men in question engage in intentionally self-destructive or risky behavior in a way that is symptomatic of their nonintegration.

Charef's *Miss Mona* comes on the heels of his pioneering *Le thé au harem d'Archi Ahmed*—which helped launch *cinéma beur* as a genre. The film tells the story of Samir, an immigrant who can't make ends meet and is picked up by a trans sex worker (played by veteran actor Jean Carmet). "Mona" becomes Samir's pimp for the purposes of profit but also to eventually help Samir buy identification papers. The film depicts the trans Miss Mona as an enabler of Samir's descent into ruin, but also as his possible savior: in this way, the film reinforces the idea of trans space as an intermediary place where wayward immigrants first find shelter. In a way, Mona has taken pity as a minority figure on another minority subject with his back to the wall. In Charef's film, homosexuality is depicted as a constructed condition foreign to immigrants, acquired via their necessary adaptation to a "depraved" urban environment in Europe, part of their necessary sexual entrepreneurship. Over time and repeated exposure Samir learns to find men attractive, especially if they are of the boyish type. This initiates his downfall, because it is his newly acquired ephebic lover who steals all the money he has saved, provoking a tragic chain of events. Just as Mona overcomes Samir's initial reticence and the pair starts to make money, Samir gets ensnared in a robbery gone wrong, and ends up being arrested by the police after an identity check on the metro. In many respects, the film presents noteworthy subversions of the miserabilist immigration story: Samir seems to form a surrogate family with the trans Miss Mona (and unexpectedly) her own trans father in their sunny mobile home. However, Samir ultimately blames his sexual and financial ruin on the unsympathetic urban environment of Paris, with its many false hospitalities and commerce in human bodies.

While the harsh conditions of the European urban environment would seem to call for coalition-building between struggling sexual and ethnic minorities, as modeled in the success of female trans intermediary spaces, several films instead make the point that a strong isolationist tendency has separated these communities. Self-ghettoization and the *communautarisme* so dreaded by French republicans are shown to dissolve what could have been a natural alliance between sexual and ethnic minorities. The makers of these films underscore that the *repli communautaire* (the tendency to fall back on one's own community) is not the sole province of ethnic minorities, it also concerns sexual minorities: this state of affairs recalls Eric Fassin's warning to gay and lesbian activists singling out banlieue homophobia not to forget that the gay "ghetto" was also accused of self-ghettoization only a decade ago (see chapter 1). In *Les témoins*, it is the gay doctor Adrien who condemns Mehdi's easy crossing of communities, his touristic foray into the homosexuality of which Adrien is a more "fitting" owner. He tells Mehdi's wife, Sarah, his close friend, that he cannot understand how she could overlook Mehdi's sexual experimentation and simultaneously welcome him back into her life, that she's "completely masochistic," asking her somewhat homophobically, "does it not bother you that he sleeps with boys?" Adrien's rejection of the couple formed by Mehdi and Sarah is revelatory, revealing him to be an enemy rather than a friend of budding coalitions (Sarah especially had supported Adrien's campaign battling the outbreak): "Well I was wrong. I understand now that you've chosen your camp, and I'm not sure we can remain friends." Adrien's fixation with and avoidance of Mehdi betrays the draw and the repulsion of ghetto-breaking practices that Mehdi incarnates. Adrien's self-isolation, however, comes at a moment in the 1980s during which Euro-American AIDS activists often felt abandoned by their governments, as well as by society in general which for the most part stood idle while the epidemic ravaged the gay community. This explains in part Adrien's sentiment that community self-sufficiency was the only possible recourse for gay men at that point in time.

The frustration Adrien feels regarding Mehdi—a bisexual Franco-Arab man who can "pass" as straight and enjoy occasional clandestine homosexuality, without ever suffering from being visually identified as "gay"— is often echoed in other works of gay auteur cinema. Such films identify with some envy a bisexual Franco-Arab ability to pass between discrete communities at leisure: a parallel in the world of nonfiction would be the interview subject Majid, profiled with frustration by Franck Chaumont in *Homo-ghetto*, and his talent for "passing" in both ethnic and gay enclaves (see chapter 1). From the homonormative point of view, Arab men's clandestine passages "in the night" are made to seem dishonest, symbolizing the rupture of a public contract which has it that identities should be visible, and more importantly, that one must prioritize sexual identity just as much if not more than ethnic identity. This imperative stands even as the Franco-Arab characters in these films resist the very concept of "sexual identity," in practice if not speech: characters may show attraction to a greater variety of love objects than they admit to when interrogated.

Téchiné similarly dramatizes the competitive communitarianisms dividing the gay community itself, locating tension in discriminations that pertain to age and race. The director stages a very philosophical confrontation between ethnic and white queer characters through Mehdi and Adrien: their competition is examined through the prism of their simultaneous sexual attraction to Manu, and in their different means of access to their love object. Their rivalry is exacerbated by the jealousy both feel for each another, with Adrien closer to Manu as a friend (closest, importantly, at the end of Manu's tragically short life) while Mehdi was closer to him as a lover. When Manu and Adrien first meet in a cruising park, before Mehdi comes into the picture, Adrien raises a social grievance he has long held. This comes after Manu lets on that he might not be interested in Adrien because of the evident age difference between them, a justification that allows Manu to avoid having to reject him on the grounds of looks. However, this does not soften the blow for Adrien: "It revolts me to hear that. That's where the real segregation is. With gays, there are no barriers of class or of religion; we are the champions of the melting pot. The only taboo left is that of age, we have a lot of progress to make on that front. All right, goodbye mountain boy." Adrien ties this missed connection to a gulf between two generations of homosexuals: the first seasoned by a more embattled past and its experience of persecution, and the second coming of age in the film's present, a present that annoyingly reminds Adrien that homosexual solidarity has been overshadowed by solidarity with cultural and ethnic others. Previously, the radical gay liberation group Front Homosexuel d'Action Révolutionnaire (FHAR), for example, had occasionally geared its activism around the "sexiness" of immigrant and "Arab" causes (see chapter 5). Adrien also suggests that while homosexuals as a class have grown sensitive to race, even pretending to be "postracial," ethnic minorities have yet to meet sexual minorities "in the middle." Such remarks paint a picture of ingratitude, describing the way in which an allegorized ethnic minority class has not abided by the terms of an implicit social contract, neglecting the etiquette of progressive coalition building. Such a conflict, only nascent in the 1980s, has a parallel in the French press landscape of today. Eric Fassin has unpacked the conceptual dangers of setting the ethnic *banlieue* against the tolerant *centre-ville*, of pitting concerns for sexual and racial justice against each other.[57] The scene from *Les témoins* avoids this trap, however, when it draws connections between sexual and ethnic minorities in unexpected ways, as occurs when Adrien asks Manu a flurry of private questions, to which Manu replies, "Are you a cop? Do you want to see my papers, or something?" The experience of police scrutiny and interrogation is one that immigrants, minorities, and homosexuals shared at this time, when gay cruising was still criminalized and racial profiling rampant. Manu also exposes Adrien's latent desire to police sexuality, to call a young renegade to homosexual order. This, of course, foreshadows Adrien's later competitive showdown with the actual policeman Mehdi.

Téchiné presents *mixité*—the positive commingling of different genders, races, classes in a given space—as a possible antidote to the communitarian entrenchment outlined earlier between sexual and ethnic minorities. In doing so he echoes currents of left-wing discourse in France, wherein *mixité sociale* has been a fixture of the Socialist Party platform as part of urban renewal programs in the suburbs (more recently, *mixité sociale* has become part of center-right discourse as well). *Mixité*, however, departs from its status as an innocuous buzzword favored across political parties when it is employed, with some symbolic violence, as a countermodel to minority desires for community, as a tactic to break apart ethnic enclaves. This occurs, to give a variety of examples, with antigang legislation that shades off into restrictions on group assembly, with exhortations for minorities to leave the banlieue or the ghetto in order to succeed, with the social policies aiming to break-up "excessively large" families living together in social housing, and finally with directives encouraging the separation from husbands—who are consistently portrayed as abusive or polygamous—and by extension families. Queer of color analysis has already uncovered the ways that the solutions proposed for socioeconomic problems in US minority communities often take the form of a demand for heterosexual order and stability in order to set up the appropriate building blocks for capitalist salvation.[58] Such solutions have consequences for the existence of sexual diversity, whether in the *banlieues* or the American inner cities. The films addressing the question of harmony between communities often distinguish between a spontaneously forming *mixité* (Téchiné, Lifshitz) and a coercive *mixité* that is more the result of outside directives than internal desires. Sometimes a value almost universally acknowledged as positive can generate resentment when imposed and not volunteered by the people concerned.

Mixité in the first spontaneous sense—a celebration of difference rather than of uniformity and commonality—provides a "visual answer" to some of the vexing problems of representation outlined earlier in this chapter. In Richet's films, we find a clearly articulated resentment against visual surveillance, against which banlieue youth rebel. The scenes in which urban France's various figures come together in chosen *mixité*, one that takes place within banlieue privacy during lulls in police interruption, disconnect the idea of cinema's visual surveillance from that of policing and social regulation.

220 / SEXUAL UNDERGROUNDS

Summary

In this chapter, I explore cinematic portrayals of immigrant and minority sexual subcultures and undergrounds. While most French production on this topic operates in a hyper-expository mode, revisiting all the hot-button issues of recent immigration debates, several films attempt the formally challenging task of depicting sexual clandestinity of ethnic minorities without destroying it. Auteur directors working against dominant media representations here seek to rehabilitate a vilified Arab body. While they have been instrumental in increasing the visibility of Arab actors, they perhaps unintentionally typecast them in sexually "dissident" roles. The casting of Arab actors in gay roles becomes in my argument a kind of assimilation process, both in regard to the film industry and to larger society: Arab actors demonstrate their acting skills and commitment to sexual tolerance by taking roles that are assumed to contravene their cultural customs. There is a pressure, I argue, to manage and regulate the sexuality of minority subjects that emerges not only in featured characters but also more implicitly in directorial cues. Three films especially illustrate the ways in which ethnic sexualities are managed and policed: André Téchiné's *Les témoins*, Jacques Audiard's *Un prophète*, and Jean-François Richet's *Ma 6-T va cracker*.

In *Un prophète*, the homophobic environment of the French prison system suddenly morphs into a magic-realist school in which Malik learns to appreciate the difference between positive and negative homosocialities. The film also provides a quite queer meditation on survival instincts in prisons, depicting how Malik repeatedly turns a devalorized or vulnerable position into one of strength, displaying remarkable adaptation and performance skills. In *Les témoins*, one character in particular helps us understand the dynamics of sexual policing to an exemplary degree: the Franco-Arab policeman Mehdi. Like the prison environment in *Un prophète*, the police order is another social constellation in which homosociality can provide the conditions for exploring homosexuality. Both environments are somewhat closed orders that shield men's homosocial activities from suspicion, providing clandestinity for sexual explorations outside of public view. The evolution of Mehdi's character throughout the film causes the viewer to interrogate what surveillance and clandestinity may mean at this historical junction. *Ma 6-T va cracker* also homosexualizes the police force. The film opposes the "perverse" police authority to the heterosexualized heroes of the banlieues, embellished and glorious in revolt. Policewomen are shown to symbolically control male sexuality in one scene, and in another *banlieusard* men find themselves rejected from a nightclub where they hoped to meet women. This situation of bottled-up sexual frustration eventually culminates in violence against material property. In one of the film's most memorable sequences, an Arab young man is arrested and homosexually abused by three policemen who have strong Southern French accents and seem well-versed in colonial-era stereotypes about Arabs. The left-leaning Richet's depiction of fascist homosexuality is informed, I submit, by an earlier representational tradition in communist production. A final group of films investigates the sex worker and the transsexual as intermediaries with unique exposure to Arab men in the liminal spaces of the metropolis. For them, escaping surveillance is a requirement for survival. In the next chapter, I examine a filmic domain that makes no qualms about exposing clandestine minority sexualities: pornography, and in particular, ethnic porn, a lucrative genre that banks on making the secret known.

5 /   Erotic Solutions for Ethnic Tension:
Fantasy, Reality, Pornography

> *Tarek . . . he's the boss of the projects . . . have to say . . . he knows how to*
> *fight . . . best not to challenge him. Heard that he has a giant cock. . . . Some*
> *guys saw it after soccer practice in the showers. With his buddies, he goes down*
> *to the basement where they have a squat all laid out. There, they smoke, tag the*
> *walls, and when possible . . . they fuck in groups. But sluts in the projects are*
> *hard to find . . . Tarek is a "Natural Born Fucker!" His balls are always full.*
> SKARLAONE IN THE COMIC STRIP "DEBOITAGE DANS LA CAVE"[1]

As the previous chapters on film and literature have shown, cultural
representations of the sexual politics of immigration and diversity have
managed to get at the heart of French anxieties and projections where
journalistic analyses have often fallen short. In early cultural production about the banlieues, writers and directors chose modes of ethnographic "realism" to relate their stories. However, the fantastical, surreal,
or fictional accounts that have depicted banlieue life arguably say more
about anxieties regarding these areas than hyperrealistic portrayals that
aim for sociological accuracy. One cultural medium, often disparaged,
manages to capture particularly well the exaggerated sexual projections
and tensions I am speaking of: pornography. In many ways, pornography
provides more explicit culminations of the processes I have analyzed in
the previous chapters. In this chapter, I examine how the French porn
industry channels and manipulates tensions and fears related to the immigration debate and the place of Arabs in France, at times offering erotic
"remedies." This has culminated in a new porno trope: *porno ethnik* (ethnic porn), or pornography involving men and women of color, usually
Arab or black. I begin by discussing the output of three French directors
who were the first to feature Franco-Arab actors in gay male pornography: Jean-Daniel Cadinot, Jean-Noël René Clair (better known under his
pseudonym JNRC), and Stéphane Chibikh, cofounder of the gay porn studio Citébeur. I also consider heterosexual pornography featuring Franco-
Arab women, and ask whether this field of production is so different in its
representations of minority sexuality that it precludes comparison with

homosexual pornography. Furthermore, I focus on tropes of sex tourism to North Africa, the hypersexualization of single immigrant men, the "eroticization of poverty" as regards both women and men, the hijab as striptease, and the so-called homo thug type. Through recourse to my own interviews with directors and actors, articles in the mainstream and alternative press, and DVD content, I will argue that in this case pornography, often seen as apolitical, does tackle issues of undigested colonial memory and contemporary race relations in a much more forthright (if politically incorrect) way than do the traditional journalistic media. In addition, I explore how avant-garde artists in France have recognized the political import of pornography, incorporating its provocative tropes into their work.

One of the most unapologetic and fantastical forms of sexualization, pornography responds to the dystopian visions of immigrants and their descendants circulating in the French mainstream. Many productions featuring Franco-Arabs have engaged with the alleged breakdown of *mixité* (social mixture) in the banlieues.[2] Numerous media exposés on *tournantes* (gang bangs or gang rapes[3]) have focused on this breakdown, controversially suggesting that collective youth rape is a feature specific to banlieue populations; sociologists, including Laurent Mucchielli, have questioned both the ethnicization of rape and also the "novelty" of *tournantes*, pointing to many earlier examples of collective rape epidemics in French society. The pornography world has in turn produced an erotic exaggeration of these controversies to nightmarish, and sometimes humorous, extremes.

Until recently, pornography, as a cultural medium, has been dismissed as a legitimate branch of academic inquiry in France. The pornography wars in feminist circles, as well as the emergence of respected pornography scholars across the Atlantic have changed this. Pornography remains a multibillion dollar industry whose viewership numbers in the hundreds of millions: it is both a highly capitalistic enterprise with real elements of exploitation, as well as a forum for the expression of sexual fantasy and intimacy not hindered by representational and political red lines. Porn directors do not have to justify or apologize for objectionable content, because they can cite the supposed lack of intentionality at the center of desire and sexual preferences.[4] The central role of fantasy in pornography entails that one cannot so easily compare it with other forms of cultural representation. One also has less control over what one desires when viewing porn, leading to instability of viewer response. The process of identification with characters on-screen is one that changes fundamentally when one passes from cinema to erotica: porn movies allow their viewers to desire and fantasize about what they find ethically or politically repulsive in a way that most other genres do not (with the exception, perhaps, of horror movies). As discussed in chapter 2, psychoanalysis often offers ways out of conundrums in the politics of representation by opening up the psychoanalytical terrain of fantasy as a space where desire is not limited by one's identifications in the so-called real world: one can fantasize about high-risk, extremist, or dangerous behaviors that one politically opposes. Pornography proved divisive among feminists and the LGBT community often sparred over its acceptability and legitimacy as a form of cultural expression.[5] Echoing this division, in the corpus of films at hand, the possibility of identification with mainstream porn actors differs according to whether one is watching homosexual or heterosexual pornography, and importantly, according to whether one is a man or a woman. In most cases, gay consumers can project themselves into any gay porn actor's experience while straight male viewers may not so readily want to or be able to project themselves into the experience of female performers, and female viewers may find that heterosexual porn is tailored to the straight male's pleasure and not their own, which explains women's recourse to woman-authored porn or, with increasing frequency, their preference for gay male porn over straight porn.[6] In gay porn, however, there may be other barriers to identification between viewers and actors that go beyond their shared gender (race, effeminacy, role): in other instances, however, these same factors of differentiation can actually spur identification, especially where fetish is involved or racial difference is eroticized. The element of fantasy—by which, for instance, decided antiracists can find enjoyment in watching mirror images of themselves racially humiliated on screen—opens up a space for frank conversation about inadmissible desires that nevertheless animate social space, a space difficult to establish in holier-than-thou and progressive-to-a-fault activist circles. At the same time, some of the very best and most advanced academic writing on pornography has managed to neglect questions of race so apparently suffusing the production, and even more so questions of empire and colonialism.

In France, art-house film directors—such as Virginie Despentes, Catherine Breillat, and more recently Christophe Honoré—increasingly have been exploring the grey area between art film and pornography, with porn stars cast in starring and unconventional roles. Honoré's L'homme au bain (2010; Man at Bath) starred the gay porn actor François Sagat, who was discovered by the French "homo-thug" porn studio Citébeur.[7] Sagat, a Caucasian actor who began his porn career cast as an Arab, found transatlantic fame with World of Men (2006), Arabesques (2006), and L.A. Zombie (2010).[8] These American porn producers notably cast Sagat in a series of Arab and Middle-Eastern–themed films, confirming his initial ethnic molding by the French Citébeur studio: from the sex tourism scenes in Lebanon in *World of Men* to the carpeted sex labyrinth of *Arabesque*.

Honoré's *L'homme au bain* merits further consideration as it dismantles the stereotype of the banlieue as a no-go zone for homosexuals. Honoré has been a veteran of pensive films reflecting on gay urban subjectivity in a time of evolving family relationships and AIDS; in this film however he decided to explore banlieue homosexuality. *L'homme au bain* is a distinctly nonmiserabilist film, which discards the portrait of banlieue homosexualities as schizophrenic and wrapped up in down-low secrecy; instead, the film depicts the banlieue in counterpoint to the mainstream media as a relative paradise of spontaneous sexual opportunity and unchallenged homophilia. This homophilia can be understood in the sense of loving the same sex as well as loving those who are culturally or socially similar, a nonpejorative way of referring to *communautarisme* (communitarianism), a word that carries mostly negative connotations in France.[9] The complex banlieue space represented by the director, however, does have some problematic aspects, incarnated, for instance, by the American artist character who lives in a banlieue apartment seemingly to be closer to the raw "ethnic" masculinity he fetishizes and uses as inspiration for his artwork. Interestingly, the film explores the contrasts and also interactions between upper- and working-class homosexualities via the central relationship of Emmanuel (François Sagat) and Omar (Omar Ben Sellem). In this pairing, it is the Franco-Arab who represents metrosexuality and the white character who represents a thuggish-looking *banlieusard*. After a somewhat violent fight with his boyfriend, Omar, an artist/filmmaker type, leaves for New York on a promotional film tour, where he pursues a fling with an NYU student of the hipster variety. This provides for a representational contrast between the banlieue world of athletic and hypermasculine men of color, and the Manhattan aesthetics of rock-infused hipsterdom with its scruffy, skinny, androgynous, and mostly white young men. Rather than suggesting that metrosexuality and banlieue virility are opposed, the director considers them logically complementary as two pieces of a human relationship that respond to each other, boyfriend dramas notwithstanding. Instead of portraying banlieue men as intellectual and aesthetic voids (as is the case in much mainstream television), the film insists that they wield their own artistic potential and have always been an object of fascination for artists: after too much time spent alone thinking over their fight, Sagat draws a giant, well-executed romantic portrait of the boyfriend he sorely misses on the walls of their shared

In Christophe Honoré's *L'homme au bain* (2010; *Man at Bath*), the banlieue is a fertile cruising ground under cover of masculinity.

apartment. In the film, Sagat also makes connections with intellectual and cultural elites just as easily as he does with urban men from his own neighborhood (recalling the "passing" and social mobility of the Majid case study in chapter 1). The film's optimistic tone, as far as sexual opportunity and affective contentment are concerned, is arguably informed by actor Sagat's channeling of porn studio Citébeur's aesthetics as well as the "ethics" of the banlieue as a sexually promising zone, producing a reinterpretation of the banlieue as a center rather than satellite of sexual liberation. With this in mind, I now consider ethnic pornography by Cadinot, JNRC, and Chibikh, who, through the ostensibly improbable filter of pornography, tackle issues of colonial memory, immigration, hospitality, and contemporary race relations in a forthright and unapologetic way.

Exploiting Exploitation

In Chibikh's Citébeur productions, we see macho, multiethnic youths carrying out a playful eroticization of their delinquent "menace" to society. Delving further into this connection between crime and alternative sexuality, Nacira Guénif-Souilamas helps contextualize the way that modern-day *banlieusards* help illustrate the theories of the 1970s gay French intelligentsia on this topic, as evidenced by Michel Foucault. Here she speaks of the media's current caricatural portraits: "Virilism, that out-rageous expression of masculinity constrained to its strict sexual limits, offers the advantage of illustrating the ideological proximity already un-derlined by Foucault between perversion and delinquency, which, as is publicly notorious, the Arabs of the projects practice in equal measure."[10] While Citébeur productions often explore the erotics of resistance against the state, attempting a reading of pornography in the hopes of finding political engagement becomes complicated in light of that market's highly capitalistic nature and often untrustworthy entrepreneurs, who may dis-guise material gain in the colors of radicalism.

In 2008, Antoine Barde of Studio Press, the business team that releases the popular Citébeur video series, offered his thoughts on the place of ethnic porn in the European market.[11] The *Cité* in Citébeur refers to the projects: the series is one in which the *racaille* (thug) stereotype abounds. Several videos pit suburban Arab and black teens in sportswear and chains against symbols of the negligent or abusive French state, such as policemen and administrators, on whom the actors repeatedly carry out what appears to be a sexualized revenge. The dénouements of the often hilariously inappropriate plots rarely deliver on their original menace, often concluding with both sexual partners deriving pleasure from the encounter, though perhaps for different reasons.

Because they display so well the simultaneous demonization and eroti-cization of "ethnic" virilities in France, it is worth citing amply from the Citébeur corpus of clips, full-length films, comic strips, and erotic fiction. The titles of video releases evoke themes at the intersection of immigra-tion, sexuality, and urban blight: the humorous eroticization of urbaniza-tion and the lack of green spaces (*Bitume te met dans la lune* [Pavement makes you see stars][12]), the infiltration of the Mediterranean and the de-mographic redefinition of France (*Med in France*; *Med* is also shorthand for Mohammed), or the transformation of the dingy sites of gang bangs and gang rapes into zones of pleasure (*Caves à plaisirs* [Pleasure cellars]). The phrasing of *Caves à plaisirs* raises some very salient class dimensions, first of all because of the wine connoisseur connotations of cellars, which in a very different banlieue context can also refer to the disaffected stor-age areas below housing project towers. This creates an ironic architec-tural oddity: spaces designated in one instance for the collection of fine and expensive wines are now being used as hangout spaces by impover-ished banlieue youth mostly of Muslim background (who supposedly do not drink alcohol). The fact that these spaces were also used to launch a pornotrope now as common as the locker room scene in US production (i.e., the French trope of the cellar gang bang) seems odd at first; but on second thought, it is in keeping with the hedonistic qualities of both alcohol consumption and orgies.

Barde and his partner, Chibikh, started from a desire to provide an alternative to the formulaic and "colorless" output of the main porn studios, which they considered conformist. Business exploded, and in 2008 Barde bragged that Citébeur was the highest-selling gay porn DVD studio in Europe. The partners were instrumental in turning the new consumer category of "ethnic porn" into a market force. Faced with aggressive yet playful images of Franco-Arab men dominating what are alleged to be their white oppressors (policemen, prison guards, snobs of the bourgeois elite),[13] many in the gay establishment media—especially in the pages of mainstream gay-interest magazines such as *Têtu*—criticized Citébeur as a step backward and away from a humanist, egalitarian model of twenty-first-century gay relations.[14] At the same time, a gay consumer public searching for something new and slightly disturbing quietly bought Citébeur productions and spread the name.

The mainstream gay press critiqued Chibikh, who now shies away from media engagement, for choosing to film in caves, those basements converted into congregation spaces that are often used as a symbol of suburban squalor, the site of a kind of nonbourgeois listlessness, while also being the supposedly preferred site for *tournantes*. Chibikh was accused of eroticizing poverty and romanticizing the daily routine of confrontation that dominates miserabilist representations of the suburbs. As with many sexual subcultures (S&M, bareback, intergenerational), the gay press saw in Citébeur productions a form of renegade or even outlaw sexuality. The mainstream seemed pained at the studio's popularity, as depictions of the erotics of conflict might "jeopardize public acceptance of homosexuality" and would also "represent astonishingly bad PR."[15] In 2003, the "Porno" rubric of the then leading gay-interest magazine *Têtu* profiled the emergent Citébeur studio, which had just released its first full-length DVD, *Wesh cousin* ('Sup, bro?). Journalist Louis Maury headlined the article "Cantique de la racaille" (Praise song for thugs), describing the release as a "porn video [that], with its rascal show-offs sprucing themselves up in front of the camera, is as irritating as it is exciting."[16] Under the subheading, Maury added, "Stéphane Chibikh, the director, explains himself [*s'en explique*]," as though Chibikh had been an undisciplined enfant terrible in need of a call to order. Maury captured the ambivalent strategy of Citébeur marketing, halfway between provocation and entertainment, always engaging the viewer. Declaring the human subjects caricatural, Maury preferred to focus on the "astonishing authenticity" of the lighting and sound, perfectly rendering the surrounding urban environs, an authenticity which he then positively compared with the "realist" production of porn predecessor Jean-Noël René Clerc, better known under his pseudonym JNRC, who is notorious for his scenarios involving immigrants and construction workers hard-up for cash, often looking desperate and barely interested. More charitable than most journalists, Maury allowed Chibikh (who had not yet forsaken media appearances) to respond to the echo chamber of one-way critique:

> In the face of criticism, the young man listens, takes notes, and justifies his choices, . . . [displaying] a disconcerting conversational ability [*un tchatche qui désarçonne*] and an undeniable sense of precision that rests upon a term that has become his catch phrase: *authenticity*.
> "Why deform reality to make it more presentable?" he asks from the start. "I didn't want to make it 'pretty,' but rather to make it 'real.' In this film, everything is na-tu-ral!"
> [Chibikh] addresses, point by point, our objections. The actors' look? "They dress the way they want." The dialogue? " . . . If you have a big dick, you brag about it. The masturbation scenes in my film resemble no others; these are interactive scenes. Filming this type of scene can often be annoying; for the spectator just as much as the actor. Here, the actor turns on and excites the spectator; with his own words. I won't make him say things to furnish the scene."[17]

Maury and Chibikh deploy the highly ambivalent term *authenticity* in very different, perhaps incompatible ways, such that the debate about representational accuracy arrives at a relativist dead-end: Chibikh insists the acting realistically approximates banlieue codes while Maury finds the actors' behavior exaggerated (compared to what?). Maury's surprise at Chibikh's collected eloquence and entrepreneurial spirit is somewhat surprising with its ambiguous assumptions about Chibikh's lack of education. Maury also assumes a majority opinion of sorts behind his own objections, collapsing an entire gay viewing public—which may love Citébeur just as it is—with his own point of view. In his book on the bareback subculture and its accompanying pornography in contemporary San Francisco, Tim Dean warns against the tendency to bring moral judgment, whether positive or negative, against subcultures, as this could result in obstacles to gaining a full and comprehensive analysis of that subculture.[18] Bareback culture has faced accusations all too familiar to practitioners of clandestine homosexuality, namely, the internalization of homophobia, and a destructive instinct which is then brought to bear on one's own body. Internalized self-hatred would explain the dominance of virilism (defined here as the rejection of effeminacy) within clandestine, communitarian homosexualities, a dominance that Dean finds widespread in bareback subcultures as well.[19] Citébeur is indeed the pornographic complement to a subculture of clandestine and often anonymous sex in the banlieues, a subculture that often resists exposure and is thus difficult to represent on screen: Citébeur has emerged from this subculture but also has helped to expand it beyond its original limits when disseminating videos about it. This fact also explains the preponderance of masks and sunglasses, which here serve a deliberately erotic purpose: in much other homosexual erotic production, a pixelated or hidden face causes frustration. Dean is useful here for the way he lays out the linkages between a given sexual subculture and its pornography, especially as it concerns subcultures that shy away from outside scrutiny. For some of these subcultures, only the pornographic tip may register as visible or analyzable by an outside audience. While Dean's analysis is eminently useful in terms of understanding unconventional fantasy lives and viewing pornographic worlds and audiences as essential elements of a subculture, his views on the place of racial fetishization in fantasy productions like porn differ from mine.[20]

Another critique persistently raised against porn containing objectionable content has to do with viewer response. Some critics have said that porn provokes the sometimes problematic acts that it represents when its viewers imitate them with their partners, a notion disseminated not just by antipornography feminists such as Catherine Mackinnon but also French politicians such as Ségolène Royal (see chapter 2). Some journalists warned of Citébeur's possibly nefarious effects on gay individuals whose sex lives were already, in their view, dictated by what they saw on screen. What would happen if, say, Citébeur viewers decided to return to the closet in order to experience the clandestine pleasure depicted? In terms of subcultural porn, such a claim does not hold water if the acts and subcultures depicted were already in existence long before their pornographic echo could be heard.[21]

Against Maury's assumptions of coercion, of directorial cues that reinforce stereotypes, and of artificial exaggerations of virility, Chibikh insists on free will and the creativity born of it. Citébeur scenes, to him at least, do not seem as artificially rehearsed or professionally edited as mainstream productions. In a way, free will is wrested from the consuming viewer and offered to the denying performer. The interaction between viewer and performer that Chibikh speaks of stems from his productions' special feature, distinctive in European gay porn—that the actors in many solo scenes are relentlessly conversational and interpellative, bordering on sexual harassment. These clips channel the negative stereotype of young men of color and their aggressive pick-up lines in public, in the Paris metro for instance, a rare place of cross-class and cross-race interaction. Against the accusations of Franco-Arab actors "provoking" supposedly white viewers with denials of bodily access (their clothes don't always come off, nor do their hats and sunglasses), the direct eye contact and sustained verbal address to the spectator establish a visceral connection that is difficult to refuse.

The following passage from the DVD jackets for the *Wesh cousin* series illustrates this concept of provocative yet inviting engagement: "You will check out my huge rod [*grosse tige*] and you will want it. Impossible not to! Look me right in the eyes and submit to my power. I know you are dying of envy for me to stuff it in your mouth and for me to detonate your little butt which is overheating and wet from checking out my huge caliber [member/weapon]. Let yourself go, damn it!" Employing the imperative case while offering the services of a guide, this monologue plays on ethnographic stereotypes of the native informant by turning that guide into a bossy drill sergeant, who reads the transparently aroused body language of spectators who find a reluctant attraction to being dominated. These scenarios depart from the assumption that the Franco-Arab partner vengefully derives a one-way satisfaction at the expense of the white subject: the objective for the Franco-Arab character is still to produce unparalleled pleasure in the recipient. This comes despite the prevailing encouragement in the gay mainstream media for ever more versatile sexual roles in homosexual relations, an injunction that is part of a sexual modernity that looks down on excessively virile and exclusively active men.

Stereotypes and Victimology

Though journalists ridicule Citébeur's commerce in stereotypes, they often fail to remark that these bothersome "types" until then had been noticeably absent from French gay pornography. Citébeur productions evidence an awareness and manipulation of stereotypes below the surface. Mireille Rosello's work is useful here in illuminating just how stereotypes are "declined"—conjugated, altered or rejected—when those stereotypes are redeployed to encourage the taking of social and postcolonial justice.[22] In the *Têtu* article, stereotypes were not investigated but rather avoided. If they were ever mentioned at all, it was as a contagious label associated with something reprehensible (e.g., "this director engages in stereotypes, therefore the entire production is invalid"). In some Citébeur pornography stereotypes are deployed, I argue, with a level of sophistication that approaches that of the reappropriations Rosello mentions in her explanation of how one can decline stereotypes while also embodying them:

> The double movement of inhabiting while displacing can be achieved through a combination of the two meanings of the word "declining," for if "declining" evokes delicate decisions and potentially strident political statements when referring to what we do to invitations, the same word also refers to an apparently innocent and quite socially meaningless activity. I am thinking about what we do to German, Latin, or Greek nouns when we learn the grammatical rudiments of such languages. . . . Remembering that stereotypes are also or perhaps above all a manifestation of what is mechanical in our language, I will treat declensions as an interesting combination of fixed roots and variable endings.[23]

If we think of the willfully exaggerated and provocative Citébeur dialogue quoted earlier, it succeeds in creating a similar ambiguity between the "stridently political" and the cliché. This dialogue approaches a humorous register that edges the spectator into an unstable state, in which he or she laughs at and is simultaneously excited and unsettled by the eye-winking recognition of stereotypes brought into a metasphere, as if to say, "I know that you know that I know what this is about." The stereotype's harmful repetitive power is defused by highlighting it in such a laughably evident way, or in Rosello's framing "paying attention."[24] The scene's racialized tension is sublimated at the same time into the forgettable and drowsy world of postorgasm (for the consumer as well as the actor), during which the "offense" of the pornographic material is diluted into an afterthought.

Citébeur's Arab producer exploits the negative portrayal of banlieue youth as macho delinquents, while somehow casting these young actors in flattering and chest-thumping roles that have drawn the ire of the gay mainstream and praise from the avant-garde and radical fringe. Rosello's analysis of how Arab characters exploit the stereotype of the Arab as thief to their advantage, proves useful here. Going beyond the question of why novels by Franco-Arabs would harmfully reproduce offensive stereotypes about their own communities, Rosello pays attention to how theft can be redefined. She examines filmmaker and novelist Mehdi Charef's *Le thé au harem d'Archimède* (1985; *Tea in the Harem*), a pioneering work of Franco-Arab banlieue cinema which was adapted from Charef's novel *Le thé au harem d'Archi Ahmed*. The film showcases a theft scene in which two young men, one Arab (Madjid) and one Caucasian (Pat), commit an act of theft, with Madjid stealing a metro passenger's wallet before passing it on to Pat, because Pat would appear less suspicious. The victimized passenger takes the bait of course, angrily searching Madjid while ignoring a laughing Pat, feeling both duped and worse, racist when the search does not recover the wallet. Rosello reads the act in a way that emphasizes how Madjid is able to literally profit from the reproduction of anti-Arab stereotypes:

> Madjid is obviously quite aware of the existence of stereotypes, but he does not suffer from them. He has learned how to use them and to send them back to potential aggressors. For him, stereotypes are baits that he uses to tempt other human beings. Madjid never seems to suffer from internalized racial prejudice. He is not interested in what the man thinks. He has no desire to convince him that Arabs are not all one thing or another. . . .
>
> In order to adopt Madjid's position, it is not enough to be that ethnic Other who must constantly protect himself against stereotypes: It is more important to have become aware of the perverse dynamic that puts each potential victim of ethnic stereotypes in a complex position. Both can suffer from the internalizing of stereotypes and use them as if they were a perfectly mastered foreign language. The principle is to have the last laugh.[25]

Madjid accepts stereotypes as a fact of life and uses them as objects of temptation in a seduction scheme: a technique that recalls similar erotic processes at work in Citébeur. In Madjid's case, as with the provocative marketing of Citébeur, the "white" party's stereotypes about Arabs are not registered as injuries but rather opportunities for material gain. The producers of the pornography do not suffer for inadvertently confirming the stereotype, but rather *steal* it when they seize it, transform it, and gain from it. One might argue that the "Arab" does not win at the end of the day if he or she is commodified by pornography, no matter how rule bending. However, the self-conscious theatricality of the performers and the mocking of the would-be white consumer complicate the commodification of the Arab body, such that one could read Citébeur as an Arab commodification of white stereotypes about Arabs. Citébeur is a far cry from the figure of the *beur complexé* (Arab with psychological complexes) who crumbles whenever he falls into an ethnic pattern devalorized by society. Rather than winning over racists, the "last laugh" becomes the greatest prize, and in a certain way it becomes bad sportsmanship not to laugh, to frown at the politically incorrect humiliations of white performers on display: the duped, robbed party becomes equivalent to the disturbed viewer of pornography who didn't get the joke and let offense get in the way of pleasure.

Rosello also sheds important light on the role of white witness and audience reception in assessing the impact of stereotypical representation. She examines the figure of Pat, Madjid's white partner in crime, and says that we, the viewers, are thoroughly entertained by this scene, because "Like Pat, safe at the other end of the car, we are both aware of the existence and power of stereotypes and delighted to witness an act of reappropriation."[26] I submit that Pat is equivalent (in the analogy with Citébeur) to the viewer who can laugh at the aggressive masculinity on display, without being wounded by it. Rather than showing alarm at becoming an accomplice to a visual crime, this relaxed consumer of Citébeur pornography, like Pat, looks on amusedly from a safe distance, which is perhaps itself an offensive subject position (due to the privilege of never being suspect or visible, a privilege one gets away with). Yet from that advantageous position of "white invisibility" comes not escape but applause, encouragement, and a position of solidarity with ethnic minorities that accepts and eroticizes sexual "revenge" against white privilege through porn that processes and at times may alleviate racist injury through erotic consumption. Like Pat, the imagined white viewer is offered an opportunity to move beyond an essentialized white role, identifying "unexpectedly" with the Arab virile thug rather than the victim of the shared racial category.

The place of witnesses brings up a recurring question often addressed to ethnic porn producers: Who is their target audience? Is the projected viewer a member of the "white petit-bourgeoisie" in need of exoticism and brute sensuality? Is it the marginalized Franco-Arab closeted gay *banlieusard* who wants to "stick it" to the man? Maury, it must be stated, had opened his article with an almost insecure admission: "Without being frightened virgins or uptight bourgeois, one can get slightly irritated, right off the bat, while watching *Wesh cousin*." Chibikh responds to Maury's question about reductiveness with a critique of his own: "It's easy and reductive to say that . . . in the videos online and in this film, I mix some *beur* (Franco-Arab) with some French, because the combination is realistic. White people are attracted to *beurs*, and vice versa. In terms of the viewing public, it's the same: I want to attract whites and *beurs*."[27] Chibikh alleviates fears of racial enmity, divided publics, and non-*mixité* by evoking the capacity of eroticism and mutual attraction to encourage social mobility and encounters outside of comfort zones and community limits. One cannot be sure whether Chibikh means by this that all manner of people are attracted to each other in general (*mixité* meaning social mixture), or whether a specific attraction emerges from the eroticization of difference (in terms of race, social status, or power). The result is the same, however, with the added *mixité* benefit of being exposed to other types one might not have discovered in ethnically uniform pornography.

François Sagat, aka "Azzedine"

Porn star François Sagat, who declares himself inspired by Arab culture, has achieved worldwide fame as a Caucasian actor discovered peripherally by consumers searching for Arab men. With his inked scalp evoking Pharaonic Egypt, a giant Islamic crescent and star gracing his back,[28] sculpted physique, and versatile performing abilities, Sagat is one of porn's most recognizable stars and Citébeur's most famous export. Sagat showed a keen interest in fashion, art, cinema, and photography early on in his career, and later on arthouse and queer film directors such as Bruce LaBruce and Christophe Honoré recruited him to star in their films *L.A. Zombie* and *L'homme au bain*, respectively. He achieved crossover success in the horror genre, playing an addict in *Saw VI*.[29] Sagat (born in Cognac, France, of Slovak ancestry) got his porn start doing Arab drag as a sweatpants-wearing *banlieusard* with an aggressive stare under the stage name Azzedine, an Islamic honorific which means "the honor, esteem, or glory of religion." That he was uncircumcised and frequently denied Arab heritage in interviews did nothing to stop his Arab fame. In many ways, Sagat exploits this erotic "esteem" of religion in the way he eroticizes Islam on his own body, while he also capitalizes on the still pervasive stereotype that Muslim men, while outwardly conservative, are sexually adventurous and potent: unlike, Charef's character Madjid or Citébeur producer Chibikh, he is not exploiting a stereotype that victimizes a race or class to which he belongs. Sagat declared a long-standing love and respect for Arab men and Arabic culture in interviews, and that his crescent tattoo is an "eye-winking" gesture to the Arab men who watch him.[30] Perhaps Sagat's greatest feat of image engineering has been to make the French-Arab street style he eroticizes and performs intelligible to an arthouse audience around the world. In this way, Sagat was both able to pay his respects to the Arab culture that was instrumental to his success, and also venture into more avant-garde horizons, via his collaboration with Australian photographer Elvis di Fazio in a performance piece titled "Don't Panic I'm Islamic."[31] Borrowing from the amateur public service announcements that have proliferated on the Internet in the face of fear-mongering about the Islamization of the West, the performance piece takes inspiration from the suburban landscape of Western Sydney where a numerically significant Muslim population has taken up residence, and makes a strident statement in favor of multicultural acceptance. The video, structured as a triptych, shows Sagat inhabiting the dual role of a third-generation mother and son, donning a burqa and a panoply of Arab street fashions, respectively. Sagat reintroduces the Citébeur body language and articles of clothing that channel *banlieusard* swagger and street style, all symbols of combative posture which are again milked for their eroticism: running shoes with loose laces, wifebeater, fanny pack, boxing sweats, boxing attire, diamond studs, athletic shorts exposing muscular thighs. As the son, Sagat repeatedly pulls a gun out of his shorts for phallic emphasis, getting hyped up on his own virility, glaring at targets; one of which is the viewer. We notice an appendage that seems out of place, a tacked-on hair extension that resembles the back of a mullet but also adds an androgynous motif. At the same time, within the other frames of the triptych, the mother character, who has been smoking shisha and blowing it through the opening in her burqa, also glares at the camera (her eyes evoking the familiar stares on *National Geographic* covers) and begins a slow striptease that reveals that she is wearing the same shoes as Sagat, eventually becoming her son. The epilogue at the conclusion of the performance piece states: "In this piece, François Sagat reflects on the battle of masculinity vs. femininity, traditional vs. modern society and how this transition from traditional to modern created a whole subculture which has (unfortunately) become a victim of discrimination by both traditional and modern sides." This explanation echoes my argument in chapter 2, detailing the ways that the "dysfunctional" Muslim family unit—made up of the delinquent son, the self-censoring mother, and the absentee father—has become a key engine of fearmongering about Islam. The piece also emphasizes the proximity between the self-censoring mother and delinquent son, with the former enabling and encouraging the latter in the recycling of patriarchy. However, the piece finally opts for queer optimism, underlining that what they share is an androgyny that only becomes visible beyond the smoke and the burqa. The artist statement also identifies the cultural, or more precisely subcultural, stakes of the performance on display: the artists show that the subculture emerging from Muslim suburbia is rife with aesthetic merit and possibility as well as gender bending. However, this aesthetic and queer potential is always under threat of erasure from pressures of discrimination, accusations of nonassimilation, and the awareness that one constitutes a "problem" for the host society.

"Don't Panic I'm Islamic!" alerts porn actor François Sagat in Elvis Di Fazio's video short. Here Sagat channels the androgynous synergy between a burqa-clad mother and her swagger-filled son, on the periphery of the Western metropolis. (Courtesy of Elvis Di Fazio.)

The Banlieue's Erotic Premises

The presence of firearms in the Citébeur erotic strategy, creatively channeled by Sagat, raises the specter of *insécurité* (lack of security) in the banlieues, a daily feature of the French evening news. In Citébeur, we witness the *insécurité* that imperils private property (theft, home invasion), but also bodily invasions that, in their rehearsed violence, blur the line between sadomasochism and personal *insécurité*. Antoine Barde, Chibikh's business partner, is unapologetic about this violence and refuses to consider as pathological the controlled masochism on display—according to Barde, consumers enjoy watching white (and sometimes Arab) men humbled or humiliated on-screen by thug types. This mock violence, he insists, could be the main draw for a significant portion of viewers who purchase their DVDs. The presence of firearms, albeit fake, in the videos is just one point of controversy in the Citébeur erotic strategy: "We don't support, of course, the use of firearms," assured Barde, who seems seasoned by his PR role designed to calm down worried media inquirers who might see in Citébeur a sort of incitement to violence. In important ways, Citébeur has a paradoxical effect of addressing the fear of violence, sabotaging the expected outcome and cliché of conflict while telling another story in its place, not necessarily flattering for the parties involved, but not apocalyptic either. Much criticism of the studio revolved around the accusation that its rehearsed violence appeared too "real," that its actors did in effect such a good job that perhaps they were not acting at all. This critique shades into familiar, racist tropes that assume men of color's propensity for anger and violence, their greater degree of authenticity, and, most importantly, an inability to merely simulate or perform rage, which translates into an inability to distinguish between representation and reality. This pattern of representation harkens back to the rhetoric of the Algiers School and its afterlives in France, whereby experimental psychiatrists determined that Arab and Muslim men were prone to anger, sexual violence, and perversion, and lacked essential psychological capacities to distinguish shades of reality, resulting in an extreme, simpleminded literalism (see chapter 2). This projection of literalism onto racial others also affects power differentials between actors, usually an element of eroticism in ethnically uniform porn. Here, the power imbalance between Arab top and white bottom for some (squeamish critics) seems to depart from representation and approach reality. As theorists of sexuality have explained, the exhibition of power often intimidates because it seems "incompatible with freedom," but power in Citébeur is a perpetually moving entity, taken away from bottoms and given to tops (and sometimes vice versa), and is never permanently consolidated in one type of individual.[32] This aligns with Foucault's analysis of power: the movement and "exchange" of power (a term with less hierarchical associations) shows that power is constantly on the move, with an agency of its own, and it is this dynamism of unexpected "power exchanges" that generates drama and excites the viewer.[33] One gains the sense, watching Citébeur, that performers are more excited by the channeling and exhibition of power than questions of domination, such that domination can generate pleasure in both dominator and dominated as they enjoy the spectacle.

Chibikh's upbringing, with Kabyle and Harki parents,[34] born and raised in the French suburbs, perhaps explains an investment in the French urban environment, whereas producers such as the late Cadinot fetishize North Africa and its sex tourism. Some critics of Citébeur, however, say it is animated by the same mechanisms of exoticism and colonial othering that animated Cadinot's production values, turning the banlieue into a postcolonial repository of colonial desire and anxiety. Yet, with Citébeur, it is hard to ignore just how much the colonial tropes have been overturned. In the tourism literature of André Gide or Joe Orton, for instance, the predominant figure of desire was the androgynous North African youth of rare beauty, taken as a figure of alterity against which to evaluate European subjectivity by comparison: one remembers Gide comparing his sickly "European" body to that of exuberant, bronze-skinned North African boys and young men. In Citébeur that image has been exchanged for the often obscured Franco-Arab model, who is the opposite of naked: somber and grinning provocatively under his baseball cap, wearing sun glasses or a Palestinian keffiyeh even when indoors. Actors are purposefully dissimulated by the cinema verité style of Chibikh's handheld camera, which playfully hides actors in a way that frustrates the viewers' desire for nudity, yet simultaneously generates the eroticism of delayed reward when more of the actor is exposed. This returns to journalist Maury's frustration about Citébeur being as irritating as it is exciting, a result of Citébeur's upending of conventional porn marketing, which has it that the entire action must cater to the visual satisfaction of the consumer. Though Citébeur does eventually give the client what he (or she) wants, as with any pornographic production, the consumer is actually paying to have the actors visually frustrate him (or her, as there are female fans of this production).

For Barde, Chibikh's coproducer, the so-called authenticity of a clandestine sexuality thought to thrive in the banlieue space is essential to Citébeur's appeal. This is in large part due to the "forbidden, because of the danger and the possibility of surprise" that keeps that sexuality erotic. For the filmmakers, this tension between secret and discovery provides a gold

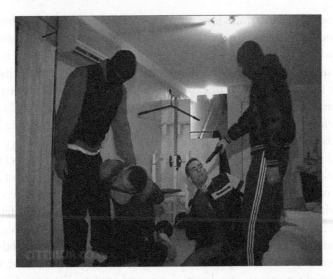

Porn studio Citébeur, specializing in *racaille* or thuggish banlieue men, gives new meaning to the term "power exchange."

mine of eroticism for patrons bored with a "modern" gay mainstream. "It's a tension which you feel on film," says Barde. "Many times, while filming in stairwells or basements, we've startled policemen who, in a state verging on shock, said it was the first time they had seen anything like this, or even imagined such a thing were possible, in the projects at least."[35] In this anecdote, Citébeur sabotages the structures that oppose the state apparatus and its personnel to a surveilled Arab community. Barde and Chibikh here use the serendipitous occurrence of *banlieusard* homosexuality as a ruse, a surprise, or even a consciousness-raising initiative against established French anxieties about racial and sexual difference. When those accustomed to a monochromatic banlieue (here, policemen) discover its sexual diversity, the hope is that they may take a startled step back and leave more room in the consideration of Franco-Arab subjectivities for sexual alterity and the dispersal of ethnic stereotypes.

The studio toes an ambivalent line by exposing sexual practices represented and valorized as private. The way that Citébeur's visual conventions evidence contradiction (in the way it exposes sexual activity eroticized as hidden) establishes striking parallels with other infamous forms of pornography, such as bareback, in which the normal imperative to show evidence of male orgasm (the money shot) conflicts with the "commitment to internal ejaculation."[36] As Linda Williams explains in *Hardcore: The Frenzy of the Visible*, hardcore has a special commitment to maximum visibility, which distinguishes it from the gradualist, progressive visibility fostered by erotica. Citébeur charts an innovative path in the way it seeks to make visible, not the body parts of its actors, but rather the techniques and instruments they use to hide themselves and establish anonymity (through the use of sunglasses, ski masks, hoodies, darkness, night cameras, basements, abandoned buildings).

In discussing the innovation of Citébeur, it may be tempting to describe its producers as capable of circumventing the representational clichés that sometimes bog down gay visual culture. In such a view, this postcolonial production, in which homosexuality mostly occurs in a clandestine mode, appears to exist above and before categories—that is, before nomenclature regarding identities and roles—and thus appears able to rejoin a lost golden age that may have existed prior to the naming and identifying enthusiasm Foucault declared concurrent with the medicalization of homosexuality that dates to the late nineteenth century. In travel and sex tourism literature, this age before categories and identifications is purported to have survived in Middle Eastern cultures (see chapter 3). In casting Arab men who have sex with men without ever describing themselves as gay,[37] Citébeur establishes a bridge between Arab sexual cultures in North Africa and those of the diaspora in the banlieues.

From *Beur* to *Beurette*, a Political Loss

Postcolonial pornography has a highly lucrative heterosexual side of course. As with gay productions, Orientalist tropes have often been recycled from times past, visible in the proliferation of titles (most often made for men by men) depicting harems, the sexual despotism of Arab men, as well as forced or voluntary unveilings that become erotic events following the sequence of a striptease. One of the trendiest figures emerging in post-1980s porn has been that of the *beurette* (Franco-Arab woman) in French heterosexual pornography. It has become difficult if not impossible to perform Internet searches about nonsexual aspects of *beurettes*, so prevalent is their sexualization online. As with Citébeur and its promotion of the *racaille*, heterosexual porn studios have promoted the "girl from the projects" into a recognizable and sought-after type, such that zeitgeist publications like *Les Inrockuptibles*, which follows trends in pornography closely, have dubbed this trend *La mode beurette*.[38] Citébeur and *beurette* productions strongly differ, however, in terms of the directors' proximity and identification with the actors, and in terms of the existence of an arguably political activism on display. In gay productions, the intended audience can more easily identify with the actors, in contrast to the heterosexual production, which is usually designed for the gratification of a hypothetically white male viewer. Heterosexual porn featuring *beurettes* does not showcase scenarios of resistance, role reversal, or social reckonings to the same extent, even though it takes as one of its central figures the virile woman or gang member in the banlieues (see chapter 1). As *beurette* porn star Yasmine describes, the *racaille* (female thug) role is one that provided her the means to emerge (as in her breakout title *Yasmine et ses amies* [Yasmine and her girlfriends]). It is a role she has avoided ever since, as it represents for her an unflattering image of a *beurette de service* (token Arab, but also, Arab at your service) who hustles in the projects, for whom nothing is too degrading as long as it involves money. In the 2007 investigative report "Les Marocains et le X: une histoire charnelle" (Moroccans and the X-rated: A carnal story) organized by francophone Moroccan magazine *Tel Quel*, the editorial writers described the France-born trope, as well as its later infiltration of the Moroccan sexual imaginary, in the following terms:

> *Beurettes* are cast in scenes that derive from the image of the "Muslim woman from the banlieues who wants to slum it with riff-raff [*s'encanailler*]." The discourse is always the same: a virgin girl wants to emancipate herself from moral pressures, to "let loose and have a good time" [*s'éclater*] as it is often specified, to uproot herself from "poverty," to get her "thug-girl" on, but without forgetting to put on her headscarf which she removes little by little as the film progresses. This mass of clichés seduced Moroccans, who saw resonating within it their own erotic imaginary. "This archetype of the transgressed religious taboo is just as valid in the reality of Moroccan life. Prostitutes are increasingly donning the headscarf . . . as it is an excitement factor for clients . . ." explains [the sexologist] Aboubakr Harakat.[39]

Interestingly, for Yasmine, the fantastical Orientalist tropes of *The One Thousand and One Nights* appeal to her above and beyond the more contemporary and urban roles available in banlieue pornography. This comes in total opposition to Citébeur's rejection of the service-oriented and sex tourism–enabling Arab boy figure as a disempowering relic of the colonial era. Though Yasmine enjoyed a stratospheric yet temporary success, at the end of her journey she was underpaid, subject to extremely difficult working conditions, and eventually dropped by the mega studio Dorcel when her contract expired. She spoke very bitterly of her experience at Dorcel and her attempts to branch out—without support from her former employer—into film, publishing, or modelling.[40] The prevailing representations of Franco-Arab women in heterosexual pornography for male audiences are, I maintain, less engaged with addressing postcolonial discrimination as an injustice to be dealt with on the level of sexual representation. There are of course exceptions, as in some women-directed crossover films that engage with the porn world: *Baise-moi* (Fuck me, incorrectly translated in its English version as *Rape Me*), which had been released to a wide audience in France and had enjoyed some international success. It starred two *beurette* porn stars—Karen Bach (now deceased) and Rafaella Anderson, playing a prostitute and *racaille* rape survivor, respectively—who go on a killing spree and sex binge. Unlike the case of Citébeur, it is clear that the intended audience for mainstream heterosexual porn featuring Arab women is not the Franco-Arab subject or even the white male viewer who would enjoy seeing women of North African background "heroically" employing sexual weapons toward anticolonial or antiracist ends.

In terms of audience, *Tel Quel* documented how the vogue for *beurettes* moved from France to Morocco, the ancestral homeland of many *beurette* actresses. The francophone culture magazine also explained the subsequent "Moroccan-ization" of this trope that occurred when Moroccan fans began making their own films, and placing market demands for models "closer-to-home" in terms of looks, figure, and especially their ability to speak in *darija* or (Moroccan) dialect. One of the journalists involved in the investigative report, Hassan Hamdani, gives an ultimately pessimistic verdict on the promise of such representation to bring about anything positive in terms of ethnic visibility and empowerment:[41]

> Racism and sexism are two breasts upon which the producers of this sector are now feeding. By investing in realist XXX porn in the mid-nineties, they have inundated the market with films in which the ethnic component was the draw-in. The Arab has not escaped from marketing and even less from racial prejudice. . . . Following the example of the American sites, the women don the veil, except that in France, this piece of cloth is invested with Islam in order to also sell the religious prohibition being transgressed. These sites warn that their content has nothing to do with Islam. Nevertheless, it's the "Muslim woman who's letting go" that one is being sold. . . . A "Yasmine," as liberated as she may be, cannot serve as an example, Moroccan or otherwise.[42]

In an interview with the same magazine, the actress Yasmine invoked here stated that she is a practicing Muslim.[43] When asked about the current image of Arab women today, she lamented the loss of "certain traditional values": when the interviewer expressed surprise at her remark, she expressed her own surprise at his question. Interestingly, the journalist Hamdani conservatively deprives her of role model status in the name of progressive values, while Yasmine the porn star shows a more open-minded understanding of a moral conservatism that can be available to anyone, no matter the judgment placed upon their profession. Also, in the quote itself, it is assumed the male viewer could make a distinction between practicing Islam and engaging with pornography exploiting the erotics of the veil, while the same distinction is not allowed for Yasmine. In this ongoing comparison between Citébeur and heterosexual postcolonial porn, it should be noted, however, that testimony from Citébeur actors about their experiences is not as readily available: their experiences dealing with the studio may have been as problematic as Yasmine's, if not as well documented.

Domestic-Exotic Men

Citébeur was not the first French studio to take an interest in Franco-Arab models. Cadinot's *Harem* (1984), was the first full-length production to feature North African men prominently, following the sex tour of a solitary, slight French youth (known in the gay vernacular as the "twink" type) on location in Morocco.[44] The film was innovative albeit very Orientalist, exiting the hexagonal frame while at the same time drawing on stock ideas of an unlimited sexual *souk* or marketplace just a plane ride away. One Orientalist motif—the idea of the perilous, labyrinthine, yet seductive Casbah—suffuses the film's description on the Cadinot website:

> Everything starts in the hammam. In the humidity of the bath-house, a young Frenchman discovers Arab sensuality with a handsome stallion. It's love at first sight. But the young Moroccan disappears within the narrow streets of the Casbah upon exiting the establishment. Our young hero follows him in hot pursuit through the populated streets . . . he gets lost in the souk where he soon discovers, in the boutique store-rooms, the very special hospitality of the Oriental merchants. Bronze bodies follow one after the other, even an ebony body, perhaps one of the most beautiful ephebes of the Cadinot collection.[45]

Cadinot's ethnic porn often touts the consistent and nearly magical power of white skin to turn Arab men bisexual. In his entry on the recently deceased Cadinot (1944–2008) for the *Dictionnaire de la pornographie*, the scholar Christian Fournier connects Cadinot to the philosophy of the Homosexual Front for Revolutionary Action (FHAR) in the 1970s, saying

that: "Harem . . . seems to illustrate the famous FHAR manifesto claiming the 'right and the desire of French fags to go off and get laid in Morocco.'"[46] On the Cadinot website, the promotion around the film mentioned that a flurry of gay charter flights to North Africa had been booked
in the wake of the film's release.[47] At his death, Cadinot was eulogized in
the mainstream gay press for being a champion of diversity, with journalists making the point that pornography can be in the vanguard of making
France a more inclusive society, even if the images may occasionally be
exploitative. In the period prior to his death, Cadinot focused exclusively
on Arab and Franco-Arab models, culminating in a six-part series titled
Nomades.[48] Some featured performers, however, including Ilmann Bel,[49]
disclosed in interviews that filming conditions were less than ideal. Cadinot, he said, would recruit Franco-Arab men born in urban France and
ask them to play the roles of North African boys with thick accents ac-
costing European tourists while on location in North Africa. Bel spoke
of being flown to Cadinot's vacation home and of a tension-filled filming experience during which his request to play both active and passive
roles was denied, as Cadinot preferred casting him exclusively as a macho, aggressive top. This casting decision does cause one to reconsider the
reproaches often levelled at Franco-Arab porn performers (such as excessively virile and sexist) by gay and straight commentators alike: these
reproaches should in some high-profile cases be directed toward porn's
directors of that virilism.

Well-intentioned attempts to valorize Arab subjects thus sometimes
run the risk of assigning Arab men to a highly limited role. Prominent
director JNRC was also one of the first to emphasize Arab "beauty" with
the release of his Studio Beurs series. Like Cadinot, JNRC showed a pre-
dilection for what he called bisexual "men of the South," a term strangely
reminiscent of what the translator of *The One Thousand and One Nights*,
Richard Burton, termed the "Sotadic Zone" of pederastic enthusiasm:
inside the zone—which covered much of the Mediterranean—sodomy
reigned, regardless of sexual object choice. JNRC spoke at length in interviews of his *beur* favoritism in an almost mystical language of enchant-
ment, as if *beurs* were a final frontier for those who have experienced all
thrills and breached all limits. The following passage could be mistaken
for *nostalgérie* (discourse invoking nostalgia for French Algeria): "I have
lived in the Maghreb in a climate of human warmth. Here [in Paris], people have no sense of orientation. The Marais, it terrifies me. There is such
a sadness. . . . When I return to Marseille, a Mediterranean city, I find my
favorite [Arab] dropouts once again." Why mention "dropouts"? Asked
what kind of actors he chooses, and according to what criteria, JNRC

responds without sarcasm, almost fondly: "Hoodlums, people recently released from jail, on the road to marginalization. These people suffer from a lack of affection, they don't have confidence in themselves. I reflect a positive image back at them, I flatter them, I take care of them. . . . I do social work."[50] Perhaps unconsciously, here JNRC cuts an exploitative figure, swooping down to redress the *misérabiliste* mess of punctured Arab self-esteem and atrophied affectivity. JNRC has made a career out of eroticizing the risks involved in exposure to other cultures, classes, and masculinities: something evidenced in his point about actively seeking out "social cases" for his castings. In 2011, JNRC's risky recruitment efforts were abruptly halted while on a scouting trip in Eastern Europe: he was arrested in Bulgaria under contested circumstances for violating that country's pornography laws.[51] JNRC makes ambivalent assertions about the "men of the South" he recruits, finding in them a reminder of warmth but also the loss of a once common homosocial affectivity that North Africans, among other groups, may have suffered as a result of immigration to France, a loss that stretches over several generations. Claims like JNRC's are often observational and difficult to evaluate in part because they are caught in the crosscurrents of various essentialisms and counter-essentialisms, between openness to cultural difference and the reactivation of stereotypes.

This is one of JNRC's recurrent concerns: the perceived difference in affectivity and human warmth between the European North and the Mediterranean. He echoes other writers who have spoken vaguely of a timeless Mediterranean or Arab hospitality. The sociologist Guénif-Souilamas has historicized this pattern of affective nostalgia and attempted to track its evolution through immigration and subsequent generations, describing a distinctive North African social "warmth" characterized sometimes, but not always, by a fluid line between male homosociality and homosexuality. Immigration can impact affective traditions brought from the home country, and these traditions may evolve at their point of origin as well. Sexual customs in North Africa and the Mediterranean are not immune to change, especially in light of colonial and postcolonial relations. Sex tourism, misunderstandings between tourists and locals, and sometimes outright exploitation, has over time produced a hostility to a homosexuality suddenly seen as Western and no longer implanted in local cultures, as historians of Gay Tangier have explained.[52]

JNRC's ethical concern is complicated by the eroticism he juxtaposes with his "social work." He searches out the masculine "hardness" borne of physically taxing or contentious lives, all while trying to bring some pleasure and softness to his actors' lives in the form of sexual service:

actors ("men from the street," "men of Eastern Europe") are serviced by seasoned gay bottoms in an eager assistant role. Clair contrasts men of color to sad and bitter Parisian gays: it seems as if he detects a certain vitality and affective exuberance in North African men that he wishes to preserve from the harshness of urban and immigrant life in France, hence his concern. In this somewhat romanticized view, porn is not a cause of affective atrophy but rather a remedy against it. The meaning of JNRC's gesture is furthermore vexed because his comments about social cases reinforce stereotypes of minority dependency on the state. Though essentialist, the porn director does bring up something rarely broached, the evolution of affectivity through waves of immigration between North Africa and postcolonial France. Guénif-Souilamas explains that the image of Franco-Arabs has often been locked into a stereotype by which the modern elements of banlieue tensions, poverty, and a survivalist machismo born of these conditions have been fixed as the transhistorical components of essential North African masculinity, regardless of how "tender" affectivities have been outside of these circumstances in previous epochs, places, and pages. This stereotypical imprisonment within virility creates Franco-Arabs who are unable to comprehend the so-called representative French values of equality of the sexes and sexual tolerance that are said to reign in the center of power, in Paris: metrosexual enclaves that she ironically calls "sites of enlightened reconciliation."[53] It is this perception of the unadapted, forever macho Arab or immigrant youth that seems to have informed gay pornographers in their marketing of "rough types."

Summary

A series of persistent and interrelated tropes run through gay and straight "ethnic" erotica: the hypersexualization of single immigrant men; the eroticization of banlieue poverty as regards both women and men; the veil as striptease; and the homosexual thug type or homo thug (*caillera gay*). Pornography stands outside the requirements of political correctness—it elucidates, but also exaggerates and distorts the sexualization of immigration and race relations. Porn studios have seized upon quite serious contemporary scandals involving everything from postimmigration exploitation, sex tourism, *tournantes*, sexual violence, and *insécurité* in the suburbs. Instead of heightening anxieties, the gay productions at least have sought to bring about a strange, and strangely effective, civic therapy using exaggeration, fantasy, but also honesty about the fears that may cause ethnic segregation in city space. Though Arabs are, in mainstream gay productions, more the objects of fantasy rather than the producers of fantasy, Arab performers also eroticize themselves in a way that is initially meant to frustrate, rather than excite, the assumed white viewer-consumer. Heterosexual "ethnic" pornography, made most often by heterosexual men for other heterosexual men, has not been as effective in providing politically subversive images, in exploiting the exploitation so to speak. Finally, this erotic recasting of the demonized banlieues as a space of cleverness, creativity, pleasure, and harmony allows for a crucial interrogation of pornography's low cultural status, its academic marginalization, and its limited political potential.

Conclusion: The Sexagon's Border Crisis

Recent events in France and Europe have highlighted the trends discussed in this book. The massive influx of refugees fleeing Middle Eastern countries has magnified the image of migrants as young, male, and Muslim (in spite of the large-scale presence of women and children). These developments have pushed extreme-right parties that were once the laughing-stock of Europe into prominence and unprecedented electoral victories.[1] French writer Michel Houellebecq, whose past comments earned him a court date for "racial insults and incitement toward religious hatred,"[2] published *Soumission* (*Submission: A Novel*) on the day of the Charlie Hebdo attacks: the novel imagines a doomsday scenario only eight years away at which point, during the 2022 elections, in a political atmosphere increasingly polarized between the far-right and Islamic parties, France elects its first Muslim president. This demographic apocalypse is also sexual: Polygamy is legalized, child brides proliferate, and women return to homemaking. Christianity, the narrator François reflects, is indeed a religion for women as Nietzsche affirmed, powerless in France to defeat virile Islam.[3] The novel's title, which symbolizes both Muslims' attitudes in regard to their religion as well as the capitulation of Westerners faced with its force, evokes the French submission thesis developed in chapter 2 which harbors secular male impotence at its core.

The event that most significantly sexualized the European immigration debate did not actually happen in France, although its aftereffects shook up the French intellectual world. On New Year's Eve 2016, Cologne, Germany, saw a wave of reports of sexual assaults committed by men of Middle Eastern and North African descent, according to police accounts. In 2015, Germany and in particular Chancellor Angela Merkel were lauded for their model response to the refugee crisis afflicting not just Syria but also Iraq, Afghanistan, and East Africa: by year's end, the country had welcomed more than one million refugees.[4] However, the events in Cologne marked a turning point that culminated in the increased unpopularity of Germany's asylum policy and political threats to Merkel's rule, with her approval rating sinking to a four-year low after the attacks.[5] This despite the fact that the crimes could not conclusively be linked to the Syrian refugee crisis.[6]

The Cologne attacks became the object of a polemic in France pitting a group of academics against the Algerian writer and journalist Kamel Daoud. In an op-ed piece entitled "The Sexual Misery of the Arab World" published in the New York Times, Daoud, who had just recently won the Prix Goncourt (the French equivalent of the Pulitzer Prize) for Meursault, contre-enquête (The Meursault Investigation), wrote that after the Cologne attacks, "people in the West are discovering, with anxiety and fear, that sex in the Muslim world is sick, and that the disease is spreading to their own lands."[7] In response, a group of academics, which included many experts on Algeria, penned a letter of protest against Daoud's sexual demonization that accused him of "recycling the most stale orientalist clichés."[8] After accusations of Islamophobia even from former allies, a dismayed Daoud declared that he would quit journalism for good and focus on his literary career.[9] Daoud, who had reported from the front lines of the Algerian civil war in the 1990s, had earned an upstanding reputation as a bold critic of Islamism in his home country of Algeria and had thus become an ally of the secular Left in France. However, his generalizations about a timeless sexual deviancy found in all the "lands of Allah" (to borrow his words) struck many as phantasmatic and poorly researched. The Daoud affair marked an important turning point because it brought "sexual demonization" into the mainstream: I argue elsewhere that Daoud's characterizations of Muslim sexuality went mostly unchallenged because of his membership in the "secularist select," which is counted on to say the otherwise unmentionable about European Muslims in the guise of self-criticism.[10]

After my initial research phase, another major political development occurred in France: the Mariage pour Tous (Marriage for All) campaign which eventually led to the legalization of gay marriage and adoption (though not surrogacy) in 2012. At the political level, the campaign was artfully articulated by Christiane Taubira, then minister of justice in the Hollande government, a French woman of color of Guyanese descent.

This provided for a special convergence of interests as many LGBT activists and allies were enamored of her vivacious defenses of the law against the Catholic Right's insistence on preserving the "traditional" family unit. After Taubira made her memorable speeches on the floor of the National Assembly, an author friend joked that "gays no longer wanted to marry each other, they want to marry Christiane Taubira." She finally resigned from her position in 2016 over disagreements with President Hollande over a controversial proposed civil rights amendment: removing French citizenship from dual-national citizens convicted of terrorism, a proposition that threatened to create two categories of citizenship (one for single nationality French citizens and one for dual nationals). Though the amendment did not pass, the episode underlined a problem at the level of priorities for the French Left, in which sexual progressivism seemed more popular an issue than the defense of citizenship rights. The contrast in responses to Taubira's two courageous actions underlines this: the enthusiasm for her support of gay marriage eclipsed the support offered her in the wake of threats to citizenship rights after the 2015 terrorist attacks. Those who would have been affected most directly by the proposed law were citizens who possessed both French citizenship and a passport from former French colonies or protectorates in Africa, a group that is one of the primary foci of this study.

Members of this group, straddling two or more countries, remarkably had faced "special" treatment when it came to the application of the gay marriage law, as it was precisely countries with a former colonial relationship to France that were made exceptions to the law's provisions. In a strange twist that has consequences for homosexuals of North African origin and their partners, the immigration rights afforded by the shift in marriage laws stopped short of naturalizing citizens of Algeria, Tunisia, and Morocco because of bilateral accords originally designed to protect French citizens' rights in certain countries, and vice versa.[11] In Algeria's case, the 1962 Evian Accords concluding the War for Algerian Independence dictate these terms, acknowledged by French law in Article 202-1, line 2 of the Civil Code. As it stands, gays and lesbians from this list of countries can only marry in France if their spouses happen to be French: a gay marriage involving two Moroccans, for example, would not be allowed. The French government has no (current) plans to renegotiate these bilateral accords as they affect more than just marriage: rather, the government has encouraged those affected to take up their case with the courts. LGBT activists protested that the law was thus not in fact universal, with one news comic redubbing the law "Marriage for (almost) everyone" while it depicted a disappointed biracial couple.[12]

The gay marriage debate also had notable repercussions in antiracist circles. Comparable to the rhetoric in *Homo-ghetto*—which states that banlieue homosexuals are locked in zones of nonrights, in territories lost to the French Republic, or that the banlieue and the city center are evolving at two different speeds—one antiracist activist invoked the idea that gay *banlieusards* live in different dimensions of time and space, albeit for very different reasons.[13] "Indigenous time" is a concept formulated by Houria Bouteldja, an activist and spokesperson for the group Les Indigènes de la République (The Republic's Indigenous), to denote the realities and circumstances that animate the lives of *banlieusards* and minorities and, more importantly, to describe the pace of evolution (or preservation) that these people set for themselves, absent pressures from the outside to change or evolve. Bouteldja, no stranger to the ire of the establishment Right and Left, generated controversy for her remarks on the TV program "Ce soir où jamais," when she was asked to give her opinion on the Marriage for All debate:

> I don't have an opinion about the legitimacy of homo demands but I do have an opinion about the universality of a demand for a homosexual identity. I will tell you straight up, this debate doesn't concern me. . . . I am situated in the history of postcolonial immigration and in the working-class neighborhoods. If I am asked about this issue where I am, because I do not have a universal point of view where I am, I say that this question doesn't concern me. Because if you take a microphone and go into these neighborhoods . . . and ask people about their problems, the spontaneous answers will be about housing, police harassment, or discrimination, unemployment. . . . I bet gay marriage won't come up. That doesn't mean there aren't gay practices in these neighborhoods, it means it's not a priority issue and that people are dealing with things that are more important and urgent.[14]

On the same program, Bouteldja made a distinction between the definite existence of same-sex practices in underprivileged neighborhoods and the "demand for a political identity," which she believes is not universal. She essentially called the focus on gay marriage as the LGBT community's sole goal an example of white, upper-class concerns, because of the emphasis on financial equality with heterosexual couples, succession rights, and family planning. For her, banlieue sexual minorities face the same "urgent" challenges (police harassment, discrimination, poverty, unequal access) as their outwardly heterosexual neighbors and do not express a need for the gay marriage campaign. Critics could reply, however, that banlieue sexual minorities do not articulate solidarity with gay marriage because they can't do so openly: however, this alleged lack of enthusiasm among banlieue sexual minorities is no different from criticisms leveled by US minorities at the gay marriage campaign and the way it sidelined intersectional issues of race and class,[15] as well as people of color's greater vulnerability to STDs and homophobic violence and their lesser access to medical treatment.[16] Bouteldja's insistent inculpation of white privilege has ruffled many feathers in a country where the invocation of privilege has brought up the specter of "antiwhite racism" (especially on the political Right), a conjunction of terms that for some critics evokes racism itself in the way it allows a dominant class to assert victimhood at the hands of the dominated.[17]

After speaking on the TV show, Bouteldja was accused of homophobia and unfavorably compared with Frigide Barjot (unofficial spokesperson of the anti–gay marriage campaign),[18] while newscasts increasingly highlighted the presence of Muslims and people of color among the anti–gay marriage camp, no matter how numerically small. It was this notion—that Muslim groups, antiracist people of color, and the Catholic Right would all be on the same page—that prompted Bouteldja to speak out and clearly set herself apart from the Catholic Right, as well as from Muslim groups seduced into homophobic national belonging.[19] She explained that she was not opposed to but rather nonenthusiastic about gay marriage, underlining that residents of underprivileged neighborhoods were actually more neutral than the media might like: not especially homophobic, but not especially gay-friendly either.[20] She expressed wariness about a French (gay) universalism that would once again assume that the goals of the white majority were necessarily shared by citizens of color. Like Stéphane Chibikh, the cocreator of Citébeur (see chapter 5), she had to explain herself before a skeptical audience to recover the meaning of her own words. Her essay also marked the convergence of the antiracist Far Left and Joseph Massad's theses in Desiring Arabs (see the introduction): like Arabs in the Middle East on whose sexual instability the homo-hetero binary was imposed, banlieusards of all stripes would be subject to a gay imperialism that paves over dissident local sexual cultures. The Bouteldja episode highlights the way the French mainstream media, which routinely calls her anti-French, was actually quite oblivious of the queer and the latter's partially French roots. Michel Foucault, for instance, respected the local particularities of sexual cultures by setting the birth of homosexual identity in a specific time and place in Western Europe—the French mainstream commentators critiquing her would still have to make an effort to be properly Foucauldian. She invoked queer theorist Judith Butler's vocal opposition to the militarization of gay culture at the very moment that "gender theory" was raised as the anti–gay marriage camp's enemy number one: that camp had mobilized to rid school curricula of any trace of gender theory,[21] a fact that again marks Boutledja's nonalignment with the Catholic Right. Importantly, Bouteldja's position cannot be confused with a kneejerk pro-Muslim stance, because she also rejects as paternalistic the outwardly more sympathetic stance that tolerates homosexuals as God's creation and reserves judgment for a conversation between them and their maker. Beyond the limitations of the French Right and Left, of the secular and religious, she proposes: "[the] decolonial position [which is one that] does not view homosexuals as baby seals, a species deserving of protection or contempt, but as social subjects. It is a position that develops a political formulation free of a pathological or paternalistic relationship with homosexuality but refuses to align itself with the white agenda. This is far from homophobia. It is in fact its opposite."[22] This political formulation deviates from the homonormative agenda when it attempts to decolonize homosexuality by invoking the long history of homoeroticism in Islamic lands which, Bouteldja says, "was displaced during the long colonial night." A position that rejects one kind of homosexual culture in favor of another, much like Majid's dismissal of public homosexuality in favor of discreet homosexuality in chapter 1, cannot easily be passed off as homophobic if it merely reflects a dispute among sexual minorities about how to be.

Bouteldja explains that banlieue subjects may voluntarily reject "progress" when it excludes them, as well as embrace elements of their past in order to better affirm themselves: in this way she gives an illustration of the proregressions I theorize in the introduction and chapter 1. The Arab same-sex practices displaced in the "colonial night" are the object of a recovery operation in postcolonial France, where they have survived despite all attempts to shame or eradicate them, albeit in reconstructed form: this would be evident in Majid's attempt, for instance, to reorganize a sexual network of Arab "cousins for cousins" who have the sense of vice and discretion he prefers. Bouteldja actually uses an expression very similar to proregression to describe the space-time of Les Indigènes de la République and the way the group refuses the Eurocentric model of linear time that builds toward progress but inevitably leaves people of color outside of that progress. She calls "productive regression" that which seems like a "regression but is in fact progress from the point of view of the overall interest of the racialized people."

While Bouteldja's vision aims to recover the displaced sociosexual links that Arabs can call "ours" and "authentic," my view of proregression is different in that it does not aim to restore a lost authenticity, but rather stresses the modernity and unprecedentedness of *banlieusard* sexual cultures that eroticize old Arab social customs and Islamic bonds. In this way, I may accept a chronology that lines up with the Eurocentric model of linear time, because I believe banlieue subjects who embrace regressive clandestinity do so as Muslim Europeans produced by the circumstances of contemporary Europe: these subjects do not seek to recover so much as to create sociosexual bonds among Muslim Europeans and Europeans of color. In this sense, I agree with Fouad Zeraoui's view in chapter 1 when he says that French black and *beurs* are agents of creative change on the cutting edge of not only fashion but also self-styling in general.

What many antiracist defenses of discreet sexual subcultures leave out—and indeed what I mostly leave out here but hope to return to one day—is the existence of queer effeminacy and flamboyancy in the banlieues, that is, gender expressions that cannot "pass" and do not always have the option of discretion. Over the course of writing this book, I have tried not to fall into the trap of denying effeminacy in the attempt to defend queer virility cultures against too hasty condemnations. This effeminacy has a real but admittedly embattled status in the banlieues and French communities of color, and should not be confused with the relaxed and public effeminacy on display in gayborhoods. In *Homo-ghetto*, Chaumont alludes to effeminate men with indomitable spirits who nevertheless use the vernacular of the banlieues and are seasoned fighters ready to defend their place in a dense urban environment. While one should not romanticize confrontation nor seek to "save" others from it, it is important to recognize that effeminate subcultures have existed and continue to exist in the banlieues, sometimes in a mode of resistance. These subcultures are on prominent display at Zeraoui's Black Blanc Beur dance parties (see chapter 1), where groups of young effeminate black men, arranging themselves in cliques channeling American vogue and ballroom culture, are commonly referred to as *les beyoncés*, in a naming gesture that designates their plurality, independence, and proverbial fierceness. Now documented by American hipster outlets (they were called "Proletarian French Voguers" in the *Fringes* series on Vice.com),[23] *les beyoncés* are plainly visible in the Paris metro, traveling in large groups often in the company of women: in this sense, they mirror the ways that queer Muslims have forged alliances first with the Muslim women in their midst, often borrowing pages from one another's life and survival manuals, sharing strategies for straddling communities and negotiating tempered liberties (see the introduction). The *banlieue's* effeminate subcultures need not be divorced or extricated from a sense of urban belonging. For example, Lasseindra is a black French voguer (whom Vice.com calls a "drag queen" but who other publications refer to as trans[24]) who also founded the French ballroom vogue scene and was recruited by New York's House of Ninja (popularized in Jennie Livingston's documentary *Paris Is Burning*): in 2013, Lasseindra participated in the StreetStar international urban street dance festival in Stockholm and took home the top prize as an openly trans contestant competing against cis-women before an urban hip-hop audience that rewarded her despite its alleged sexual intolerance.

Framing the Sexagon

Though far from comprehensive, *Sexagon* offers five interconnected perspectives into the sexualization of immigration. Recurring tropes and persistent figures cross boundaries of art and discipline, establishing a continuum of representations that filter cultural and ethnic difference through the prism of sexuality. This Western strategy, of comprehending the other's cultural difference by expressing it in the more "intelligible" language of sexuality, has precedents in the Orientalist output of old. There are contemporary and political factors involved, however, when this translation of cultural difference into sexual difference happens in postcolonial, postimmigration Europe. The terms *sexual modernity, sexual democracy,* and *sexual citizenship* were coined to qualify our new sexualized hierarchies of cultural capital. These terms emerged when those cultural custodians vested with the highly unstable task of defining Europe opted for sexual vocabularies as the best language for expressing Europe's singularity. The reasons for this choice, as a wide array of thinkers cited here have suggested, have to do with the perception that immigrant and immigrant-issued attitudes toward sexuality are so different from the mainstream that they present one of the last remaining platforms with which to establish a civic gap between white European citizens and minority residents otherwise indistinguishable from them. Some activists, thinkers, writers, and filmmakers have pushed back against this turn of events by stressing the hypocrisy, regression, and xenophobia inherent in defining Europe this way. Still others have sought to locate a more current and even subversive modernity in the often vilified gender expressions of minorities, promoting the banlieues as centers rather than suburbs of French culture. Thus, a battle of representations has broken out on the slippery terrain where culture meets politics in multiethnic France: it has been fomented by the recasting of the issue of cultural assimilation as a sexual one, as well as by the initially slow but now increasing consciousness that such a recasting has taken place.

The Banlieue as Maker of the Queer

Gay and feminist activist journalism has contributed to the sexualization of discourse about the banlieues, often in nonemancipatory ways that work against the interests of those they are meant to defend (see chapter 1). Activist journalists who are invested with a responsibility to protect sexual diversity in many instances end up repressing it, especially when the sexuality in question does not conform to normative ideas of femininity or homosexuality by embracing virility cultures. This applies to activist journalists covering women's and gay and lesbian rights as well as race and the effects of racism. Investigative reports that purport to reveal the untenable living conditions of women and sexual minorities in the banlieues are often seen to commit journalistic and ethnographic abuses. Stereotypical trends in banlieue representation have recently become objects of critique for those represented, with *banlieusards* discontent with the portrayal of their living spaces increasingly opting for disengagement with the media. One of these media distortions revolves around an increasingly prominent gender expression among young banlieue women—what I've termed *nongendered virility*—displayed most spectacularly by girl gangs. Nongendered virility presents special obstacles for mainstream feminist attempts to "save" banlieue women, as these interventions often condemn the virile assertiveness these women view as key to agency and respect in their communities. In rejecting the combative virility of banlieue women, these activist journalists reveal themselves to be more concerned with preserving essentialist notions of femininity, than with protecting all forms of gender expression as they originally intended. Female gang members are not the only subjects whose combativity is dismissed in light of their "dangerous virility"; veiled women who engage in activism and educate themselves also find their resistance invalidated due to a nonconforming gender expression, in which the hijab is virilized and turned into armor.

Media commentators and activists have minimized and often mocked the resistant posture in many of these ethnic minority displays of virility, ridding them of all political significance. Since virility is purported to constitute the dominant law in the banlieues, any strategies of coping or resistance that embrace virility lose all subversive content and are met with verdicts of "false consciousness." French diversity activists Fadela Amara and Franck Chaumont, among others, have highlighted the internalization of patriarchy that supposedly becomes apparent when virility is wielded by women, sexual minorities, and other marginalized groups.

By confining the meaning of virility to banlieue spaces (rather than considering the effect of the interplay between the banlieue and the city center) such analyses conveniently gloss over the resistant or nonnormative potential of a strategic virility that arises in border confrontations, or when banlieue subjects enter the city center—that is, they ignore virility as survival, negotiation, coping, or play.

Critiques of banlieue and Islamic virilities have originated in feminist circles but have recently branched out. Following in the footsteps of women's rights campaigns, new sexual rights campaigns are being pursued in the banlieues under the rainbow flag. Though the intention of coming to the aid of homosexuals encountering homophobia is laudable, such interventions sometimes harm the subjects they intend to assist in the way they define homosexuality as incompatible with (and thus foreign to) the banlieues. This makes it impossible for activists and critics to acknowledge a banlieue homosexual identity; it also directs banlieue homosexuals toward the sole "solution" of escape to the city center. In this context, all banlieue homosexuals must always already be sexual refugees.

Two figures keep reappearing in arguments about the dangers to sexual diversity that virilism in the banlieues poses: the homo-thug and the proud *banlieusard* homosexual. These two figures are exceptional in the sense that they express no need to (and often refuse to) disassociate their banlieue and sexual identities. Though the heavily edited interviews with these banlieue homosexuals exude an undeniable sexism, they also exhibit significant queer traits often glossed over in the rush to condemn virility. Within gay enclaves like the Marais, virility can be turned into a tool for underlining cultural difference, class difference, and even sexual preferences. The homo-thug's queer use of virility, which is different from a queering of virility, includes an eroticization of clandestine encounters that are often deemed to be an ancient relic of the homosexual past by the gay mainstream, rather than a product of newer urban relations.

In recent years, the coalition of activists advocating on behalf of sexual minority issues in the banlieues has splintered somewhat. The former activist turned nightclub and online entrepreneur, Fouad Zeraoui, for example, now opposes miserabilist discourse on banlieue sexual minorities, though he used to be a proponent of such discourse ten years earlier. Whereas alarmist discourse on the banlieues often invokes an atemporal machismo, Zeraoui speaks in terms of evolution and gradual change for the better. He does not necessarily contest the grid of an inevitable progress toward (sexual) modernity: while accepting this frame of reference, however, he emphasizes how banlieue youth could actually embody modernity's cutting edge, especially when it comes to the worlds of fashion, music, and sports. The creativity emerging from banlieue clandestinity, combativity, and virile performance has more often been recognized by cultural actors than activists. Within an atmosphere of miserabilist discourse that suffocates alternative representations of the banlieues, Zeraoui presents the evident "happiness" he observes in his nightclubs as a political counterexample. He also dismisses miserabilism in his questioning of the often uncontested fact that ethnic sexual minorities are the most victimized of victims. He highlights the upward mobility and visibility of gay and lesbian Arabs in a society that regards androgyny and metrosexuality as modern. Zeraoui criticizes the call for homosexuals to flee the banlieue, underlining that those *banlieusards* pushed into domestic exile would merely be exchanging one communitarianism for another.

Psychoanalysis's Family Terrible

In my examination of the sexualization of diversity and immigration through psychoanalysis—a discipline that has since its foundation expertly unpacked the sexual undercurrents in both culture and politics—I contend that a significant part of the sexualization of these debates stems from the fact that psychoanalysts have had an unusually prominent voice within them. This sexualization targets three figures who present a portrait of culturally informed sexual aberration: the turbulent adolescent, the veiled or (self-)censoring woman, and the impotent father. Much in the same way that the figure of the dominant immigrant male and the submissive immigrant female mutually reinforce each other, these three figures of a "dysfunctional" family unit participate in setting up a chain of failure that reinforces miserabilism. Many parallels exist between the French psychological rhetoric and the alienating "culture of poverty" arguments targeting blacks and Latinos in the United States.[25] Queer of color analysis echoes throughout these readings, in the way it has outlined how liberal ideology defined the "bourgeois nuclear family model" and fitness for citizenship in opposition to African-American "sexual, familial, and gender relations."[26]

Islam, as a complex system of signs, has fascinated many Francophone psychoanalysts since Freud's brief consideration of the Islamic faith in *Moses and Monotheism*. Muslim subjects, both during the colonial and decolonization eras, have regarded psychoanalysis with deep ambivalence, as many abuses were committed in the name of the experimental science, as Frantz Fanon reminds us in his criticisms of the infamous Algiers school. A certain kind of ethnopsychiatry existed back then, a highly othering one that assumed a permanent "Muslim madness," and also a permanent Muslim perversity. A very different school of ethnopsychiatry emerged after decolonization, one that declared itself sensitive to the immigrant condition in a way that a universalist (some might say a French republican) brand of psychoanalysis could not. However, this branch of ethnopsychiatry has consistently had to prove, not always convincingly, that it has severed links with colonial ethnopsychiatry. Several critics have pointed out that both old and new ethnopsychiatrists dispute the universality of Freudian psychoanalysis, albeit for ideologically conflicting reasons.

The adolescent is a theoretical and sexual figure highlighted for various reasons in this literature. In much francophone North African psychoanalytical writing, adolescence is represented as a period of sexual maturation but also as the psychological boiling point of society, the place where society might let off steam for the sake of the well-being of the whole. Culturalist interpretations surface when it comes to explaining why adolescent violence has allegedly proliferated in France among populations of immigrant origin. One school of thought suggests that suddenly intimidating adolescents have merely taken advantage of the gap left by fathers too busy with work, disabled by injury or unemployment, or too defeated by life in France to fulfill their role as authority figures. As a consequence, filiation models get scrambled and the second generation cannot improve upon the first, because it no longer respects its elders. Another school of thought suggests that, in the Franco-Arab case, the killing of the hobbled father has occurred much too easily, with disorienting consequences for the son who must take his place.

French psychoanalysts of a conservative stripe have reified this reading. Michel Schneider in particular has spoken of banlieue adolescents of Islamic origin as key figures in his diagnosis of the psychopathology of political life in France.[27] Alluding to an over-mothering, neutering France that has caused amnesia in Caucasian men in regard to their masculinity, Schneider says that "hyperviolent" and "hypersexual" youth issued from immigration are the only figures to have escaped society's "counterproductive" feminist education. France's progressive education of its citizens, Schneider says, has managed to discipline men, except for those youth of immigrant origin who have not passed through those processes of cultural reeducation. This state of affairs derives from what he calls the slow degradation of the "symbolic order," in which the father should be the figure who guarantees the function of the whole, but who cannot educate his children about how to treat women or bring discipline to bear on his sons if that father happens to be a (disoriented) Muslim immigrant.

There are precedents to Schneider's placement of banlieusards at the fault lines of a national psychodrama. His intervention can be linked to an interpretive tendency in psychoanalytical literature by which society's indigestible or unmanageable psychologies have been directed toward the periphery. For the purpose of this discussion, such a move occurs because the banlieues would represent that part of the psychological whole where residents have not yet adopted the "self-civilizing" mechanism that re-presses impulses seeking release in violent pleasure: they appear to lack a super ego. In this schema, it is only a matter of time before "terrorism" and, in the banlieue dystopia, "sexual terrorism" enter the picture. This sexualization of Arab violence has a history that predates the banlieue context. Surveying the work of the Algiers School, Richard Keller shows how stereotypes of North African sexual violence were already spreading in the late nineteenth century, culminating in midcentury recommenda-tions at the political and police level to curb immigration to France for "psycho-sexual" reasons.

The "self-censoring woman" is the second member of this family pa-thologized by psychoanalysts. The Tunisian-born analyst Fethi Benslama took her as a point of departure for his study of what the hijab "means" symbolically to Muslims, anchoring his analysis in the veil controver-sies that gripped France starting in the late 1980s. The French headscarf ban in schools of 2004 importantly targeted conspicuous religious sym-bols: Benslama's 1998 critique anticipates the irony of this prohibition in light of the veil's symbolic function of limiting "showiness." He bases his symbolic analysis on the protective role of the hand versus the (evil) eye in Arab-Islamic culture writ large: the hijab in this schema lines up with the hand, against hypervisibility and exposure. In the period be-tween the two most prominent controversies, state arguments against the hijab arguably shifted from secularism-based rationales to platforms that advocated for values of equality and complementarity of the sexes. Benslama speaks of the hijab's importance in Islamic relations between the sexes, making intriguing use of the story of the Prophet's first wife, Khadija. In this, he reflects a striking adherence to an officialized French understanding of relations between the sexes, in which complementar-ity, I argue, is of supreme importance. However, if one takes his analysis to its logical conclusion, one can "paradoxically" see why a headscarf ban might jeopardize harmony between the sexes rather than encour-age it.

The stigmatization of the hijab impacted the formation of the new ethnopsychiatry in France. Colonial ethnopsychiatrists had tried to dis-miss or actively repress local forms of Islamic spirituality or mysticism, since these "relics" (including the hijab) were seen as unacceptable com-petitors with modern Western medicine and progress. Postcolonial ethnopsychiatrists, however, incorporated symbols from immigrants' spiritual cosmologies as tools useful for the psychoanalysis of these patients. The distinction between public and private realms becomes increasingly politicized and sexualized in Benslama's theories about how the hijab, removed in private but worn in public, produces eroticism.

The last figure rounding out the dysfunctional immigrant family arranged by this group of psychoanalysts is the unemployed, emasculated, or impotent father. As we have seen, much has been written about the failure of the sons of immigrants to integrate the rule of the father: some authors state that this failure occurs because the fathers of these sons were infantilized or dehumanized as easily disposable manual workers. Tahar Ben Jelloun, now better known as a novelist, wrote a psychiatry doctoral thesis about the affective and sexual suffering male workers underwent as a result of immigration to France. He noted a startling incidence of solitary, immigrant men being sent to psychiatry wards due to complaints of impotence. Ben Jelloun argues that impotence is merely the physical expression of a lack of affective welcome in the host country. It may also have resulted from the impossibility of intimacy with one's spouse for workers who could not take return trips home, at a time in the early 1970s before family reunification laws had come into effect. All of these factors culminate in a revolt against reproduction itself (impotence) and a psychosomatic refusal to project oneself generationally into any kind of French future.

Ultimately, the strongest point of conflict in debates about immigration and psychoanalysis has to do with individualism. After diagnosis of this family's "dysfunction," these psychoanalysts recommend an individualist exit from what is deemed to be a dangerous group or communitarian psychology at the family's core. Against this recommendation for reasons of cultural sensitivity, new ethnopsychiatrists have argued with this group of thinkers over whether the imperative for individuality reflects the intrusion of republican ideas into psychoanalysis. Ethnopsychiatrists call attention to the importance of ethnic belonging as a tool that can help cement the psychologically crucial building blocks of filiation between generations: thus, ethnopsychiatrists have often argued for immigrants' rights *not* to assimilate, to preserve a communitarianism that is a sign of health rather than social exclusion. These thinkers have described the ways in which "republican" psychoanalysis amounts to yet another form of epistemically violent assimilation, replacing a functional form of filiation (immigrant families) with an often elusive and aspirational one (national filiation). Ethnopsychiatrists have in turn been criticized for calling back immigrants (who may *want* to assimilate) to their origins, privileging old links that are destined to weaken over time with integration in the host country. Some radical and queer activists have also criticized the "forced" psychological assimilation of immigrants and their descendants for related reasons. They declare that conservative psychoanalysts now target ethnic minorities in the same way they had targeted homosexuals and transsexuals in the past. After pathologizing sexual difference, this conservative strain of psychoanalysis has deployed the same community-breaking arguments about "invalid" lifestyles and lack of appropriate psychological grounding against immigrants and their progeny.

The Arab Boy's Blowback

In the literature at hand, taking affective revenge for a past injustice does not have to take the form of a sexual encounter. Often, its strongest examples come in the form of a practiced indifference, when Franco-Arab characters frustrate the desires of non-Arab admirers with the aim of denying sexual reciprocity to those who have denied them socially. In many of the works profiled here, reciprocity is a casualty of the breakdown of hospitality within postimmigration circumstances. The estranged Arab and white parties position and consolidate themselves against one another in a hierarchy, through a process of critical alterity or by defining oneself against the other's difference. When French writers of European origin derive a sense of identity by contrast against what they are not, namely, "macho" North African men, this leads to a deprivation of subjectivity and, most importantly, intellectual and cultural aptitude in the Franco-Arabs described. Disappointed admirers such as Mitterrand and Cardon have voided the personalities of their lover interlocutors, as their portrayals of Franco-Arab "dullness" made clear. What some authors view, with noticeable frustration, as the opacity of Franco-Arab subjectivities can instead be read as a minority strategy of resistance against exploitation; the Moroccan writers Mohammed Choukri and Mohammed Mrabet frequently had male characters present stubborn walls of silence to European tourists, clients, or tricks. A wariness perhaps conducts these sometimes real, sometimes literary subjects—chided by Barthes and Cardon for their sexually "uncooperative" behavior—to forgo a sexual reciprocity that might itself have gone perilously unreciprocated had they engaged in it. This fear is expressed in Taïa's rewriting of typical sex tourism dynamics, when M'hamed offers René his body but receives nothing in return. Tali, however, in *Incomparable*, departs from the resentment-filled trope of "writing back," by writing simultaneously (Camus and Tali agree to present their material at the same time), and in the process realizes that what seemed like an enchanted encounter actually gave way to an astonishing gap in cultural and political understanding, upon the discovery of which each party goes their own way.

However, Franco-Arab writers more recently have decided to revamp this story of disenchantment for contemporary circumstances. One method has been to create white characters that obtain an almost subaltern status in light of the intensity of their own unreciprocated desires for Franco-Arabs. Nina Bouraoui illustrates this with her exploration of sexual psychology, masculinity complexes, and cross-ethnic attraction in *Avant les hommes*. Taïa has his sexual tourist taken captive by the poignancy of a situation in which he cannot help but sympathize with the spectacle of M'hamed's suffering before him, impossible to ignore. The teenage Jérémie in *Avant les hommes* suffers from his failure to communicate his subjectivity to his love interest Sami, his desire just as painfully closeted as his Arab love object is free. Jérémie's desire is perilous, inducing vertigo and disorientation: it is far removed from the structuring recourse to "critical alterity" seen in Cardon, Barthes, and Mitterrand.[28] This deterritorialization is all the more marked because Jérémie's object of admiration has, in contrast, such a secure grounding in his own identity, at least the way Jérémie perceives it. Sami' s internal compass has thrown off Jérémie's in light of its proximity. His infatuation with Sami leads to an unbearable confrontation with the roots of his psychological fragility. Such sexual disorientation sets off an identity crisis in Jérémie, made manifest in a cry for help to Sami: Jérémie wants to be collapsed with the object of his desire in a way that would cast off the threat of hierarchy and submission, to move from being weaker than Sami to as strong as Sami. Thus, the psychological logic behind Jérémie's ethnic solidarity reveals itself to be an erotic coveting of Sami's more solid mind and body.[29] Bouraoui's novel illustrates how in urban France the figure of the Arab boy has become a coveted anchor for fragilized masculinities and, most importantly, a source of suffering that can lay the foundations for the homosexual's poetic lament.

Like Koltès, the playwright Jean-Marie Besset—author of *Les Grecs* and *Grande école*—has employed Franco-Arab lovers as foils through which white characters must face their own privilege. His production expands upon literary explorations of interracial relationships already underway in postcolonial North African literature (Ben Jelloun, Choukri, Mrabet), literature that can in part be taken as a rejoinder to the way European and American authors depicted encounters between white and Arab men in North Africa (Gide, Orton, Burroughs, Ginsberg, Barthes). Besset and Koltès find themselves in a unique situation: they are continuing with the examination of interracial and cross-class relationships normally kept hidden, while at the same time shielding them from view. They have succeeded at the paradoxical task of exposing clandestine sexuality, while in some way also respecting its secrecy and its continuing appeal in a France that supposedly does not need clandestine sexuality.

While gay Franco-Arab authors speaking as native informants have found considerable success, sometimes the writers selected as flag bearers for sexual liberation provide narratives that cause guilt rather than gratification in their audiences. Taïa, for instance, derails a cliché storyline of erotic fiction—the tourist meets the native—redirecting it toward a suddenly nonerotic, sociopolitical space. Taïa makes the point that the sexual exploitation of Moroccans has often been eclipsed by the sexual liberation of the voyagers and writers doing the exploiting, almost as if to excuse it, since those European and American gay men were indeed oppressed in their home societies. One injustice does not justify another, however, and Taïa describes what might happen had these voyagers been sensitive to the obvious imbalances of power and indeed freedom inherent in sex tourism, whether gay or straight. Authors such as Taïa, O., Tali, and Bouraoui have answered contemporary calls for the disclosure of ethnic sexuality, while at the same time offering destabilizing answers. They have disclosed unusually frank stories of adolescent sexuality, have presented critical views of sex tourism, and have explored the fractures of European masculinity. To varying degrees, writers from Mitterrand to Bouraoui have fashioned Franco-Arab men as virilities of reference, as figures against which to measure masculinity, as well as, more insidiously, degrees of culture, intellect, and emotional sensibility.

Image Control

From Malik's soft-spoken knight of the Islamic prison to the benevolent policeman in Téchiné's *Les témoins*, the representations of men surveyed here recover Franco-Arab virility from its usual condemnation. Directors switch codes such that machismo becomes a perhaps misunderstood chivalry. These alternative representations insist upon the caring aspects of virility as well as the fact that virility remains constantly "in demand" in French society. By presenting Franco-Arab virility as a possible force for social stability rather than delinquency, they shed light on the ways that Arab (sexual) education might paradoxically guarantee respect for sexual diversity and gender equality. The directors also tackle the issue of Arab homophobia (normatively described as endemic to Arab machismo) by including otherwise virile characters who blur the line between homosociality and a more clandestine, behind-the-scenes homosexuality. These directors present figures with homosexual inclinations (if not identities) who respect an all-important public-private distinction. On a symbolic level, Audiard's *Un prophète*, with its parallels between the figures of the *arabe de service* and the *homo de service*, mixes the Arab-Islamic and the queer such that the Franco-Arab protagonist eventually takes a page from the queer playbook, overcoming his "masters" by aping their codes and subverting them. Most remarkably, the film's protagonist abandons his criminal associations and turns to an Islamic, straight and narrow path due to the instructions of a homosexually inclined Arab inmate.

Some formative works of banlieue cinema have also meditated on the increased policing of "outlaw" *banlieusard* sexualities. Jean François Richet's films depict hostilities between delinquents and authorities in a way that focuses on the sexual tenor of their opposition: two homosocial orders competing for phallic dominance. In a somewhat masculinist sense, the police divisions are portrayed as white, right-wing, xenophobic, and homosexually perverse, while the multiracial banlieue youth appear heterosexually dynamic, their attempts at courtship, love, and procreation unnaturally thwarted by the authorities. Harassed in banlieue spaces of assembly the youths refer to as private and the police call public, the Arab and black protagonists express frustration with the lack of opportunities for intimacy to occur naturally, building up a sexual misery that sometimes violently explodes. Richet highlights the homosexualized aggression erupting between police and delinquents as reminiscent of sexual dynamics belonging to a recent colonial past not properly digested. Stereotypes about the supposed perversion of *pieds-noirs* jump through history to make their way into banlieue cinema, mingling with some Marxist portrayals of homosexuality as a symptom of bourgeois decadence.

Téchiné connects France's contemporary police force to its colonial past through the psychodrama of a singular protagonist: a Franco-Arab policeman who is also the leader of a vice brigade cracking down on prostitutes and homosexuals in the early 1980s. Through this unique character, Téchiné launches a discussion about whether police surveillance might share parallels with a type of Arab Big Brother surveillance: the director eventually suggests that fears of such a correlation are unfounded. As is common in his films, Téchiné flips a condemned trait of ethnicized virility—surveillance—so that it instead becomes a form of care and concern. This switch crucially allows for life-saving (and sometimes erotic) contact when danger presents itself and the Franco-Arab "savior" character steps in. Ethnicized virility is valorized, but also challenged, in many of the films discussed here by sexually "enlightened" homosexual figures and their heterosexual allies who lecture Franco-Arab men about their sexual hypocrisy and the need to disclose one's intimate life as a sign of liberation. It becomes clear that the policing of sexuality can occur from more than one vantage point.

The spaces most policed by vice squads and cops have often been immigrant and red-light districts populated by a diverse group of loosely defined "refugees"—immigrant, economic, sexual—who come from all corners of life to converge in a singular urban *mixité*. Since *mixité* has been enshrined as an official French policy recommendation for countering communitarianism, the state's repression of this alternative *mixité* via the police is singled out with much irony by these directors. One of the most represented *mixités* in these films occurs between trans women and hypervirile *banlieusard* men. This kind of contact is enabled by a flexible Arab sexuality that can also open itself to homosexuality after a preceding exposure to trans women. Franco-Arab men and trans women on the economic margins are united again in sex work, portrayed very bleakly in the early production at least as an inevitable last resort after failed job searches and repeated social exclusions.

Communitarianism, usually a charge leveled at immigrants in the suburbs, is lobbed back at the city center via depictions of bourgeois or aristocratic enclaves, gentrified homosexual ghettos, or exclusive centers of higher learning, all of which seem to resort to contact with ethnic minorities only for the duration of a clandestine sexual release. In contemporary times, and despite a characteristically French aversion to identity politics, ethnic and sexual identities are constantly being asserted in a shared public space, sometimes engaging in what has been labeled "Oppression Olympics." Accepting that these communities should face off in competition, several directors have attempted to map the power differentials and shifting hierarchies that demarcate them. These nightmare scenarios of alienation between ethnic and sexual minorities, however, need not pan out, with alternative visions of social harmony emerging from an unlikely source of cultural production: pornography. As becomes clear, the forces that divide these communities are also the key to their erotic reconciliation.

Is Autoeroticism Possible?

In the passage from fad to fad in postcolonial porn (spanning colonial nostalgia for Arab servility to the eroticization of postcolonial violence in urban France), what may have been irretrievably lost is a sense of how Franco-Arabs view and eroticize themselves, absent the influence of predominantly white market forces. In a way, Citébeur's Arab fan base may not have come into existence had it not been for the expected white viewership. Chibikh, Citébeur's creator, has insisted that his company was born of a desire to fill a colorless vacuum, and the success of his enterprise and recruitment point to a familiarity with a preexisting network of men who have sex with men in the banlieues. Another matter that complicates these claims about a mainly white audience, is that it is not always certain whether the imagined viewer is indeed a white male. The self-fulfilling autoeroticism of featured *banlieusard* actors—as well as the "dirty talk" addressing an imagined fellow *banlieusard* instead of a white, middle-class viewer—have created dynamics in which the metrosexual city center has been entirely forgotten as a point of reference. These dynamics have created an inter-banlieue, self-sufficient erotic market, similar to that described by Christophe Honoré in *L'homme au bain*.

In this gay ethnic pornographic corpus spanning four decades, directors have gone from riads in Morocco, to the Sultan's harem, to immigrant construction sites, all the way to the disaffected basements of peri-urban housing projects in search of the domestic exotic. In the interim, the figure of the Arab male has undergone a parallel evolution: from a servile ephebe waiting on colonial tips, to a "straight" immigrant hustler desperate for cash, to a macho, sporty *banlieusard* who makes French whites serve him, a role to which they happily assent. Meanwhile, in heterosexual productions, this turning-of-the-tables outcome has not transpired; even the *beurette caillera* (female thug), who in other cultural venues has been variously assertive, combative, and androgynous (see chapter 1), loses these traits in a male-authored striptease that sees her brought back to submissive femininity and economic dependency. In Citébeur films and comics, objectionable stereotypes abound but do not completely victimize those they frame, because the *banlieusard* director has managed not only to exploit the ethnic exploitation for his own material gain, or for the power trips of his performers, but also to secure the increased recognition of Arab and *banlieusard* male aesthetic merit in fashion and avant-garde film. While playing on stereotypes of the banlieue as a "danger zone" of *insécurité*, *clandestinité*, and general lawlessness, a selection of ethnic porn films have managed to take the French city center's worst fears (and fantasies) about its banlieue neighbors and suggest erotic solutions where one sublimates violence into excitement and entertainment.

Exit the Sexagon

My intervention locates the frustration of France's cultural guardians with insubordinate banlieusards and Muslims in a particular source: ethnic virility cultures, whether male or female. This virile designation encompasses not only the banlieues, but also such large and internally diverse entities as immigration and the religion of Islam. In this way, the presence of North African Muslims and their descendants in France is consistently felt as "masculine," and conversely, historical "Frenchness" and whiteness are coded as feminized or androgynous, the victim of un-wanted macho advances. Ethnic sexual minorities themselves become a battleground in this equation, torn as they are between imperatives to honor one but never two sides of their identity: leave the banlieues and sever ties with the Muslim community in order to embrace the public sexual liberation of the city center, or affirm an ethnic communitarian-ism and shield one's sexual expression from public view. The choice of some gay French Arabs and Muslims to sever ties instead with their sup-posed city center salvation, falling back on clandestine sexual networks for satiation, has baffled those trying to "save" them. Clandestinity has been a conceptual focus of this book, intertwined as it is with ethnic vi-rility cultures. Myriad examples have highlighted ways that immigrant and sexual undergrounds may come to resemble one another, in the way that both seek to escape the scrutiny of an often reproachful officialdom, whether that of the police or sexual modernity. This officialdom believes that the impenetrability of these undergrounds resistant to assimilation has to do with an ethnic virilism that possessively guards and imprisons those within its domain, especially if these prisoners may want to take steps toward Frenchness. In the face of sexual demonization, Arab sexual "outlaws" and their artist admirer allies have challenged the sentence of "never queer" and offered instead some postcolonial queerings of French homo- and heteronormativities: in a climate that calls for queer Arabs and Muslims to prioritize their sexual identities over other attachments, these queerings have creatively bonded sexuality to race, religion, and class in a way that conserves their intersectionality, and ultimately, the modernity of ethnic virility cultures.

Acknowledgments

This book is the result of a persistent frustration with the representation of Arab sexuality in France and around the world, rife with misinformation, distortions, and Orientalist inheritance. Nacira Guénif-Souilamas has been a role model in her courageous rethinking of the paradigm that locks all French Arab men into macho straitjackets and French Arab women with headscarves into submission; this book might not have been conceptually possible without her first steps, as well as the hours spent on the Parisian park bench near her home where she so kindly oriented me in the right directions. Fred Meshreky shared the research years with me and opened my eyes to a different banlieue, telling stories from his lived experience as a teacher in the French public school system. Arm in arm, the legendary Hélène Hazera has personally curated for me all that is beautiful, eccentric, vivacious, and queer in Paris for many years now: her endless gifts of fine Arabic music and debauched literature have caused me to happily exceed my baggage restrictions every time; she is a UNESCO monument unto herself. Rachel Pollack and Mathilde Labbé, those two awesome ladies, made Wondaland, our apartment on the Boulevard Henri IV, my family home away from home, as did my birthday brother John Rogove. Danilo Scholz, and Loumia Ferhat showed me what nightlife means in Paris, and I hope to have shown them what it means in the United States. Aladdin Charni and Julien-Friant Zeroug tuned me in to their exciting nocturnal pulse and I smiled trying to keep up. David Ansari combines tennis, beer, and late nights in a way I find wonderful. Nick Rees-Roberts has been a familiar and trusted *terrasse* companion and confidante, an ally and confidence builder on an academic circuit short on solidarity. His wonderful friends who became my friends, Anissa and Günther, exemplify cosmopolitan Paris. While it's customary to thank people, places are also deserving of gratitude: *la BBB* was a window into another world, more realistic than the one on TV, and in many ways it prompted my first interrogations of the banlieue prison sentence for homosexuals.

Stateside, Joseph Massad has been an invaluable mentor, friend, and an endless source of bawdy laughter. As a young graduate student, and before that a journalist concerned with the Western sexual liberation of victims in the Arab/Islamic world, reading his interventions rearranged my thinking in at first difficult, but ultimately edifying ways. I am indebted to him for amplifying my project in such a way that it could be considered on a continuum with the historical and colonial demonization of Arab sexual diversity. Jarrod Hayes is another paradigm breaker whose work taught me that the direction of sexual liberation could be reversed from South to North. Todd Shepard's great honesty and political integrity are a model to learn from: he showed care in criticism in a way I hope to emulate. The trio of courses I took in the Department of French at Columbia University, with my eventual advisor Madeleine Dobie, opened my eyes to the merit and possibilities of Franco-Arab studies: going to class was like "church" and I was always thirsty for more. Tremendously generous with her time, she taught a once brash journalist caution, measuredness, and a greater respect for the rigor that goes into quality academic writing. Emmanuelle Saada pointed me toward authors and sources that blew open what I had thought were unexplored fields, exposing me to the already ample French corpus at the intersection of race and sexuality on the one hand, and psychoanalysis, literature, and activism on the other. With her no-nonsense efficiency, she pushed me to improve my argumentation with eminently useful tips, and generally set the bar very high for writing in French. In my current post at Smith, I find myself repeating to my own students everything she advised me to do. The late Phil Watts was a radiant face of encouragement who brightened gloomy days and spoke and acted with elegance: in our cohort he was universally loved. Pascale Hubert-Leibler taught me that teaching is the priority and helped me secure a job at a teaching college, in addition to being a rock of support. Meritza Moss and Benita Dace held down the department fort and made going to the office a source of pleasure rather than dread: I will never forget their sunny smiles or the crazy conversations we had. Muhsin Al-Musawi took a chance and gave me my first real publishing opportunities in Arab studies and his attentive readers helped radicalize the points that were hiding in my research. My classmates became my friends and we all became one another's cheerleaders: Lamya Al-Kharusi (my Omani sister); Cheryl Eve Leung (Orifithe te pathe le bonjour); Yasmine Khayyat who was the sweetest of roommates and a comforting presence in my life; Pandora O'Mahony Adams and her Irish solidarity and hospitality; Rahel Fischbach my German sister; Maytha Al-Hassen (dancer and web communicator extraordinaire); Aleksandra Perisic (keeps it real at concerts and in the classroom) and her partner Jacques, who so amiably hosted my partner and I on so many an occasion; Sarah Jean Lazur for her humor and sense of justice; Elizabeth Marcus for her infectious zest for life; Kami Jones for her grace and consistent friendship; and Veli Yasin who in his precocious ways is continuing on toward doing ever greater things. I want to thank each and every foot soldier in the near-death experience called Advanced Arabic. NYC friends who enriched my doctoral studies are too numerous to list all: special thanks to Julian Marley McBride, Hani Khalil, Natacha Poirier, Devon Thomas, Claire Sulmers, Robert Camacho Roman, Vlad S, Elisa Lee, and Lucas Shapiro.

I would not have been able to complete this book on time without the support at Smith College. I want to thank my French studies colleagues for believing in me and allowing me creative pedagogical outlets that most of my professor friends can only dream about: Eglal Doss-Quinby, Ann Leone, Hélène Visentin, Janie Vanpée, Martine Gantrel, Jonathan Gosnell, and my current mentor, Dawn Fulton. Thanks are due to Christiane Métral for mentoring me and being so amiable. Jennifer Blackburn has gotten me out of more pickles than can fit in a Maille jar. My new affiliation with the Program for the Study of Women and Gender has also provided an invaluable circle of peers who "get" what I was trying to say the first time. I am proud of this department, the intellectual core of Smith which keeps everyone honest when it comes to privilege in all its forms. Thanks to Lisa Armstrong for pulling me in; Kevin Quashie and Gary Lehring for co-teaching and co-playing tennis; Ambreen Hai for confronting Islamophobia with me, Jennifer DeClue for our heart-to-hearts; and Darcy Buerkle, Carrie Baker, Daphne Lamothe, Cornelia Pearsall, and Naomi Miller for welcoming me into their midst. Teaching at a women's college has sharpened and sensitized my thinking around issues of gender and sexuality, as have the students who do not simply swallow information but challenge me to convince them of my convictions. The students in Immigration and Sexuality and French Islam immediately grasped the insights I had spent years trying to articulate, and they in turn have become experts educating family members at the holiday dinner table about Islamic and banlieue issues that escape our news streams.

On the road to publication, numerous peers pushed me at the right moment and in just the right ways so that the stars aligned. My Smith mentor Susan Van Dyne refined my prospectus and got Andrea Stone to workshop it into better shape with me. The trusted Vinay Swamy challenged me to take ownership of my claims. In conversations that stretched from Northampton to Baltimore, Mireille Rosello listened, offered edifying feedback, and taught me to take a larger and more ethical view of the discipline. William Spurlin, the most entertaining dinner companion, wrote missive upon missive educating me about the dynamics of the publishing world. Denis Provencher has offered quick, clear advice at various junctures which has proved to be golden. Kathryn Kleppinger has been not only a friend but also an inclusive colleague who has extended numerous invitations. Tarek El-Ariss read an earlier version of this text and gave useful pointers, especially for chapter 1. Ann Pellegrini made the key connection by sending on my work to Richard Morrison, my current editor, a righteous friend who has reassured me at every nerve-racking step of the way. Michael Koch and his keen eyes and mind helped get the book in its best shape.

This project would not have been feasible without important financial and logistical support from the following sources: Smith College's Start-up, Connections, and CFCD funds, the FLAS fellowship, Columbia University's Kaufman Memorial fellowship, the ENS Paris fellowship, and the GSAS summer stipends. I also thank the following institutes, universities, and administrators for inviting me to speak and workshop the materials in this book: George Washington University; Ralph Heyndels and the University of Miami, Johns Hopkins University; the Homonationalism conference at the CUNY Graduate Center; the righteous Maya Mikdashi at NYU's Kevorkian Center; the CRASC in Oran, Algeria; the amazing William Leap at the American University in Washington, DC; the Institute for Comparative Literature and Society at Columbia University; David Ansari at the University of Chicago's Self and Subjectivity group; Agustin Villalpando and Lars Ivar Owesen-Lein Borge at the Universidad Del Claustro de Sor Juana in Mexico City; Suzanne Schneider-Reich at the Brooklyn Institute for Social Research; Nellie Boucher and the AALAC working group at Amherst College; the incredible superhero duo of Sahar Amer and Martine Antle; and the dearly departed Larry Schehr who gave me my first opportunity to speak at the University of Illinois at Urbana-Champaign.

In random conversations and outings, numerous people contributed to this book without knowing or being on the record. Khaled Beydoun and Will Youmans, you are communicators and big brothers extraordinaire. Alex Shams, Maya Mikdashi, Gianfranco Rebucini, Nadya Sbaiti, you bring me reassurance and hope: I always feel better after reading what you've written. Ruby Tovar and Sanjay Makhijani, I could speak to you for hours and salute your activism. Chadia Chambers-Samadi, you are my favorite MLA and conference partner. Long-time friends Philippine Demeestere, Natasha Case, Jamila Pierson-Jase, Justine Jones, Yong-Ha Jeong, Greg Baker, you all left an indelible stamp. Cecilia Miniucchi, you helped raise me. Ock-Ju Noh, you taught me what an occasion is and always made me feel like a dignitary. Lucy Mott, Alice Stanners, and Lucy Mitra, you enhanced the Anglophone world. Sama Adnan and Marc Michael, you are elegant models in more ways than one. Sarah and Boback Ziaeian, you've made me feel I'm part of your family. Vincent Message and Chloe Korman, I so enjoy the privilege of being admitted into the writerly life you've dared to dream. Yoram Elkaim, thank you for being such a good friend and including me in your always interesting life. Frédéric Nauczyciel, you do in art what I try to do in writing. My penpal Hytham El-Rayah, your words always dazzle me. My journalism mentors Lamis Andoni, Daniel Hernandez, Alan Mittelstaedt, Laurie Ochoa, and the late Doug Ireland, you've all emboldened me in invaluable ways. Christen Mucher, Nusrat Chowdhury, and Pinky Hota, thank you for making me feel so much less alone during my first years on the job. Ira Wolf, Jim Ault, and Rogelio Miñana, thank you for your returns and for being such good sports. Dafne Muntanyola-Saura, Luca Ponsi, Jake Schwartz Walker, and Asa Calthorpe, you bring gold to my childhood memories and I appreciate your enduring friendship.

My loved ones help me remember what my ideals are and what my objectives were. My mother and father, to whom this book is dedicated, embody Bernard-Marie Koltès's notion that immigrants make for a "happening" place. Both crossed the Atlantic and left what were very sedentary families to chart a new life: the magnitude of their journey has brought a greater respect for those Mediterranean migrants who have left everything behind. Among the endless life lessons I have learned from my mother is how to properly be a model (second-generation) immigrant: the kind who does not keep quiet, or wait till things get better, or accept the intolerance of neighbors as a necessary step toward assimilation. She is a woman whose sense of dignity goes beyond residency, rootedness, or time. My father is my role model in style, humor, optimism, and creativity and also my best bud: his acceptance and popularity in new countries and situations still gives me hope for the immigration project. To those proud to call me a "doctor" (who can't cure anything)—grandma Amna, uncles Sami, Tariq, and Awad, aunts Awatif, Madawi, and Farida, cousins Faisal, Ahmed, Hanouf, Nahar—thank you for being so good to me growing up. My Austrian family is also a consistent presence in my thoughts—Herfried, Monica, Nina, and Max—you are my European lifeline. Thanks also to Luis Carrasquillo, his father, Gary, and his sisters, Sonia and Joanny, who make up my home away from home in Massachusetts. Lou, it has been thrilling to see the world—its beauties but also its injustices—through your eyes these last few years.

Notes

Introduction: Enter the Sexagon

1. Tariq Ramadan, "Islam et homosexualité," Tariq Ramadan (blog), May 28, 2009, accessed November 13, 2015, http://tariqramadan.com/islam-et-homosexualite/. Unless otherwise noted, all translations from the French are my own.

2. Banlieues are multiethnic, working-class neighborhoods and housing projects in the French suburbs where immigrants and their descendants have been concentrated. Initially built as a way to alleviate the housing crisis following the recruitment of immigrant workers in the 1960s and 1970s, the towers that dot the banlieues have often been tied, in mainstream media accounts, with social inequality, insalubrious living conditions, sub-par educational opportunities, and ethnic and religious radicalization.

3. Franck Chaumont, *Homo-ghetto: gays et lesbiennes dans les cités: les clandestins de la République* (Paris: Le Cherche Midi, 2009).

4. Conrad Hackett, "5 Facts about the Muslim Population in Europe," Pew Research Center, January 15, 2015, accessed November 13, 2015, http://www.pewresearch.org/fact-tank/2015/01/15/5-facts-about-the-muslim-population-in-europe/.

5. See Fatima El-Tayeb, *European Others: Queering Ethnicity in Postnational Europe* (Minneapolis: University of Minnesota Press, 2006), 110: "There is an unwillingness to seriously engage him, accept him as an intellectual peer who is a genuinely European intellectual. . . . Instead, there often is an antagonistic approach, driven by an immense sense of suspicion, a desire to 'unmask' him, to show the thoroughly foreign radical behind the mask of the Westernized liberal."

6. Mayanthi L. Fernando, *The Republic Unsettled: Islam, Secularism, and the Future of France* (Durham, NC: Duke University Press, 2014), 241, 250.

7. Ramadan launched an international call for a moratorium on corporeal punishment, stoning, and the death penalty in the Islamic world; elsewhere he has been instrumental in stressing the existence of "Islamic Feminism," a conjunction of terms that many staunch secularists and some feminists consider contradictory. See Tariq Ramadan, "An International Call for Moratorium on Corporal Punishment, Stoning

and the Death Penalty in the Islamic World," Tariq Ramadan (blog), April 5, 2005, accessed November 13, 2015, http://tariqramadan.com/blog/2005/04/05/an-international-call-for-moratorium-on-corporal-punishment-stoning-and-the-death-penalty-in-the-islamic-world/.

8. El-Tayeb, *European Others*, 101.

9. Caroline Fourest, *Frère Tariq: discours, stratégie, et méthode de Tariq Ramadan* (Paris: Grasset et Fasquelle, 2004).

10. See Ramadan, "Islam et homosexualité": "What we behold today are sick [*malsain*] and ideologically-oriented campaigns. Affirming one's convictions while respecting other persons does not suffice: it becomes necessary for Muslims to condemn the Koran, to accept and promote homosexuality: the proof of their modernity would come at this price."

11. Isabelle Lévy, *Soins et croyances: guide pratique des rites, cultures et religions à l'usage des personnels de santé et des acteurs sociaux* (Issy-les-Moulineaux, France: Éditions Estem, 2002), 149. See also Ramadan, "Islam et homosexualité."

12. Tariq Ramadan, "De la charia à l'islamophobie, de l'homosexualité au statut de la femme," Tariq Ramadan (blog), April 22, 2011, accessed November 13, 2015, http://tariqramadan.com/blog/2011/04/22/de-la-charia-a-lislamophobie-de-lhomosexualite-au-statut-de-la-femme/.

13. It is nonetheless semantically problematic to assert that the word *homosexual* appears in the Koran. Ramadan does not cite specific passages to make his case. Anything resembling the word's referent—exclusive and identitarian sexual preference for the same sex—is even harder, if not impossible, to find in Koranic passages without running into obstacles of anachronism. At the very least, the question involves a high degree of undecidability. Khaled El-Rouayheb, in *Before Homosexuality in the Arab-Islamic World, 1500–1800* (Chicago: University of Chicago Press, 2005), one of the only nonsensationalist works on the topic, looks at Islamic legal traditions in the Arab-Islamic world between 1500 and 1800 and states that sodomy and homosexuality cannot be confused easily. He adds that "the relevant passages of the [Koran] do not specify which sexual acts had been committed by the people of Lot," and that jurists, rather than employing a term such as *homosexuality*, "operated instead with a set of concepts" such as *liwat*, or sodomitic relations, and *ubnah*, men who desire anal intercourse. Taken together, these concepts still do not match up to "instances of one overarching phenomenon" (6). In this, El-Rouayheb does not differ much from Michel Foucault and his distinction between "sodomites," practitioners of sexual acts, and "homosexuals," a term that is much more extensive (and recent) in that it derives identity from acts. Here, the assertion that homosexuals didn't exist in the Arab-Islamic word paradoxically serves to demonstrate that male-male sexual relations were tolerated, in that "homosexuality" was not a legal category to be targeted.

14. Joseph Massad, *Desiring Arabs* (Chicago: University of Chicago Press, 2007).

15. This aggrandizement of the intolerance of minorities versus majorities will be familiar to those who followed the fallout after California's Proposition 8 (which sought to eliminate the right of same-sex couples to marry) in the fall of 2008. The large African-American turnout during that election was blamed for the "yes" vote, which mattered statistically less than, for instance, the white male vote in favor. See Marisa Abrajano, "Are Blacks and Latinos Responsible for the Passage of Proposition 8? Analyzing Voter Attitudes on California's Proposal to Ban Same-Sex Marriage in 2008," *Political Research Quarterly* 63, no. 4 (2010): 922–32.

16. Fernando, *Republic Unsettled*, 238.

17. Ramadan, "Islam et homosexualité."

18. See the HM2F website, accessed November 14, 2015, http://www.homosexuels -musulmans.org.

19. As Gayatri Gopinath notes— citing Stefan Helmreich's analysis of the term *diaspora*—the roots of the term refer back to the scattering of seeds and thus sperm (a definition she uses to begin to explain the problematic absence of female perspectives in South Asian diasporic production): "The original meaning of diaspora summons up the image of scattered seeds and . . . in Judeo-Christian . . . cosmology, seeds are metaphorical of the male 'substance' that is traced in genealogical histories. The word 'sperm' is metaphorically linked to diaspora. It comes from the same stem and is defined by the OED as 'the generative substance or seed of male animals.'" See Gayatri Gopinath, *Impossible Desires: Queer Diasporas and South Asian Public Cultures* (Durham, NC: Duke University Press, 2005), 5. See also Stefan Helmreich, "Kinship, Nation and Paul Gilroy's Concept of Diaspora," *Diaspora: A Journal of Transnational Studies* 63, no. 4 (Fall 1992): 245.

20. The French population descended from the European settlers of colonial Algeria.

21. *Beur* is back slang for *Arab*.

22. *Rebeu* is another back slang variant of *Arab* that postdates *beur*.

23. Nacira Guénif-Souilamas, *Des beurettes* (Paris: Hachette Pluriel, 2003).

24. While the term *Franco-Maghrebi* can be used when referring to a large class of subjects united in a postcolonial situation, it is no less problematic than using the term *Arab*. Dismissing the terms used by the minority protagonists is not a neutral act, because this dismissal allows the majority group to ignore the minority's request to be identified in the way it finds affirming. *Rebeu*, which means "Arab," presents a demand in a way that *Maghrebi*, which means hailing from the Maghreb (Tunisia, Algeria, Morocco), does not. The term *rebeu* is also marked by the creative argotic scrambling practiced by the French descendants of North African immigrants. More precisely, *rebeu* is a second, reappropriating scrambling of *Arab* after the first scrambling (*beur*) was co-opted by mainstream political and media organizations who sought to latch on to a trend.

25. Moreover, the terms derived from *Arab* arguably have a meaning independent of an ethnic identity originating in the parents' emigrant countries: Berber and Kabyle subjects might use the term *rebeu* without acknowledging an Arabic heritage. These various derivations of *Arab* refer to a local branding, itself related to common experiences and performances produced in postempire, metropolitan France.

26. See El-Tayeb, *European Others*, xxii: "I suggest that the complex interactions of race, religion, migration, and colonialism haunting the presence of minorities of color in Europe might be best explored through a shift away from a vertical look at one ethnic group, covering various generations and their move from home to host country, toward a horizontal perspective crossing various ethnic and national divides."

27. Ian Buruma, "Final Cut: After a Filmmaker's Murder, the Dutch Creed of Tolerance Has Come under Siege," *New Yorker*, January 2005, cited in El-Tayeb, *European Others*, xxxii.

28. As many ethnographies, memoirs, and anecdotal experiences attest, French citizens with Spanish, Italian, Portuguese, or Armenian surnames—as well as Europeans hailing from former French Algeria—have viscerally recalled experiences of discrimination based on skin color, and have remembered with sorrow the aspersions

of "being less French" hurled against them. Yet, in other instances, French citizens of foreign but European origin have not had their "French-ness" questioned, and have managed to pass in a way that those West African, Antillean, and North African immigrants have not. In this book, I occasionally will use the term *white* not to reify the category of "whiteness" in France but rather to comment on representations in which racial difference is clearly stressed, as well as to comment on situations in which passing as white affords distinct advantages.

29. Even if one ignores postdecolonization immigration from North and West Africa, France's long history of population shifts, annexations, occupations, intermarriage, settlement of colonies, and the repatriation of French citizens concurrent with decolonization have yielded a singular demographic situation, in which the isolated "French stock" (*français de souche*, also a term that resonates with the Far Right) could potentially be made up of, for example, any combination of Germanic, Roman, or Gallic, as well as Spanish, Italian, Portuguese, Armenian, Polish, Jewish (Sephardic and Ashkenazi), or Lebanese elements.

30. Gérard Noiriel, *Le creuset français* (Paris: Seuil, 2006).

31. The Schengen agreement of 1985, later incorporated into the 1997 Amsterdam Treaty, called for eliminating the internal borders of the European Union so as to enforce a single, external border and allow the free passage of persons within.

32. Although Fortuyn was not killed by a Muslim, the perpetrator cited Fortuyn's "scapegoating of Muslims" as a factor in targeting him.

33. Section 2: article 8 de la Loi Informatique de 1978, Legifrance, accessed November 15, 2015, http://www.legifrance.gouv.fr/affichTexte.do?cidTexte=JORFTEXT00000 0886460.

34. Fernando, *Republic Unsettled*, 248–49.

35. Jasbir Puar, *Terrorist Assemblages: Homonationalism in Queer Times* (Durham, NC: Duke University Press, 2007), 20.

36. See Todd Shepard, *The Invention of Decolonization: The Algerian War and the Remaking of France* (Cornell, NY: Cornell University Press, 2008); and "'Something Notably Erotic': Politics, 'Arab Men,' and Sexual Revolution in Post-decolonization France, 1962–1974," *Journal of Modern History* 84, no. 1 (2012): 80–115.

37. Kristin Ross, *Fast Cars, Clean Bodies* (Cambridge, MA: MIT Press, 1994).

38. The field of cultural studies has its limitations, and of course many critics. They take issue with the insistent return to the internalization of power structures in the individual. In my discussion, I will not attempt a full-fledged application of its methods; rather, I draw on the aspects that are useful in bridging the problematic gap between narrow textual readings that isolate literary works from sociological and anthropological arguments.

39. When employing the term *discourse*, I mean both the repeating and recognizable representational patterns that come together in the shape of a theme of social relevance, as well as that which Michel Foucault referred to in coining the expression "incitement to discourse."

40. Sayad Abdelmalek, *The Suffering of the Immigrant*, trans. David Macey (Cambridge, England: Polity Press, 2004).

41. Loïc Wacquant, *Parias urbains: ghetto, banlieue, état* (Paris: La Découverte, 2007).

42. Alec Hargreaves, *Multi-Ethnic France: Immigration, Politics, Culture and Society* (London: Routledge, 2007).

43. Carrie Tarr, *Reframing Difference: Beur and Banlieue Filmmaking in France* (Manchester: Manchester University Press, 2005); Kathryn Kleppinger, *Branding the "Beur" Author: Minority Writing and the Media in France* (Liverpool: Liverpool University Press, 2015).

44. Nacira Guénif-Souilamas, *Les féministes et le garçon arabe* (Paris: Editions de l'Aube, 2004).

45. Jarrod Hayes, *Queer Nations* (Chicago: University of Chicago Press, 2000).

46. Marlon Ross, "Beyond the Closet as a Raceless Paradigm," in Henderson and Johnson, *Black Queer Studies: A Critical Anthology* (Durham, NC: Duke University Press, 2005), 162.

47. Roderick Ferguson, *Aberrations in Black: Toward a Queer of Color Critique* (Minneapolis: University of Minnesota Press, 2003), 69.

48. An Anglo-American bias often colors the otherwise decentralizing logic of queer theory. This bias permeated earlier currents of gender and gay and lesbian studies, and proponents hoped queer theorists would depart from it. Joseph Massad, among other critics, has explained that even those at the vanguard of queer theory (he references Judith Butler's early work) have at times processed their understandings of non-Western sexualities through the homosexual/heterosexual binary without regard for that binary's relevance to the culture at hand; see Massad, *Desiring Arabs*, 40. Butler has since become one of the loudest adversaries of "sexual nationalism," famously refusing a prize bestowed on her by the organizers of the 2011 Berlin Pride event. During her refusal speech, she critiqued the latent homonationalism suffusing the festivities and the organizers' proximity to military interests. She also highlighted the anti-immigration rhetoric advanced by some prominent LGBT personalities and organizations in Germany. See Judith Butler, "I Must Distance Myself from This Complicity with Racism, including Anti-Muslim Racism," Civil Courage Prize refusal speech, Christopher Street Day, June 19, 2010, accessed November 19, 2015, http://www.egs.edu/faculty/judith-butler/articles/i-must-distance-myself/.

49. Ferguson, *Aberrations in Black*.

50. Gopinath, *Impossible Desires*, 11.

51. El-Tayeb, *European Others*, xlv.

52. Gopinath, *Impossible Desires*, 11.

53. Lisa Duggan, "The New Homonormativity," in *Materializing Democracy Toward a Revitalized Cultural Politics*, ed. Dana D. Neslon and Russ Castronovo (Durham, NC: Duke University Press, 2002): 175–94.

54. Les Indigènes de la République was formed in 2005 as an anticolonial group on the premise that colonialism is an unfinished business whose influence persists even in postcolonial France. The group calls for renewed decolonization of hierarchies that still demarcate white Frenchmen from Frenchmen of color. These people of color are named indigenous not because they are the historic ancestors of the French nation, but rather because they would still insidiously be restricted, in contemporary France, to the status of the colonial "indigenous," a name commonly used in the colonial era to refer to the colonized, who were subject to a different legal system (*le code de l'indigénat*).

55. Houria Bouteldja, "Universalisme gay, homoracialisme et 'mariage pour tous,'" Les Indigènes de la République, translated by Decolonial Translation Group as "Gay Universalism, Homoracialism, and Marriage for All," accessed June 21, 2016, http://www.decolonialtranslation.com/english/gay-universalism-homoracialism-and-marriage-for-all.html.

56. See Ross, "Beyond the Closet," 176: "Poststructuralist theories of sexuality frequently build a case for the instability of sexual identities by using black bodies as their stable foundation, as the deep well of empirical evidence on and beyond which their own fluid identities can be playfully manipulated and differentiated."

57. Mehammed Mack, "Scènes des genres au Maghreb. Masculinités, critique queer et espaces du féminin/masculin," book review, *Modern and Contemporary France* 22, no. 4: 551–53, http://www.tandfonline.com/doi/full/10.1080/09639489.2014.891578.

58. Saba Mahmood, in *Politics of Piety: The Islamic Revival and the Feminist Subject* (Princeton: Princeton University Press, 2005), explains how Muslim women active in Cairo mosques derive power from inhabiting rather than subverting norms.

59. Nilüfer Göle, *Interpénétrations: Islam et l'Europe* (Paris: Galaade Editions, 2005), 28.

60. The location of the Sexual Nationalism conference in the Netherlands is revelatory given that it is a country where multiculturalism and sexual rights are often at odds in media and political rhetoric. In 2002, far-right homosexual politician Pim Fortuyn was murdered by Volkert van der Graaf, who, at trial, cited Fortuyn's targeting of Muslims and "weaker members of society" as motives for the killing.

61. Credit goes to one of the anonymous readers at Fordham University Press for offering *illogic* as an apt term for describing this phenomenon.

62. Jytte Klausen, "Rotten Judgment in the State of Denmark," Salon, February 8, 2006, http://www.salon.com/2006/02/08/denmark_3/, cited in El-Tayeb, *European Others*, 82.

63. For a discussion of the study, see El-Tayeb, *European Others*, 130, citing Hiske Arts and Anita Nabha, "Education in the Netherlands: Segregation in a 'Tolerant' Society," Humanity in Action, http://www.humanityinaction.org/knowledgebase/6-education-in-the-netherlands-segregation-in-a-tolerant-society; for the official report, see Forum, Instituut voor Multiculturele Ontwikkeling, *Homoseksualiteit en gedeeld burgerschap* (Utrecht, Netherlands: Forum, 2003).

64. See El-Tayeb, *European Others*, 100: "The West thus is forced to travel back in time and reface challenges that it would have already overcome, at least within its borders, had it not been infused with a population arriving not only from a different space, but also a different time."

65. See Éric Fassin, "Homosexual City, Homophobic Banlieue?," trans. Christina Mitrakos, Metropolitiques, March 9, 2011, http://www.metropolitiques.eu/Homosexual-City-Homophobic.html. Fassin writes: "The (clash) thesis by Samuel Huntington in 1993 that caused a big stir after the Cold War, was recast ten years later, after September 11, by Ronald Inglehart and Pippa Norris, as a 'sexual conflict of civilizations,' a war of values where the status of women is the main issue and Islamism, the main enemy."

66. Maxime Cervulle and Nick Rees-Roberts, *Homo Exoticus: race, classe et critique queer* (Paris: Armand Colin, 2010).

67. See Puar, *Terrorist Assemblages*, 2: "At work in this dynamic is a form of sexual exceptionalism—the emergence of national homosexuality, what I term 'homonationalism'—that corresponds with the coming out of the exceptionalism of American empire. Further, this brand of homosexuality operates as a regulatory script not only of normative gayness, queerness, or homosexuality, but also of the racial and national norms that reinforce these sexual subjects. . . . The fleeting sanctioning of a national homosexual subject is possible, not only through the proliferation of sexual–racial subjects who invariably fall out of its narrow terms of acceptability, as others have

argued, but more significantly, through the simultaneous engendering and disavowal of populations of sexual-racial others who need not apply."

68. Gopinath, *Impossible Desires*, 14.

69. See Hiram Perez, "You Can Have My Brown Body and Eat It, Too!," *Social Text* 23, no. 3–4 (2005): 171–91. Perez speaks of queers of color who do not participate in gay upward mobility as eroticized but also expelled from homosexual dignity: "the mobility that modern gay identity requires is not universally available. Here we encounter trouble in the form of noncanonical bodies (not surprisingly, also quite brown bodies) nonetheless interpellated as gay. Gays who cannot properly be gay" (177).

70. El-Tayeb, *European Others*, 128.

71. For more on gentrification and gay-friendliness, see Colin Giraud, *Quartiers gays* (Paris: PUF, 2014), and Sylvie Tissot, *Good Neighbors: Gentrifying Diversity in Boston's South End*, trans. Catherine Romatowski and David Broder (London and Brooklyn, NY: Verso, 2015).

72. In his post 9/11 study of the multiethnic New York City neighborhood of Jackson Heights and its ongoing gentrification, Martin Manalansan explains that in the age of homonormativity, race and class may become, as Fatima El-Tayeb summarizes, "more important than sexuality with regard to access to public space" (El-Tayeb, *European Others*, 125). See Martin Manalansan, "Race, Violence and Neoliberal Spatial Politics in the Global City," *Social Text*, nos. 84–85 (Fall–Winter, 2005): 141–56.

73. In the introduction to *Impossible Subjects*, Gopinath writes that South Asian diasporic writers also find queerness in the home rather than without it.

74. El-Tayeb, *European Others*, 99; In French cultural production, escape from the home or the banlieues as a whole can be found in multiple genres. For representative examples, see the following films and memoirs: Samira Bellil with Josée Stoquart, *Dans l'enfer des tournantes* (Paris: Editions de la Seine, 2005); *Lila Says*, directed by Ziad Doueri (Samuel Goldwyn Films, 2005), DVD; *La squale*, directed by Fabrice Genestal; and *Chaos*, directed by Coline Serreau (Bac Films, 2001), DVD.

75. Gopinath, *Impossible Desires*, 15.

76. Ibid., 25.

77. Massad, *Desiring Arabs*, 164 (footnote in excerpt omitted).

78. See Guénif-Souilamas, *Les féministes et le garçon arabe*, 74–75: "Cut off from a rich and complex past, [the young men of the *banlieues*] are here reduced to the grin of the vicious macho man, constrained to conform to an exacerbated sexuality which can only earn them opprobrium and serious legal problems. Virilism, that outrageous expression of masculinity contained within its strict sexual limits, offers the advantage of illustrating the ideological proximity already underlined by Foucault between perversion and delinquency, which, as notoriously, the Arabs of the projects practice in equal measure. These accumulators of deviance are thus doubly reprehensible in light of the rules of civility, indexed upon those of sexual correctness. . . . Delighting those who hold them in contempt, they would relay in a docile way the homophobic representation of the world that has long prevailed in the Catholic West, just as that representation is becoming politically incorrect. [This glosses over] the idea that this betrays their past and shuts them up into a present without a future."

79. Ibid., 75.

80. Ibid., 68–70. Observers of French society may protest that French men also practice accolades (*la bise*) that might be met with suspicion, from an American perspective, for instance. Guénif-Souilamas emphasizes that the colonial tragedy occurs

when the sight of a kiss on the cheek gained a negative connotation when French men observed it in North African men. Ordinarily *la bise* is (was) an aspect of a "Mediterranean" heritage belonging to both French and North African men, but here it becomes an unbearable reminder of French proximity to Arabness. In the Franco-Arab youth generation, the disappearance of the *bise* occurs for roughly the same reasons of distaste for ambiguous homoaffectivity. This is ironic because the youth generation, which arguably strives to assert cultural pride, has altered its behavior because of negative outside perceptions that aim to belittle North African social customs.

81. See Fassin, "Homosexual City": "From the sexist housing projects to the homophobic (hood), a landscape is being drawn where the border between the city and the *banlieue* separates 'them' from 'us:' it is being expressed mainly in terms of gender and sexuality, in the name of what I've suggested to call 'sexual democracy.'"

82. The politicians and commentators who have renovated French values in this way exclude from sexual democracy those immigrants and minorities "culturally foreign to these values emblematic of modernity." Stressing the post-9/11 rhetoric of the "us versus them" narrative, Fassin speaks of the way that certain political actors, such as US neoconservatives, have articulated an "end-of-history" telos that supposes a sexual clash of civilizations that terminates not just in liberal democracy but "sexual democracy." This democracy is distinctly noninclusive, more closely resembling an elite Greek democracy; it rejects cultural and ethnic difference on the basis of culturalist attributions of sexual intolerance.

83. See Éric Fassin, "National Identities and Transnational Intimacies: Sexual Democracy and the Politics of Immigration in Europe," *Public Culture* 22, no. 3 (2010): 507–29; and Éric Fassin et al. "Homophobie = Identité Nationale?," *Le Monde*, June 28, 2008.

84. See Fassin, "Homosexual City": "Europe, however, puts forward a particular variation of this rhetoric: indeed, in a context marked by increasing immigration restrictions more than by a war on terror, it is not about exporting 'our' values, but about preserving them. In other words, the dividing line between 'them' and 'us' on this side of the Atlantic appears like an inner border that divides the space of European nations according to cultural origins: sexual democracy would draw the limit between the city and the *banlieue*."

85. See ibid.: "The figure of the 'ghetto' can serve as a point of reference here. In the 1990s, the "gay ghetto" was denounced and the gay community was called on to be discreet. The republican rhetoric, in the name of universalism, was opposed to any 'American-style' communitarianism. In the 2000s, we get a sense that the situation is reversed; we still criticize the 'ghetto,' but it designates the projects and no longer the Marais (Paris's gayborhood). And now the *banlieue* is criticized for forcing homosexuals to remain discreet: these "stowaways of the Republic" should be freed from their home community in order to blossom in the gay community."

86. See ibid.: "Still largely not thought of, is less the opposition between the two [ghettoes] than their relationship, in other words, between the 'homo-ghetto,' these [social housing] projects that are today portrayed as homophobic prisons, and the 'ghetto homo,' that in no way escapes the racial logic that pervades society (and sexuality): they mirror each other. The culturalism ascribed to the banlieue thus contributes to the problem that it claims to describe and denounce. Thus, we ought not ignore homophobia in the projects, but describe it without reinforcing it, by avoiding the traps of a rhetoric that in opposing 'them' to 'us,' forces the former to define themselves

in opposition to the latter, as if reacting to the clear conscience of a sexual democracy, not devoid of racism, where the expectation is alas, the most often, imposed only on the (Other)."

87. Roderick Ferguson in *Aberrations in Black*—his incisive study of capital, sexuality, and race in the American context—describes the way that capitalism triggers the nonnormative sexual diversity it elsewhere opposes to the ideals of gender and sexuality associated with citizenship. This happens when the immigrant working class, with its multiplicity of origins and sexual customs, is solicited for work as well as for assimilation and Americanization programs. In this way, sexual "diversity was, in large part, the outcome of capital's demand for labor" (14). This process, when transposed to the French context, bonds the waves of Muslim working-class immigrants to the introduction of sexual diversity, when these immigrants bring nonnormative sexual customs with them. This diversity would persist in the banlieues through their children, still seen as attached to their immigrant ancestry. This correlation has an obvious impact on the notion that the banlieue *only* represses sexual diversity, instead of fostering it.

88. *Misérabilisme*, or "miserabilism," denotes a representational trend that stresses inevitable (socioeconomic) failure, an inescapable cycle of poverty on various levels, and an incapacity to improve upon previous generations. In this way it resembles the culture of poverty arguments often deployed against US minorities, as well as the literary genre of "misery lit."

89. People often differentiate between androgyny and metrosexuality. While androgyny can be associated with both men and women, metrosexuality is most often used to refer to men. The *metro* root offers an indication of how cities give rise to this marker, as it refers to a hyper-attentive care of the self, self-styling, and fashionable nature that reflect how they have tapped into a city's pulse. Metrosexuals have often been called modern-day dandies. Metrosexuality, like androgyny, is not a marker of orientation and does not necessarily line up with bisexuality; although, when used as an insult, metrosexual often is code for homosexual, especially of the closeted kind.

1 / The Banlieue Has a Gender: Competing Visions of Sexual Diversity

1. *Les terres froides*, directed by Sebastien Lifshitz (Agat Films et Cie, 1999), film.

2. *La cité du mâle*, directed by Cathy Sanchez (ARTE Productions, 2010), documentary. The title is a play on the phonetic similarity between *mâle* (male) and *mal* (evil), conflating masculinity with a tendency toward evil in the projects.

3. See Anaëlle Verzaux, "La cité du mâle: la contre-enquête," Bakchich.tv, December 17, 2010, site discontinued, archived version available at http://admi.net/archive/ www.bakchich.info/La-Cite-du-male-la-contre-enquete,12681.html. In response to the controversy, Daniel Leconte—who introduced the documentary on ARTE and provided its voice-over narration—insisted that consent forms had been collected, that all testimony had been recorded with cameras in plain sight. He suggested that Laïb wanted to retract her name in light of threats she had received, thus confirming the film's thesis of unrestrained male dominion in the banlieues; see Guillaume Weill-Raynal, "Retour sur 'La cité du mâle': la vérité selon Daniel Leconte," L'Obs avec Rue89, October 3, 2011, http://rue89.nouvelobs.com/2010/10/03/retour-sur-la-cite-du-male -la-verite-selon-daniel-leconte-169327.

4. "La fixeuse du documentaire 'La cité du mâle' condamnée à 4 mois ferme," *Le Monde*, October 14, 2011, accessed November 20, 2015, http://www.lemonde.fr/societe/article/2011/10/14/la-fixeuse-du-documentaire-la-cite-du-male-condamnee-a-4-mois-ferme_1587945_3224.html.

5. ARTE has a long history of sensationalist reporting on Muslims, the banlieues, and sexism, often questioning Muslim immigrants' ability to adapt to French values. See Mona Chollet, "Sur Arte, un 'féminisme' anti-immigrés," *Le Monde Diplomatique*, October 1, 2010, accessed November 20, 2015, https://www.monde-diplomatique.fr/carnet/2010-10-01-Arte. On Ladji Réal's reasoning for launching his *contre-enquête* to Sanchez's documentary, see Emilie Guédé, "La cité du mâle: une contre-enquête pour dénoncer les dérives des medias," *Les inrockuptibles*, October 16, 2010, accessed November 20, 2015, http://www.lesinrocks.com/2010/12/16/actualite/la-cite-du-male-une-contre-enquete-pour-denoncer-les-derives-des-medias-1122114/.

6. Bertrand Cassaigne, "Les médias et la banlieue," *Ceras*, January 2008, accessed November 20, 2015, http://www.ceras-projet.com/index.php?id=2864.

7. *La squale*, directed by Fabrice Genestal (Cine Nomine, 2000), and *Bande de filles*, directed by Céline Sciamma (Hold Up Films, 2014).

8. *La journée de la jupe*, directed by Jean-Paul Lilienfeld (ARTE Films, 2008), made-for-TV film.

9. Literally, "Neither whores nor submissives"; the official English translation, "Neither sluts nor doormats," captures neither the antiprostitution elements that elicited some critique from sex worker organizations at the group's founding nor the idea of submission that vaguely suggests a simultaneously gendered and religious deference to Islam.

10. See Fernando, *Republic Unsettled*; see also, Mayanthi L. Fernando, "Save the Muslim Woman, Save the Republic: Ni Putes Ni Soumises and the Ruse of Neoliberal Sovereignty," *Modern and Contemporary France* 21, no. 2 (2013): 147–65; Stéphanie Marteau, "Ni putes ni soumises: un appareil idéologique d'Etat," Movements, October 22, 2011, http://mouvements.info/ni-putes-ni-soumises-un-appareil-ideologique-detat/; and Catherine Raissiguier, "Muslim Women in France: Impossible Subjects?," *Darkmatter*, May 2, 2008, http://www.darkmatter101.org/site/2008/05/02/muslim-women-in-france-impossible-subjects/.

11. Fadela Amara and Sylvia Zappi, *Breaking the Silence: French Women's Voices from the Ghetto*, trans. Helen Chenut (Berkeley: University of California Press, 2006), 69–75. Though Amara perhaps seeks to diagnose an alleged problem, and thus opts for the explanatory power of categories, she reproduces an enthusiasm for anthropological types prevalent in colonial-era writing. This enthusiasm has also been found in recent *banlieue* fiction that introduces the unseasoned observer to the *banlieue* via a cartography of social types.

12. Ibid., 70.

13. Pascal Duret, *Les jeunes et l'identité masculine* (Paris: Presses Universitaires de France, 1999).

14. Amara, *Breaking the Silence*, 65–66.

15. Ibid., 73–74.

16. The veiled young women seem to be the "defense" to the *banlieue* rioters' "offense" in commentary depicting the banlieues as a battleground manned by violent Muslims, as Tayeb explains in regard to Germany: "Veiling thus becomes a convenient

act of self-segregation and simultaneously aggression, the female version of the male youth setting the suburbs on fire" (Tayeb, *European Others*, 104).

17. John Bowen, *Why the French Don't Like Headscarves: Islam, the State, and Public Space* (Princeton: Princeton University Press, 2008).

18. In the video, Diam's appears to shop for an ideal man in a "human" shopping center, enumerating the various celebrities and musicians he should look and act like; with the help of some girlfriends, Diam's dresses and undresses a human mannequin, critiquing the different looks put together amidst giggles. See Diam's, "Jeune demoiselle recherche un mec mortel," YouTube, accessed November 21, 2015, https://www.youtube.com/watch?v=akceZqkxCcY.

19. S. P., "Diam's s'en prend violemment à Fadela Amara," *Elle*, January 25, 2010, accessed November 21, 2015, http://www.elle.fr/People/La-vie-des-people/News/Diam -s-s-en-prend-violemment-a-Fadela-Amara-1128094; and G. G., "Fadela Amara et sa violente critique envers Diam's," *Voici*, February 11, 2010, accessed November 21, 2015, http://www.voici.fr/news-people/actu-people/fadela-amara-sa-violente-critique -envers-diam-s-341708.

20. Judith Halberstam, *Female Masculinity* (Durham, NC: Duke University Press), 1–8.

21. Giraud, *Quartiers gay*, and Fassin, "Homosexual City, Homophobic Banlieue?"

22. Chaumont, *Homo-ghetto*, 17.

23. For instance, the hip culture magazine *Les Inrockuptibles* uncritically recycled the findings of Chaumont's book in an article entitled "No home for homos: Two steps from the city center, the projects' gay and lesbian youth are living in social hell." See Hugo Lindenberg, "Pas de quartiers pour les homos: à deux pas des centres-villes les jeunes gays et lesbiennes des cités vivent un enfer social," *Les Inrocks*, September 30, 2009, accessed November 21, 2015, http://www.lesinrocks.com/2009/09/30/actualite /societe/pas-de-quartiers-pour-les-homos-1137118/.

24. I examine this notion of unrestrained youth revolting against the assimilationist deference their parents displayed toward French superiors in chapter 2.

25. Kenneth Lewes, *Psychoanalysis and Male Homosexuality* (Lanham, MD: Jason Aronson, 1999).

26. Michael Walonen, in *Writing Tangier in the Postcolonial Transition* (Farnham, England: Ashgate, 2011), has inventoried perceptions of North Africans—and in particular, Moroccan men—among European and American travelers and writers in mid-century Tangiers: "The Moroccan 'Arab' male took on a very particular sexual allure for those attracted to them, as Greg Mullins notes. Accorded much of the same exotic virility and untrammeled sexualized masculinity as commonly attributed to black men, the 'Arab' was prized as someone bisexual or 'sexually undifferentiated' rather than gay, and hence 'a man whose masculinity is uncompromised'" (22).

27. As I explain in the section on nightlife entrepreneur Fouad Zeraoui later in this chapter, these clubs have at times rejected patrons exhibiting a *banlieusard* appearance. As an aside, my own personal experience echoes this: when traveling in groups to gay clubs with friends of North African background, those members of our group wearing attire associated with the banlieues (sneakers, sweatpants, diamond studs, high socks, and flak jackets) were denied entry, even though the dress code was casual. At heterosexual clubs, Malek Boutih, a politician and former president of SOS Racisme, found repeated evidence of such door policies when sending identically dressed patrons of

different ethnicities to nightclubs. See Clotilde Alric, "Discrimination: la Cour de cassation confirme la validité juridique du testing devant les tribunaux" LegalNews-Notaires, June 12, 2002, accessed November 21, 2015, http://www.legalnewsnotaires .com/index.php?option=com_content&view=article&id=82009&catid=944:non -categorise&Itemid=230.

28. Such sites include: Kelma (https://www.kelma.org), Citébeur personals (http:// citebeur.com/en/pagesperso/galerie), and Planet Romeo (https://www.planetromeo .com), as well as the apps Grindr and Scruff.

29. Chaumont, *Homo-ghetto*, 20–21.

30. The trope of the Franco-Arab man who polices sexuality is explored in André Téchiné's *Les témoins* (2007; *The Witnesses*). See also the portrait of the character Mehdi in chapter 4.

31. *Le plafond de verre*, directed by Yamina Benguigui (Bandits Productions, 2006), film.

32. See, for example, Michael Luongo, *Gay Travels in the Muslim World* (Binghamton, NY: Haworth Press, 2007); and Jehoeda Soefer and Arno Schmitt, *Sexuality and Eroticism among Males in Moslem Societies* (Binghamton, NY: Haworth Press, 1992).

33. It may be tempting, when interpreting Majid's account of his own sexual disposition, to categorize him as an MSM or "man who has sex with men"—A term common in the disciplines of sociology and public health, to describe patterns of sexual practice that are not necessarily identity-affirming, nor exclusively homosexual, or that may involve insertive rather than passive sex (though non–identity-affirming MSMs who opt for the passive role are an important component as well). Not normally used for self-designation, the term has sometimes been criticized for reifying an identity-affirming understanding of homosexuality (since it remains a designation of types of persons), despite being coined to avoid this. Majid, as we have seen, identifies as homosexual and does not resort to this vocabulary.

34. Kim Roselier, "Momosexuel: L'Histoire de momo, le lascar homosexual," Momosexuel (blog), accessed November 21, 2015, http://momosexuel.blogspot.com/.

35. Majid subsequently recounts an anecdote about a man who wanted him to bring dirty sneakers to their rendezvous so he could smell them, better known as a *plan sket*, eroticized on porn sites such as SketBoy.com. The cellars of housing projects are often the location for fantasized gang-bangs. See Chaumont, *Homo-ghetto*, 23–24.

36. From the same chapter ("Majid: pédé et racaille"): "The liberated relationship the Gauls have with their own homosexuality shocks him: 'At first, I had relationships with Europeans, but I didn't like it because they are too frank, they tell you they liked the fucking they got and they want to do it again.' For him, what with homosexuality being a form of deviance, it is inseparable from the secret, from clandestinity, from guilt. Which is exactly what excites him: 'The Maghrebis, they are more embarrassed [*gêné*], they have a sense of vice and that's what I prefer'" (Chaumont, *Homo-ghetto*, 22–23).

37. The famous Franco-Arab actor Roschdy Zem exemplified this in a famous scene from Liria Begeja's *Change-moi ma vie* (2000; *Change My Life*). Playing a transvestite North African prostitute, he meets the fantasy demand of a white French client nostalgic for North Africa by dressing up in traditional country attire and sensuously separating grains of couscous with his fingers, while the client pleasures himself, in a scene of grotesque and somewhat tragic comedy.

38. Tim Dean, quoting D. W. Winnicott, in *Unlimited Intimacy: Reflections on the Subculture of Barebacking* (Chicago: University of Chicago Press, 2009), 35. See also D. W. Winnicott, *Playing and Reality* (London: Routledge, 1991), 41.

39. See my analysis of Christophe Honoré's film *L'homme au bain* (2010; *Man at Bath*) in chapter 5.

40. Gopinath makes this point in regard to representations of lesbian desire in Bollywood cinema: "Indeed the most enabling and nuanced instances of queer female desire on the Bollywood screen transpire not through the representation of explicitly queer coded, visible "lesbian" characters but rather through evoking the latent homoeroticism of female homosocial space" (*Impossible Desires*, 25).

41. José Esteban Muñoz, *Disidentifications: Queers of Color and the Performance of Politics* (Minneapolis: University of Minnesota Press, 1999).

42. Tim Dean dignifies this sexual alternative to individualism with the term *ethics*, in this preview of *Unlimited Intimacy*: "Far from a sign of the failure to commit to a single partner, cruising entails a commitment to something more than just individuals. Rather than rationalizing gay men's cruising habits as the inevitable yet dysfunctional outcome of heteronormative social arrangements and discriminatory laws, then, the final chapter considers what it might mean to adopt an ethic of cruising as a way of life" (175).

43. Ferguson, *Aberrations in Black*, 21.

44. Tayeb, *European Others*, 105.

45. My point here is not to deny the homophobic and sexist violence that does exist in *banlieue* spaces, but to stress the journalistic erasure of the *banlieue*'s sexual diversity, as well as its particular strategies of negotiating queer identity and finding avenues of sexual expression in circumstances very different from those in the city center.

46. In 2012, he became a counselor for press relations in the cabinet of Aurélie Filippetti, then minister of culture and communication, and in 2014, he obtained a position in then Minister of Education Benoit Hamon's cabinet.

47. Marteau, "Ni putes ni soumises: un appareil idéologique d'etat."

48. After twenty years (1995–2015) in print, *Têtu* has since become an online-only magazine. See Franck Chaumont and Fouad Zeraoui, "Débat *Têtu*: gays de banlieue: faut-il en sortir pour s'en sortir?," Kelma (blog), November 2009, accessed March 3, 2012, http://blog-gay.kelma.org/gays-en-banlieue (site discontinued).

49. This ambivalent attitude of attraction and repulsion colors many other situations in which Muslims may represent "spice" or an acceptable level of difference in European neighborhoods that are gentrifying. Speaking of the construct of the "creative city," Fatima El-Tayeb describes how the dominance of white, middle-class man (who may move to ethnic neighborhoods for cultural capital) is never really endangered by "the Muslim community, which provides color, exotic food, and sexual objects but also stands for restrictive morality, crime, and poverty" (*European Others*, 125).

50. Daniel Garcia, "L'avant-garde soluble dans le Marais?," *Le Nouvel Observateur*, February 28–March 6, 2002.

51. Fouad Zeraoui, "La soirée Black Blanc Beur (BBB)," Kelma, accessed June 19, 2016, http://www.kelma.org/soiree_bbb.php.

52. The club night then moved on to a variety of locales—including the venerable rock-n-roll disco La Loco adjacent the Moulin Rouge, the Montparnasse tower, and

the Champs-Elysées—before returning to its Pigalle birthplace, where it still resides as of June 2016.

53. SO36 Nightclub organizers, "Gayhane: House of Halay," So36, http://so36.de/regulars/gayhane/.

54. Gopinath, *Impossible Desires*, 21.

55. Gopinath detects a similar ambivalence in her study of South Asian public cultures, which "function to name the myriad cultural forms and practices through which queer subjects articulate new modes of collectivity and kinship that reject the ethnic and religious absolutism of multiple nationalisms, while simultaneously resisting Euro-American, homonormative models of sexual alterity" (ibid., 20).

56. Beyoncé and Sean Paul, *Baby Boy* (Scott Storch and Beyoncé Knowles, 2003), CD.

57. Both Fassin ("Homosexual City, Homophobic Banlieue?") and Rees-Robert and Cervulle (*Homo Exoticus*) offer critiques.

58. No minors have been sentenced to death in peri-urban France for sex crimes, as happened infamously in Iran in 2006 with the much-mediatized hangings in Mashad. Using Iran as the ultimate homophobic model in LGBT discourse presents its own problems, not least because of the country's rich literary and artistic heritage of homosexual practices if not identity, but also because, in the Mashad case, those allegedly sentenced to death for homosexuality in human rights parlance were accused of other crimes (rape and theft), making it difficult to isolate the "crime" of homosexuality, as explained in a pivotal article by Richard Kim (by mentioning this article, I do not want to take anything away from the injustice of sentencing minors, or adults, to death for whatever "reason"). See Richard Kim, "Witness to an Execution," *Nation*, August 15, 2005, accessed November 15, 2015, http://www.thenation.com/article/witnesses-execution.

59. Gaël Klement, "Homosexualité des bobos, homophobie des prolos?" *Revue L'Anticapitaliste*, no. 58 (April 2014), accessed June 23, 2016, https://npa2009.org/idees/homosexualite-des-bobos-homophobie-des-prolos-0.

60. P. G. Lange, "Publicly private and privately public: Social networking on YouTube," *Journal of Computer-Mediated Communication* 13, no. 1 (2007), accessed October 6, 2012, http://jcmc.indiana.edu/vol13/issue1/lange.html.

61. Marc Endeweld, "Drague homo: vive le plein air," *Les Inrocks*, August 15, 2013, accessed November 15, 2015, http://www.lesinrocks.com/2013/08/15/actualite/drague-homo-vive-le-plein-air-11416391/.

62. Dean, *Unlimited Intimacy*, xii.

63. Gérard Noiriel, *Le creuset français* (Paris: Seuil, 2006), 48.

64. Michel Foucault, *The History of Sexuality*, vol. 1, trans. Robert Hurley (New York: Vintage, 1990).

65. Leo Bersani, *Homos* (Cambridge, MA: Harvard University Press, 1996).

66. The gay-friendly Brahim Asloum also appeared in the April 2010 special edition of *Têtu*, "Spécial beurs: les nouveaux Delon." *Têtu* came out with cover-to-cover exposés on minority themes every couple of years.

67. Didier Lestrade, "La moustache et les gays," Didier Lestrade (blog), December 2, 2010, accessed November 22, 2015, http://didierlestrade.fr/porno/article/la-moustache-et-les-gays.

68. Madonna, *Vogue* (Sire, 1990), CD, and *Paris Is Burning*, directed by Jennie Livingston (Miramax, 1990), film.

69. Delphine Aunis, "Tecktonik KIDS (Photos: Takao Oshima)," *Têtu*, April 2008.

70. Guénif-Souilamas, *Les féministes et le garçon arabe*.

71. Prominent examples of media personalities who present metrosexuality are the Canal+ presenter Ali Baddou, Chakib Lahssaini of NRJ 12, the out choreographer and frequent TV guest Kamel Oualli, and the chronicler Mustapha El Atrassi on Laurent Ruquier's variety show, *On est pas couché*. Ruquier, a well-liked media personality, is one of the most prominent openly gay journalists in France. Notably, one of the acts featured on his show are the *lascars gay* ("gay thugs") portrayed as comical by virtue of the juxtaposition of homosexuality and *banlieue* values. In this sense, the *lascars gay*, played by actors Majid Berhila and Hugues Duquesne, present an ambiguous case, both increasing the visibility of homo thugs, while at the same time making their existence seem aberrantly strange. This mockery, I contend, repeats the homonormative censorship of *banlieue* sexual instability. See Luc Sonzogni, "Les Lascars Gay" (Splendid Playhouse, Paris, 2012).

72. His point echoes what I will explore in chapter 2: psychoanalyzing commentators of *banlieue* affairs have routinely called for the imperative of individual escape from the dominant group psychology that supposedly restrains *banlieue* and immigrant populations.

73. Zeraoui develops the point at the end of the *Têtu* debate: "Young people really have a whole set of signposts to help orient them [*un vivier de repères*] that is much more significant [than before). The witness accounts in your book are not all there is, full of pain and so on, there is something else, a real interface of exchange, of encounters. People are no longer isolated. . . . I'm much more optimistic, things are evolving in the right direction. The matter is taking care of itself [*ça s'arrange*], thanks to sexuality. The Internet has allowed for a true *mixité*, more than one can imagine."

2 / Constructing the Broken Family: The Draw for Psychoanalysis

1. Slavoj Žižek and John Millbank, *The Monstrosity of Christ* (Cambridge, MA: MIT Press, 2009), 86.

2. The Algiers School, established in the 1920s, refers to a group of psychiatrists practicing in Algeria. The school's practitioners were known for their experimental willingness to focus on ethnicity and culture as tools for understanding indigenous psychology and especially "Arab madness." Prominent members included Antoine Porot and his son Maurice, as well as Don Côme Arrii. See Richard Keller, *Colonial Madness: Psychiatry in French North Africa* (Chicago: University of Chicago Press, 2007), 138.

3. Ranjana Khanna, *Dark Continents: Colonialism and Psychoanalysis* (Durham, NC: Duke University Press, 2003).

4. Jalil Bennani, "La psychanalyse au Maroc," in *Le sacré, cet obscur objet du désir?* (Paris: Editions Albin Michel, 2009), 36.

5. Bennani, "La psychanalyse au Maroc," 35.

6. Malek Chebel, *Psychanalyse des mille et une nuits* (Lausanne, Switzerland: Payot, 2002).

7. While Chebel's vivid accounts of the sexual diversity of Islam are a welcome change from representations that emphasize a total lack of such diversity, his views on Arab heritage and especially sexual customs may have been impacted by political

292 / NOTES TO PAGES 81–84

events such as the Algerian civil war of the 1990s. As one of my readers suggested, his long-standing focus on Islamic sexuality could be seen as an attempt to save from historical oblivion exactly that which the Algerian Islamists were trying to repress in the way of sexual dissidence; his mission is a historiographic battle so to speak.

8. Joan Scott, "Ursula Hirschmann Annual Lecture on Gender and Europe: Sexularism," European University Institute, April 23, 2009, accessed June 21, 2016, http://cadmus.eui.eu/bitstream/handle/1814/11553/RSCAS_DL_2009%20_01.pdf;jsessionid=A7596F760E063B5054809B38DD37D950?sequence=1.

9. Didier Fassin, "L'ethnopsychiatrie et ses réseaux. L'influence qui grandit," *Genèses*, no. 35 (1999): 146–71.

10. Tobie Nathan, and many others who support ethnopsychiatry in its current venture, have argued in their own defense that attention to cultural particularity and especially filiation is an absolute requirement of successful psychoanalytic therapies. A mere similarity, in terms of attention to cultural particularity, is not sufficient to reduce the new ethnopsychiatry to the old one: the first accepts that cultural difference can be used as a therapeutic tool, the second defines cultural difference in order to stigmatize it. Furthermore, Nathan and his allies have been very vocal about the symbolic violence against immigrants that results from forced assimilation with French republican norms, arguing for a right to difference and communitarianism. In contrast to Nathan et al., critics such as the sociologist Didier Fassin and the prominent psychoanalytic essayist Fethi Benslama believe that the new ethnopsychiatry—even though comprised of left and far-left thinkers that declare themselves "antiracist"—shares tendencies with the colonial one. By referring to filiation and cultural roots, these critics say the new ethnopsychiatry imprisons subjects within their ancestry and origins, preventing evolution, assimilation, and the establishment of new roots in the host country. Some critiques have gone so far as to describe Nathan and others as modern-day snake oil peddlers who have reaped great financial benefit from their innovative methods, which have yielded spectacular albeit, some would argue, unethical, unscientific, and most crucially nonuniversal results.

11. Khanna, *Dark Continents*.

12. See Keller, *Colonial Madness*, 4: "At different periods and from different perspectives, the field was less a weapon in the arsenal of colonial racism, than it was a tool for the emancipation of the colonized, an innovative branch of social and medical science . . . a discipline in crisis, and a mechanism for negotiating the meaning of difference for Republican citizenship."

13. Tahar Ben Jelloun, *La plus haute des solitudes* (Paris: Le Seuil, 1977), 20.

14. Ibid., 169.

15. Tahar Ben Jelloun, *Hospitalité française* (Paris: Le Seuil, 1997).

16. See Ben Jelloun, *La plus haute des solitudes*, 168: "What is impotence, for a man to whom one has taught that 'sexuality valorizes,' but a failed suicide . . . ? The negative diagnosis is the start of something else, the start of death, meaning the 'will' to cease existing sexually, to cease being present in the world according to the dialectic of *jouissance* and, in the specific case of Maghrebis, to no longer perpetuate themselves via new progeny. Due to this state of affairs, relations with other people prove impossible or at least difficult, except if that person is able to penetrate into the only dialectic that the now impotent man is capable of practicing: that which begins his death march, that which legitimizes his existential refusal, that which permits the only possible denunciation of a political and economic system which can only ignore the individual

as a living, that is to say, desiring being. The psychotherapist is called upon to be this person."

17. Elisabeth Badinter, *XY: de l'identité masculine* (Paris: Odile Jacob, 1992), 24.

18. Badinter is infamous, in some circles, for declaring that her conclusions about the "fragility" of masculinities in Western society do not apply to men outside of Western civilizations, and that, if she calls for increased tolerance for the expression of masculinity at all, it is not for the excessive virilities of non-European men who haven't been subjected to the same "emasculation." This analysis echoes right-wing psychoanalyst Michel Schneider's comments on immigrant men.

19. Jalil Bennani with Alain Braconnier, *Le temps des ados* (Casablanca, Morocco: Éditions Le Fennec, 2002).

20. Ibid., 174.

21. See my discussion of adolescence and creativity in relation to fashion in chapter 1.

22. Bennani and Braconnier, *Le temps des ados*, 146.

23. Ibid., 10.

24. Ibid., 144.

25. Ibid., 27.

26. Ibid., 46.

27. Ibid., 20.

28. Ibid., 43.

29. Ben Jelloun, *La plus haute des solitudes*, 91.

30. Bennani and Braconnier, *Le temps des ados*, 65.

31. Michel Schneider, *Big mother: Psychopathologie de la vie politique* (Paris: Odile Jacob, 2005).

32. Camille Robcis, "How the Symbolic Became French: Kinship and Republicanism in the PACS Debates," *Discourse* 26, no. 3 (Fall 2004): 110–35.

33. Ibid., 116.

34. Michel Schneider, *La confusion des sexes* (Paris: Flammarion, 2007), 130.

35. Schneider, *Big mother*, 10.

36. Ibid., 9.

37. Didier Fassin, one of Nathan's greatest critics, has employed such language in the title of an essay about political attitudes toward discrimination—"Du Déni à la denegation: Psychologie politique de la représentation des discriminations"—while other analysts have sought to understand issues affecting the banlieues in psychopathological terms. Schneider takes upon himself the special mission of deconstructing political psychopathology, because he believes that, unlike Freud in his time, psychoanalysts today "rarely focus on the world as it evolves [*comme il va*], and do not make the necessary links between the mental troubles they heal and the collective representations amongst which they live" (*La confusion des sexes*, 14). Like many psychoanalysts claiming filiation with Freud, Schneider seeks to ground within psychoanalysis' formative period his own amalgam of collective psychology (evident in politics) and individual psychology. See Didier Fassin, "Du Déni à la denegation: Psychologie politique de la représentation des discriminations," in *De la question sociale à la question raciale*, ed. Eric Fassin and Didier Fassin (Paris: La Découverte, 2006); and Jean Jacques Rassial, ed., *Y a-t-il une psychopathologie des* banlieues? (Toulouse, France: Erès, 2002).

38. Schneider, *Big mother*, 185.

39. Fassin, *Liberté, egalité, sexualité*.

40. Schneider, *Big mother*, 49.

41. Ibid., 20.

42. Ibid., 11, 13.

43. Ibid., 46.

44. Ibid., 54.

45. Ibid., 84.

46. Ibid., 186.

47. Ibid., 58.

48. "The Islamists think—wrongly—that the West is a castrated male. At the same time, we can hypothesize that America's aggressors launched their assault with the conviction that the West was condemned to disappear, precisely because it had blurred or erased the traditional roles delegated to man and woman. Ever since the Gulf War, women's access to US army units, even to combat posts, had perhaps convinced those warriors that the Western world's final hour had come. It must not be omitted, that in our very own banlieues, where delinquency is often the work of boys issued from Arabic Islamic countries, the fact that girls manage to 'get out' and succeed remarkably [*s'en sortent de façon remarquable*] according to studies, as well as the fact of their upward mobility, take on the meaning of a threat originating with women. And there, once more, the presence of women in the police, the *fliquettes*, has managed to reinforce a feeling of the end of authority. . . . Just as much as woman and her status, what menaces the sexual identity of terrorists seems to be the way Western women and men seem to reinscribe sexual difference" (ibid., 234).

49. Yann Moix, *Partouz* (Paris: Editions Grasset, 2004), 64.

50. Schneider, *La confusion des sexes*, 266.

51. Cited in Khanna, *Dark Continents*, 2.

52. Benjamin Stora, *La gangrène et l'oubli* (Paris: La Découverte, 2005).

53. Schneider, *La confusion des sexes*, 251.

54. Laurent Mucchielli, *Le scandale des "tournantes: dérives médiatiques, contre-enquête sociologique* (Paris: Editions La Découverte, 2005).

55. Fassin, *Liberté, egalité, sexualité*, 131.

56. Royal cited in ibid., 171.

57. Ibid.

58. Ministère de la Culture et de la Communication, *La violence à la télévision* (2002), http://www.culture.gouv.fr/culture/actualites/communiq/aillagon/rapportBK .pdf.

59. Ibid., 25.

60. Tania Modleski, *Feminism without Women: Culture and Criticism in a "Post-feminist" Age* (Abingdon, England: Routledge, 1991), 69.

61. Bennani, *Le corps suspect* (Paris: Editions Galilée, 1980), 44.

62. Ben Jelloun, *La plus haute des solitudes*, 59.

63. Ibid., 88.

64. Ibid., 90.

65. Fethi Benslama, "The Veil of Islam," translated by Emiliano Battista and Sigi Jöttkandt, *S: Journal of the Circle of Lacanian Ideology Critique*, no. 2 (2009): 24.

66. Famed anthropologist Françoise Héritier produced such discourse in an interview, when she explained that what she "has tried to show is that the anatomical, physiological, and functional difference of the sexes . . . is at the basis of the fundamental opposition which allows us to think. Because thinking is first of all classifying,

classifying is essentially discriminating, and the fundamental discrimination is based on sexual difference." Françoise Héritier, "Pacte Civil De Solidarité: 'Aucune Société N'admet De Parenté Homosexuelle,'" interview by Marianne Gomez, *La Croix*, November 9, 1998, 16.

67. Robcis, "How the Symbolic Became French."

68. Benslama, "The Veil of Islam," 25.

69. India was symbolically the next "neighbor" over, much more similar to Christianity's trinity with its plural deities. In Lévi-Strauss' description, Indian spirituality was less patriarchal and prohibitive than Islam: "Today, it is behind Islam that I contemplate India; the India of Buddha, prior to Muhammad who—for me as a European and because I am European—arises between our reflection and the teachings which are closest to it . . . the hands of the East and the West, predestined to be joined, were kept apart by it. . . . The West should return to the sources of its torn condition: by way of interposing itself between Buddhism and Christianity, Islam islamized us when, in the course of the Crusades, the West let itself be caught in the opposition to it and thus started to resemble it, instead of delivering itself—in the case of the inexistence of Islam—to the slow osmosis with Buddhism which would Christianize us even more, in a sense which would have been all the more Christian insofar as we were to mount beyond Christianity itself. It is then that the West has lost its chance to remain woman." Claude Levi-Strauss, *Tristes tropiques*, cited in Slavoj Žižek, "A Glance into the Archives of Islam," Lacan.com, accessed June 30, 2016, http://www.lacan.com/zizarchives.htm#_ftn1.

70. Ibid.

71. Bennani, *Le corps suspect*, 43.

72. Ibid., 44.

73. Michel Schneider, "Mère, delivre-nous du sexe," *Champ Psychomatique*, no. 27 (2002–2003): 31.

74. Ibid., 232.

75. Ibid., 235.

76. Khanna, *Dark Continents*, 6.

77. This relates to the tendency in radical homosexual cinema and activist circles to cast Franco-Arab characters exclusively as sexually dominant or "active" at the risk of restricting Franco-Arab masculinity to such stereotypes and making Franco-Arab effeminacy or passivity inconceivable. See chapter 4; see also Maxime Cervulle, "French Homonormativity and the Commodification of the Arab Body," in "Queer Futures," special issue, *Radical History Review*, no. 100 (2008): 171–79.

78. Schneider, *Big mother*, 235.

79. Shepard analyzed how *pied-noir* men were cast as violent, perverse, obsessed with proving their virility, and most of all, fundamentally different from the idealized Metropolitan French in regard to relations between the sexes. This distinction helped make the case for separation between France and Colonial Algeria, because the masculinity of *pieds-noirs* was cast as un-French and too close to the supposed mores of North Africa. See chapter 4.

80. Schneider, *Big mother*, 236.

81. Ben Jelloun, *La plus haute des solitudes*, 32.

82. Keller, *Colonial Madness*, 3.

83. Schneider, *Big mother*, 276.

84. Keller, *Colonial Madness*, 16.

85. Ibid.

86. Maurice Porot, "L'Ecole Algérienne de Psychiatrie et son initiateur: Le Professeur Antoine Porot," *L'Algérianiste*, no. 62, n.d., accessed April 9, 2012, http://cerclealgerianiste2607.fr/Chapitres/Site%20Internet%20Cercle%20National/www.cerclealgerianiste.asso.fr/contenu/sante3204.htm (site discontinued), archived at http://archive.is/vgAU. See also, "Porot (Maurice Marie-Joseph)," in *Qui est qui en France: dictionnaire biographique de personnalités françaises vivant en France, dans les territoires d'Outre-Mer ou à l'étranger et de personnalités étrangères résidant en France*, 14th ed. (1979–1980) (Paris: Editions Jacques Lafitte, 1979).

87. René Charpentier cited in Keller, *Colonial Madness*, 146.

88. Charles A. Hirsch, "La criminalité des Nord-Africains en France est-elle une criminalité par défaut d'adaptation ?," *Revue Internationale de Criminologie et de Police Technique* 13, no. 2 (April–June, 1959): 129–41.

89. Mehammed Mack, "L'impact de 1962 sur la théorie psychoanalytique de la dépendance, et ses échos dans les débats Français sur l'immigration," paper presented at the 1962: Un Monde conference in Oran, Algeria, October 14, 2012.

90. Antoine Porot and Jean Sutter, "Le 'primitivisme' des indigènes Nord-Africains: Ses incidences en pathologie mentale," *Sud Médical et Chirurgical*, April 15, 1939: 226–41.

91. Jean-Claude Scotto, "Professeur Jean Sutter (1911–1998)," *L'Histoire de l'Algérie Médicale*, Santétropicale.com, accessed February 21, 2014, http://www.santetropicale.com/santemag/algerie/hist/index.asp.

92. Keller, *Colonial Madness*, 17.

93. Ibid., 102.

94. Don Côme Arrii and Antoine Porot, "Impulsivité criminelle chez l'indigène algérien," *Annales Médico-Psychologiques* 90, no. 2 (December 1932): 588–611.

95. Arrii, "De l'impulsivité criminelle," 40–41.

96. Adolphe Kocher, *De la criminalité chez les Arabes au point de vue de la pratique medico-judiciaire en Algérie* (Paris: J. B. Baillière et fils, 1884), 103–6.

97. Yvan Gastaut, *Immigration et l'opinion en France sous la Vème République* (Paris: Seuil, 2000), 111–14.

98. Keller, *Colonial Madness*, 208

99. See chapter 1 and also John Bowen's study of French Christian and secular reactions to the headscarf in public space. Many respondents used the expression *cela m'aggresse* (it makes me feel that I am under aggression) when speaking of their impressions upon seeing a headscarf. John Bowen, *Why the French Don't Like Headscarves*, 174.

100. Benslama, "The Veil of Islam," 14–26.

101. Both Benslama and Nathan are disciples of the founder of modern ethnopsychiatry, Georges Devereux, both worked with immigrants in Paris suburbs and published groundbreaking books about their conclusions, both were instrumental in setting up university clinics and connecting training to research (Nathan at Université Paris VIII and Benslama at Paris VII), and both launched influential psychoanalytical journals (Nathan: *La Nouvelle Revue d'Ethnopsychiatrie*; Benslama: *Cahiers Intersignes*).

102. Didier Fassin, "L'ethnopscyhiatrie et ses réseaux. L'influence qui grandit," *Genèses*, no. 35 (1999): 146–71.

103. In his essay "Psychoanalysis, Islam, and the Other of Liberalism," Joseph Massad takes Benslama to task for what he explains are unexamined biases that prejudice

the latter's conclusions. Benslama's *insoumission* (nonsubmission, resistance)—which carries a special meaning in light of the loose translations of "Islam" as "submission"— would in Massad's argument be against "Islam" as a father in an Oedipal formation. In his essay, Massad calls the translation "submission" erroneous, and mentions an array of more precise alternatives, for example, "deliverance," which importantly do not contain an element of subjugation (198). Massad states that the persistence of Islam in North African and Arab public consciousness creates a deep narcissistic injury in psychoanalytical thinkers writing on the subject from France. Joseph Massad, "Psycho-analysis, Islam, and the Other of Liberalism" *Psychoanalysis and History* 11, no. 2 (2009): 193–208; Fethi Benslama, *Déclaration d'insoumission: à l'usage des musulmans et de ceux qui ne le sont pas* (Paris: Editions Flammarion, 2005).

104. Benslama, "The Veil of Islam."

105. François Gaspard and Farhad Khosrokhavar, *Le foulard et la République* (Paris: La Découverte, 1995).

106. Christine Delphy, *Classer, dominer* (Paris: La Fabrique, 2008).

107. Benslama, "The Veil of Islam," 15.

108. Ibid.

109. Joan Wallach Scott, *The Politics of the Veil* (Princeton: Princeton University Press, 2007).

110. Fernando, *Republic Unsettled*, 230.

111. Benslama, "The Veil of Islam," 16.

112. Jean-Jacques Delfour, "François Bayrou, censeur sémiologue," *Libération*, October 20, 1994.

113. François Bayrou, "Interview," *Libération*, October 10, 1994.

114. Keller, *Colonial Madness*, 206.

115. Ibid., 205.

116. "In controversies over Muslim girls wearing headscarves in French public schools, the radical polarization of French politics, and the sentiment of rising insecurity linked to immigration in peri-urban France, psychiatrists and psychoanalysts have offered elaborate interpretations designed to sway public debate. In so doing ethno-psychiatrists have prodigiously developed the legacy of their colonial forbears, yet they have also taken the profession in a new direction. Where colonial psychiatrists intervened regularly in public debates about colonial policy, ethno-psychiatrists in a globalizing France have remade themselves in the model of engaged Paris intellectuals" (ibid., 206).

117. Ibid.

118. As colonial ethnopsychiatrists showed, the debate over the headscarf and its polyvalent symbolism sometimes is rerouted back to men to the detriment of the women who actually wear it. In the contemporary period, rarely is a veiled women interviewed by the media, or considered independently from the commentaries of male theologians (when included side-by-side, this gives the appearance that the theologians speak for them). Even the *Stasi* commission, the body of experts that was charged with holding hearings and laying the groundwork for what came to be the 2004 headscarf ban in schools, declared that it "had heard enough" after only two veiled women gave testimony. Rarely is it suggested that the headscarf is a covenant between God and women, despite many Muslim women's declarations that the head-scarf is worn out of modesty before God, not man.

119. Benslama, "The Veil of Islam," 22.

120. Ibid., 16.

121. Ibid., 18.

122. "Est-ce que c'est pris en charge?" Info-depression, accessed November 26, 2015, http://www.info-depression.fr/spip.php?article30.

123. Fassin, "L'ethnopscyhiatrie et ses réseaux," 146.

124. See Bennani, *Le corps suspect*, 41: "The immigrant's faculty of speech, seeking a place to express itself, will address itself to the medical field to speak his subjectivity. It will be spoken but not without risks. . . . We have seen it: one might recognize the psychic fact, only to better pervert it. One might make speeches about difference, only to better exclude it."

125. One of Didier Fassin's consistent critiques is that lower-income patients addressed to ethnopsychiatric services have no other recourse but to pursue that option.

126. Keller, *Colonial Madness*, 187.

127. Marie-Hélène Bourcier, *Sexpolitiques: Queer Zones 2* (Paris: La Fabrique Editions, 2005), 68–75.

128. Khanna, *Dark Continents*, 5.

129. Jean-Michel Hirt, *Le miroir du prophète: psychanalyse et Islam* (Paris: Grasset, 1993), 111.

130. Ibid.

131. Schneider, *Big mother*, 90.

132. See the portraits of intentionally clandestine young men in Franck Chaumont's *Homo Ghetto*, analyzed in chapter 1.

133. *Sans-papiers* (literally, "without papers") translates to "undocumented" and refers to the large group of migrants who have rallied together (especially since the 1990s) to make demands for a regularized status in France.

134. Amara and Sylvia Zappi, *Breaking the Silence*, 63.

135. Bennani, *Le temps des ados*, 42.

136. Schneider, *Big mother*, 61.

137. Sigmund Freud, *Moses and Monotheism* (New York: Vintage Books, 1939), 118.

138. Hirt, *Le miroir du prophète*, 11.

139. See Schneider, *Big Mother*, 136: "The desire to get rid of the father by interiorizing the law he represents, the 'guilt toward the father,' has, it seems, strongly declined, and the loss of a moral sense in very young delinquents must be connected to the historical decline of the Oedipal complex on the paternal side of things [*sur son versant paternel*]. It's a major change in the psychopathology of delinquency: those who break the law no longer recognize the legitimacy of sanction . . . their [violence], called gratuitous, without cause nor stakes, is the product of those who have not gotten into conflicts with their parents, something necessary for their maturity."

140. Ben Jelloun, *La plus haute des solitudes*, 60.

141. Keller, *Colonial Madness*, 209.

142. Ben Jelloun's latest novel, *Leaving Tangier* (London: Penguin, 2009) features a Moroccan immigrant who practices a homosexuality of economic necessity, moving in with a Spaniard whom he is not attracted to at first; the novel connects sexual with social dissatisfaction in a way that recalls Ben Jelloun's initial psychiatric study.

143. Guénif-Souilamas, *Les féministes et le garçon arabe*, 68. These diagnoses of social malaise informed by rushes to modernity recall Kristin Ross's work in *Fast Cars, Clean Bodies*. In that study she correlates new relationships to industrial and commercial objects with changes in social policies and attitudes, linking banlieue consumerism

with a disaffection with the Algerian war experience, a disaffection that in turn caused a certain neglect of the influx of Algerians into France.

144. Bennani, *Le corps suspect*, 35.

145. Ibid., 45–46.

146. Ibid., 46.

147. Ben Jelloun, *La plus haute des solitudes*, 8.

148. Ben Jelloun, "Comparative Approaches to Middle Eastern Literature: Leaving Tangier," talk delivered at the Department of Middle Eastern and Islamic Studies, New York University, October 22, 2010. Ben Jelloun went on to state: "When I was doing my doctorate, I found myself taking care of immigrants who were coming in for the specific problem of sexual impotence, there were only immigrants coming in for that. The boss of the hospital was a sexologist [*sexologue*]. I thought when he hired me I would do interpretation. The boss was so racist. He would say, I don't understand this nonsense [*charabia*], work it out with your compatriots. I became a psychotherapist by myself, that's why I did my doctoral thesis."

149. Ibid.

150. Abdelmalek Sayad, *The Suffering of the Immigrant* (Cambridge, England: Polity Press, 2004).

151. Ben Jelloun, *La plus haute des solitudes*, 30.

152. After introducing universalism as a defining French republican value, Robcis provocatively concludes her essay—on French civil unions (PACS) and the monumental resistance they faced from psychoanalyst opponents—in the following way: "Since the symbolic and citizenship appear to be linked, at least as they were deployed throughout the PACS discussions, one could wonder . . . why 'France' insists on remaining singular while its inhabitants are, increasingly, multiple" ("How the Symbolic Became French," 132).

153. Tobie Nathan, "De la fabrication culturelle des enfants: Réflexions ethnopsychanalytiques sur la filiation et l'affiliation," *La Nouvelle Revue d'Ethnopsychiatrie*, no. 17 (1991): 15.

154. Tobie Nathan, *Nous ne sommes pas seuls au monde* (Paris: Les Empêcheurs de Penser en Rond, 2001), 71.

155. Massad, "Psychoanalysis, Islam, and the Other of Liberalism," 206–7.

156. See especially the chapter "ZAP la psy," in Bourcier, *Sexpolitiques*, 251–71.

157. Samira Bellil with Josée Stoquiart, *Dans l'enfer des tournantes* (Paris: Gallimard, 2003), 16.

158. Bourcier, *Sexpolitiques*, 72–74.

159. Bellil, *Dans l'enfer des tournantes*, 16.

160. Bourcier, *Sexpolitiques*, 74; Philippe Bernard, "La commission Stasi recherche les lignes d'un compromis sur la laïcité," *Le Monde*, October 28, 2004.

161. Nacira Guénif-Souilamas, *Des beurettes* (Paris: Hachette Pluriel, 2003), 60.

162. See the chapter "ZAP la psy," in Bourcier, *Sexpolitiques*, 251–72.

163. Bennani and Guillebaud, *Le sacré, cet obscur objet du désir?*, 18.

164. Keller, *Colonial Madness*, 181.

165. Bennani, *Le corps suspect*, 52.

166. "The individual treatment of the person must not be the sole response to this suffering, which necessarily requires a collective treatment, emanating from social actors and public decision-makers" (ibid., 174).

167. Keller, *Colonial Madness*, 211.

168. Guénif-Souilamas, *Des beurettes*, 73.

169. Fethi Benslama, "L'illusion ethnopsychiatrique," *Le Monde*, December 4, 1996.

170. Keller, *Colonial Madness*, 218.

171. Fethi Benslama, "Épreuves de l'étranger," in *Le Risque de l'étranger: Soin psychique et politique*, ed. J. Ménéchal (Paris: Dunod, 1999), 60.

172. Michèle Pons, "Kabyle sous la peau: renversement dedans/dehors dans les épisodes aigus de jeunes patients immigrés de seconde génération," *Nouvelle Revue d'Ethnopsychiatrie*, no. 5 (1986): 89–92.

3 / Uncultured Yet Seductive: The Trope of the Difficult Arab Boy

1. Renaud Camus and Farid Tali, *Incomparable* (Paris: P.O.L., 1999), 116–17.

2. Kathryn Kleppinger explores questions of Franco-Arab authorial agency in the media and resistance to restrictive interpretations of these authors' works. See Kathryn Kleppinger, *Branding the "Beur" Author: Minority Writing and the Media in France* (Liverpool: Liverpool University Press, 2015).

3. Catherine Simon, "La Voix étouffée de l'homo moyen-oriental," *Le Monde des Livres*, December 9, 2011, accessed on November 27, 2015, http://www.lemonde.fr/livres/article/2011/12/08/la-voix-etouffee-de-l-homo-oriental_1614676_3260.html.

4. Shu-mei Shih and Françoise Lionnet, eds. *Minor Transnationalism* (Durham, NC: Duke University Press, 2005), 18.

5. Kleppinger, *Branding the Beur Author*, 213, quoting from the television program *Le grand journal*, Canal +, November, 2, 2004.

6. Marc Endeweld, "Maroc: Abdellah Taïa explique l'homosexualité à sa mère," *Têtu*, April 16, 2009, accessed on April 10, 2010, http://www.tetu.com/actualites/international/maroc-abdellah-taa-explique-lhomosexualite-a-sa-mere-14451 (site discontinued); Zineb Dryef, "Maroc: Abdellah Taïa, l'homosexualité à visage découvert," *Têtu*, May 4, 2009, accessed on April 10, 2010, http://www.tetu.com/2009/05/04/news/international/maroc-abdellah-taia-lhomosexualite-a-visage-decouvert-7/ (site discontinued); and Catherine Simon, "La voix étouffée de l'homo Moyen-Oriental," *Le Monde des Livres*, December 9, 2011, accessed on April 10, 2010, http://www.lemonde.fr/livres/article/2011/12/08/la-voix-etouffee-de-l-homo-oriental_1614676_3260.html.

7. Although Rachid O. technically came "out" before Abdellah Taïa, he did not make as much of a splash in the Moroccan press, with discussion around his reception limited to France and its North African diasporas. This discrepancy between the authors relates to O.'s relative shying away from the media and reluctance to stake out positions that politicize sexuality.

8. See El-Rouayheb, *Before Homosexuality in the Arab-Muslim World*.

9. Taïa's impact on French literary and extraliterary discourse is complex. While in his novels he does not take a prescriptive attitude in regard to what kind of sexual liberation, if any, should be encouraged, in his public engagements he speaks of homosexuality in North Africa and homosexuality in France as transhistorical identity categories. For instance, a chapter on cohabiting with a lover in Paris in the 2000s might be found in the same collection of vignettes as a chapter exploring adolescent sexuality in 1980s Morocco. He has very vocally reproached family members and Moroccan society as a whole for their attitudes toward sexuality in the French press, as well as in the Moroccan francophone press. In the Moroccan *Tel Quel*, Taïa penned an alternately combative and reconciliatory letter to his family as well as to Morocco in general,

entitled "Homosexuality explained to my mother." That Taïa's mother, as he describes, is illiterate, complicates the meaning of his gesture and the whole matter of the intelligibility of sexual dissidence. He does not critically meditate, to the extent that other thinkers have, on the possible effects of geographic displacement and globalization on local sexual cultures: in so doing, he opens himself up to a critique suggesting that he reifies a universalist notion of homosexuality. Like his compatriot O., Taïa chooses to write in French, from France, about sexuality involving mostly North African subjects: one of his more recent novels, however, *Le jour du roi*, was translated into Arabic by Lebanese publisher Dar Al-Adab in 2011. See Marc Endeweld, "Maroc," and Abdellah Taïa, *Yom Al Malek* (Beirut, Lebanon: Dar Al-Adab, 2011).

10. Péroncel-Hugoz's critique and Taïa's response are included in Péroncel-Hugoz and Taïa, "Homosexualité à la Marocaine," *Actuel*, no. 47 (2010): 50–51.

11. Ibid.

12. Ibid.

13. Rachid O., *Chocolat chaud* (Paris: Gallimard, 1998) and *L'Enfant ébloui* (Paris: Gallimard, 1999).

14. O., *L'enfant ébloui*, 110–11.

15. Abdellah Taïa, *Le rouge du tarbouche* (Paris: Éditions Séguier, 2005). The chapter title "Terminus des Anges" borrows the name William Burroughs bestowed on Tangiers in *Naked Lunch* (New York: Grove Press, 2013). In the francophone context, "Le Terminus" is a popular name for bars and cafés adjacent to train stations, collecting a gallery of sad figures by night's end.

16. Choukri and Mrabet wrote (disparagingly) of gay sex tourism but did not identify outwardly as gay.

17. Taïa, *Le rouge du tarbouche*, 113.

18. See Jehoeda Soefer and Arno Schmitt, *Sexuality and Eroticism among Males in Moslem Societies*; and Michael Luongo, *Gay Travels in the Muslim World* (Philadelphia: Haworth Press, 2007).

19. Taïa, *Le rouge du tarbouche*, 122–23.

20. Joseph Boone, "Vacation Cruises; or, the Homoerotics of Orientalism," *PMLA* 110, no. 1 (January 1995): 89–107.

21. Mireille Rosello, *Postcolonial Hospitality: The Immigrant as Guest* (Stanford, CA: Stanford University Press, 2001).

22. Frédéric Mitterrand, *La mauvaise vie* (Paris: Robert Laffont, 2005).

23. Mitterrand insisted that, despite these admissions, he had made no compromises with Ben Ali: Agence France Presse. See "Frédéric Mitterrand assure qu'il n'a pas fait de 'compromis' avec Ben Ali," *Le Point*, January 20, 2011, accessed on November, 27, 2015, http://www.lepoint.fr/monde/frederic-mitterrand-assure-qu-il-n-a-pas-fait-de -compromis-avec-ben-ali-20-01-2011-130438_24.php.

24. "Beyond Thailand and sexual investments enabled by mass tourism, gay exoticism poses the question of people reminiscing about colonial eroticism. The Mitterrand affair pulls up a mirror to a sexual culture where colonial tensions, socioeconomic precarity and racialization organize fantasies and representations" (Rees-Roberts and Cervulle, *Homo exoticus*, 13–14).

25. Frédéric Mitterrand, with Abdellah Taïa, *Maroc, 1900–1960: un certain regard* (Arles, France: Actes Sud, 2007).

26. *Avril brisé*, directed by Liria Begeja (Canal +, Les Films du Sémaphore, 1987); and *Change-moi ma vie*, directed by Liria Begeja (Pan Européenne Edition, 2001), film.

27. *Mon copain Rachid*, directed by Philippe Barassat (La Vie est Belle Films, 1998), film.

28. Sami Bouajila, a Franco-Arab actor whose early gay roles helped introduce him to a wider audience, remembers being acutely aware of touristic interest in Arab adolescents, and the fact that Arabs could have a special sex appeal. In an interview with *Têtu* magazine, the unspecified journalist conducting the interview writes: "In the interview we broach questions that directly bring up desire and . . . gay porno sites specializing in *beurs*. With no subject off limits, Bouajila explains: 'If I had wanted to exploit the image of the Arab sex symbol, I would have done it even more, believe me! Already, when I was little, and I would go to Tunisia, we were aware of the existence of sex tourism with little Arabs.'" Sami Bouajila, "J'entretiens une vraie schizophrénie," interview, *Têtu*, July–August, 2011. Bouajila's consistent homosexualization on-screen is discussed in chapter 4.

29. Another Franco-Arab, out, gay writer who sexualizes his siblings, Farid Tali, meditates abstractedly on his relationship to bodies through his brother's death, in the novel *Prosopopée* (Paris: Editions P.O.L., 2001).

30. Emmanuel Berretta, "Frédéric Mitterrand a oublié son 'copain Rachid': un film relance la polémique," *Le Point*, October 15, 2009, accessed on November, 27, 2015, http://www.lepoint.fr/actualites-medias/2009-10-15/frederic-mitterrand-a-oublie-son -copain-rachid/1253/0/386186.

31. Mitterrand, *La mauvaise vie*, 320.

32. Interestingly, in the erotica market, gay porn studio Citébeur (which specializes in ethnic and banlieue men) has successfully marketed just such sexual revenge scenarios to a European audience, openly reveling in the fantasy of raping the French establishment and its representative figures (see chapter 5).

33. Mitterrand, *La mauvaise vie*, 169–70.

34. Ibid., 170.

35. Jérôme Dupuis, "L'écrivain Frédéric Mitterrand au pied de la letter," *L'Express*, October 14, 2009, accessed November 30, 2015, http://www.lexpress.fr/actualite/ politique/l-ecrivain-frederic-mitterrand-au-pied-de-la-lettre_794410.html.

36. Frédéric Mitterrand, *La mauvaise vie*, 18.

37. The title alludes to the handsome "Farid" whose name translates to "unique" or "singular" in Arabic.

38. Boone, "Vacation Cruises," 90.

39. I place "innocent" in quotation marks because Camus later founded a political party around the notion of *in-nocence*, a neologism whose elucidation requires some further context around his biography and his collaborations.

40. Renaud Camus, *Tricks: 25 Encounters* (New York: Saint Martin's Press, 1981).

41. Renaud Camus, "Le site du parti de l'In-nocence," accessed November 30, 2015, http://www.in-nocence.org/index.php.

42. Camus, "Le site du parti de l'In-nocence."

43. In addition to his anti-immigration rhetoric, Camus has made statements expressing anti-Jewish xenophobia. In what later came to be known as the "Camus affair," the author reproached, in his published 1994 journal, the publicly funded radio station France Culture for what he deemed the overrepresentation of Jews and Jewish themes on its program "Panorama." For a summary of Camus's anti-Semitism, see Marc Weitzmann, "De l'in-nocence: à propos de *La Campagne de France*, de Renaud Camus," *Les*

Inrockuptibles, April 18, 2000, accessed on November, 27, 2015, https://www.renaud
-camus.net/affaire/weitzmann.html.

44. Camus has declared agreement with the recent analyses of the Front National
(distancing himself from its negationist and anti-Semitic heritage), and has professed
his admiration for such anti-immigration polemicists as Eric Zemmour and Alain
Finkielkraut. See "Renaud Camus et la 'contre-colonisation': interview de l'écrivain
Renaud Camus," *agoravox.tv*. May 2010, accessed on November 30, 2015, http://www
.agoravox.tv/tribune-libre/article/renaud-camus-et-la-contre-26634.

45. Sylvie François, "Apéro Goutte d'Or: Sylvie François livre la liste des soutiens
officiels," Novopress, June 14, 2010, accessed on April 6, 2012, http://fr.novopress
.info/60784/apero-goutte-dor-sylvie-francois-livre-la-liste-des-soutiens-officiels/.

46. Renaud Camus, *Abécédaire de l'In-nocence* (Paris: Editions David Reinharc, 2010).

47. Under Marine Le Pen, daughter of founder Jean-Marie Le Pen, the party
has made great electoral gains and increasingly defined the tenor of the immigration debate: in the 2012 presidential election, Marine outdid her father and obtained
nearly 18 percent of the vote. In 2014, the party won the most seats of any party in the
French election for the European parliament. See Thomas Wieder, "Européennes: large
victoire du Front National," *Le Monde*, May 25, 2014, accessed on November 30, 2015,
http://www.lemonde.fr/politique/article/2014/05/25/europeennes-large-victoire-du
-fn_4425528_823448.html.

48. Renaud Camus, "La Nocence, instrument du grand remplacement," In-nocence,
December 2010, accessed on November 30, 2015, http://www.in-nocence.org/index.ph
p?page=editoriaux&edit=edit_46_main.html.

49. Renaud Camus, *Le grand remplacement* (Paris: Editions David Reinharc, 2011).

50. Ivan Valerio, "Pour Marine Le Pen, la théorie du 'grand remplacement' relève du
'complotisme,'" *Le Figaro*, November 2, 2014, accessed on November 30, 2015, http://
www.lefigaro.fr/politique/le-scan/citations/2014/11/02/25002–20141102ARTFIG00145
-pour-marine-le-pen-la-theorie-du-grand-remplacement-releve-du-complotisme.php.

51. Frédéric Martel, a frequent critic of Camus, takes up Didier Lestrade's book on
rightward gay trends, in "Comment Sarkozy va tenter de récupérer le vote gay par la
peur de l'Islam" [How Sarkozy will attempt to win the gay vote through fear-mongering about Islam], *L'Express*, February 1, 2012, accessed on April 6, 2012, http://www
.lexpress.fr/actualite/politique/comment-sarkozy-va-tenter-de-recuperer-le-vote-gay
-par-la-peur-de-l-islam_1078081.html. In addition to sections on Caroline Fourest and
Camus, Lestrade's book contains a section on Frédéric Mitterrand, in which he takes
the minister to task for sex tourism; see Lestrade, *Pourquoi les gays sont passés à droite*.

52. Roland Barthes, *Incidents*, trans. Richard Howard (Berkeley: University of
California Press, 1992), 28. A new edition of *Incidents* includes contemporary color
photographs of alluring South Asian men in addition to North African young men,
even though *Incidents* recounts memories of encounters in North Africa. See Roland
Barthes, *Incidents*, trans. Teresa Lavender Fagan (Kolkata, India: Seagull Books, 2010);
for the photography, see Bishan Samaddar, "Roland Barthes *Incidents*: Photographs by
Bishan Samaddar," seagullindia.com, accessed on November 30, 2015, http://seagull
india.com/samrc/incidents/incidents.html.

53. Barthes, *Incidents*, 28.

54. Camus and Tali, *Incomparable*, 12.

55. Ibid., 23.

56. "Ca c'est passé comme ça—Patrick Cardon," host Frédéric Mitterrand, *PinkTV*, May 23, 2010, accessed on November 30, 2015, http://television.telerama.fr/tele/magazine/ca-s-est-passe-comme-ca,1590805,emission5870291.php.

57. Patrick Cardon, *Le grand écart ou tous les garcons s'appellent Ali (vignettes postcoloniales)* (Paris: L'Harmattan, 2010).

58. "Ca c'est passé comme ça—Patrick Cardon," host Frédéric Mitterrand.

59. Cardon, *Le grand écart*, 52.

60. Ferdinand Oyono, *Houseboy*, transl. John Reed (Long Grove, IL: Waveland Press, 2012).

61. Camus and Tali, *Incomparable*, 9.

62. Boone, "Vacation Cruises," 102.

63. Ibid., 102. Footnote omitted.

64. See Jonathan Dollimore, *Sexual Dissidence* (Oxford, England: Oxford Paperbacks, 1991), 250: "The homosexual is involved with difference . . . because, contrary to what (a critique of sexual tourism) implies, she or he has, in historical actuality, embraced both cultural and racial difference. The relationship to these other kinds of difference has, for some homosexuals, constituted a crucial dimension of their culture. Sexually exiled from the repressiveness of the home culture . . . homosexuals have searched instead for fulfillment in the realm of the foreign. Not necessarily as a second best. . . . That this has also occurred in exploitative, sentimental, and/or racist forms does not diminish its significance; if anything it increases it. Those who move too hastily to denounce homosexuality across race and class as essentially or only exploitative, sentimental, or racist betray their own homophobic ignorance."

65. This greater faith in the educational prospects of girls was made evident in the documentary *La cité du mâle* (see chapter 1).

66. Camus and Tali, *Incomparable*, 111–12.

67. A *harki* is a descendant of indigenous Algerians who collaborated with France during the Algerian war of independence.

68. Camus and Tali, *Incomparable*, 30, 100.

69. Ibid., 100.

70. For a more substantive discussion of the distinction between these types of "sexual" solidarities, see chapter 12 ("Homosexuality and Anti-colonialism") in Robert Aldrich, *Colonialism and Homosexuality* (New York: Routledge, 2003).

71. This was a parody of the famous 1971 "Manifesto of the 343" circulated by French feminists who advocated for the legalization of abortion in France. See FHAR, *Report Against Normality*. 1971. See also chapter 5 for an analysis of the FHAR.

72. Ilmann Bel, *Un mauvais fils* (Saint Martin-de-Londres, France: H et O Editions, 2010).

73. Nina Bouraoui, *Avant les hommes* (Paris: Stock, 2007).

74. See *Mes mauvaises pensées* (Paris: Stock, 2005), winner of the Prix Renaudot in 2005.

75. Nina Bouraoui, *La voyeuse interdite* (Paris: Gallimard, 1991).

76. *Tarik el hob*, directed by Rémi Lange.

77. Nina Bouraoui, *Poupée Bella* (Paris: Le Livre de Poche, 2005).

78. The author adopts the perspective of an adolescent male in *Le bal des murènes* (Paris: Fayard, 1996).

79. Bouraoui, *Poupée Bella*, 9.

80. Nina Bouraoui, *Garçon manqué* (Paris: Livre de poche, 2000).

81. Bouraoui, *Avant les hommes*, 40.

82. El-Rouayheb, *Before Homosexuality in the Arab-Islamic World, 1500–1800*; and David Halperin, *How to Do the History of Homosexuality* (Chicago: University of Chicago Press, 2002).

83. Michel Houellebecq, *Les particules élémentaires* (Paris: Editions J'ai Lu, 2000).

84. See Guénif-Souilamas, *Les féministes et le garçon arabe*, 63: "We live in the moment of porous borders between the sexes, in the epoch of the attenuation of social differences between sexes, we live under the sign of the euphemizing of persistent, sexual, biological differences, even a confusion of genders, all of these processes being activated and provoked by the denunciation of the millennial domination of men over women, the precise clinic of its forms and intensities. In this context, those Arab boys—and their acolytes, blacks and '*petits blancs*' (white boys or thugs) from working-class areas—seem wedded to an ahistorical machismo, its presence forbidden in those sites of reconciliation between the sexes which we pretend are peaceful, rejected to the sidelines of this unprecedented process of social transformations of sexual identities, prevented from participating in them but expected to serve them by inhabiting the role of counter-example, of the unadapted."

85. Bouraoui, *Avant les hommes*, 57.

86. Ibid., 56.

87. Ibid., 40.

88. Ibid., 57.

89. Pierre Bourdieu and Jean-Claude Passeron, *Les héritiers* (Paris: Les Editions de Minuit, 1964).

90. Elisabeth Badinter's *XY* discussed the cultural consequences of deficient or excessive mothering, while Michel Schneider, with *Big mother*, penned an alarmist treatise on the controlling influence of the maternal at the political level (see chapter 2).

91. Houellebecq, *Les particules élementaires*.

92. Bouraoui, *Avant les hommes*, 78.

93. Ibid., 79.

94. Bouraoui, *Poupée Bella*, 22.

95. The term *taulard*, derived from *taule* (prison), in a French gay context corresponds to a popular pornographic type: the repeat offender; see the section on the Citébeur studio in chapter 5. These references to shaving and thuggery bring up a striking intertext with Gaël Morel's film *Le clan*, which depicts the aesthetic practices of a group of Franco-Arab men who appear violent in terms of body language, verbiage, and in the way they seek to eradicate any "feminine" traces of hair. These practices of shaving and their relationship to the self-fashioning of masculinity are also explored in a notable 2000 interview between nightlife entrepreneur Fouad Zeraoui and the then president of the antidiscrimination group SOS Racisme, Malik Boutih. The state-sponsored activist had suggested that the practice of shaving off ethnic markers like curls and body hair, seen in the self-stylings of *banlieue* youth, constituted a form of self-hatred and body shame. *Le clan* (*Three Dancing Slaves*), directed by Gaël Morel (TLA, 2004), DVD. Mehammed Mack, "Body Image and Arab Masculinity: A Conversation with Malik Boutih," paper presented at Sex in France Since 1958 conference, Johns Hopkins University, September 20, 2013.

96. Bernard-Marie Koltès, *Dans la solitude des champs de coton* (Paris: Editions de Minuit, 1986).

97. Bernard-Marie Koltès, *La nuit juste avant les forêts* (Paris: Editions de Minuit, 1988).

98. Bernard-Marie Koltès, *Le retour au désert* (Paris: Editions de Minuit, 1988).

99. Bernard-Marie Koltès, *Une part de ma vie: entretiens (1983-1989)* (Paris: Editions de Minuit, 1999), 20.

100. Bernard-Marie Koltès, *Combat de nègres et de chiens / Carnets* (Paris: Editions de Minuit, 1989), 34. Koltès wrote the play after a year spent traveling through Nigeria, Guatemala, Nicaragua, and Mexico in 1978.

101. Koltès, *Une part de ma vie*, 115.

102. Ibid., 127.

103. Bernard-Marie Koltès, *Plays*, ed. David Bradby (London: Methuen Drama, 1997), 13-24.

104. A striking intertext exists between this scene and the one in Mehdi Charef's *Le thé au harem d'Archi Ahmed*, considered the first *beur* novel. In Charef's book, two young men (one white, one North African) steal a metro rider's wallet by playing on stereotypes. The white thief steals the wallet but the victim's attention immediately shifts to the North African accomplice. After the victim roughs him up physically and verbally, performing a humiliating body search that turns up nothing, the victim is left feeling embarrassed and worse, racist. In *La nuit*, Koltès also shows how the plausibility of stereotypes can be manipulated, this time, so as to turn stereotypes about gay cruising and ethnic hustling into an opportunity for exploitation and theft. See chapter 5 for a fuller unpacking of Charef's passage.

105. Géunif-Souilamas, *Les féministes et le garçon arabe*.

106. Koltès, *Plays*, 195.

107. Ibid., 191.

108. Ibid., 26.

109. See Ben Jelloun, *La plus haute des solitudes*, and Sayad, *Suffering of the Immigrant*.

110. See Malika Amaouche, "Invisibles et indicibles sollicitations: jeunes hommes pratiquant de nos jours la prostitution dans une gare parisienne," *Les jeunes et la sexualité*, ed. V. Blanchard, R. Revenin, J. J. Yvorel (Paris: Autrement, 2010). In these films, young Arab men experiment with bisexuality out of economic necessity at first, before developing a taste for being "kept" (cared for, in every sense) by an older, more established person (of any gender, including trans women). This person supplies an alternative maternal or paternal role for the immigrant or the Franco-Arab youth, who is often *en rupture familiale* (a runaway without family contact). *Un fils* in particular contains a harrowing scene that evokes the metro theft scene in *La nuit*, wherein a gang of young Arab delinquents brutally beat up the Franco-Arab protagonist suspected of homosexuality and prostitution, eventually triggering his suicide. See *Wild Side*, directed by Sébastien Lifshitz (Maïa Films, 2004), film; *Un fils*, directed by Amal Bedjaoui (ML Productions, 2003), film; *Miss Mona*, directed by Mehdi Charef (KG Productions, 1987), film; and *Welcome Europa*, directed by Bruno Ulmer (Solaris, 2006), film.

111. Here Guénif-Souilamas details the evolution of a homoaffectivity developed in North Africa which then was put to the test in France. She attaches this phenomenon to a process of slow cultural amnesia, chipping away at North African customs: "The second episode of memory amputation takes place here, in France, within the personhood of the fathers and the repression of their inappropriate customs [*usages déplacés*]. . . . Let's imagine for a minute the reaction of a foreman or a French colleague at the sight of workers arriving in the morning for work at the assembly line, and

saluting each other with accolades punctuated by an exchange of kisses" (*Les féministes et le garçon arabe*, 68–70).

112. Guénif-Souilamas, in *Les féministes et le garçon arabe*, writes:

> With the passing decades of factory wear and tear, the 'immigrant Maghrebi workers' learned the handshake, the relational commodity that they procure by loosening the stranglehold of suspicion and rejection, orienting their corporeal *hexis* toward the Western to remove disapproval. . . . The loss of the accolade is the fruit of an asymmetrical contact between two worlds inheriting the same Mediterranean past but still rendered foreign to one another by the colonial era.

> By adopting the same restraint as their fathers, by seeking out new codes of salutation, the sons of immigrant workers did not renew the abandoned gestures. They swerved toward the gestural codes of the African-American ghettos, breathing into them an Arabic tonality, the hand on the heart punctuating the handshake. (68–70)

113. Yannick Butel, "Koltès, capitalism et dramaturgie: 'la botte, le papier gras et les maîtres chanteurs', suivi de 'une césure linguistique'", in *Koltès maintenant et autres Métamorphoses* (Bern, Switzerland: Peter Lang Publishing, 2010), 61.

114. Rosello, *Postcolonial Hospitality*, 176.

115. It is a short step to the real-life nightclub analogy, in which flirtatious and seemingly overconfident young men make extravagant attempts to woo a mate: conventional wisdom holds that they strike these Casanova poses to impress their peers, rather than the person they are trying to seduce; however, these attempts at contact, especially when occurring away from the peer group, can indicate a desire to break out of solitude, as sociologists have indicated. See Eric Marlière, *Les jeunes et la discothèque* (Paris: Editions du Cygne, 2011).

116. Leo Bersani, *Homos* (Cambridge, MA: Harvard University Press, 1996), 53.

117. Koltès, *Une part de ma vie*, 30.

118. Koltès, *Plays*, 203–5.

119. Elaborated by Rees-Roberts and Cervulle, the "erotics of poverty" designate a specific gay hybrid between class tourism and sexual tourism. Visible in Christophe Honoré's *L'homme au bain*, among other films, it finds its most exemplary expression in pornography, for example, in Citébeur productions and the films of Jean Noël René Clerc (JNRC). For an in-depth discussion of representative films and their themes, see chapter 5.

120. *Grande école*, directed by Robert Salis (Pyramide, 2004), film.

121. Jean-Marie Besset, *Grande école* (Arles, France: Actes Sud, 1995), 54–55.

122. See Gopinath, *Impossible Desires*, 4. Gopinath elaborates on how the children of the diaspora in Europe themselves contain the reminders of past imperial violence in their bodies. Through queer desire, which escapes the strictures of heterosexist regulation, these reminders find their way into the open and break the silence confining colonial violence to their ancestors' generation.

123. As film scholar Carrie Tarr has noted, many films exploring Franco-Arab social and romantic malaise suggest the countryside and especially places along the ocean (the Atlantic Coast, the French Riviera) as refuges from the city's hostility. These become sites where "love" can blossom outside the surveillance and pressures of urban life. See Carrie Tarr, *Reframing Difference: Beur and Banlieue Filmmaking in France* (Manchester: Manchester University Press, 2005).

124. The play establishes a striking intertext with Pasolini's *Teorema*, in which a mysterious and handsome man introduces himself into an upper-class Milan family,

having sexual relations with the daughter, the mother, the son, the father, and the maid, only to leave just as suddenly as he arrived. As in Besset's play, in which the racial other takes the place of the subject of a different class, bourgeois life is upended after this destabilizing but also "missionary" visit: all characters become more "honest" with themselves, pursuing their repressed desires or ambitions. The father hands over control of his factory to the workers, the mother pursues sexual liberty, the son becomes an artist, and the maid returns to her village as a holy woman. The daughter, however, seems bewildered and outside the circle of liberation. The cinema of Pasolini, it has been suggested by some, is a kind of asynchronous antidote to miserabilist representations of ethnic and working-class men in a multitude of different contexts. *Teorema*, directed by Pier Paolo Pasolini (Euro International Film, 1968), film.

4 / Sexual Undergrounds: Cinema, Performance, and Ethnic Surveillance

1. Some of the films that have most famously vilified immigrant or Franco-Arab virility include *La squale* and *La journée de la jupe*, as well as the controversial TV documentary *La cité du mâle* (see chapter 1).

2. See Nilüfer Göle, *Interpénétrations: l'Islam et l'Europe*.

3. Hélène Hazera, interview by the author, July 1, 2011.

4. *Ma 6-T va crack-er*, directed by Jean-François Richet (Actes Proletariens, 1997), film; *Grande école*, directed by Robert Salis (Pyramide, 2004), film.

5. *Têtu* magazine (December 2011). See also Chloé Breen. "Jamel Debbouze : 'J'avais parfois l'impression d'être moi-même un homosexual,'" Purepeople, November 15, 2011, accessed on November 27, 2015, http://www.purepeople.com/article/jamel-debbouze-j-avais-parfois-l-impression-d-etre-moi-meme-un-homosexuel_a91154/1.

6. *Pédale* means both "faggot" and "pedal" and *dure* means "hard"; the title is a pun and roughly translates into "hard/tough faggot" or "pedal hard."

7. *Un Prophète*, directed by Jacques Audiard (Why Not Productions, 2009); *Pédale dure*, directed by Gabriel Aghion (Galfin, 2004); *Le clan*, directed by Gaël Morel (Sépia Productions, 2004), and *Chouchou*, directed by Merzak Allouache (Warner Brothers France, 2003).

8. See Maxime Cervulle and Nick Rees-Roberts, "Le cinéaste gay et le garçon arabe," in *Homo Exoticus*, 81–109.

9. Another important exception to the stereotype is *Pépé le Moko* (1937), directed by Julien Duvivier, which features the character of Inspector Slimane, a detective of North African descent, who, like Mehdi in *Les témoins*, is portrayed with a marked degree of sexual ambivalence, barely hiding feelings of attraction for the subject of his manhunt, the escaped French robber Pépé.

10. *La fille du RER*, directed by André Téchiné (UGC Films, 2009), film.

11. *Le Monde*'s mea culpa, printed in an editorial titled "La faute et le défi" (July 15, 2004), read: "This news story sounded much too right. But there you have it, what is believable [*vraisemblable*] is not what's real."

12. The depiction of Corsicans in the film is monolithically negative, with few redeeming aspects apart from the very fragile fair-weather agreement between Rahim and the Corsican crime boss César, whereby they exchange services for protection and meager benefits. The prevalent stereotype according to which Corsicans are the most racist toward North Africans is not critically assessed or nuanced over the course of the film.

13. Farhad Khosrokhavar, *L'Islam dans les prisons* (Paris: Jacob Duvernet, 2004).

14. This trope of "revenge from within" also appears in other films on ethnic minority sexuality. For instance, in *La squale*, teenage girls defeat the young men tormenting the community by posing as easy girls and penetrating to the core of that underground. Less empowering, more self-destructive examples include *Baise-moi* (2000; *Rape Me*), directed by Virginie Despentes and Coralie Trinh Thi, in which a victim of rape wields her sexuality to better set up intimate encounters with the victims of her ensuing killing spree. Lastly, *Les amants criminels* (1999; *Criminal Lovers*), directed by François Ozon, showcases a female high school student who wants to murder a Franco-Arab classmate she (falsely) accuses of gang rape; she lures him in by incarnating the "bourgeois slut" character she believes he fantasizes about.

15. The French subtitles at this juncture mistranslate the verb *iqra* as "speak," taking away from the miracle of the Prophet Muhammad being able to read while illiterate.

16. Richet is using abbreviated slang in the style of graffiti and rap lyrics that often mix letters and numbers. The number "6" when combined with the French pronunciation of the letter "T" registers as *cité* or "housing projects." The French argotic *crack-er* is a more anglicized spelling of the verb *craquer* which can mean "to snap or break apart." The verb also links up to the drug trade, as in crack cocaine. In my loose translation, I chose "blow" over "snap" to give a sense of the pressure building toward explosion that the film sustains.

17. *De l'amour*, directed by Jean-François Richet (Les Films Alain Sarde, 2001), film.

18. Psychoanalyst author Michel Schneider controversially suggests that the figure of the female cop in the banlieues represents an intolerable sexual liberty to Muslim youth (see chapter 2).

19. Much other banlieue cinema examines interruptions into banlieue courtship, with ample references to lovers sent to prison. Richet's subsequent film *De l'amour* focuses on this explicitly, showcasing a young woman (Virginie Ledoyen) imprisoned on a shoplifting charge and then raped in custody by a corrupt police officer. Meanwhile, her Franco-Arab boyfriend, a dedicated factory worker, tries to liberate her from the outside. Such a representation flips the traditional trope of incarceration that fixes suspected criminals as male and of minority background by locating the nonminority partner inside the prison, with the savior-of-justice role falling to her Franco-Arab boyfriend. In the film, Ledoyen's character is of Italian background, but racialized as nonminority by the cop who abuses her.

20. Tom of Finland, *Tom of Finland XXL*, ed. Dian Hanson (Cologne, Germany: Taschen, 2009).

21. Shepard, *Invention of Decolonization*.

22. Philippe Hernandez, "Lettre d'un pied-noir à un pied-noir," *France-Observateur*, March 15, 1962, 10.

23. Pierre Nora, *Les Français d'Algérie* (Paris: Julliard, 1961), cited in Shepard, *Invention of Decolonization*, 201.

24. *Ma 6-T va crack-er* is not the only film in which *pieds-noirs* have been depicted as possessing a strange, high-strung, obsessive focus on the sexual. Connecting with Shepard's study of how *pieds-noirs* were sexually distinguished from the metropolitan French, Téchiné's *Les roseaux sauvages* (1994; *Wild Reeds*) depicts the sexual "awakening" of four young people in 1960s provincial France at the moment of Algerian independence. It features a darkly intelligent, brooding high school student (Frédéric Gorny) who arrives in the middle of the school year because of the Algerian War;

a palpable influence at the high school, he seems to bring on sexual and political upheaval wherever he goes. Aggressive and also slightly effete, he has much more life experience than his classmates, having already rushed through a precocious adolescence while others were still finding themselves. He seems to perceive more easily the sexual dimension of power relations between men, and sees the potential for homosexuality everywhere. He proves instrumental in getting the protagonist (Gaël Morel) to recognize his own sexual orientation.

25. Shepard, *Invention of Decolonization*, 186.

26. For an analysis on communist views of homosexuality, see Jeffrey Weeks *New Internationalist*, no. 201 (1989), accessed December 6, 2015, http://www.newint.org /features/1989/11/05/politics/; and "The Last Word: Gay Liberation," *Jump Cut: A Review of Contemporary Media*, no. 16 (1977): 39–40, accessed December 6, 2015, http://www.ejumpcut.org/archive/onlinessays/JC16folder/edlGayLibern.html.

27. Karl Marx, in *Pre-Capitalist Economic Formations*, trans. Jack Cohen (London: International Publishers, 1964), famously heterosexualized ideal social relations by saying that the "direct, natural, and necessary relation of person to person is the relation of man to woman" (134).

28. Ferguson, *Aberrations in Black*, 7.

29. In this context, *la volaille* can refer to the police but also to the unjustifiably rich and overstuffed. The use of the term *niquer* to describe *fucking* is inherited from Arabic. While various explanations exist for how Arabic vocabulary has been integrated into French argot, prominent suggestions have highlighted the influence of North African immigrants on the language, the tendency of *pieds-noirs* to use Arabic swear words, and finally, and more controversially, the tendency of reserving dirty words for another language in order to preserve the "cleanliness" of a native language. See Farid Aitsiselmi, ed, *Black, Blanc, Beur: Youth Language and Identity in France* (Bradford, England: University of Bradford, 2000).

30. Henri Alleg, *The Question* (New York: George Braziller, 1958).

31. Shepard, *Invention of Decolonization*, 199.

32. In the preface to *The Question*, Sartre writes: "In this way exploitation puts the exploiter at the mercy of his victim, and the dependence itself begets racialism. It is a bitter and tragic fact that, for the Europeans in Algeria, being a man means first and foremost superiority to the Muslims" (32).

33. Frantz Fanon, *Black Skin, White Masks* (London: Pluto Press, 1986), 123.

34. Hernandez, "Lettre d'un pied-noir," 200.

35. Frantz Fanon, *The Wretched of the Earth* (New York: Grove Weidenfeld, 1963), 39.

36. *J'embrasse pas*, directed by André Téchiné (Bac Films, 1991), film.

37. Although it is possible that Mehdi's allegiance to France's patriotic forces stems from a *harki* status (Algerian "Arab" proponents of French Algeria), Mehdi's background is not substantially detailed in the film, apart from a Hand of Fatima pendant hanging from his neck. However, in later arguments with Adrien—the doctor also in love with Manu—Mehdi does show an embattled ethnic pride and assertively rejects what he suspects are French stereotypes about Algerians. In general, Téchiné portrays *harkis*, patriotic Franco-Arabs, as well as Arab administrators in French Algeria very sympathetically, as if to generate pathos for Algerians and Franco-Arabs who have stretched out their hands in vain. Such a portrayal also supports the idea of a will

toward *métissage*—sexual, cultural, and political—that was clipped in the bud: it is later revealed that Manu's late father was an Arab Algerian politician in French Algeria.

38. Such designations of morality policing as revolution recall other cinematic precedents: *Battle of Algiers* (1966), directed by Gillo Pontecorvo, features a scene in which the anticolonial National Liberation Front (FLN) enacted revolution by cleaning up the Casbah neighborhood of Algiers, both physically and "morally."

39. *From Here to Eternity*, directed by Fred Zinneman (Columbia Pictures, 1953), film.

40. In the popular *L'Italien* (2010), directed by Olivier Baroux and starring Kad Merad, the Algerian protagonist leads a double life as an Italian in order to obtain a job, girlfriend, and swank apartment. In Malik Chibane's *Hexagone* (1994), a Franco-Arab protagonist poses as Italian to woo the object of his affection, a blond member of the far-right Front National party from Brittany.

41. See DVD extras, *Les témoins*, directed by André Téchiné (UGC Films, 2007), DVD.

42. Eric Fassin and Clarisse Fabre, *Liberté, égalité, sexualités: actualité politique des questions sexuelles* (Paris: Belfond, 2004).

43. D. Vaillancourt, C. Beyrer, and V. Gauri, *Evaluation of the World Bank's Assistance in Responding to the AIDS Epidemic: Brazil Case Study* (World Bank, 2005); and Joint United Nations Programme on HIV/AIDS and the World Health Organization, *AIDS Epidemic Update: Special Report on HIV Prevention* (United Nations, December 2005).

44. *Change-moi ma vie*, directed by Liria Begeija (Pan Européenne Edition, 2001), film.

45. *Wild Side*, directed by Sébastien Lifshitz (Maïa Films, 2004), film.

46. *La chatte à deux têtes*, directed by Jacques Nolot (Elia Films, 2002), film.

47. Although some prominent trans activists have underlined the commercially exploitative aspects of the "Escualita" soirée, it is nevertheless well-attended and still ongoing. See the Escualita website, accessed December 6, 2015, http://www.escualita .com. See also Luc Arbona, "Trans Paris Express," *Les Inrocks*, May 7, 2001, accessed December 6, 2015, http://www.lesinrocks.com/2001/07/05/musique/escualita-trans -paris-express-11223237/.

48. Though the film is not devoid of violence, the lone incident occurs within a male homosexual dynamic, when a Franco-Arab youth pushes a man who had been aggressively propositioning him; this follows several other vignettes depicting other immigrant youths engaging in homosexuality, complicating the question of homophobia in such a space.

49. *Origine contrôlée*, directed by Zakia and Ahmed Bouchaala (M6 Films, 2001), film; *Miss Mona*, directed by Mehdi Charef (KG Productions, 1987), film.

50. *Rue des figuiers*, directed by Yasmina, Yahiaoui (Kinok Films, 2005), film. Nini is the author of *Ils disent que je suis une beurette* (Paris: Fixot, 2001); he also wrote the screenplay for Philippe Faucon's filmic adaptation of the same novel, Samia (Canal+, 2000).

51. *Chaos*, directed by Coline Serreau (Bac Films, 2001), film.

52. *Welcome Europa*, directed by Bruno Ulmer (Solaris, 2006), film.

53. Thomas Sotinel, " 'Welcome Europa': Dérives sur les trottoirs de l'Europe des riches," *Le Monde*, January 29, 2008, accessed December 6, 2015, http://www

.lemonde.fr/cinema/article/2008/01/29/welcome-europa-derives-sur-les-trottoirs-de
-l-europe-des-riches_1004884_3476.html.

54. Bruno Ulmer, "Note d'intention du réalisateur," accessed December 6, 2015,
http://www.solaris-distribution.com/welcome-europa/.

55. Tahar Ben Jelloun, *Leaving Tangier* (Mt. Pleasant, SC: Arcadia Books, 2009). At
a 2010 book talk, Ben Jelloun spoke of how he grounded the novel in his observation
of actual migration, and explained that the protagonist Azel considers his prostitution
a slight against his masculine identity, in a novel that often intertwines political and
sexual relationships between countries just as it does between persons. See Ben Jelloun,
"Comparative Approaches to Middle Eastern Literature."

56. *Un fils*, directed by Amal Bedjaoui (ML Productions, 2003), film.

57. See Fassin, "Homosexual City."

58. Ferguson, *Aberrations in Black*, 20.

5 / Erotic Solutions for Ethnic Tension:
Fantasy, Reality, Pornography

1. *La bande dessinée* (Paris: Citébeur, 2012), 2. The illustrator's name, Zgeg, translates
to "penis" in Arabic argot, a word now common in French slang. The title of the comic
strip roughly translates into "In and out of the cellar" (*deboitage* means to take out,
dislocate, or disconnect an object that is placed inside another object, such as a pipe or
knee bone; here it takes on a sexual meaning).

2. The term *mixité* refers to a mixture of different social groups, ages, genders,
ethnicities, and classes. It is a criterion often considered auspicious for the peace and
prosperity of a given neighborhood.

3. A *tournante* is a "gang bang" or "gang rape," depending on whether the reference
is to consensual or nonconsensual sex.

4. Exceptions must be made for discussions gathering steam on the Internet in
regard to sexual racism in personal ads, which render racial preferences blameworthy.

5. Dean, *Unlimited Intimacy*, 115.

6. Dean explains the differing relationship of homosexual and heterosexual communities to pornography, a distinction located in sexual difference: "Porn consumption has long been normative in gay relationships in a way that it is unlikely to become
in heterosexual relationships, at the very least because imbalances of power between
the sexes aren't at stake when everyone involved in the pornography—actors, producers, distributors, consumers—is male" (ibid., 109). While critical analysis of heterosexual pornography attaches great importance to how sexual difference is represented, the
same cannot be said of gay pornography. What unites gay porn with straight hardcore,
in Dean's understanding, is a concern with "maximum visibility" and "curiosity about
the body's interior" (ibid., 110). However, other kinds of difference that might stand in
for sexual difference and could be eroticized in the same way are crucial to gay porn's
forms of representation and dramatic techniques: masculine and feminine, top and
bottom, white and nonwhite, rich and poor, gay-for-pay and gay-for-pleasure.

7. *L'homme au bain*, directed by Christophe Honoré (Les Films du Bélier, 2010),
film.

8. *World of Men: Lebanon*, directed by Collin O'Neal (TLA, 2006); *Arabesque*,
directed by Chris Ward (Raging Stallion, 2006); and *L.A. Zombie*, directed by Bruce
LaBruce (Wurstfilm, 2010), film.

9. *Communautarisme* refers to the tendency of minority groups (sexual, ethnic, or religious) to stick together and thus form somewhat segregated or uniform communities, an outcome that (apart from the sexual minority case) can also be the result of decisions regarding the concentration of the urban poor in designated areas.

10. Guénif-Souilamas and Macé, *Les féministes et le garçon arabe*, 74.

11. Antoine Barde of Citébeur, interview by author, summer 2008.

12. Bitume is the name of one of Citébeur's most famous actors.

13. This was the case at least in the initial output, in which active and passive roles were racialized, Arabs always active and Caucasians always passive. The production has since switched up the role assignments in unpredictable ways.

14. For more on the interracial revenge porn trope in the American context, see the controversy surrounding the gay porn film *Ni**a's Revenge*, directed by Dick Wadd (Dick Wadd Productions, 2001), DVD. See also Dean, *Unlimited Intimacy*, 156–57.

15. Dean, *Unlimited Intimacy*, 9.

16. Louis Maury, "Cantique de la racaille," *Têtu*, July–August 2003, 36. The title of the article alludes to the Flore Prize–winning novel of the same name by Vincent Ravalec, *Cantique de la racaille* (Paris: J'ai lu, 1999).

17. Maury, "Cantique de la racaille," 36.

18. See Dean, *Unlimited Intimacy*, x: "I contend that an unclouded view of this subculture may be gained only by checking the impulse to either criticize or defend it."

19. See Johann Hari, "The New HIV Threat," *Independent*, November 7, 2005, cited in Dean, *Unlimited Intimacy*, 3: "They internalize the homophobia of the culture around them, and act it out on their own bodies."

20. In *Unlimited Intimacy*, Dean takes Dwight McBride, author of *Why I Hate Abercrombie and Fitch*, to task for misunderstanding how fantasy and fetish work at the psychoanalytical level, accusing McBride of taking a naïve, humanistic view of the possibility of interracial relations free of fetishization. Mcbride's book points out how black men are often either objectified as man-phalluses by those with black fetishes or rendered invisible in contemporary youth consumer cultures, exemplified by Abercrombie and Fitch and similar stores, which implicitly valorize whiteness and its cultural associations. While Dean is correct that in many ways there is no sexual relation—including interracial, unmediated by language and the social messaging that informs the racing of sexual subjects—this perspective depoliticizes the issue of sexual racism in the gay community, a problem that has largely been excused by appeals to semiotics and the authority of fantasy to want what it wants. My approach seeks to keep Dean's attention to the presence of fetish at the center of every sexual exchange, while also keeping in mind the white privilege inherent in discounting men of color's charges of sexual racism, as well as injuries suffered from it. See also Dwight McBride, *Why I Hate Abercrombie and Fitch: Essays on Race and Sexuality* (New York: New York University Press, 2005).

21. Dean, *Unlimited Intimacy*, xi.

22. Mireille Rosello, *Declining the Stereotype* (Dartmouth, NH: University Press of New England, 1998).

23. Rosello, *Declining the Stereotype*, 10. (Thanks go to Denis Provencher for reminding me of Rosello's possible relevance for analyzing ethnic porn.)

24. See Rosello, *Declining the Stereotype*, 11: "One sense of 'declining' involves paying attention to the formal characteristics of the stereotype so as to control its devastating ideological power. In practice, this type of declining encompasses ironic repetitions, carefully framed quotations, distortions and puns, linguistic alterations, double

entendres, and self-deprecating humor. Declining a stereotype is a way of depriving it of its harmful potential by highlighting its very nature."

25. Ibid., 56–61.

26. Ibid., 59.

27. Maury, "Cantique de la racaille," 36.

28. Sagat's crescent tattoo is most apparent in (and one could say made for) one of the sexual positions directors often cast him in: doggy style, in which the actor playing the top gets a clear view of the eroticized Islamic imagery.

29. *Saw VI*, directed by Kevin Greitert (Lionsgate Films, 2009), film.

30. Explaining the origin of his crescent tattoo, Sagat said: "It's a mix between the Turkish flag and the Tunisian or Algerian sign. I would say it's a '*clin d'œil*' for Arabic men. A people and culture that I really love and respect, even if I was born Christian and Caucasian. I love Algerian men. They are really beautiful. I did it when I was 20 years old, in January 2000. I'm still wondering why I choose [*sic*] it, I did not choose it for religious purpose. I'm not Muslim. But it is a beautiful sign and the top of my back is a good place for it." See "François Sagat, the Man behind the Mask: Part 2," interview by Rob Evers, *Beautiful Mag*, July 14, 2006, accessed December 7, 2015, http://beautiful.blogs.com/beautiful/2006/07/franois_sagat_t_1.html.

31. Elvis Di Fazio, Ron Wan, and François Sagat, "Don't Panic, I'm Islamic," Vimeo, accessed December 7, 2015, https://vimeo.com/111341729.

32. See Dean, *Unlimited Intimacy*, 166.

33. Ibid. Incidentally, "The Power Exchange" is the name of a pansexual venue in the San Francisco sex club scene Dean analyzes.

34. Algerian Muslim soldiers who fought on France's side during the Algerian war of independence.

35. Barde, interview by author.

36. Dean, *Unlimited Intimacy*, xii.

37. In Citébeur's comic book, simply called "La bande dessinée," all the featured Arab men are tops, and all the white men are bottoms, save for one half-Arab, half-white character who is versatile. This configuration aligns passive homosexuality with whiteness in the way all the characters' sexual preferences are associated with their ethnic origins, not their nationalities.

38. For more on the *mode beurette* in French heterosexual porn, see Éric Fassin and Mathieu Trachman, "Voiler les beurettes pour les dévoiler: les doubles jeux d'un fantasme pornographique blanc," *Modern and Contemporary France* 21, no. 2 (2013): 199–217.

39. Mehdi Sekkouri Alaoui, "Les Marocains et le X: une histoire charnelle," *Tel Quel*, January 9, 2008, accessed July 7, 2012, http://m.telquel-online.com/archives/296/couverture_296.shtml (site discontinued).

40. Philippe Vecchi, "Yasmine, ex-égérie Dorcel: 'Maintenant je sais pourquoi je suis devenue hardeuse,'" Les Inrocks, January 9, 2011, accessed December 7, 2015, http://www.lesinrocks.com/lesinrockslab/news/detail-de-lactualite/t/57329/date/2011-01-09/article/yasmine-ex-egerie-dorcel-maintenant-je-sais-pourquoi-je-suis-devenue-hardeuse/.

41. See Hassan Hamdani, "Les Marocains et le X: Une histoire charnelle," http://m.telquel-online.com/archives/296/couverture_296.shtml (site discontinued): "On American sites, the Arab girl is sold enrobed in pastel veils, half belly dancer, half Sheherazade [*sic*] in Walt Disney's Aladdin. This is the Orientalism of bazaars. In France,

the Thousand and One Nights are not the most in demand, but the [producers'] imagination is still limitless, according to the principle: always more (shady). The client wants the sordid and that's what he'll get, from the demonized banlieue and *beurettes* presented as overworked maids [cosettes frustrées], ready to do whatever it takes to exit their social and sexual impoverishment."

42. Ibid.

43. Religious faith is not unheard of in the adult film industry; many American performers, male and female, declare themselves practicing Christians; for example, mega-star Jenna Jameson, formerly a devout Catholic and now a convert to Judaism. See Zoe Nauman, "Cooking Up a Kosher Storm! Adult Film Star Jenna Jameson Ditches Bawdy for Bat Mitzvahs Converting to Judaism for Love," *Daily Mail*, June 12, 2015, accessed 6 July 2016, http://www.dailymail.co.uk/tvshowbiz/article-3122331/ Cooking-kosher-storm-Adult-film-star-Jenna-Jameson-ditches-bawdy-bat-mitzvahs -converting-Judaism-love.html.

44. *Harem (Sex Bazaar)*, directed by Jean-Daniel Cadinot (Cadinot Productions, 1984), film.

45. "*Harem (Sex Bazaar)*," accessed July 6, 2016, http://cadinot.fr/en/dvd/detail/ 13285-harem/.

46. *Dictionnaire de la pornographie*, ed. Philippe Di Folco (Paris: PUF Editions, 2006).

47. Jaap Kooijiman, "Pleasure of the Orient: Cadinot's Maghreb as Gay Male Pornotopia," *Place, Sex and Race* 22, no. 1 (2011): 97.

48. *Nomades*, directed by Jean-Daniel Cadinot, Cadinot.fr, accessed December 6, 2015, http://cadinot.fr/fr/dvd/detail/11756-nomades/Accessed 3/13/2012.

49. Ilmann Bel, *Un mauvais fils* (Saint-Martin-de-Londres, France: H + O Editions, 2010).

50. "Les Documents Ethniks et Gays: Interview de Jean Noel René Clair," interview by Fouad Zeraoui, Kelma, n.d., accessed March 17, 2012, http://www.kelma.org/pages/ documents/jean_noel_rene_clair.php.

51. "JNRC: l'interview exclusive," interview by Didier Lestrade, Minorites.org, October 10, 2010, accessed December 10, 2015, http://www.minorites.org/index.php/ 2-la-revue/861-jnrc-l-interview-exclusive.html.

52. Michael K. Walonen, *Writing Tangier in the Postcolonial Transition: Space and Power in Expatriate and North African Literature* (Farnham, England: Ashgate Publishing, 2011).

53. See Guénif-Souilamas and Macé, *Les féministes et le garçon arabe*, 63: "In this context, the Arab boys . . . seem to be condemned to an atemporal machismo, forbidden during daylight hours in those sites of enlightened reconciliation between the sexes, spaces we pretend to be peaceful. The boys are banished to the confines of this foreign process of social transformation of sexual identities, they are prevented from participating in it but counted on to serve it by taking the role of the counterexample, of the unadapted."

Conclusion: The Sexagon's Border Crisis

1. "La victoire du Front national à la Une de la presse étrangère," *La Tribune*, December 7, 2015, accessed on December 10, 2015, http://www.latribune.fr/economie/france/ regionales-la-victoire-du-front-national-a-la-une-de-la-presse-etrangere-533762.html.

2. In 2001, Houellebecq had told the magazine *Lire* that "Islam is the world's dumbest religion." In his novel *Platforme* (Paris: Flammarion, 2001), which unlike the aforementioned comment is a fictional account about sex tourism and the Israel-Palestine conflict, one character thinks out loud: "Every time I learned that a Palestinian terrorist, or a Palestinian child, or a Palestinian pregnant woman had been shot full of bullets in the Gaza Strip, I felt a thrilling enthusiasm at the thought that there was one less Muslim on Earth" (357). While reviewers were careful not to confuse fiction and reality, they noted that the novel's protagonist shared Michel's name and age, and the novel's intrigue borrowed freely from current events, French presidential politics, and the Israel-Palestine conflict. See "Islam: Houllebecq relaxé," *Le Nouvel Observateur*, October 22, 2002, accessed on December 10, 2015, http://tempsreel.nouvelobs.com/culture/20021022.OBS1729/islam-houellebecq-relaxe.html.

3. Michel Houllebecq, *Soumission* (Paris: Flammarion, 2015).

4. Rick Noack, "Germany Welcomed More Than 1 Million Refugees in 2015. Now, the Country Is Searching for Its Soul," *Washington Post*, May 4, 2016, accessed July 9, 2016, https://www.washingtonpost.com/news/worldviews/wp/2016/05/04/germany-welcomed-more-than-1-million-refugees-in-2015-now-the-country-is-searching-for-its-soul/.

5. Patrick Donahue, "Merkel's Popularity Drops to Four-Year Low After Cologne Attacks," *Bloomberg News*, January 15, 2016, accessed July 9, 2016, http://www.bloomberg.com/news/articles/2016-01-15/merkel-s-popularity-drops-to-four-year-low-after-cologne-attacks.

6. Of the fifty-nine suspects announced by the Cologne prosecutor, two were Syrian, three German, three Tunisian, twenty-one Moroccan, and twenty-five Algerian. Only five of these suspects were eventually investigated for sexual crimes. The German media had connected the sexual assaults to an infamous phenomenon native to another national context: *taharrush*, which means "harassment" in Arabic, was used to describe sexual attacks against protestors in Tahrir Square during the years of the Egyptian Revolution. Though Egyptians were not among the suspects in Cologne, invoking the term *taharrush* made it seem like group sexual violence was a borderless feature of all Arab societies that could logically make its way to Europe through the movement of refugees. See Angie Abdelmonem, Rahma Esther Bavelaar, Elisa Wynne-Hughes, and Susana Galán, "The 'Taharrush' Connection: Xenophobia, Islamophobia, and Sexual Violence in Germany and Beyond," *Jadaliyya*, March 1, 2016, accessed July 9, 2016, http://www.interviews.jadaliyya.com/pages/index/23967/the-%E2%80%9Ctaharrush%E2%80%9D-connection_xenophobia-islamophobian.

7. Kamel Daoud, "The Sexual Misery of the Arab World," *New York Times*, February 12, 2016, accessed July 9, 2016, http://www.nytimes.com/2016/02/14/opinion/sunday/the-sexual-misery-of-the-arab-world.html?_r=0.

8. Collective, "Nuit de Cologne: 'Kamel Daoud recycle les clichés orientalistes les plus éculés," *Le Monde*, February 11, 2016, accessed July 9, 2016, http://www.lemonde.fr/idees/article/2016/02/11/les-fantasmes-de-kamel-daoud_4863096_3232.html#PbyaDiDH4rUYBed8.99.

9. Mehammed Mack, "Kamel Daoud: Sexual Demonization and the Secularist Select", *Jadaliyya*, March 9, 2016, accessed July 9, 2016, http://www.photography.jadaliyya.com/pages/index/24029/kamel-daoud_sexual-demonization-and-the-secularistn.

10. Ibid.

11. The full list includes Algeria, Poland, Morocco, Bosnia-Herzegovinia, Montené-gro, Serbia, Kosovo, Slovenia, Tunisia, Laos, and Cambodia. "Le 'mariage pour tous' exclut les homosexuels algériens," Algérie-focus (blog), June 21, 2013, accessed July 1, 2013, http://www.algerie-focus.com/blog/2013/06/21/le-mariage-pour-tous-enfin-sauf-pour-les-algeriens/.

12. Gaëlle Dupont, "Onze nationalités exclues du mariage pour tous," Le Monde, August 27, 2013, accessed July 9, 2016, http://www.lemonde.fr/societe/article/2013/08/27/onze-nationalites-exclues-du-mariage-pour-tous_3467000_3224.html

13. Houria Bouteldja, "Gay Universalism, Homoracialism, and 'Marriage for All,'" Decolonial Translation Group, February 12, 2013, accessed July 1, 2013, http://www.decolonialtranslation.com/english/gay-universalism-homoracialism-and-marriage-for-all.html.

14. Houria Bouteldja, "Ce soir où jamais," November 6, 2012, hosted by Frédéric Taddeï, France 2 Télévision.

15. Imara Jones, "Marriage Is Great, but Many LGBT People of Color Need Job Safety," Colorlines, April 11, 2013, accessed July 1, 2013, http://www.colorlines.com/articles/marriage-great-many-lgbt-people-color-need-job-safety.

16. Melissa Dunn and Aisha C. Moodie-Mills, "The State of Gay and Transgender Communities of Color in 2012," Center for American Progress, April 13, 2012, accessed July 1, 2013, https://www.americanprogress.org/issues/lgbt/news/2012/04/13/11493/the-state-of-gay-and-transgender-communities-of-color-in-2012/.

17. Sadri Khiari, "Y'a-t-il un racisme anti-blanc?," Les mots sont importants, March 10, 2006, accessed July 1, 2013, http://lmsi.net/Y-a-t-il-un-racisme-anti-blanc.

18. Robin D'Angelo, "Plus forts que Frigide Barjot, les Indigènes de la République dénoncent l'impérialisme gay," Street Press, February 6, 2013, accessed July 1, 2013, http://www.streetpress.com/sujet/74580-plus-forts-que-frigide-barjot-les-indigenes-de-la-republique-denoncent-l-imperialisme-gay.

19. At one anti–gay marriage demo that took place in February 2014 after the law was passed, organizers invited Muslims to lead the protest with a large banner stating "French Muslims Say 'No' to Gay Marriage." The headline of Le Nouvel Observateur's report borrows a snippet of a conversation between two marchers, a Muslim and a non-Muslim, overheard by the reporter that day: "It's great that you Muslims are here. We (Catholic Caucasians) are much too nice." Ramses Kefi, "A la Manif pour tous: 'C'est bien que vous soyez là, les musulmans. Nous, on est trop gentils,'" Nouvel Observateur, February 2, 2014, accessed July 19, 2016, http://rue89.nouvelobs.com/2014/02/02/cest-bien-les-musulmans-soyez-est-trop-gentils-249576.

20. Bouteldja, "Gay Universalism."

21. Stéphane Kovacs, "Théorie du genre à l'école: la polémique prend de l'ampleur," Le Figaro, January 30, 2014, accessed July 9, 2016, http://www.lefigaro.fr/actualite-france/2014/01/30/01016-20140130ARTFIG00364-theorie-du-genre-a-l-ecole-la-polemique-prend-de-l-ampleur.php.

22. Bouteldja, "Gay Universalism."

23. Gabrielle Culand, "Fringes: Proletarian French Voguers," Vice, March 20, 2014, accessed July 9, 2016, http://www.vice.com/video/french-drag-queen-dance-battles.

24. Lasseindra, "Interview de Lasseindra," by Jérémie Patinier and Tiphaine Bressin, Des ailes sur un tracteur éditions, September 24, 2012, accessed July 9, 2016, http://www.desailessuruntracteur.com/Voguing-a-Paris-l-interview-de-Lasseindra-Ninja-House-of-Ninja-pour-le-livre-Strike-a-pose-Histoire-s-du-Voguing_a41.html.

25. As Kobena Mercer, in *Welcome to the Jungle: New Positions in Black Cultural Studies* (London: Routledge, 1994), has argued in the US context, early American social science rooted the dysfunctionality of families of color in their sexual eccentricity and differing structures: "Assumptions about black sexuality lie at the heart of the ideological view that black households constitute deviant, disorganized and even pathological familial forms that fail to socialize their members into societal norms" (150–51). The casting of family dysfunction for reasons of racialized sexual difference is a key process studied in this book.

26. Ferguson, *Aberrations in Black*, 20.

27. Schneider, *Big mother*.

28. See Bouraoui, *Avant les hommes*, 31–32: "When I think of him, I'm jumping from a plane without a parachute, I'm free falling . . . I feel like a lost dog."

29. "I could throw myself upon him, take hold of his neck, make him fall and crush my penis against his, I could follow him and then hide, I could call him by my first name (as if we had exchanged identities)" (ibid., 66).

Index

Printed and bound by CPI Group (UK) Ltd, Croydon, CR0 4YY

09/06/2025

14685656-0004